GW01377051

Essential Writings

Supported by a grant from the John Templeton Foundation
... *exploring the creative interface between science and religion*

Chiara Lubich

Essential Writings
Spirituality • Dialogue • Culture

Compiled and edited by
Michel Vandeleene

English-language editors
Thomas Masters and Callan Slipper

New City
London

First published in Great Britain
by
New City
Unit 17
Sovereign Park
Coronation Road
London NW10 7QP

©2007 New City Press, New York and New City, London

Translated by Bob Cummings, Jerry Hearne, Thomas Masters, Eugene Selzer and Callan Slipper
(revised and edited by Thomas Masters and Callan Slipper) from the Italian
La dottrina spirituale
© 2006, Città Nuova Editrice, Rome, Italy

British Cataloguing-in-Publication Data:
A catalogue record for this book is available from the British Library
ISBN 978-1-905039-00-5

Cover design by Paulo Silva
Back cover photograph Horacio Conde
Typeset by Belen Velasco
Printed and bound in Great Britain by the Cromwell Press, Wiltshire

Contents

To the Readers. xi

Introduction xiii

The Spirituality of Unity in the Christian Vocation xxi

Editor's Preface. xxxi

Part One
Mysticism for the Third Millennium
Key texts of the spirituality of unity

The Beginnings. 3

A New Way of Christian Living 12

Two Sides of the Same Coin 16
    Our aim: "May they all be one" – 16; The key: Jesus crucified and forsaken – 19

A Spirituality of Communion. 27

Look at All the Flowers. 33

The Way of Unity. 36

Mary in the Focolare Movement 38

A Legacy: Be a Family 48

And the Focolare Was Born 49

Part Two
A New Look at Faith

The core facts of revelation and of the Christian life viewed in the light of the spirituality of unity

A God Who is Love. 55
> What is essential today – 55; How I met you – 56; God is within – 57; Love the One who is Love – 58; God our brother – 59; God is powerful; he is the Omnipotent – 60; No one ever showed such concern for humanity – 61; Thoughts: Grant that I may love you – 62; Live within – 63; Thoughts: With the Almighty – 63; You exist. This is how it is – 65

Our "Yes" to God 66
> Seeing with new eyes – 66; The only good – 69; Partnership – 70; A sanctity of the people – 71; A note of solemnity – 74; With feet on the ground – 74; Time is fast escaping me – 75; Thoughts: Improve always – 75; Not mine but yours be done – 76

The Art of Loving. 77
> The little seed – 77; Our brothers and sisters – 78; The exam – 79; As yourself – 79; If your eye is simple – 80; Enlarge our heart – 81; Lord, give me all who are lonely – 81; In love what counts is to love – 82; Once we have known God – 82; Love is what matters – 83; Christians' attire – 84; There are those who do things for love – 84; When we have known suffering – 85; Thoughts: Nothing is small if it is done out of love – 86

Jesus Forsaken 88
> There is no thorn without a rose – 88; A paradoxical purpose – 89; The cross – 89; I have found you – 91; The sun must set – 92; The hour that awaits us – 92; Eli, Eli, lema sabachthani – 93; Lament – 93; We would die – 94; Where is the slavery? – 94; "I know only Christ and Christ crucified" – 95; Thoughts: The foolishness of love – 96

"The Dream of a God" 98
> Unity, a divine word – 98; The words of a father – 98; He wants to give us heaven – 99; Love generates communion – 100; When unity is complete – 101; If we are united, Jesus is among us – 102; Christ will be my cloister – 102; If a city were set on fire – 103; One city is not enough – 105; Thoughts: Bend but never break – 108

Church as Communion 110
> A myriad of shining pearls – 110; The Mother – 111; Laity like us – 112; Passion for the Church – 112; Christ through the centuries – 113; The lives of the saints – 115; Launched to infinity – 116; To become saints as Church – 117; Thoughts: Like the angels – 118

The Word that Gives Life 120
> Nourished on the Word – 120; The truth makes us free – 120; The Golden Rule – 121; A divine balance – 123; Watch – 125; If we were to live the beatitudes – 125; They do not pass – 126; Thoughts: To be re-evangelized – 127

Jesus in the Eucharist 129
> In the bosom of the Father – 129; When you are offering your gift – 130; His, and our Mass – 130; Inconceivable – 131; Gratitude – 132; Thoughts: Heaven on earth – 133

Mary, the Flower of Humanity 135
> As a heavenly plane sloping – 135; "Explanation" of God – 136; My soul magnifies the Lord – 137; How beautiful the Mother – 137; Two hearts of flesh, clothed in virginity – 138; Thoughts: The Desolate – 139; I have only one mother on earth – 139; Because I want to see her again in you – 140; The All-Beautiful – 141

The Holy Spirit, the Unknown God 143
> Mary and the Holy Spirit – 143; You sanctify – 144; Often love is not love – 144; Thoughts: The inner Master – 146; The abyss inside me – 147; Thoughts: With Mary – 147; Like an empty chalice – 148

Living Life. 150
> Life – 150; Whatever happened to boredom? – 151; The light of a candle in the sun – 152; If a soul gives itself to God sincerely – 153; You are everything, I am nothing – 154; What really matters – 154; But you not pass … – 155

The Final Hour 157
> Still more beautiful – 157; Thoughts of gold – 158; Stars alight in heaven eternally – 159; Death which is the beginning of Life – 161; Towards our homeland – 161; A love that continues – 164; Thoughts: The rehearsal – 164

Part Three
Reflections of Light upon the World

*Basic notions of the charism of unity
and their practical applications in the
Church and the world*

The Attraction of Modern Times 169
  Alongside others – 169 "Have faith, I have conquered the world" – 169; Invasion of love – 171; We have a great responsibility – 172; The resurrection of Rome – 173; Like a rainbow – 177

The Family: Treasure Chest of Love 179
  A living cell – 179; Family and Love – 180; As in the family, so in society – 183; The family is our future – 185

The Talents and Gifts of Women 195

In the School of Jesus: Philosophy and Theology 201
  The charism of unity and theology – 204; The charism of unity and philosophy – 209

Persons in Communion 215
  Jesus the teacher – 215; The charism of unity and education – 219; Every life calls for love – 224; The charism of unity and psychology – 225

The Charism of Unity and Politics 230
  People of God – 230; Mary, bond of unity among nations – 231; Divine diplomacy – 233; More wisdom in government – 235; Reflections: Universal brotherhood – 235; The Movement for Unity in Politics – 236; A united Europe for a united world – 247; Politics based on communion – 257; For an interdependence based on fraternity – 264

The Charism of Unity and Economy 269
  The "Magna Carta" – 269; Underdeveloped Christians – 269; The heavens protest – 273; Towards an Economy of Communion – 274; Fundamental concepts of the Economy of Communion – 278; What kind of work is done by the Economy of Communion? – 286

The Charism of Unity and the Media 290
    Communication and unity – 290; Mary and communication – 298

The Charism of Unity and the Arts 304
    The Madonna of Michelangelo – 304; Art, "a new creation" – 306; The Beautiful – 307; God who is beauty, and the Focolare Movement – 307; Artistic vocation — a talent for unity – 317

360° Dialogue 320
    With Movements and various charisms within the Catholic Church – 320; With other Christians – 325; With our elder brothers – 333; With the world religions – 337; The Focolare Movement's experience of interreligious dialogue – 344; With Muslims – 348; With people of convictions not based in religion – 354; On reasons to share our lives – 358

To the Youth. 360
    A united world: an ideal that becomes history – 360; To the children – 366

Epilogue 369
    The vineyard of Jesus forsaken – 369; The secret – 369; Simply "Thank you"! – 370

Bibliography. 371

Significant Dates and Events 383

The Focolare Movement. 393

Notes. 399

Index. 411

To the Readers

If my words in this book have any value, it is to be attributed to the charism that the goodness of God wished to entrust to me: a gift of the Spirit which by its nature, as other similar gifts poured out on the human race, is meant to be given to everyone in the world who wishes to receive it.

I hope that some glimmer of his light and some gleam of the true love issuing from him may give a new impetus to those who have already received its benefits, and touch, illuminate, spur on, comfort, guide to noble goals men and women of our times, of every age, race, faith, and culture.

Chiara Lubich

Introduction

The modern Christian prays again and again for unity among believers; the last hundred years have seen a previously unimaginable passion developing for the reconciliation of separated Christians, and every Christian leader in the world is bound to make reference to this and to endorse such a passion.

But it is all too easy to think of this as somehow not much more than the negotiating of a comfortable consensus. What Chiara Lubich's writings — and the whole witness of the Focolare Movement — challenge us to is the discovery of what unity really means: not simply unity between believers, but the unity that alone will heal the terrible and murderous conflicts between human beings the world over. From the very beginning of the Movement, the governing theme and calling has been the call to "make yourself one." And from the very beginning, Chiara has insisted that this first and foremost involves dispossession. Each of us stands in a condition of separateness, clinging to our markers of identity; and these markers of identity readily become defences and barriers against each other.

To "make myself one" is not simply to strip away what makes me who I am; I couldn't do that even if I tried. And reconciling love comes from the real and distinct subsistence of a person made in God's image, not from a psychological vacuum. But it does involve stripping away those habits that allow me to anchor my security in what sets me apart from others. Only so do I become reliant on God alone, and become the agent of his love, not of my own good will, moral energy or spiritual resourcefulness. In this way only do I share in Christ's act — Christ making himself one with humanity, in a process that culminates in his dereliction on the cross and his cry of forsakenness.

So Chiara can write, in a memorable and definitive phrase, that "we need to know how to lose God within us for God in our brothers and sisters." As Christ himself empties himself of anything that could be called a private or self-enclosed relation to God the Father so that he may be at one with the dark and confusion of the human relation to God, so too for us (Phil 2). And as Christ rises from the dead not simply as a human individual resuscitated but as the Head of the Body, the community of the new creation, as the giver of the Holy Spirit, so we, in passing through this painful dispossession, enter into the new network of relationships that is the realm of the Spirit, in which there is no longer any intimacy with God that is not also intimacy with and compassion for the human other.

So it is that the life of God the Holy Trinity acts itself out in our lives. We are taken into Christ's desolation, with our defences broken down, our habits of isolation and superiority challenged at their root. As St John of the Cross said, over four hundred years ago, Christ is never more actively doing the Father's will than when he enters into the powerlessness and darkness of his death; so we in sharing his cross open ourselves to the Father's will, with our confidence in our own resources taken away. And when this happens, when God's love is allowed to move in us, it is the Spirit that begins to work, binding us not only to the Father through Christ but to one another in Christ. As we begin to receive Christ from each other in mutual love, we are led into a deeper level of joy than we could have imagined, something that goes far beyond mere feelings of well-being.

"Love must be distilled to the point of being only the Holy Spirit," writes Chiara; "It is distilled when it passes through Jesus forsaken." The simple but devastating truth is that God will fully act and live in our world when and only when we ask God to be himself in us — not for benefits and comforts and securities of any sort but for himself. And this is frightening to ask because it seems to be launching us into uncharted waters. As individuals we can only gain the courage to begin and to pursue this calling as we grow into the life of the Body and learn from those who have stepped out before us — above all from the saints and especially from Mary.

There will be some non-Roman Catholic readers who find themselves surprised, even shocked, by the central importance of Mary in Chiara's exposition. But she makes it absolutely clear why this is so: we have, she says, too often approached Mary as if she were not herself a disciple — the first "follower" of Jesus. The whole life of the Church of God is, historically speaking, rooted in her discipleship. She makes room in her heart and her body for Christ to be born. She experiences the threat and terror of being with Christ as the Holy Family flees into Egypt, leaving the slaughtered innocents behind. She faces the suffering of apparent separation from her son in his adult ministry, yet follows still, uncomprehending. She takes her stand with him in his desolation; and then, as Chiara wonderfully puts it, she becomes more than just a "follower." As she waits with the apostles for the gift of the Spirit, she enters the new creation where she with them is "transformed into him" by the gift of the Spirit. With all the company of Christ's people, she makes real the

Body that is his beloved community, as she once made real the physical body of God's Son in her consent to the angel's message.

The human intimacy between Mary and her Son must have been an extraordinary thing, as Chiara reminds us. Yet when we travel with her into the mystery of Christ's desolation and resurrection, it is not simply a human intimacy that we are given. Like her, we receive a hidden life that will gradually transfigure every aspect of our being. So too, we should not be too fixated on having an imagined human intimacy with her. She goes on "mothering" the Church, and, like a mother, most of her work is out of our line of sight. She pours in her strength, her gentle love, her nourishment, whether or not we understand her or sense her presence like that of another person. She is our sister in faith as well as our mother; but much of the time we experience her in this latter role even as we recognize how we stand alongside her, because she has laid the foundations of faith for us in her journey. Scripture tells us little about her, little of the sort that would enable us to celebrate her great heroic holiness or her miracles. The great Catholic novelist, Georges Bernanos, commented that Mary in the Bible works no miracle except to be the place where the greatest of all miracles occurs, the Word of God becoming human. In this "poverty" of hers, she opens the door of grace to us and shows us an essential dimension of the love of the Trinity. It is like a mother's love in that it is rooted in the absolute bestowal of life, something deeper than any single limited gift.

The Focolarini are called to be a "living rosary" — that is, they are to be walking Mary's path. They are to be followers of Jesus; they are to be people in whom Jesus comes to life through the Spirit; they are to be a place where God's absolute gift of life can come through into the world, bringing others to new birth and feeding them with the glory and strength of God made flesh. Mary, says Chiara, lived "between two fires," the Spirit and Christ — the Spirit bringing Christ to life in her, Jesus himself calling to her as a human other to love. And so we live also between two fires, the inner attention to God's love in silence and adoration and the Jesus who dwells in our midst if we are met together in his name, that is, loving one another (Mt 18:20).

"Between two fires;" that is an unforgettable evocation of what it means to live and pray as a Christian. And the stark honesty of Chiara's description of the cost we must face in this condition prevents what she writes from being sentimentally consoling, or the emphasis on Mary being some kind of regressive pietism. As Chiara says, this is very much a spirituality for our age, when we cannot avoid or lie about the depth of human suffering, mental and physical, that disfigures the world. And the only response that will really meet this is the response of God in Christ — stepping over the boundaries, making yourself one. "Jesus forsaken is the God of our times." This brings no magical solution, no instant healing; but it radically changes the nature of the whole world we live in. So the act of making yourself one in and with Jesus, of walking with Mary and allowing Jesus' life to come alive in us — this has immense implications for what is possible in the world of politics and economics. The Focolare Movement is about these possibilities as well — certainly not just the creation of cells of spiritual peace.

Much of the writing represented here shows Chiara's engagement with this complex world of public policy and rhetoric. She bravely challenges politicians to confront the results of the lack of unity in their world — the divisive, point-scoring language, the short-term and partisan projects, the collusion with ethnic and class rivalries ... And the goal of this is not (God forbid) to create another party, but to prompt some shared thinking (and praying) about how politics of any colour can help to form truly active citizens who are conscious of their responsibility for each other — not passive consumers, but agents for Christ who will work to allow God's action to move freely and build common understanding and purpose. So too she challenges Europe to conceive of the aims of European unity as only a step towards universal justice and solidarity. And she puts into healthy perspective the debates over the public role of faith in Europe, insisting that no political goals are worth discussing that do not have their roots in the recognition of the spiritual possibilities of citizens — that God-given possibility and challenge to "become one," to leave rivalry and defensiveness behind. This doesn't "just happen;" it needs inspiration and grace. And so the part that can be played by small and dedicated networks of believers is crucial, perhaps as never before. To the anxiety that encouraging religious groups breeds factionalism and violence, Chiara's reply is, naturally, that the whole motivation and rationale of these new faith-based networks in Europe is the transcending of all kinds of tribalism — including the religious variety.

The effect this can have also on the world of economics is spelled out in relation to the vision of an "Economy of Communion," a set of principles and practices that directs the profits of business towards the support of job-seekers and the encouragement of generous giving as well as towards the internal needs of a business for development and expansion. In a pungent phrase, Chiara characterizes the churches as "underdeveloped," as we once characterized the "Third World." The lack of material development in disadvantaged countries is matched by the lack of spiritual development among those who call themselves Christians because they do not see these questions of economic justice as fundamental. The "Economy of Communion" is about helping believers (and not only believers) approach economic life with spiritual imagination. At a time when several economists are sharply questioning models of economics based on some mysterious set of "purely" economic goals and desires and demanding that human factors be introduced — environmental and social concern, the measuring of cost in these terms not only in a balance sheet — the Focolare vision is timely and practical. The real problem of secularization, it could well be said, is the acceptance by Christians of the terms in which the wider society sets the problems. If we are serious about our belief in the new creation, we cannot rest content with that.

These examples, though, show that what the Movement is advocating on the basis of Chiara's theology is not some ambitious plan for religious domination, the denial of independence to the world or an ignoring of the real and sometimes tragic complexity of its affairs. It is simply a matter of learning a few basic skills in daily living and human relating, and allowing them to make a difference to whatever broader responsibilities we exercise. When we do this, we are likely to discover that far more is possible than we ever dreamed. And — crucially — if we are truly acting on the basis of "making myself one," the effect is not to divide the world into the doers of good and those poor souls who are "done good to;" it is to break the barrier, to allow real validity to the experience of the other and to help the emergence of *mutual* dependence.

This also affects what Chiara writes about communication. If it is true that the Word of God communicated most completely in the wordless cry with which he died on the cross, there can be no real communication for the Christian without silence, attention and solidarity — those things which are, or ought to be, in the DNA of the believer, as Chiara puts it. Communication is never the passing on of some bundle of information — or some package of propaganda — from one "owner" to another, any more than the active love that engages with the poor is a matter of the rich discarding a few spare possessions; it is a creative process in which people matter more than media, and in which new relations emerge.

And this creative dimension is, of course, a major factor in understanding how we are to relate to people of other faiths and none. If we begin, once again, with willing identification with the other, taking the initiative in love, we may be astonished at what is possible. It remains "proclamation" because it is a living out of what we believe, of the character of the threefold God revealed in Jesus Christ; it is not a nervous "liberal" compromise. But it is proclamation that allows the other to be who they are, hoping that they feel themselves invited to listen in return. It is an extraordinary fact that the

Focolare Movement includes non-Christian associates (including several thousand Muslims) despite its clear theological and spiritual foundations in the Christian gospel. The vocation of becoming one with the other is something, says Chiara, that prompts the right kind of curiosity in people; and out of this friendship arises. The Spirit can move between people of different faiths if we are acting in conformity with Christ and stepping across the boundaries of comfort. In a multicultural environment, the Movement is entirely at home, and has clear and simple lessons to offer about engagement with those we encounter as strangers and guests. Tolerance alone is no recipe for creativity; the Christian has to go beyond and make possible real silence in each other's presence, not trying to foresee or foreclose what God may bring out of an encounter.

All that Chiara writes here is about a very special group of people in the Church — by which I don't mean Focolarini, special as they are, but *laypeople*. She is writing about the specialness of the ordinary baptized man, woman and child, and she reminds us more than once of the lay status of the saints, including Our Lady. We forget so easily that Jesus himself was not a "professional" holy man, a priest or even a rabbi: he was a son of Abraham, a man born into the covenant people in order to extend that covenant to the ends of the earth and create countless more children of Abraham from every tribe and tongue. The distinctive vocation in the Church of the priest or of someone living a vowed life as a monk or sister is there to serve the calling of the whole people, whose collective calling is the great new fact that Jesus brings into being. Once again, we are referred back to ordinary skills, ordinary and simple disciplines for living, not exceptional techniques. This is about the life of the person in relationship, in family and society, letting himself or herself be moulded bit by bit into that vital exchange of life and love that is Christ's Body, learning to allow God in his love to tell them who they are — not society or family, certainly not fashion or profession or race, or even religion in terms of human institutions. We are who we are as disciples not because we identify ourselves as belonging to something called "Christianity," but because we have come to life in relationship with Jesus, the maker of the world who stepped over the threshold dividing creator from creation and became one with what he had made. How extraordinary and how tragic that we can make even that into another defence, another way of occupying and defending safe territory.

But God remains, and God is faithfully ready to take advantage of even the smallest motion of real trust and love, to take any opportunity of bringing his life to live in our lives. Once again, we should remember that this is not about heroism, about exceptional and memorable deeds to be publicly celebrated. Just as much as St Thérèse's teaching, this is a "little way;" and just as much as the "little way," this is a call to the full radicalism of the cross of Jesus. Because it is about two great facts — the unchangeable love of God for each person he has made and the unchangeable purpose of God to build on earth an image of his perfect Trinitarian life by coming to live in our hearts — the message of Chiara Lubich is unaffected by passing fashions of thought, politics, culture and so on. But for the very same reason, it is sharply and sometimes uncomfortably contemporary; it offers the hope of transformation in even the most apparently unfree and dark corners of our deeply shadowed world. It sets before us a lifetime's work, yet it is never more than can be drawn out of the shortest and simplest passage of Scripture. And in all these ways, it is true theology — which must always be nothing more than a reflection on and an induction into true discipleship: into the indwelling love of Father, Son and Holy Spirit.

Rowan Williams
Archbishop of Canterbury
Lambeth Palace, October 2006

The Spirituality of Unity in the Christian Vocation

Christian mysticism

A person God chooses for one of his projects is like the brush in an artist's hand or the pen between a poet's fingers. This image, in various forms, often appears in the sayings of the mystics. Indeed it expresses well, in its utter simplicity, what mystics clearly see in their relationships with the One to whom they have dedicated their existence. It expresses their awareness of their role in all that flows from their actions: without hesitation they recognize that its inspiration and its author lie elsewhere. The image of brush or pen, at first glance, could seem to downgrade human creativity's contribution. But the painter needs a brush to paint and the poet needs a pen to write. And the grace of God too, as Augustine teaches, can do nothing without a person's free participation. The theology of the Eastern Church even speaks of synergy, of something done by both partners, where the initiative belongs to God, but nothing happens in the human world without us making a clear choice and opening ourselves to God.

For these reasons Mary's "let it be done" to the angel is the model for every kind of divine activity in the world and every genuine cooperation in it by a creature. Mary, St. Thomas Aquinas writes, said her yes in the name of the whole human race, and upon her human yes depends the greatest and most amazing thing God has ever done: the incarnation of his Son, Jesus Christ. So Mary's yes in some way is the shape of every other yes said to God, whether said before or after Jesus' birth, unfolding in time and space the full meaning and impact of the Word's coming among humankind.

Synergy therefore, where the human creature, following God for the good of all, experiences the meaning and the goal of his or her freedom and personal identity, in a paradoxical, immediate, life-filled combination of receptivity and activity. At the beginning of the twentieth century, the philosopher Henri Bergson tried to describe the new and unexpected personality of the mystic who by grace, and in complete though hard-won freedom, enters into transformative union:

> *Now* it is God who is acting through the soul, in the soul; the union is total, therefore final ... for the soul there is a superabundance of life. There is a boundless impetus. There is an irresistible impulse which hurls it into vast enterprises. A calm exaltation of all its faculties makes it see things on a vast scale only, and, in spite of its own weakness, produces only what can be mightily wrought. Above all, it sees things simply, and this simplicity, which is equally striking in the words it uses and the conduct it follows, guides it through complications which it apparently does not even perceive. An innate knowledge, or rather an acquired ignorance, suggests to it straightaway the step to be taken, the decisive act, the unanswerable word. Yet effort remains indispensable, endurance and perseverance likewise. But they come of themselves, they develop of their own accord, in a soul acting and acted upon, whose liberty coincides with the divine activity.[1]

Cases like those described by Bergson certainly contain a special grace coupled with a specific mission to fulfil. Still, in its essence Christian mysticism is simply the achievement — in the "already" but "not yet" of history — of the vocation every Christian is called to in faith and reaches through charity. Through our incorporation in Christ by the Holy Spirit in baptism, as Christians we are brought to perfection through Christ's personal self-communication in the Eucharist. The surprising exclamation of the apostle Paul, "I have been crucified with Christ; it is no longer I who live, but Christ who lives in me" (Gal 2:19-20), explains the meaning of Christian existence both as gift and calling to identification with Christ, where, as a member of Christ's Mystical Body, each of us becomes his or her true self.

The light and truth of unity

This substantial and well thought-out selection of Chiara Lubich's writings gives us an opportunity to encounter this experience, highly relevant today. While what is presented here is strikingly original, all the elements of a genuine and powerful mysticism can be recognized, a mysticism with an effective and understandable way of becoming incarnate in our times. Indeed, these pages echo with the Word of Christ who is the same "yesterday, today and forever." Still, this same Word is spoken, welcomed and offered with an accent that makes it surprisingly up-to-date.

As the Second Vatican Council said: "God, who spoke of old, uninterruptedly converses with the Bride of His beloved Son; and the Holy Spirit, through whom the living voice of the Gospel resounds in the Church, and through her, in the world, leads into all truth those who believe and makes the word of

Christ dwell abundantly in them."[2] God speaks to the Church today too, and through it to the whole human race. This is because God wants the Church to be open to everyone and to be the home of all. And today humanity has entered into a new and dramatic era of its history: the era of the global village inviting us all to become a single family. So it is not by chance that the specific word of Jesus that Chiara Lubich feels called to relive and witness to is: "May they all be one" (Jn 17:21). It is one word among the many said by Christ, but it is at the heart of his message and his life — it is the dream of the Father, the most solemn prayer of the Son made flesh, the crucial yearning at the core of each human being, and the great sign of our times.

This particular word did not overwhelm Chiara in a dazzling vision. Her discovery came rather from reading the Gospel in the darkness of an air raid shelter, in the northern Italian city of Trent, accompanied by the fury of the bombs during the Second World War. It was, as she says, as if the words of chapter seventeen of John's gospel were lit up from within. Here, before the hour of his passion and death, Jesus turns to the Father. He utters mysterious words full of meaning that could not be easily understood by a woman just twenty years old, even though providentially it seems she had been made ready for them.

"Look," she wrote in a letter at the beginning of the 1940s, "I am a soul passing through this world. I have seen many beautiful and good things and I have always been attracted only by them. One day (one indescribable day) I saw a light. It appeared to me as more beautiful than the other beautiful things, and I followed it. I realized it was the Truth." These words contain, perhaps, the secret of Chiara's life: sincere, full of love, unclouded by any other agenda, an openness to the light of God made known in the truth, goodness and beauty of the world round about her. One day this was revealed to her eyes, as if completely new, in the most beautiful of the children of Adam, in Jesus who said of himself: "I am the truth" (Jn 14:6). It was a light not only concentrated in him, but shining out from him, illuminating other persons and things, events and situations. It launched Chiara and those who immediately followed her, all fascinated by the light, on a divine adventure where they discovered the golden thread that, through and in Jesus, binds everyone and everything into one. This light is the love of God; indeed, it is God himself who is Love and who has shown himself as Love by giving to us what is most dear to him and most his, his only begotten Son.

The secret — Jesus crucified and forsaken

Believing in this love is the beginning and, at the same time, the high point of Christian faith as Chiara Lubich rediscovered it. For her, as for the New Testament and the undivided tradition of the Church, the light and the love of the Father have a name and a face: Jesus crucified. From the very first steps of her spiritual adventure, she had an attitude of radical openness, unburdened by human expectations, in the face of her experience of God's light.

So Chiara was guided to discover and to choose, among the sufferings of Jesus, the one most hidden and interior, yet the deepest and most tragic. That is, the extreme aloneness and meaninglessness of the cross, of being forsaken by that Father-God he still knows with absolute certainty to be Love. It is the cry of the ninth hour: "My God, my God, why have you forsaken me?" (Mt 27:46) which shows the extremes Christ's love urged him to go through for our sake. Chiara does not doubt or hesitate: if Jesus has loved us this much, feeling separation from God in order to make himself our neighbour and to reunite us to the Father, then this cry, this face of Jesus as the Forsaken One will be the one Ideal of her life.

The word "May they all be one" then finds the secret of its fulfilment in the cry of forsakenness. Only those who, with and in Jesus, are ready to live in the faith of love that conquers the huge and often humanly impossible trial of forsakenness, in the thousands of forms it takes in human existence — only these can make this word their life's ideal. Thanks to Jesus forsaken, recognized and welcomed as the one good, unity is no longer a utopia: it becomes history, humanity's real history. This is the originating core and guiding principle of these essential writings. Chiara Lubich's spirituality springs from the free, exclusive choice of Jesus forsaken that allows Jesus himself to pour into her heart those streams of living water and light which, as the Word of the Father made man, he brings down from heaven to earth to communicate in their fullness to all.

Indeed, in its early years the story of Chiara Lubich and her work goes through a period of intense illumination. In 1949, as Chiara puts it, "It seemed that God wanted to give us an intuition of some of his plans for our Movement. We also understood better many truths of the faith, particularly who Jesus forsaken was for humanity and for creation — he who recapitulated all things in himself."[3] It was a founding moment, one with clear parallels in the story of the great charisms, the great spiritual Movements that have arisen throughout the centuries of Christ's Church.

Going to God together: the Trinity and mutual love

One fact, however, is completely original, at least in the degree of its intensity and in its specific fruits: in keeping with the unity Christ wills — the unity Chiara Lubich and her Movement feel called to witness to and promote in the world — this experience is radically a shared one. It is about going to God together, and Christians are called in Christ to be "one heart and one soul," a teaching that Jesus, like a divine sculptor, deeply and permanently etched on Chiara's soul. We need not avoid our neighbours to stay in God's presence. We have to love them as ourselves, recognizing in them the face of Christ, especially in the poor, the lonely, those who suffer in any way at all: "As you did it to one of the least of these my brothers, you did it to me" (Mt 25:40). This must be done to carry out the will of the Father. When love becomes mutual in Christ to the point of reaching, through Jesus forsaken, the real unity which we celebrate sacramentally in the Eucharist, we enter with our brother or sister into the place Jesus has brought us. That is, the kingdom of God which is the bosom of the Father, where everything is love and communion, light and joy, and each thing belongs to all: "all that is mine is yours" (see Jn 17:10).

Here is what's new about Christianity, what sums it up: the revelation of God as the Trinity of Love, the inexpressible and inexhaustible communication of Self to Self and to creation, and thus the vocation of human creatures to be, each on his or her own and all together, "sons in the Son." The truth, novelty and beauty of what Chiara Lubich teaches about spirituality consists — through the breath of the Holy Spirit — in helping to bring about today the light and grace of the unity Christ has realized in human history. So it is a teaching both utterly traditional and prophetically creative. Like a branch grafted onto the ancient trunk of the Church's experience and doctrine, helping it flower anew, it is traditional, and because of its original perspective on the once-and-for-all revelation of Christ, it is creative.

As already suggested, Jesus forsaken himself is both traditional and creative, especially when recognized and welcomed for who he is: the revelation of love and so, the key to unity. This "glance at the core of faith," as Hans Urs von Balthasar would say, reshapes Christian life and truth from top to bottom. Archbishop G. B. Montini, later Pope Paul VI, recognized this in the 1950s when Chiara Lubich presented her gospel-based intuition to him. The "new" element (though ancient as the gospel itself) of this spirituality is indeed the existential understanding, in the light of Jesus forsaken, of the Trinitarian love between the Father and the Son in the communion of the Holy Spirit.

And this Trinitarian love is the pattern and dynamic thrust of human existence. This new element is lived out in all of humanity's expressions — ecclesial, social, cultural — and at every level of human life — personal, communal, social — with all the necessary consequences. It is a love that makes the presence and action of the risen Christ in history something we can experience. Indeed he promised: "I am with you always, to the end of the age" (Mt 28:20). But we have to do our part to set free his presence into the world: we must live united in his name (see Mt 18:20), putting into practice that will of his that sums up all others: "Love one another as I have loved you" (Jn 15:12). This is how he comes to dwell among us as Emmanuel, God-with-us.

Balancing contemplation and action

And this Trinitarian love is the basis for the unity in distinction between the religious and the secular aspect, between the ecclesial and the social aspect of the Movement founded by Chiara Lubich. In other words, it is the dynamic balance between contemplation and action. Not by chance does one of Chiara's most famous passages begin by speaking of "the great attraction of modern times," which she deftly describes as "to penetrate to the highest contemplation while mingling with everyone, one person alongside others." The pages of this collection fully document the successful synthesis of these two essential and complementary dimensions of the Christian spirit.

This, it could be said, is common to every true spirituality, even if the dominant feature in one spirituality is contemplation and in another is action. But Chiara has realized the centrality of Jesus forsaken as the key not only to union with God but also to unity with her brothers and sisters. So she has identified the Archimedean point that unites, without confusion, the vertical, divine nature with the horizontal, human nature both of the experience of Christ and of those who, with serious commitment, join the community of his followers. This perspective allows us to speak of a mysticism for the dawn of the third millennium, a mysticism that also brings us back to the most genuine mysticism at the origins of Christianity. That is, the mysticism of Jesus and Mary, where vertical union with God was lived among those who were their brothers and sisters, and with them, in the service of all people in the everyday affairs of life.

The Christian of the future, as Karl Rahner pointed out a few decades ago, will either be a mystic, one who lives the experience of God in the world, or he or she will simply not exist. It is not hard to see how and why — without any compromise or watering down — a spirituality like the one that comes from Chiara Lubich's charism is adapted to every human condition and to every kind of vocation in the Church and in society. Perhaps this is why a layperson, a woman, was chosen to be its bearer. And not by chance did Chiara Lubich's spirituality and her Movement from the very beginning, even before the Second Vatican Council, draw ever-greater numbers of men and women, priests and bishops, men and women religious from countless spiritual families, the married and the unmarried, young people of all ages and older people, from every nation on earth. It has produced a modern school of holiness open to all. And this holiness is a holiness of the people summed up in faithfulness to love as the essence of the gospel and, in this love, to one's own vocation as the fulfilment of God's specific will for each person. All this takes place in a communion lived with everyone, going beyond every kind of diversity based on culture, social class, or walk of life, where in fact these differences are seen as gifts to be offered and put in common with all that others bring with them.

Open to dialogue with everyone

In addition, the gospel imperative, "May they all be one," combined with passion for the disfigured face of Jesus forsaken meant that the dynamism of this charism could not stay locked inside the Roman Catholic Church. And, in fact, in harmony with the ecumenical movement, the spirituality of unity soon spread among Orthodox, Lutherans, Reformed, Anglicans … still today it is moving to recall the spontaneous and especially intense sympathy between Chiara Lubich and the Ecumenical Patriarch Athenagoras I of Constantinople. He, as in their various ways did many other leading figures among the Churches, recognized in Chiara's spirituality the common and fertile ground of the gospel of love. And living the gospel with one's gaze fixed on the crucified Christ — who was ready to give everything to re-establish unity between the Father and his brothers and sisters — can, as this man, a Father of the Church in our times, prophetically loved to say, speed up "the hour of the one chalice."

In the last few decades, the meeting with the great religious traditions of humanity and with some of their most important leaders has been even more unexpected, and perhaps more fascinating. In these encounters, Chiara Lubich has acted as an ambassador of peace, of dialogue and of brotherhood to the whole world: from Jerusalem to Tokyo, from Chiang Mai in the north of Thailand to the Malcolm Shabazz Mosque in Harlem, from meetings with

Hinduism to contacts with Islam. What opens up surprisingly new and apparently unbridgeable ways is always the same spirit that urges us to look at Jesus forsaken who, according to the teaching of Paul, knew how to strip himself of every richness (see Phil 2:7) so as to make himself one with all (see 1 Cor 9:22). Those who model their existence on Jesus forsaken become in him living witnesses — first in being and then through words — of what most specifically belongs to the gospel. That is, they give witness to the love that is able to become the other, so that the other too may welcome freely the same precious gift Christ's disciples know they have received freely and bear in earthen vessels. Then, when the other's time comes, the same gift may be given to whoever wants to receive it.

Chiara Lubich's spirituality seems to have been developed precisely for energizing and fleshing out that "aggiornamento" of the Church's life required by the current era of human history, and which John XXIII spoke of when he called the Second Vatican Council. For the first time as Bishop of Rome, in 1984 John Paul II met the Focolare Movement at its centre at Rocca di Papa in the hills near Rome. Having heard there a summary of the Movement's spirit, structure and activities, it is not surprising that he recognized in it, in miniature, the features of the Church as laid out by the Council. That Church is not on the defensive, enclosed by a siege mentality. Rather, aware of its identity and mission as "a sign and instrument of unity" for the whole world, it is open to dialogue with everyone, in joyful and credible witness to the crucified and risen Christ. It is a Church committed, as *Novo Millennio Ineunte* desires, to living the spirituality of communion before everything else.

Foundations for a cultural paradigm shift

What Chiara Lubich teaches gives witness to a paradigm shift in the history of Christian spirituality, by going from the primacy of the individual to a balance between persons and communion — which is in line with the aspirations of Vatican II and our needs today. In addition, moreover, it is a spirituality rooted in the mysticism of Jesus, true God and true Man, living again today through the unity of those who belong to him. So it lays down the kind of foundations needed for a significant cultural paradigm shift. In a troubled and sometimes even tragic way our era demands such a shift with some urgency and, in different and even contradictory forms, we can begin to grasp its outlines.

Such an impact is not new in the history of Christian spirituality. A new charism generates from within itself a cultural style shaping the character of those aspects of human and social life in which it is called to participate. We've only to think of the effects of Benedict of Nursia's "pray and work" and the birth of Europe, of Francis of Assisi's ideal of "Lady Poverty" and the flowering of medieval Christianity, or of Ignatius of Loyola's "for the greater glory of God" and the emergence of the modern era. Theology, philosophy, social, economic and political organization, the arts and even the scientific study of nature have all been influenced, at times even profoundly marked by the mystical inspiration of these great saints.

This is not an overly bold suggestion, because the charism of unity's original view of Christian revelation and the vision of the world it unfolds cannot but cast its own light on all these levels of human existence. The third part of this anthology shows this. It presents the first intuitions derived from the charism, already put into practice in their respective fields, in various areas of human study and action. Indeed for some years now a group (the Abba School) of academics and scholars competent in a variety of disciplines have gathered around Chiara Lubich with the idea of making explicit what could be called the cultural potential of the spirituality of Jesus forsaken and of unity. The Abba School's methodology and its objective are ambitious, almost risky. In our time, modernity is uncovering the crisis of the subject and accompanying that, the fragmentation of knowledge. At the same time, there is an explosion of all the complexities of multiculturalism together with the unrelenting emergence of globalization with its opportunities and dangers.

The Abba School seeks to rediscover the centre that enlightens and gives truth, trying not to suffocate it in some kind of over-simplified uniformity yet at the same time not to get lost in a relativizing multiplicity of perspectives. What the School seeks is a celebration of genuine diversity gathered into the One that is Three because it is Love. The shadow of the absence of God weighs upon so many parts of contemporary culture. In the light of Jesus forsaken, who Chiara Lubich unhesitatingly recognizes as "the God of our times," even this reality can be interpreted and illuminated as that "collective dark night of an era." This "collective dark night" prepares the dawn of a new civilization of love where the principal actors are all the members of the whole human family in its multifaceted expressions and richness.

The Work of Mary

Among all that could be said, I think we should remember one thing. The Movement that has arisen from the charism of unity is known everywhere as the Focolare Movement. But according to the Roman Catholic Church its official name is the Work of Mary. Its General Statutes explain this in these words: "The Work of Mary bears this name because its characteristic spirituality, its ecclesial form, the variety of which it is composed, its universal expansion, its relationships of collaboration and friendship with Christians of different Churches and ecclesial communities, with persons of various faiths and of goodwill, and its lay and female presidency, demonstrate the particular link it has with Mary most holy, mother of Christ and of each human being, of whom it would like, insofar as it is possible, to be a presence on the earth and almost a continuation." So the Work of Mary is another way of speaking of Mary at work in the Church and among humanity today.

Here, perhaps, we should look for the simplest and deepest inspiration for a charism so rich, new and universal. It is a presence of Mary. We can recognize in it what von Balthasar first described as the "Marian profile" of the Church, where he said it is as fundamental and definitive for Christianity as the apostolic and Petrine profile, if not indeed more so.[4] Mary, as I mentioned at the beginning of my few words, gave Jesus to the world. For this reason she formed a background for him so that, in a unique way, he could shine his light upon us and could carry out the greatest revolution of all time, which Mary sang prophetically in her Magnificat. Chiara follows the same way, so that today Jesus can continue and bring to fulfilment his work, "May they all be one."

Piero Coda, Professor of Fundamental Theology,
Lateran Pontifical University, Rome

Editors' Preface

Translating and editing these "essential writings" of Chiara Lubich has deepened our respect not only for her intellectual and spiritual depth, but also for her power, skill, and elegance as a writer. Trying to express her in English has been a challenge! But we have attempted as far as we are able, by every word chosen, every punctuation mark placed, every sentence crafted, every passage arranged, to take readers as close to her as possible. Chiara writes with a distinctive voice and we have tried to preserve that. Of course, every translation fails to some extent, but we have sought to overcome the various obstacles in such a way that the reader may enter into something of the same conceptual and spiritual space accessible to the Italian reader.

Perhaps a little of the excitement of the spiritual discovery made by Chiara, something of its simplicity, its delicacy yet its overwhelming nature, can be captured even in translation. It opens up a world in which faith is about living and living is focused on the yearning that will never be satisfied until Jesus' prayer, his last will and testament, is fulfilled: "May they all be one."

The texts in this volume have been selected and arranged with a view to entering this world. They lay bare the cornerstones of her work. Many of them are standard or, as it were, classic expositions of Chiara's vision. These texts will serve readers for years to come. In the first place they are useful for those who wish to meditate upon Chiara's spirituality to draw upon it for their lives, but scholars will also find them useful to understand more clearly the distinctive contribution of her spirituality both in itself and in its implications in practically every aspect of human activity and culture.

With this in mind, it may be good to offer readers some notions to help find their bearings in the sea of material.

Organization of this book

The book is in three parts, each an anthology of texts from the many literary genres that Chiara has used. This variety is unified in each section by the basic purpose of the part. Overall the three parts give a comprehensive picture.

The first part, "Mysticism for the Third Millennium," presents both the origins and the originality of the spirituality of unity. Consequently it unveils the spirituality's fundamental points: its focus on unity, the love for Jesus crucified and forsaken, its communitarian nature, its relationship to other traditions of spirituality in the Church, the place of prominence that Mary holds in it. It indicates the characteristic sense of family, of profound mutual belonging, that supports this unprecedented way of devoting one's life to God, particularly in the new form of vocation found within the Movement born from the spirituality — the "fourth way," the Focolare.

The purpose of the second part, "A New Look at Faith," is to consider what the spirituality means for the core experiences common to all Christians. It shows the Christian faith in a fresh light. Beginning from the realization at the root of everything else, that God is Love, it outlines the vocation of every person to be love. Certain elements of Christian experience stand out in a life of love centred on unity — among them the will of God, mutual love, Jesus crucified and forsaken, the presence of God among his people, the words of life contained in Scripture, the Eucharist, Mary, the Holy Spirit. Taken together as a way of living, these elements generate a current of culture for the world today.

Part Three, "Reflections of Light upon the World," draws out the implications of this culture. These are foundational documents, often with something of a programmatic nature. Chiara demonstrates how to generate constructive dialogue, offering ways of bringing about an alternative approach based on the gospel. Her range is enormous. She looks at families, women, and young people, theology, philosophy, education, psychology, politics, economics, communications, and art. And she also draws out the consequences of her approach for the search for Christian unity and for relations with members of other religions and with people whose convictions are not based in religion.

How to use this book

Essential Writings is comprehensive in the sweep of time it covers, from 1943 to the present, as well as in the variety of genres it contains. A single section may encompass letters or meditations originally intended for an intimate audience as well as speeches addressed to huge throngs, spiritual poems as well as transcripts of question and answer sessions with Chiara herself, aphorisms as well as academic lectures. Taken together, they reflect Chiara's literary output, which to this point has been published separately or not at all. Different readers may approach it in different ways.

- Those unfamiliar with Chiara or with the Focolare Movement may wish to begin by reading the first section in each of the three parts. These serve to orient readers towards the deeper exploration of spirituality, dialogue and culture, that each part elaborates.
- Those who already know Chiara and the spirituality of unity will find familiar passages (albeit in a fresh, often revised translation) as well as unfamiliar texts that will deepen their understanding and appreciation. Many passages have never appeared before in English translation.
- By using the table of contents and the index, those who seek material for spiritual reading or meditation can follow themes that run through all three sections of the anthology, themes that touch on the central realities and mysteries of Christian life.
- Scholars will find a wealth of primary sources that give an in-depth presentation of Chiara, the spirituality of unity, and the Focolare Movement, as well as a chronology of important dates in the life of Chiara and the Focolare Movement, a thumbnail sketch of the Movement's size and its various sections, a comprehensive index, and bibliographies of additional sources published in English and in other languages.

Concerning the sources and style

This volume contains a number of previously published passages, and the original sources are cited in endnotes. Chiara subsequently has revised some of these selections, and they are indicated as "revised" in the endnotes. Those published for the first time in this anthology are identified as such in the brief explanatory note that precedes them.

At various points the original Italian texts use italic type and capitalization of some terms for emphasis. We have retained those features in the English translation. Another feature of the original style is the occasional use of scriptural passages that are punctuated as quotations, yet actually are paraphrases of biblical matter. We indicate these periphrastic quotations in the parenthetical citation with the notation "see"; for example, on page 67 there is the citation (see Is 62:4). With few exceptions, we have used the New Revised Standard Version for biblical citations. When the wording of a scriptural passage from NRSV did not fit the author's tone or intention we have indicated with an abbreviation in the citation that another translation has been used. For other sources cited in the original text, such as papal documents, passages from the Fathers of the Church, or from other spiritual writers, we have used published English translations. In a few cases it was necessary that we make our own as indicated in the introduction to the Notes, page 401.

Chiara uses few explanatory footnotes, and where she does we have indicated them with "author" in parenthesis following the note. We have supplied other footnotes where it was necessary to explain terms strange to readers not conversant with the Focolare lexicon, to put certain statements into their historical context, to identify historical figures unknown in an English-speaking cultural context, or to address shades of meaning that the English translation could not capture.

We acknowledge the generous help of the Templeton Foundation, which has underwritten the production of the English version of *Essential Writings*. We also wish to recognize the contributions of Michel Vandeleene, who undertook painstaking and careful work as the general editor of this volume and of the original Italian version; Giovanni d'Alessandro of Città Nuova, Rome; Luisa Del Zanna of the international headquarters of the Work of Mary; Carla Cotignoli of the Focolare Information Office; Bob Cummings, Jerry Hearne, and Eugene Selzer, who did the preliminary translations; Enzo Fondi, Giorgio Marchetti, Piero Coda, Brendan Leahy, Thomas Norris and Brendan Purcell; the staff of New City Press, New York and New City, London; and the many, many others who have lent their assistance in preparing this edition.

Thomas Masters and Callan Slipper, editors

Part One

Mysticism for the Third Millennium

Key texts of the spirituality of unity

The Beginnings

A discourse at the Council Chambers of Bologna, 22 September 1997, on the occasion of her receiving the Turrita d'Argento Award. In this previously unpublished address, Chiara Lubich describes the principal stages of her story, which is linked with the birth and development of the Focolare Movement.

The welcome I received, although directed to me, was meant in a special way, I believe, for what I represent, the Focolare Movement, a religious and social movement present in 182 nations, practically everywhere in the world.

It is most widespread in the Catholic Church, but is also found in 300 other churches and ecclesial communities and among the faithful of many other religions, as well as people of goodwill who do not relate their lives directly to God.

It is all about *unity*, among individuals, groups, cities and nations, which seeks to eliminate all discrimination and dreams of a future which could be expressed as: a united world. It is accomplishing a great deal of good in the world.

I say a great deal of good, but out of all proportion to any person or persons who might be instrumental in doing it.

It is, as we say, a work of God.

That is the secret of its success.

That is due to its evangelical spirit, ever up-to-date and modern, a gospel-based, collective spirituality, known as the *spirituality of unity*, capable of generating an entirely new way of living.

Through that spirituality, men and women everywhere today slowly but decisively are trying to become, at least in the places where they find themselves, the seeds of a new people that promotes a world of greater solidarity especially with the poorest and weakest, a world more united.

This can be a spiritual resource of love supporting the various forces already leading in that direction everywhere on earth.

It has a markedly communitarian dimension; in fact it is lived by people not only individually but also as groups small and large. Inspired fundamentally by Christian principles — not disregarding but rather affirming parallel values in other faiths and cultures — it has brought unity into all areas of our world, which needs so much to rediscover and consolidate a sense of unity.

To explain it I need to relate something of the history of the Movement.

The Movement began in Trent. At the outset I had no plan in mind, no programme. The idea for this Movement was God's; it was a project from heaven. That is how it was in the beginning; that is how it has been during the 54 years of its growth.

In 1943 war raged in Trent: ruin, destruction, death.

For a variety of reasons a group of young people about my age gathered around me.

One day I found myself with my new companions in a dark, candle-lit cellar, a book of the gospels in hand. I opened it. There was Jesus' prayer before he died: "Father ... may they all be one" (Jn 17:11, 21). It was not an easy text to start with, but one by one those words seemed to come to life, giving us the conviction that we were born for that page of the gospel.

On the feast of Christ the King we gathered around an altar. We said to Jesus: "You know the way to achieve unity. Here we are. If you so desire, use us." The liturgy of the day amazed us: "Ask of me," it said, "and I will make the nations your heritage, and the ends of the earth your possession" (Ps 2:8).

We asked. God is all-powerful.

The bombardment continued, destroying some of the people and things we cherished. One loved her home; it was ruined. Another was planning to be married; her fiancé did not return from the front. My ideal was to study, but the war kept me from attending the university.

Every event touched us profoundly. The lesson God was giving us in those circumstances was clear: all is vanity of vanities. Everything passes away.

At the same time God put a question into my heart meant for all of us, and with it came an answer: is there an ideal that does not die, that no bomb can destroy, to which we can devote our lives?

Yes, there is. That ideal is God.

We decided to make God the ideal of our lives. In the midst of war, the fruit of hate, God was manifesting himself to us as Love.

Our parents sought refuge in the mountain valleys. We stayed in Trent. Some for work or study. I in order to be with the Movement that was coming to life. A flat with a few rooms became our shelter.

We found the ideal to live for. It was God, God-Love.

The Beginnings

But how could we put it into practice?

The gospel gave us the answer: "Not everyone who says to me 'Lord, Lord' will enter the kingdom of heaven, but only the one who does the will of my Father in heaven" (Mt 7:21). It is not a matter of piety or sentimentality, then. Doing the will of God; that is what matters.

But who would tell us the will of God?

Whenever the siren sounded we rushed into the shelters, unable to bring anything along other than a small book of the gospels.

In it we could find what Jesus wanted of us — his will.

So we opened it. It was wonderful. Those words which we had heard many times were illuminated as though lit from within. We seized upon them and a power, we think the Holy Spirit, led us to put them into practice.

We read: "Love your neighbour as yourself" (Mt 19:19). My neighbour. Where is my neighbour?

There beside us. In that old lady barely able to drag herself each time to the shelter. We must love her as ourselves; we must help her each time, then, and support her.

The neighbour was there in those five frightened children alongside their mother. We must take them in our arms and help them home.

The neighbour was there in that sick person confined to home, unable to go to the shelter, but in need of care. We must go there and get him medicine.

We read: "Whatever you did to one of the least of these, you did it to me" (see Mt 25:40).

People around us were in terrible conditions — hungry, thirsty, injured, without clothing, without shelter. So we cooked big pots of soup and distributed it to them.

Sometimes, poor people knocked at the door and we invited them to sit down with us: alternating one poor person and one of us, one poor person and one of us.

The gospel promised: "Ask, and it will be given to you" (Mt 7:7; Lk 11:9).

We asked on behalf of the poor, and each time we were filled with God's gifts: bread, powdered milk, marmalade, wood, clothing … which we took to those who needed it.

Here is a typical episode.

One day a poor person asked for a pair of shoes size 8½. One of us went to church before the tabernacle with this request: "Lord, give me a pair of shoes size 8½, for you in that poor person."

As she was going out of church, a young lady, a friend of hers, handed her a package. She opened it. There was a pair of shoes size 8½.

And this is only one of thousands and thousands and thousands of examples.

"Give, and it will be given to you" (Lk 6:38) we read in the gospel on another day. We gave. If we had only one egg in the house for all of us, we offered it to the poor. And what do you know, in the morning a bag of eggs arrived! It was that way with so many things.

Jesus had made a promise and he was keeping it. So the gospel was credible, it was true.

This confirmation made us fly down the path we had taken. We shared with everyone what was happening each day, and they were amazed.

Many were struck by the truth of the gospel; they wanted to experience the same thing and follow Jesus.

These astonishing new experiences of the gospel circulated from mouth to mouth. They were a small echo of the words of the apostles: Christ is risen. Now it was: Christ is alive!

The shelters where we gathered were not safe. We were constantly in danger of death. Another question came to us: is there a will of God especially pleasing to him? If we were to die, we would want to have put it into practice, at least in our final moments.

The gospel gave us the answer; it spoke of a commandment which Jesus called "mine" and "new." "This is my commandment, that you love one another as I have loved you. No one has greater love than this, to lay down one's life for one's friends" (Jn 15:12-13).

We looked each other in the face and declared: "I am ready to give my life for you; I for you, I for you; all for each one."

From that promise came the way for us to respond to the thousand daily demands on fraternal love. We are not always asked to die for one another, but we can share everything: our worries, our sorrows, our meagre possessions, our spiritual riches....

We saw our lives take a qualitative leap forward. Someone came into our group, silently, an invisible Friend, giving us security, a more experiential joy, a new peace, a fullness of life, an inextinguishable light. Jesus was fulfilling his promise to us: "Where two or three are gathered in my name, I am there among them" (Mt 18:20).

He had said: "may they also be [one] in us, so that the world may believe ..." (see Jn 17:21).

The Beginnings 7

When Christ is there in the unity of brothers and sisters, the world believes. That happened with us. Radical transformations in people occurred around us. There were many kinds of conversions, vocations in jeopardy were saved, and new ones were born.

After a few months about 500 people of all ages, men and women, from all social strata wanted to share our Ideal.*

We held everything in common, like the first Christian community.

The words of the gospel are unique, fascinating, carefully scripted, and can be translated into life. They are light for everyone who comes into this world; they are universal. When we live them, everything changes: our relationship with God, with our neighbours, with our enemies.

These words gave things their proper perspective, putting everything else in second place, including our fathers, mothers, brothers, our work ... so as to give God the first place in our hearts. That is why they carry extraordinary promises: a hundredfold in this life and eternal life as well.

This was a gospel we had not known before. Where was the usual stiff-necked piety, the drone of empty prayers, the routine faith and an inaccessible God? No, no, that was not the religion of Jesus. He does as God does. When we follow him, we give him a little and he showers us with gifts. We are alone yet we find ourselves surrounded by a hundred mothers and fathers, by thousands of brothers and sisters. We receive every kind of divine blessing which we share with those who have nothing.

There is no human situation that does not find an explicit or implicit solution in that small book that contains the word of God.

The people in the Movement immerse themselves in it. They are nourished by it. They are re-evangelized.

Finally the war ended. The followers of the Movement were able to go on to study, work and bear witness; in fact they were invited to many cities and towns to share their experiences.

From the north of Italy to the south, communities like the one in Trent flourished.

The church in Trent and in Rome, with the wisdom and experience of centuries, carefully studied the new Movement and approved it.

What happiness, new discoveries, graces and victories! That is the gospel. But from the beginning we understood that it had another side too,

---

* In the writings of Chiara Lubich, the term Ideal means the ideas, believed to have been suggested by the Holy Spirit, that are the basis of the life of the Focolare Movement. They describe both its spirituality and its structures.

that the tree has its roots. The gospel covers us with love, but it demands everything.

"Unless a grain of wheat falls into the earth and dies, it remains just a single grain; but if it dies, it bears much fruit" (Jn 12:24). That means dying.

"Every branch that bears fruit," Jesus says, "he [the Father] prunes to make it bear more fruit" (Jn 15:2). Again, suffering.

The Movement has had its share of different kinds of suffering as a result of living the gospel. But by the grace of God we have all been able to love the suffering by making our own the words of St. Paul: "For I decided to know nothing among you except Jesus Christ, and him crucified" (1 Cor 2:2).

Loving Christ crucified in every suffering is another focus of this spirituality.

During all these years the Movement was developing according to a precise plan of God, always unknown to us but revealed from time to time. It flourished among adults, youth, laity, priests, various vocations, each in its own way totally committed. These were the real force that supported the whole Movement. Around them flourished wider movements for families, for young people, for the various areas of human life and for the world of the Church as well.

With a growth that can be termed nothing less than "an explosion," the Movement in the first fifteen years crossed all the national boundaries of Europe. From 1958 on, it reached every continent.

For the Movement, 1960 marked a new stage. This was the spread of its spirit among non-Catholic Christians.

I was in Germany speaking to a group of Lutheran sisters. Three pastors who were present were rather amazed by the fact that, with such intensity, Catholics were living the gospel. In any case, this struck them, not just because we talked about the gospel but because we sought to *live* the gospel.

We were invited immediately to bring our experience to the Lutheran world.

Groups of Lutherans came to Rome almost every year. Because it was based on love and truth, a genuine fraternity developed among us that could not remain silent. Centuries-old prejudices fell by the wayside.

Cardinal Bea reminded us that when Christians of every denomination live the gospel in a profound way, they grow closer to each other, because they are becoming more like Christ.

Some Anglican ministers happened to be at a meeting between Catholics and Lutherans. They were touched by the typically warm atmosphere where long-separated Christians realized that they are brothers and sisters by baptism. They did not want anything less than that for themselves.

On 1 July 1966 at Lambeth Palace in London they arranged an audience for me with then-Primate of the Anglican Communion, Dr. Michael Ramsey. He said to me: "I see the hand of God in this Movement" and he encouraged me to bring the Movement to the Church of England.

Later on his successor, Archbishop Coggan, at Canterbury, then the next Primate, Dr. Runcie, and finally Dr. George Carey became friends of the Movement.

The Movement grew among Anglicans, Presbyterians and Baptists....

In Australia and in North and South America our life spread among many denominations.

In June of 1967 Patriarch Athenagoras, who knew something about the Movement, was waiting to see me. Athenagoras, one of the great personalities of the twentieth century, wanted to be, and I will always say this, a simple Focolarino.

Through him the Focolare Movement spread to the Eastern Orthodox.

Patriarch Dimitrios I, his successor, and the current patriarch, His All-Holiness Bartholomew I, continue in the same path.

The global spread of the Movement has put its members in direct contact with people of the major religions.

Here are two very simple examples.

I was in Thailand a few months ago, invited by some Buddhist monks to speak at Chiang Mai in the north of the country, at a Buddhist university to students and teachers, and at a temple to men and women monks and to lay Buddhists.

This most unusual event was still more surprising, if we consider that I was asked to talk about my spiritual experiences which were utterly Christian.

How did that come about?

You will understand if you know what happened before.

A Buddhist Grand Master and a disciple of his, both intelligent and open persons, got to know some members of the Movement in Asia. Afterwards they wanted to go to Italy to one of our little towns, Loppiano, near Florence, whose 800 residents try to live the gospel faithfully to build unity.

They were deeply impressed.

They were touched by the love they found and by the unity of all who lived there.

His disciple recounted: "I put my dirty shoes outside the door. In the morning they were clean.

"I left my dirty clothes outside the door. In the morning they were cleaned and pressed.

"They knew I was cold because I come from southeast Asia. They raised the heating and gave me blankets....

"One day I asked: 'Why did you do this?'

" 'Because we love you' was the answer." That overwhelmed him.

We explained various truths of Christianity for them. And, in their enthusiasm over what they experienced, they invited me to speak to their people about this marvellous reality: especially about love and unity.

My visit to Thailand was — by the grace of God and to his glory — a great success. A major way was opened for a profound dialogue to our mutual enrichment. We too, in fact, have come to admire their goodwill, their heroic asceticism and their wisdom.

Now we plan to pursue this fraternal relationship.

Here is a second example.

The founder of a great Muslim movement of two million African-Americans, Imam W. D. Mohammed, successor to Malcolm X, came to know the Movement and invited me to the mosque in Harlem, New York last May 18 to speak to 3000 members about unity and how we live it. Here too was unanimous acceptance. Now the founder and the members of his movement wish to build with us a new, more united world.

This unity has come alive among blacks and whites and is making a sensation in the United States.

Many people of goodwill who are not believers take commitments in the Movement in order to safeguard the values we hold in common: solidarity, unity, peace, human rights and liberty.

And not just that. They dedicate themselves along with all the rest of us to social action and the Economy of Communion.*

But what are the effects of the Movement?

Its fruits are immense: above all, as in the beginning, there are radical transformations. To put it in religious terms, there are conversions to God or at least to doing good, too many instances to count. Citizens are formed who carry out all their duties faithfully, with renewed awareness.

---

* For a more complete explanation of the Economy of Communion see below pp. 286-89.

To begin with, the youngest, the hope of tomorrow, are no longer immature. They act like leaders, in civil and religious life, knowing how to face difficulties. They love to be "different" because, while in the world, they are not of the world. They do not absorb the negativity the world is offering them.

The young people aim high; they prepare themselves seriously for future life; they set up projects of every kind to promote their values.

Men and women, with the highest goals, feel they are co-creators with God in building the earthly city.

Families shattered by separation and divorce are reunited and adopt children.

This collective spirituality, as you can imagine, breaks into the structures of society: economy and work, politics and ethics, medicine, education, art and so on.

In the world of the Church vocations are increasing, groups of priests and seminaries are becoming centres from which the gospel radiates, making a significant contribution to building the heavenly city.

Members of religious orders become better brothers and sisters to one another. They help to renew their communities; they rediscover their founders and their rule; they emphasize unity with their superiors, and new callings arise among them, etc.

And on and on.

Unity is the distinguishing characteristic of our Ideal, so observing the effects of the Movement is a little like watching a film in reverse.

A world immersed in secularism, materialism and indifference has brought us to so many sharp divisions, to such poverty and crises!

With the Movement, however, things go backwards, but in order to advance. The world returns to the unity of the human family as God intended when he made it.

May God, the Father of all, ever strengthen our efforts, along with those of everyone dedicated to such high ideals as these. May they be able to, as Pope John Paul II said at the UN on the fiftieth anniversary of its founding: "Build for the next century and for the new millennium a civilization worthy of the human person ...

"We can and must do it!" he continued, "and in doing so, we will see that the tears of this century have prepared the earth for a new springtime of the human spirit."[1]

That is what we all hope for.

A New Way of Christian Living

> Address to UNESCO, 17 December 1996, on receiving the Prize for Peace Education.

I am not going to speak about the history of the Focolare Movement or about its structure. The Movement is but one instrument today, along with many other worthy and deserving organizations, initiatives and efforts, for bringing unity and peace to our world.... I would rather address the secret of its success.

It consists in a new way of life, in a new way of doing things embraced by millions of people inspired by fundamentally Christian principles. Without overlooking parallel values present in other faiths and diverse cultures, but in fact embracing them, it has brought peace and unity to a world in great need of rediscovering and reestablishing peace.

This is a new spirituality, which is modern and up to date; it is the spirituality of unity.

But is it possible in our day to achieve unity and the peace it brings?

As everyone knows, the world today is beset with tensions: between North and South, in the Middle East, in Africa. There are wars, threats of new conflicts and many other evils characteristic of our age. Yet, in spite of all that, paradoxically the world is moving today towards unity and consequently towards peace; it is a sign of the times.

In the religious world, the World Conference for Religion and Peace is saying the same thing.

In the Christian world, the Holy Spirit is affirming it, and is leading the various churches and ecclesial communities towards unification after centuries of indifference and conflict.

The World Council of Churches is saying it.

Pope Paul VI said it; his teaching was laced with references to unity. Currently, Pope John Paul II is the personification of unity with his universal embrace of so many people in his travels all over the world.

The Second Vatican Council said the same thing in its documents, which continually return to this idea.

Ideologies, now partly surpassed, speak of the movement of the world to unity, as we try to resolve the great problems of today on a worldwide scale.

In the political realm, as in Europe, states are saying it as they move towards greater unity.

It is said by numerous agencies and international organizations; even modern means of communication lead to greater unity as they bring the whole world closer to being one community or family.

Yes, this is the present trend of the world.

This is the context in which the Focolare Movement and its spirituality must be viewed.

It is not lived just by individuals but by groups of people together. It has, in fact, a markedly communitarian dimension.

It is rooted in certain passages and events in the gospel that are all interlinked.

I will cite just a few of them.

It presupposes in its members a profound awareness of God for what he is. He is Love, he is Father.

How is it possible, after all, to think of peace and unity in the world without seeing all of humanity as a single family? How can it be seen as such, without a Father for all?

It requires us, therefore, to open our hearts to God the Father, who does not leave his children to their fate, but desires to walk with them, watch over them, help them and, lest they carry too heavy a burden on their shoulders, be the first to support them. Belief in his love is imperative for this new spirituality, the belief that we are loved by him personally, immensely.

Since he knows our hearts, he follows each of us in every detail, knowing even the number of hairs on our heads.... He does not leave the renewal of society to human initiative alone; he inspires and directs it.

Believe. Among the thousand possibilities that human existence offers, select him as the Ideal of your life. I consciously put myself in the attitude that each of us will assume in the future, when we arrive at the destiny to which we have been called: eternity.

Obviously, it is not enough to believe in the love of God; it is not enough to have made the great choice of him as our Ideal. God's presence and his fatherly solicitude for all of us requires each of us to be his daughter or son, to love him in turn; to fulfil day after day that particular plan of love that the Father proposes for each of us: that is, to do his will.

And we know that the will of a father is primarily that his children treat each other as brothers and sisters, by concerning themselves for each other's welfare and loving one another. They must understand and practise what can be called the art of loving.

This means we must be the first to love without waiting for the other to love us.

It means loving the other as oneself, because "You and I," Gandhi says, "are but one. I cannot injure you without harming myself."[2]

This also means knowing how to "make yourself one" with others, that is, making your own their burdens, their thoughts, their sufferings, their joys.

Now, when this love is lived by others it becomes reciprocal.

Christ, the "Son" par excellence of the Father, the Brother of us all, has left us this universal norm: mutual love. He knew it was essential if there were to be peace and unity in the world and all become a single family.

Certainly, for those who set out to move today's mountains of hatred and violence, the task is gigantic and overwhelming. But what is impossible for millions of isolated and separate individuals becomes possible for people who have made mutual love and mutual understanding the centre of their lives.

How is this possible? There is a reason.

A further incredibly important point of this new spirituality, one that is surprising and amazing, is another element from the gospel connected with mutual love. The gospel says that if two or more persons are united in real love, Christ, who is Peace, is present among them. What greater guarantee can there be for those who wish to be instruments of fraternity and peace?

This reciprocal love, this unity that gives such joy to those who practise it requires, however, a commitment that involves daily training and sacrifice.

Here we Christians come to a word full of wisdom and insight that the world does not want to hear, considering it foolishness, absurdity and nonsense.

That word is *cross*.

Nothing good, useful or fruitful is accomplished in the world without knowing how to accept fatigue and suffering, in a word, the cross.

It is not easy to commit yourself to furthering peace! It demands courage and much suffering.

But if more people would accept suffering out of love, with the suffering that love requires, it could become the most powerful weapon for bringing humanity to its highest dignity. The human race would not just be a collection of peoples, one next to the other and often in conflict, but would become a single people, a family.

God the Father has not left us to ourselves on this arduous journey. We know the Church has always been ready to offer us help.

We think of Mary, who is loved, venerated, present also in other religions. She is the mother of Jesus and of us all as well. We can go to her for inspiration, comfort and support. It is always a mother's task to gather and unite the family.

This communitarian spirituality is not exclusively connected with the Focolare Movement; it is universal and can be lived by all.

If fruitful dialogues are initiated with everyone, including the faithful of other religions and people from a wide range of cultures, they will find affirmation for the values they hold, and together we will set out to achieve that fullness of unity we so desire.

Through this spirituality, men and women of almost every nation in the world today are slowly but surely trying to be, at least in their own area, seeds of a new people, for a world more united, a world of peace, giving special attention to the poor and powerless.[3]

Two Sides of the Same Coin

> The spirituality of unity hinges on two fundamental points that Chiara Lubich compares to two sides of a single coin: unity and Jesus Forsaken. In the following two passages she explains these points.[4]

Our aim: "May they all be one"

Whenever we are asked for a definition of our spirituality, or the difference between the gift God has poured out upon our movement and the gifts with which he has graced and enriched other movements in the Church, today and throughout the centuries, we have no hesitation in replying: unity.

Unity is our specific vocation. Unity is what characterizes the Focolare. Unity, and not other ideas or words that to some degree can express other divine and splendid ways to journey towards God, like "poverty," for example, for the Franciscan movement, "obedience" for the Jesuits, "the little way" for St. Thérèse of Lisieux, "prayer" for the Carmelites, and so on.

Unity is the word that sums up the life of our movement. For us, it is the word that carries in itself every other supernatural reality, every other practice or commandment, every other religious approach.

If unity is typical of our vocation, let us take a quick look back to the beginning of our history, when its flame was first kindled, so that we can keep it alive in our hearts, or even revive it if necessary. Let us recall certain episodes and read over again the writings we have kept from that time about this idea.

We will relive especially some familiar episodes from our earliest years in Trent. The war was on. A few girls and I were huddled together in some dark place, perhaps a cellar. By candlelight we were reading the final testament of Jesus. We read through the whole passage. Those difficult words seemed to light up for us, one after another. We felt we understood them. Above all, we felt the solid conviction that what we had before us was the "founding charter" of this new life of ours, and of all that was about to be born around us.

Some time later, aware of the difficulty, if not the impossibility, of putting such a programme into practice, we felt drawn to ask Jesus the favour of teaching us how to live unity.

Kneeling around the altar, we offered our lives to him so that through them, were it his wish, he could accomplish it. As we recall, it was the Feast of Christ the King. A particular sentence from the liturgy of that day struck us deeply, "Ask of me, and I will make the nations your heritage, and the ends of the earth your possession" (Ps 2:8).

And so with faith, we asked.

Later on, joyfully and somewhat astonished, between these episodes and our aspiration for unity we would find a connection with the encyclical that Pius XII offered the world in 1943, the very year our movement was born: *Mystici Corporis* ["On the Mystical Body of Christ"].

One thing was clear in our hearts: what God wanted for us was unity. We live for the sole aim of being one with him, one with each other, and one with everyone. This marvellous vocation linked us to heaven and immersed us in the one human family. What purpose in life could be greater? As far as we are concerned, no ideal is more than this.

Let us go back to our beginnings.

Our daily programme had me giving a small morning meditation to the group of my first companions in a room called the *Sala Massaia*. We would meet at seven in the morning. During that time I felt urged within to silence any thoughts of my own in order to be open to the Holy Spirit, so he could enlighten me should he feel it useful. For this reason I would prepare myself in prayer by declaring my own nothingness and the allness of God. In front of Jesus in the Blessed Sacrament I would repeat over and over: "I am nothing, You are everything." Only after praying like this would I write down a few notes. This was the main way that God was forming us first Focolarine in this new ideal.*

Of the notes that I wrote during those years I still have one, probably from 1946. It speaks of the one thing that most appealed to the Movement coming to life: unity.

The writing draws many things together in few words, as most of my notes did. This one, after indicating the need for us to be another Jesus, seems to make the programme God had for us quite explicit:

"Before all else, the soul must always fix its gaze on the one Father of many children. Then it must see all as children of the same Father. In mind and in heart we must always go beyond the bounds imposed on us by human life

---

* In the years of the Second World War, Chiara Lubich and her first companions met as part of the Franciscan Third Order. But in 1947, Carlo de Ferrari, the Bishop of Trent, recognized the emerging group as a Movement in its own right, which was given the name the Movement of Unity. Later it was called the Focolare Movement, from which the name "Focolarine" derives.

alone and create the habit of constantly opening ourselves to the reality of being one human family in one Father: God."

The note continues:

"Jesus, our model, taught us two things alone, and which are one: to be children of only one Father and to be brothers and sisters to each other."

Further down, it emphasizes one particular virtue as being essential to acquire union with God and neighbour, which St. Paul also writes about in his letters when he spurs Christians to build unity through reciprocal love. The note says:

> A virtue that unites the soul to God ... is humility, the emptying of self. The smallest shred of the human that does not allow itself to be assumed by the divine breaks unity, and with grave consequences. The unity of the soul with God, who lives within us, presupposes a total emptying of self, the most heroic humility....
>
> Humility also leads souls to unity with others: aspire constantly to the "first place" by putting self as much as possible at the service of neighbour.
>
> Every soul that wants to achieve unity must claim only one right: to serve everyone, because in everyone the soul serves God....
>
> Like St. Paul, though free, make ourselves servants of all in order to gain the greatest number (see 1 Cor 9:19). The soul that desires to bring about unity must keep itself in such an abyss of humility that it reaches the point of losing, for the benefit and in the service of God in its neighbour, its very self.
>
> It re-enters itself only to find God and to pray for its brothers and sisters and for itself.
>
> It must live constantly "emptied" because it is totally "in love" with God's will ... and in love with the will of its neighbour, who it wants to serve for God. A servant does only what his or her Master commands.

In the following thought we can see the great revolution that this ideal can bring: "If all people, or at least even a very small group of persons were true servants of God in their 'neighbour,' soon the world would belong to Christ." Loving our neighbour in this way leads to reciprocal love, to unity, to the fulfilment of Jesus' final testament, as it states towards the end of the note.

It then specifies who our neighbour is: the person who passes us by in the present moment of our daily life. We must love that person in such a way that Christ may be born, grow and develop in him or her.

> The important thing is to have one idea of our "neighbour."
>
> Our neighbour is our brother or sister who passes us by in the present moment of our life. We must be ready to serve him or her, because in each neighbour, we serve God. (To have) a simple eye (means) to see only one Father, to serve God in our neighbour, to have only one brother or sister: Jesus.
>
> The simple eye sees in each person "a Christ coming to be." It places self at the service of all ... so that Christ may emerge and grow in them. It sees in each person a Christ being born, who must grow, live, do good, a new child of God who must die, rise, and be glorified....
>
> The soul must give itself no peace until, through its continual service, it recognizes in its brother or sister the spiritual features of Christ.
>
> By living Christ in this way ... it serves Christ in its neighbours so that they may grow in age, wisdom, and grace....
>
> This is the reason why the soul will fulfil its Ideal (Jesus' only ideal), "May they all be one" *(Ut unum sint),** when it makes use of the present moment to serve its neighbour....

So our ideal is to fulfil the prayer Jesus pronounced on Holy Thursday evening. After instituting the Eucharist and the priesthood, and having given his disciples the New Commandment, as tradition holds he descended the steps to the river Kidron, and prayed: "May they all be one" (see Jn 17: 21, 22).

All one. As long as all are not one, the "all" that Jesus surely had in mind, the Movement cannot rest. This is the end for which we were born, the purpose for which he raised us to life.[5]

The key: Jesus crucified and forsaken

If, led by a justifiable desire and also to following the Church's advice (given in order to safeguard the authenticity of the inspirations of religious families, so they can examine themselves according to the times in which the Holy Spirit brought them to life), we look back at the beginnings of the Focolare, we will see that even before we had any ideas about how to achieve unity, we had already been given a model, a figure, life for it. It was

---

* The Latin expression *Ut omnes unum sint,* often abbreviated to *ut omnes*, is taken from Jesus' High Priestly Prayer (Jn 17:21-22).

the One who truly knew how to "make himself one" with all people who have lived, who live now and who will live in the future. He was the one who made unity possible, paying for it with his cross, with his blood and with his "cry," and who gave the Church his presence as the Risen One for all times, until the end of the world: Jesus crucified and forsaken.

Our understanding of him and his reality preceded, in importance but also in time, every of other insight. If with good reason we may say that 7 December 1943 (the day of my consecration to God) is our story's beginning, but we must recall that on 24 January 1944 Jesus forsaken had already presented himself to our minds and hearts.

But let us proceed in order.

As we have done for "unity," in order to review the very first ideas we had about Jesus forsaken, let us look back on the episodes, circumstances, and the writings we still have that speak about him. They are facts and thoughts, some well-known, but we must still look back upon them for a more complete analysis.

The very first episode is our encounter with Jesus forsaken at Dori's* house. We use Dori's own words:

> We were going out to meet the poor and more than likely it was on one of those occasions that my face became infected. I was full of sores and the medicines I took were ineffective. With my face appropriately protected, however, I continued to go to Mass and to the Saturday meetings....
>
> It was cold, and it could have been dangerous for me to continue going out like that. My parents insisted on keeping me at home, so Chiara asked a Capuchin priest to come over and bring Communion to me. After receiving Communion, and while making my thanksgiving, I heard the priest ask Chiara what in her opinion was the moment during his passion that Jesus suffered the most. Chiara responded that she had always heard it was what he went through while praying in the Garden of Olives. But the priest replied, "I believe, instead, that it was what he experienced on the cross when he cried: 'My God, my God, why have you forsaken me?' " (Mt 27:46).
>
> As soon as the priest left, I turned to Chiara for an explanation of the answer she had given to him. Instead she replied: "If Jesus' greatest

---

* Doriana Zamboni, one of Chiara's first companions, to whom Chiara taught philosophy in the years 1943-44.

suffering was his being forsaken by the Father, we will choose him as our Ideal; that is the way we will follow him."

In that moment, my mind and imagination held the conviction that our ideal was Jesus with his anguished face crying out to the Father. And the mere sores on my face, which seemed to me a shadow of his own suffering, gave me joy, because they were making me a bit similar to him. Since that day, Chiara often, actually always, spoke to me of Jesus forsaken. He was *the* living personality in our lives.

One single choice ... a radical one: Jesus forsaken.

Our letters from that time emphasize it:

"Forget everything ... even the most sublime things; let yourself be ruled by one single Idea, by the one God alone who must penetrate every fibre of your being: by Jesus crucified" (21 July 1945).

"Do you know the lives of the saints? They could be summed up in two words: Jesus crucified; Christ's wounds were their rest; his blood, a healthy bath for their souls; his side, the treasure chest they filled with love. Ask of Christ crucified, through his cry of anguish, a passion for his passion.

"He must be everything for you" (21 July 1944).

Jesus forsaken was the only book we wanted to read.

"Yes, true enough I am going to college, but no book, however beautiful it may be, can give my soul such strength, and above all, such love, as Jesus forsaken..." (7 June 1944).

And further:

"But above all, learn from one book alone ... Jesus crucified, abandoned by everyone! He who cries out, 'My God, my God, why have you forsaken me?' Oh! If that divine face contorted by spasms, and those reddened eyes that look at you with goodness, forgetting your sins and mine that have reduced him to this, were always before your eyes..." (30 January 1944).

Over the years to come, from time to time we were to renew this radical choice.

A letter of 1948 says:

"Forget everything in life: office, work, people, responsibilities, hunger, thirst, rest, even your own soul ... in order to have nothing but him. This is everything ... to love as he loved us, to the extent of his experiencing for our sake even the sensation of being forsaken by his Father" (14 August 1948).

And in 1949: "I have only one Spouse on earth, Jesus forsaken. I have no God but him."

We knew nothing but him. We did not want to know anything but him. The Holy Spirit kept repeating in us: "I know only Christ and him crucified." Love for him was exclusive; it did not permit compromises.

The choice of God, which had characterized the first step of our new life, became clearer: to choose God for us meant to choose Jesus forsaken....

Jesus forsaken was the only book we read. And what did the Holy Spirit have us read in that book?

We immediately contemplated in him *the height of his love because it was the height of his suffering.* All the love of a God is revealed in Jesus forsaken.

A letter from January 1944 (a week after our first encounter with Jesus forsaken) already stated:

"Joys will come to you, suffering and anguish will come. But if you will only make the effort to see Jesus in the way I present him to you now, and always will present him to you, in the *height of suffering*, which is the height of love ..." (30 January 1944).

And, in another place:

"This is where it all lies. This is all the love of a God" (7 June 1944).

And again:

"Do you know that he gave us *everything*? What more could a God give us, that for love it seems he forgets that he is God?" (8 December 1944).

Consequently, we sensed right from the very beginning, with endless gratitude, how superb a gift our calling was to follow him:

"You don't know what fortune it is for you and for us to follow this Love forsaken!

"He, in his mysterious plans, chose us among thousands and thousands to allow us to hear his cry of anguish: 'My God, my God, why have you forsaken me?' " (8 December 1944).

Looking through these writings that we have kept from that time, we have the impression that this love for Jesus forsaken has entered, penetrated, and swept through our hearts like a fire that consumes everything, saving nothing; like a divine passion that overwhelms and completely engages our heart, mind, strength; like a bolt of lightning that illuminates everything. We saw. We understood. They were rivers of light.

Jesus forsaken enlightened us, for example, on the place suffering has in the divine economy. "Jesus converted the world with his words, with his example, and with his preaching, but he transformed it when he provided the proof of his love: the cross" (1944).

We saw in him, in his immense suffering, his divine love completely laid open, and such vision inflamed our hearts and spurred us to give value to our own personal suffering and offer it as an expression of our love for him, even to becoming in him and with him, co-redeemers.

"Just think ... God came on earth only once, and in that one time he became man and let himself be nailed to a cross! This thought gives me great strength to accept joyfully the little crosses that always seem to accompany us" (1944).

"Those who know Love and unite their suffering to the sufferings of Jesus on the cross, letting their own drop of blood lose itself in the sea of Christ's divine blood, have the most honoured place human beings can hold: to be like God come down on earth: redeemer of the world ... " (1944).

"Believe it, one minute of your life on that sickbed, if you accept it as a gift of God, is worth more than all the words of a preacher who may speak a lot, but loves God little" (1944).

"He has poured a great passion into my heart: him, crucified and forsaken!

"From the height of the cross he tells me: 'I let everything of mine fade away ... everything! I am no longer beautiful, or strong; I have no peace here; justice is dead here; knowledge is gone; truth has vanished. All that is left is my Love, which wanted to pour out *for you* the riches *of God ...* '

"This is how he speaks to me, and how he is calling me ... to follow him ...

"He is my Passion!" (25 December 1944).

"In front of him, every suffering seems nothing, and I await the small or big sufferings to come as God's greatest gifts, for this is the proof of my love for him!" (7 June 1944).

But we saw in him not only the height of suffering, and the place suffering holds in the divine economy; we contemplated in him the secret of sanctity.

"Do you remember St. Rita? In the dark corner of her room, where her two children slept, hung the crucified God-Man. He was the secret of her love: he, and he alone.

"Descending from the cross to meet her came the perfect example of patience, of forgiveness, of ever-enduring love holding strong until death, even to dying forsaken!

"He would guide her to the greatest heights of sanctity, because Rita loved Jesus crucified before anything else ... " (1948).

Because he revealed all these riches, we saw him as the pearl of great price that God was offering to us. His was a love so sublime, so extraordinary (it reduced him to becoming for us a "worm of the earth" and "sin"!), that we were convinced that no one could ever resist him; his love was so immense that no one could ever repay him!

"Oh, we have found it, yes, we have found the pearl of great price!

"Oh! Our Love!

"Oh! That man, that 'worm of the earth' ... is ours!

"The soul that has found him leaves everything to embrace him! She too, like the bride in the Song of Songs, goes in search of her treasure; she loves him, and *adores him!*

"What lover would not draw such a love to herself? I wish I could run through the world and gather hearts for him, and I sense how all the hearts in the world would not be enough for a Love so great as God's!" (15 June 1948).

We were still in only the first year of our experience when the Holy Spirit had already revealed Jesus forsaken to us as the norm of our new life. A letter from 1944 says: "As God he made that cry the norm of a new life, according to a new ideal" (8 December 1944).

It was a new spirituality, therefore, that the Holy Spirit was showering upon earth. It was a new ideal; he was calling us to be among the first to live it.

Time made everything clearer: God was calling us to Unity (we listed the signs of this vocation above), and Jesus forsaken was its secret: he was the condition to fulfil Jesus' final testament: "May they all be one."

A letter of 1948 addressed to young monks, and which describes our experience, affirms, not without surprise on our part, an existing connection between Jesus forsaken and unity with God and with one another.

"I have experienced that every soul that finds itself in the front lines of Unity, and for Unity, knows how to stand supported only by a Suffering-Love as strong as that of Jesus forsaken" (1 April 1948).

"It is for this reason, brothers, that ... we have chosen as our only purpose in life, our only aim, our everything: Jesus crucified who cries: 'My God, my God, why have you forsaken me?' It is Jesus in his deepest suffering! Infinite disunity ... to give us perfect unity that we will reach only relatively here on earth, and then perfectly in heaven ... " (1 April 1948).

And in another letter addressed to a monk:

"Try ... to embrace him.

"If I had not had him in the trials of life, this way of unity would not exist, unless Jesus had wished to raise it up elsewhere.

"Forsaken he won every battle in me, the most terrible of battles.

"But you have to be madly in love with him, who is the synthesis of all physical and spiritual suffering: the medicine ... for every pain of the soul" (23 April 1948).

Let us now read almost the entire letter written to a young monk in 1948, a letter that has as its theme: "My God, my God, why have you forsaken me?" In it we can already find the most important assertions about Jesus forsaken, which burst forth in full clarity and force: a page that sums up to some extent our thoughts about him. Right at the beginning it affirms that the one who truly understands unity is the one who loves Jesus forsaken:

"I am convinced that unity in its deepest, most intimate and spiritual aspect, can be understood only by those who have chosen as their portion in life ... Jesus forsaken who cries out, 'My God, my God, why have you forsaken me?' "

The letter then proclaims Jesus forsaken as the secret and guarantee of unity.

"Brother, now that I have found understanding in you on what is the secret of unity, I would want to speak to you about it for days on end, and I could. Know that Jesus forsaken is everything. He is the guarantee of unity. Every light about unity comes out of that cry."

It affirms that to choose him is to generate to unity an infinite number of souls.

"To choose him as our only purpose, our only aim, our life's end is ... to generate to unity an infinite number of souls."

Continuing further, the letter states categorically how already back then our emerging spirituality had two essential points: Unity and Jesus forsaken; and we speak of them as being two sides of the same coin.

"The book of light that God is writing in my soul has two aspects: a luminous page of mysterious love: Unity. A luminous page of mysterious suffering: Jesus forsaken. They are two faces of the same coin" (30 March 1948).

We understood, moreover, that it was a new light, and we wanted to protect it in order not to give "holy things" to those who are not ready for them:

"Brother, not everyone understands these words. Let's not give them to just anyone. Let Love forsaken see himself surrounded only by hearts who understand him, because they have felt him come into their lives and have found in him the solution to everything ... " (30 March 1948).

During that time we would come to define Jesus forsaken as the one most greatly Pruned, whom neither heaven nor earth seemed to want. We would say: earth does not want him, nor does heaven; and we concluded: he really can be entirely ours.

Because he had been uprooted from both earth and heaven, he brought into unity those who were "cut off," those who were uprooted from God. He was truly the way required to reach unity.

Through Jesus, in fact, we gain by losing, we live by dying; the grain of wheat has to die in order to produce the ear of grain; we need to be pruned in order to bear good fruit. That is Jesus' law, his paradox. The Holy Spirit was making us understand that in order to bring about Jesus' prayer "may they all be one" in the world, it is necessary to consume in ourselves any form of abandonment, to welcome Jesus forsaken in any disunity.

To some religious brothers, who had not obtained permission from their superiors to take part in such a new movement, we wrote in 1949:

> And have we not also understood … that the greatest Ideal a human heart could desire — unity — is just a vague dream, or just smoke, if those who desire it do not set their hearts exclusively on Jesus who was forsaken by all, even by his very Father? Doesn't this apparent separation … from your brothers and sisters, who outside the university struggle, live, and suffer for your very same Ideal, perhaps appear to you to be a small Jesus forsaken?
>
> It is only by way of embracing Jesus forsaken, so entirely wounded in body and completely darkened in soul, with all your heart, that you will be formed in unity…. Here lies the greatest secret and the final dream of our Jesus: May they all be one! And both you and we, made sharers in this infinite Suffering, will contribute effectively to the unity of all! (17 February 1949).

As we read through these first writings, we realize what our God-given charism looks towards: "May they all be one." To achieve this aim we were given a road, a key, a secret: Jesus forsaken.

Jesus came on earth so that all may be one. Jesus crucified and forsaken paid for this aim. He wants a hand from us to achieve it: the Work of Mary* has made it its specific purpose. It can accomplish it with Jesus forsaken, in him and through him.

The charism of the Focolare has come down from heaven with the specific intention of the Holy Spirit to advance Jesus' cause, which the Church must always pursue: may they all be one. To whoever those letters of our early times were addressed, they asked for one thing alone: the commitment to live for "may they all be one." It is very significant that those reached first were people of all kinds: young girls, religious, young men, and adults. It shows that this ideal was meant for everyone; all vocations were set in motion.

Some understood, and some did not. Those who were touched and enlightened felt morally committed to the ideal "may they all be one."[6]

---

* This is the name under which the Focolare Movement was approved by the Roman Catholic Church in 1962.

A Spirituality of Communion

> Selection from an address given at Milan, 9 March 1995, when receiving the Author of the Year Prize from the UELCI (Union of Italian Catholic Publishers and Booksellers).[7]

One of the more original characteristics of this spirituality of unity is its communitarian dimension.

In the two thousand years from the time of Christ, the Church has experienced the flowering of the most beautiful and fruitful spiritualities one after the other. Sometimes they occurred in the same period, adorning the Spouse of Christ with many saints, like precious pearls and diamonds.

But in all this splendour one factor has always remained constant; spirituality was focused primarily on the advance of the individual towards God.

This is a consequence of those early days when Christians lost the first fervour of the Jerusalem community in which all were of one heart and soul. With the end of persecution, they sought to preserve their own personal faith by withdrawing to the desert with the primary goal of keeping the first commandment, love of God. These were the days of the hermits.

This development preserved many Christian ideals and produced many saints, but it did not put much emphasis on the place of one's neighbour in the spiritual life. In fact the neighbour was often considered an obstacle to one's advance towards God.*

Abba Arsenius was inspired by the words: "Fly from men and you shall be saved."[8]

Many centuries later we find in *The Imitation of Christ*, a very beautiful book: "A wise man said: 'Every time I go among men, I return less a man.' "[9]

"Individual" spiritualities, in view of the mystery of the Mystical Body of Christ, are never exclusively individual, insofar as what happens in one person always has an effect on others. We see this expressed in the consistent Christian practice of praying and doing penance on behalf of others.

---

* The following quotations that today could surprise or even scandalize us need to be understood in the context of the spirituality of their time. Christian spirituality has developed historically, and over time it has become less confined to monasticism, which had been a way of protecting it.

But times have changed.

Now the Holy Spirit is inspiring people to walk together, in fact, to be of one heart and soul with all who share their convictions.

The Holy Spirit has motivated our Movement from the beginning to make this outreach towards others. In the spirituality of unity one advances towards God by going through one's neighbour.

"I — my brother — God," we say. You go to God with other people, your brothers and sisters, or rather, you go to God through others.

According to the research of our scholars, at least in the initial overview, this is the first time in the Church for a spirituality of unity like this, with its special emphasis on the communitarian dimension of the Christian life.

Yes, previously there were some such experiences, especially where love was seen as the basis of spiritual life.

For example, Saint Basil based his spirituality on the first commandment, to love God, and on the second, to love one's neighbour.

For Saint Augustine, especially, mutual love and unity had the highest value.

But Father Jesus Castellano, a recognized expert in spiritual theology, says:

> In the history of Christian spirituality it was said: "Christ is in me, he lives in me," and that is the perspective of individual spirituality, life in Christ. When it also was said: "Christ is present in my brothers," this develops the perspective of works of charity, but it falls short of saying that if Christ is in me and Christ is in you, then Christ in me loves Christ in you and vice versa ... which would involve a mutual giving and a receiving.
>
> There is also a communitarian, ecclesial spirituality of the Mystical Body.... This spirituality is a hallmark of our century, where there has been a rediscovery of the Church.
>
> The Movement gives us "something extra" with its collective spirituality and that is the vision and creation of a communion, an ecclesial life of the "Mystical Body," in which there is a mutual giving of persons and the dimension of becoming "one."
>
> Even though contemporary authors hint at this dimension of spiritual theology, what is lacking is the proposal of a concrete lifestyle, a lived experience, spelling out its simplest details as well as its more challenging demands.[10]

Contemporary theologians foresaw a communitarian spirituality in our times and Vatican II proposed it.

Karl Rahner speaks of the spirituality of the Church of the future, saying that he sees: "fraternal community in which the same all-sustaining experience of the Spirit becomes possible: fraternal community as a real and essential element of the spirituality of tomorrow." He says:

> By origin and education we older people were spiritually individualists.... Where was there a communal experience of the Spirit, clearly conceived, desired, and experienced in a general way — as it evidently was at the Church's first Pentecost — that was not presumably an accidental local gathering of a number of individual mystics, but an experience of the Spirit on the part of a community?... In the spirituality of the future as such, I suspect anyway that the element of a fraternal, spiritual fellowship, of a communally lived spirituality, can play a greater part and be slowly but courageously acquired and developed.[11]

Cardinal Montini in 1957 said that in these times what has been the exception should become the rule and that the holiness of the extraordinary individual, while still venerated, should give way to some extent to a sanctity of the people, to the people of God who become holy.[12]

In our era the reality of communion is coming to the forefront; the kingdom of God is sought not just in individual persons but in the midst of the people.*

Spiritualities characterized as individual usually make precise demands on those involved, such as:

Solitude and flight from the world to reach mystical communion with God within.

The silence that solitude requires.

Separation from others by a veil, a cloister as well as a particular habit.

The practice of all kinds of penances, sometimes very difficult ones like fasts and vigils, in imitation of the passion of Christ.

In the way of unity we do seek solitude and silence in response to Jesus' invitation to go to your room to pray, and do avoid others if they lead us to sin, but generally we welcome our brothers and sisters, we love Christ in our

---

* The apostolic letter of John Paul II, *Novo millennio ineunte*, devotes a chapter to what he calls "the spirituality of communion" (42-57).

neighbours, in every neighbour, as Christ is living in them or can be revived in them through the help we offer. We seek to be united with our brothers and sisters in the name of Jesus, who guarantees his presence in our midst (see Mt 18:20).

In the individual spiritualities it is like being in a magnificent garden (the Church), looking with admiration at a single flower, the presence of God within. In a collective spirituality we love and admire all the flowers in the garden, every presence of Christ in others. And we love him in others as we love him within ourselves.

Since communitarian life must be fully personal as well, it is our general experience when we are alone that, after loving our brothers and sisters, we become aware of our union with God. We may, in fact, pick up a book to meditate, only to find that he wants to speak within us.

So it can be said that when we go to our brothers and sisters in the right way, by loving as the gospel teaches, we become more Christ, more truly human.

And, since we try to be united with our brothers and sisters, in addition to silence we have a special love for the word, as a means of communication.

We speak in order to become one with others.

We speak, in the Movement, in order to share our experiences of living the Word of Life* or of our own spiritual life, aware that the fire that does not grow is extinguished[13] and that this communion of soul has great spiritual value. Saint Lawrence Giustiniani said:

"Nothing in the world gives more praise to God and reveals him as worthy of praise than the humble and fraternal exchange of spiritual gifts...."[14]

We speak at major gatherings in order to keep alive the fire of God's love in everyone.

When we do not speak, we write: we write letters, articles, books, diaries to advance the kingdom of God in our hearts. We use all the modern means of communication. And we dress like everyone else to avoid creating a sense of separateness from others.

In the Movement we also practise those mortifications that are indispensable for every Christian life. We do penance, especially as recommended by

---

* A sentence from Scripture that the members of the Movement strive to put into practice each month. The expression comes from Paul: "shine like stars in the world ... by your holding fast to the word of life" (Phil 2:15-16).

the Church, but we have special regard for those penances that a life of unity with others entails.

That is not easy, for the "old self," as Paul calls it,* is always ready to find its way back into us.

Fraternal unity is not established once for all; it must be renewed continually. When there is unity and through it Jesus is in our midst, we experience great joy, as promised by Jesus in his prayer for unity. When unity is compromised, the shadows and confusion return and we live in a kind of purgatory. That is the kind of penance we must be ready to practise.

Here is where our love for Jesus crucified and forsaken, the key to unity, comes in. We must first resolve all our differences out of love for him, and make every effort to restore unity.

So we pray, especially liturgical prayer such as the Mass, because it is the prayer of the Church.

Typically we use collective prayer as taught by Jesus: "If two of you agree on earth about anything you ask, it will be done for you by my Father in heaven" (Mt 18:19).

For those who follow the way of unity, the presence of Jesus in the midst of their brothers and sisters is essential.

Despite our personal inadequacy, we must always keep this presence alive.

It is precisely this that characterizes the charism of unity.

Just as two poles of electricity, even when there is a current, do not produce light until they are joined together, likewise two persons cannot experience the light of this charism until they are united in Christ through charity.

In this way of unity, everything — in our work, study, prayer, striving towards sanctity or the spreading of Christian life — takes on meaning and value, as long as we keep, with our brothers and sisters, the presence of Jesus in our midst, for that is the norm of norms for this way of life.

In this spirituality we reach sanctity if we walk towards God in unity....

St. Teresa of Avila, a doctor of the church, speaks of an "interior castle." It is the soul with the divine majesty dwelling at its centre, revealing and shedding light on everything throughout life, allowing it to overcome every sort of trial. Even though St. Teresa drew all her daughters into this experience, it is a height of sanctity that is primarily personal.

---

* Old self: in the Pauline sense, a person imprisoned by egoism, see Eph 4:22.

But then came the moment at least so it seemed to us, of discovery, of shedding light upon and building not just the "interior castle" but "the exterior castle."

We see the whole Movement as an exterior castle, where Christ is present, illuminating every part of it from the centre to the periphery.

But if we consider that this new spirituality God is giving the Church today has reached leaders in Church and society, then we see that this charism makes an exterior castle not only of our Movement, but tends to do so as well in the whole body of the Church and of society.

Pope John Paul II, speaking recently to some seventy bishops, friends of the Movement, said: "The Lord Jesus ... did not call his followers to individual discipleship but to a discipleship that is both personal and communitarian. And if that is true for all the baptized, it is true in a special way ... for the apostles and for their successors the bishops."[15]

So this spirituality, like all charisms, is for the whole people of God whose vocation is to become ever more united and ever more holy.

Look at All the Flowers

> As with other writings in this volume from the years 1949 and 1950, this text employs a "mystical" style. This passage and the others from the same period introduce strikingly new perspectives for Christian spirituality, but require care and theological discernment if they are to be properly understood.
>
> The following passage contains an early (1950) summary of the characteristic elements of a spirituality of communion, as it is described in the previous selection.

The faithful, who strive for perfection, generally seek union with God present in their hearts.

It is as if they were in a great garden full of flowers observing and admiring a single flower. They gaze on it with love, in all its details and as a whole, but they do not much notice the other flowers.

God — because of the collective spirituality he has given us — asks us to look at all the flowers, because he is in them all, and by observing them all we love him more than the individual flowers.

God who is in me, who has shaped my soul, who lives there as Trinity, is also in the heart of my brothers and sisters.

Thus it is not enough that I love him only in me. If I do, in my love there is still something personal and, considering the spirituality that I am called to live, potentially self-centred: I love God in me, and not God in God, while perfection is: God in God.

Therefore, my cell, as the souls intimate with God would say, and my heaven, as we would say, is within me and, just as it is within me, it is in the soul of my brothers and sisters. And just as I love him in me, recollecting myself in this heaven — when I am alone — I love him in my brother or sister when he or she is close to me.

And so I no longer love only silence, but also the word: the communication between God in me with God in my brother or sister. And if these two heavens meet, a single Trinity comes to be, where the two are like Father and Son and among them is the Holy Spirit.

Yes, you should always recollect yourself also in the presence of a brother or sister, but not avoiding the person, rather recollecting him or her within your own heaven and recollecting yourself in the heaven of the other.

And, since this Trinity dwells in human bodies, Jesus is there: the God-Man.

And among the two there is unity, where they are one, but not alone. This is the miracle of the Trinity and the beauty of God who is not alone because he is Love.

Therefore the soul, after an entire day of having lost God within itself willingly in order to transfer itself to God in its brother or sister (because one is the same as the other, just as the two flowers of the garden are the work of the same maker), and having done so out of love for Jesus crucified and forsaken who leaves God for God (and precisely God in self for God present or soon to be born in the brother or sister ...), returning to itself or better to God within (because alone in prayer or meditation), will encounter the caress of the Spirit who — because he is Love — is truly Love, because God cannot fall short of his word and gives to those who have given: he gives love to those who have loved.

Thus darkness and unhappiness with aridity and all other bitter things disappear leaving only the fullness of joy promised to those who have lived Unity.

The cycle is complete.

We must give life continuously to these living cells of the Mystical Body of Christ — who are brothers and sisters united in his name — in order to revive the whole Body.

To look at all the flowers is to have Jesus' vision, of Jesus who, besides being head of the Mystical Body, is everything: all the Light, the Word, while we are his words. But if each of us loses self in our brother or sister and forms a cell with them (a cell of the Mystical Body), we become the whole Christ, the Word. That is why Jesus says, "The glory that you have given me I have given them" (Jn 17:22).

But we need to know how to lose God within us for God in our brothers and sisters. And this can be done by whoever knows and loves Jesus crucified and forsaken.*

---

* The expression "to lose God within us for God in our brothers and sisters" is typical of the spirituality of unity. It refers to the need to be detached from everything, even from our own experience of God, to make ourselves one with our brothers and sisters, following the example of Jesus "who, though he was in the form of God ... emptied himself" (Phil 2:6-7) to make himself one with us.

And when the tree will blossom fully — when the Mystical Body will be completely revived — it will reflect the seed whence it was born. It will be one, because all the flowers will be one among themselves just as each is one with itself. Christ is the seed. The Mystical Body is the foliage.

Christ is Father to the tree: he was never so much so as during his forsakenness when he generated us as his children, in his forsakenness when he annihilated himself remaining: God.

The Father is root to the Son. The Son is seed to his brothers and sisters.

And it was also the Desolate who, in her silent consent to being Mother of other children, cast this seed in heaven and the tree blossomed and continues to blossom on earth.[16]

The Way of Unity

> The following passage, from 1950, in the light of the spirituality of unity, reformulates the relationship between the three traditional ways of ascent to union with God. These ways of ascent, based on the writings of the Pseudo-Dionysius the Aeropagite in the sixth century, were called purgative, illuminative, and unitive.[17]

Those who enter the way of unity, enter into Jesus. They put themselves aside in order to live Jesus. Actually, because they can only do one thing, they do not even put themselves aside; they go straight to living Jesus.

And those who live Jesus do not find themselves on a way, but on *the* Way. It is the Way on which the other ways (purgative, illuminative, and unitive), working trinitarianly, are united to one another; they join into one. Those who live Jesus are purified by this very fact, and are so enlightened as to be his very same Light.

Those who enter the way of unity do not climb a mountain with exhausting effort, but through an initial and total commitment, made out of a love that brings about a death to their own selves, a total emptying of themselves, of their entire humanity into God (and only total emptying is love), come to find themselves instead already at the top of the mountain. It is impossible to go any higher and it is rest ("Come to me … and I will give you rest"). Their journey begins on the mountain crest going all the way to God, always starting again, in the same way as before, if they should stop.

Those who enter the way of unity live as children of God right from the very start. They are perfect as the Father right from the start, as the Child Jesus was perfect while he was still a child. Their growth is more like a manifestation that could be compared to that of a tree. While the tree is no more perfect than the seed that contained it, it is the manifestation of what the seed contained.

The gospel does not really speak about climbing. It says instead: "No one who puts a hand to the plough and looks back…. " It speaks more about "entering," which presupposes a road, but on that road carrying a yoke that is easy and light.

It would be like travelling on a ray of the sun. Each one of the sun's rays is still the sun itself, but its light grows in intensity the closer it gets to the sun. It is similar for those who live unity. They live by allowing themselves to penetrate always more into God. They grow always closer to God, who lives in their hearts, and the closer they get to him, the closer they get to the hearts of their brothers and sisters.

Those who live unity are already purified and enlightened. They are an expression of living purity, in the widest sense of the word, and of living light. Those who live unity are living gospels, and by living Jesus they live these three words of his:

Those who live the word are already purified;

I will manifest myself to the one who loves me;

Those who remain united to me bear much fruit.[18]

They are three different ways, but lost in one, each way having the same value as the other. They are three, but one. And yet they are not just three, because they also contain all the other words of Jesus, and therefore, all the effects of the gospel.

Mary in the Focolare Movement

> In October 2002 Pope John Paul II wished to dedicate a year to Mary. In opening this year he added the mysteries of light to those that had made up the rosary for centuries. In a personal letter to Chiara Lubich, he entrusted this prayer to all the members of the Focolare, inviting them to "offer their contribution, so that these months may become an occasion of interior renewal for every Christian community."[19] The Focolare responded by organizing a Marian Congress in April 2003 at Castel Gandolfo (near Rome). The following text is from the talk Chiara Lubich gave on that occasion.

On 16 October of last year, the Holy Father delivered a message to me, in which he entrusted "ideally" to all the members of the Focolare the task of cooperating in highlighting and spreading the rosary during this year dedicated to it....

Now someone may ask: what did it mean for the members of the Movement, particularly for me, to have received such an assignment, such a privilege?

Above all, I felt yet again a renewed warmth towards the Holy Father, who once again wished to show a sign of trust in our Movement. And, naturally, it made me wish to carry out his desire. At the same time I had a heartfelt desire to understand the relationship between our charism and this new task that he had given us. On the one hand, an ecclesial reality such as our own is centred on living and spreading the gospel, by which we give our contribution, in the Church, to fulfilling Jesus' final testament, that is, unity. On the other, we were being asked to participate in spreading this glorious devotion to Mary.

At the time I vaguely recalled how in the beginning of the Movement, although I and all us had always loved her, at a precise moment Mary made her presence felt when the Holy Spirit, with a new charism of his, began to pour his light upon us. My thoughts did not go any further than that. I had, however, an intuition that I needed to revisit that period in our history to find the answer to my question.

And then, beyond any expectation, out of the enormous collection of papers and documents about our history, on that same day I picked up something I had from the 50s that helped me understand a little more.

The text began with the words of a song ... and continued, in diary form, with the following passage that moved me deeply:

> (One day) under a heavy bombardment, after being thrown to the ground and covered with dust that completely filled the air, almost miraculously I was able to stand up ... , and in the midst of the cries of those around me, I felt calm and very much at peace. I realized how deep a sorrow I had just felt in my soul as my life was in danger: it was the sorrow of no longer being able to recite on earth the Hail Mary.
>
> At that time I did not grasp the sense of those thoughts. Only later, after I had witnessed the beads of a living rosary coming together (the first group of Focolarine), and God, selecting people, as it were flower by flower, as he composed that Work now entirely Mary's, did I understand the cause of my lament.
>
> Perhaps it was in God's plans that praise be given to her in this age during which Popes have set such precious gems in her crown: the Immaculate One, Assumed into Heaven, our Queen! The Hail Mary I desired, though, had to be made of living words, with persons who, almost like little Marys, would give Love to the world.

The beads of a living rosary!

Living words! Other little Marys!

This is the light I was waiting for. This was, and is, the fundamental relationship between our Movement and the rosary.

It could only be this way for us, and like this reciting the rosary can have its full value, because true and authentic praise is best given by those who try to imitate the person praised.

To be able to say the Hail Mary for us, for me, would mean to build a spiritual shrine to Mary, to her glory, a glory that she, "the transparency of God," always turns back to him. And, since our Movement was to be, above all, a living rosary, then one can see why, through a divine intuition, we named it: the "Work of Mary."

After that first manifestation of Mary, for some time after we made no further discoveries about her. We thought that she might wish to be for us as she was for the early Church: to not appear in order to leave all space for

Jesus. And we compared her to a door, the door that leads to Christ, "and a door," we said, "is not a door if it does not let anyone pass."

Only later did we understand that what happened in our newly born movement could not have come about except through her influence, though her presence was hidden.

In fact, the new style of life, the "spirituality of unity," whose key points the Holy Spirit was branding upon our hearts, seemed to us almost like milk from Mary that nourished our souls.

For those truths we found in the gospel and lived (God-Love, the will of God, the Word, love for neighbour, Jesus crucified and forsaken, unity), all linked together, gave us the possibility, through mutual love, to "generate,"[20] as Pope Paul VI put it, Jesus among us: "Where two or three are gathered in my name (in my love, the Fathers of the Church explain), I am there among them" (Mt 18:20).

Jesus spiritually present among us! The same Jesus who was given physical life through Mary. As the Council says, Mary and "the Holy Spirit ... brought forth Christ ... that ... he may be born and may increase in the hearts of the faithful."[21]

For this reason, we presumed that also in that period Mary was present with the Holy Spirit.

But when the moment arrived for, we could say, her official arrival, she showed herself, or better, God revealed her to us, as great to the degree that she knew how to disappear. And she was great, great.

It was in 1949, during a period of special graces (perhaps an "illuminative" period of our history) that God wanted to tell our hearts something about Mary.

We understood, for example, that she, set as a rare and unique creature within the Holy Trinity, was all Word of God, all dressed in the Word of God. And so strong was our impression of this understanding that it seemed to us that only angels could utter something of her.

If, in fact, the Word is the splendour of the Father, Mary, so imbued with the Word of God, appeared to us as having incomparable beauty.

And it is the Magnificat that tells us how Mary is all Word of God, as it is a continuous succession of words from scripture: the Virgin Mary was so nourished by the scriptures that in her speaking she was accustomed to use its very same expressions.

And it appeared so clear to us that what characterized Mary, though in her unique perfection, should characterize every Christian: to repeat Christ, the Truth, with the personality given to each by God.

Seen in this way, with the eyes of the soul, Mary was deeply attractive to us, and in us a new love was born for her.

A new love, this love of ours, and Mary in a gospel manner responded by showing us more clearly that which made her great beyond words: being the Mother of God, Theotokos.

She was not, as we knew her from before, only the young girl from Nazareth, the most beautiful creature in the world, the heart that contains and surpasses the sum total of the love of all earthly mothers put together; she was the Mother of God.

And the slightest intuition of this mystery was enough to silence us in adoration and gratitude towards God for having done so much in a single creature.

It appeared to us, in fact, that, with this new understanding of her, Mary revealed a dimension of herself we had almost completely ignored till then.

Before that, to make a comparison, we saw Mary before Christ and the saints just as in the sky the moon (Mary) is before to the sun (Christ) and the stars (the saints). Now it was different: we saw the Mother of God as an enormous blue sky that embraces the sun itself, which is God.

God, in his infinite love for this privileged creature, had in a certain way "made himself small" in front of her.[*] "He emptied himself" (Phil 2:7) St. Paul says of Jesus. And this began in Mary's womb.

I remember how, having understood at least a little how great she was, we wanted almost to shout out to everyone that only now had we understood Mary!

Seeing Mary as all Word of God has always seemed to us to bring fruitful consequences, for example, in the ecumenical field. What joy do our evangelical brothers and sisters linked to the Movement experience when they discover in her the "personification" of the scriptures. So many have underlined the value of that discovery.

At the same time, if Mary is all Word of God, everyone can understand how Christians may see her, venerate her, follow her, after Christ, as their leader; how they sing of her, paint her, dedicate poems to her.

---

[*] St. Ephrem the Syrian in his *Hymn on the Nativity* writes: "In the womb of Mary the One who is equal to the Father from all eternity became a child: he gave us his greatness and took to himself our smallness" (*Corpus Scriptorum Orientalium* 187, p. 180).

Certainly, while Mary is indeed Mother of God, she is also quite different from all other Christians. If God himself made her so beautiful as to find his delight in her, to exalt her, as the words of the angel say: "Greetings, O full of grace, the Lord is with you" (see Lk 1:28), she deserves a special place.

We can understand then how in the Catholic and Orthodox churches we find images of Mary, and see how there is good reason for every manifestation of honour and affection that men and women address to her.

There is another aspect of Mary that has attracted the Movement since its beginnings. It is the Virgin Mary's relationship with suffering: Our Lady of Sorrows, as she is popularly called. We call her the Desolate, a name that recalls the solitude that she often met in her life, especially at the foot of the cross, that solitude in which she always knew how to lose everything in order to make herself one with God's will.

When Jesus, indicating John, said to her: "Woman, here is your son!" (Jn 19:26), she experienced a terrible trial in losing Jesus, not only because he was dying, but also because someone else was taking his place, a terrible suffering for a mother's heart.

At that moment she pronounced a *fiat* different from the first. With the first, at the Annunciation, it seemed to Mary, who since her childhood, as it is thought, had consecrated herself to God as a virgin for the whole of her life, that now she had to change her intentions. She was to be the mother of Jesus, and still remain a virgin.

With her second *fiat*, on Calvary, she renounced Jesus; only in this way did she become mother of all, acquiring countless human beings as her children.

Pope Pius XII says, "She (Mary) … offered Him (Jesus) on Golgotha to the Eternal Father … and her mother's rights and her mother's love were included in the holocaust. Thus she who, according to the flesh, was the mother of our Head … became, according to the Spirit, the mother of all His members."[22]

After these illuminations, if we can call them that, because of the love that she had showed us and because of the love that had increased in our hearts towards her, I recall that the same thing happened to us as to St. Thérèse of Lisieux when, as a child, she said, "I knew … that I was her child — I began calling her 'Mamma,' because 'Mother' didn't seem intimate enough."[23]

We felt, in a way we could never forget, that Mary was our mother. Moreover, this conviction born in us was so strong that it made us feel that Mary for us was "more a mother than our own mothers."[24]

Mary was a wellspring of inspirations in our life that here I can only list. There was a moment when, in grasping more deeply the meaning of a name attributed to her, Mother of Fair Love, we understood it was her desire to let us participate somewhat in her maternity of love. Or when we saw her as the servant of God, a mere creature recollected in front of him, adoring him. Or when she appeared to us as truly *the Daughter* par excellence, "the beloved daughter of the Father," as the Council calls her;[25] we found her so extraordinarily beautiful that we called her the Woman of Love.

Clear for us was Mary's being an *example*, a *pattern*: she represented a model for us, what we "should be," while we saw ourselves persons who "could be" Mary.

We saw in ourselves therefore the possibility of becoming a little Mary, of becoming similar to her, each a child who *alone* has the features of its mother, a conviction that was confirmed in a unique episode.

One day, years later, urged I think by the Holy Spirit, I went into church, and with my heart full of trust, I asked: "Why did you wish to remain on earth, on every point of the earth, in the most sweet Eucharist, and you have not found, you who are God, also a way to bring and to leave here Mary, the mother of all of us who journey?"

And from the tabernacle, in the silence he seemed to reply: "I have not left her because I want to see her again in you. Even if you are not immaculate, my love will virginize you, and you, all of you, will open your arms and hearts as mothers of humanity, which, as in times past, thirsts for God and for his mother.

"It is you who now must soothe pains, close wounds, dry tears.

"Sing her litanies and strive to mirror yourself in them."

I remember one day asking Mary to create a family on earth made of sons and daughters *all her*, with her same spiritual features. And who knows, maybe she had looked at us, despite our absolute unworthiness, through that prayer, that perhaps she herself had suggested.

Our Statutes, approved by the Church in 1990, say the same thing. Article 2 affirms that the Work of Mary "wishes to be, as much as it is possible, a presence of Mary on earth and almost her continuation."

Mary is the pattern and form of the Church and therefore it is evident that, in such a sublime creature, all Christians can find their model. That is how it was for us. We discovered in Mary our own form, the model of our way of perfection.

And the various moments of her life as they are presented in the gospel, even though extraordinary, appeared to us as successive steps that our own souls could look to in the different stages of the life of the spirit, to find light and encouragement.

This illumination was so strong that we called our way: *Via Mariae,* the Way of Mary.

In summary form, almost giving only the titles, here are some of its stages.

The first event spoken of in Mary's life is the *Annunciation (*Lk 1:25ff.), when the Word became incarnate in her womb.

If we try to understand the lives of some of the saints, we see that something similar happened to them.

If you were to visit the church of St. Damian, in Assisi, where St. Clare lived, the tour guide in describing that sacred place, at times says, "Here Christ was incarnated in the heart of Clare." Even though Clare of Assisi was living a very fervent Christian life, her meeting St. Francis, the personification of the word "poverty" spoken again to the world through a charism of the Holy Spirit, provoked in her something new: it made Christ grow and develop in her soul to the point of making her one of the greatest saints in the Catholic Church.

And so, when individuals meet the charism of unity and choose to make it their own, something similar happens in them as happened in Mary and in certain saints: Christ can truly grow spiritually in their hearts, as an actualization of baptism.

The second episode in Mary's life was her *visit to Elizabeth,* when she went to help her. But, as soon as Mary arrived at her house, having found in her cousin a soul so open to the mysteries of God, she felt she could communicate her great secret, and she did so through her *Magnificat*, telling Elizabeth, in this manner, of her extraordinary experience.

All who meet the Movement and choose God as the ideal of their own lives realize that in order to put this choice into practice they must begin to love. And they do love. But love is a light, and it makes them understand something of God's work in them. For the first time they grasp the golden thread of his love in their lives, about which they gladly tell their brothers and sisters what they have understood. It is their experience.

The third event of Mary's life is the *birth of Jesus* (Lk 2:7; Mt 1:25).
In the Movement one loves and is loved, because all want to love.

This reciprocal love, however, also brings about the presence of Jesus among them, which, as I mentioned before, "generates Christ" following the example of Mary.

Mary presents her Son in the Temple and *she meets the elderly Simeon*. It is a moment of joy for her, because that just and pious man confirms to her that her child is the Son of God. Yet this meeting also makes her suffer because Simeon tells her: "And a sword will pierce your own soul too" (Lk 2:35).

Those who wish to live the spirituality of the Movement pass through something similar.

This happens when they come to understand that in order to walk on this way it is necessary to say "yes" to the cross. The mystery of Jesus crucified and forsaken is announced as the foundation of the life of unity.

After the words spoken to her by Simeon, Mary soon experiences this suffering in her *flight to Egypt* (Mt 2:13ff.), in which she undergoes that persecution which was stained with the blood of many innocent children.

Adjusted to their own capacity, this happens also to those who follow the *Via Mariae*. The ideal that they live and present to the world stands in complete contrast to it. We should not be surprised then that when they begin to speak about this new life of theirs, they begin to be criticized. At such moments they must react by loving in these crosses Jesus crucified and forsaken, the Persecuted One par excellence, so that the Risen One may continue to shine in their hearts.

At the age of 12, *Jesus stays behind in Jerusalem* and speaks with the teachers in the Temple.

Mary, finding him once again, says to him: "Child, why have you treated us like this? Look, your father and I have been searching for you in great anxiety" (Lk 2: 48). And Jesus replies: "Why were you searching for me? Did you not know that I must be in my Father's house?" (Lk 2:49).

We have reached a new stage in Mary's life, in a state of soul analogous to a typical period experienced by those who have embarked on this way. In fact, perhaps after years, they sense with particular insistence the return of various kinds of temptations, of painful aridities that previously, by embracing the charism, had seemed to vanish.

These things make them suffer, and turning to the Lord, they say, "Why have you left me?" Then he seems to reply, "Didn't you know that all the good and beautiful things you experienced were mine and that you have received them only through pure grace?"

Such sufferings create a foundation of humility necessary for Christ to live and grow in them. It is the period, perhaps, of the so-called "night of the senses" of which the mystics speak.

For Mary too the loss of Jesus in the Temple had constituted, in a way, a "night of the senses": she could no longer see him nor hear his voice; his presence was removed from her motherly love.

So far as we know, after this trial Mary lived a long period of *close intimacy with Jesus*.

In a parallel way, those who humbly accept and overcome the trials mentioned before, often find a new and more profound union with Jesus.

And this period, though still containing crosses, can last for a long time.

Then *Jesus enters his public life*. Mary follows him in his mission, with her heart and at times close to his side.

For the people of the Movement this moment points to the time in their spiritual lives when, through the acquired habit of listening to the voice of Jesus in their hearts, they sense it as their own and follow it.

In his public life Jesus pronounced words of eternal life, performed miracles, formed disciples, and founded the Church.

The members of the Movement, having reached this point, experience that Jesus living in them or among them performs similar things. In them too Jesus pronounces words that have the flavour of Eternal Life. Through them too for example, he works miracles of conversion. In them too his presence forms disciples and sparks new developments for the kingdom of God.

Then Mary arrives at her hour of immolation: she is *the Desolate*. We spoke of it before.

The Movement does not lack sufferings like Mary's.

We can see, in fact, in some of the Movement's members, genuine symptoms of "the night of the spirit," when, for example, God permits that they pass through the terrible trial of being forsaken by him, or when faith, hope and charity seem to disappear.

And after the desolation? *At the centre of the Cenacle Mary* remains in the fullness of her charism of maternity towards the apostles, alongside Peter, whom Jesus had made their head.

Mary no longer "follows" Jesus: now, after the descent of the Holy Spirit, we can say she is transformed into him. As another Christ, she too works, in her own way, for the expansion of the Church.

Scaled to their own proportions, those who live the spirituality of unity also aim to reach this stage and they can achieve it. This would be the stage that the mystics call "the transforming union," when Martha is joined to Mary: a specific and unique activity for the good of the Church is united to a specific and unique contemplation.[26]

And finally, there is the hour of the *Assumption*, when God calls Mary to heaven.

Only those who have experienced this know something of this stage.

Before dying, St. Clare of Assisi said these words:

"Go forth without fear, my soul, for you have a good guide for your journey. Go forth without fear, for he that created you has sanctified you ... and loves you with a tender heart. And you, Lord, be blessed, because you created me."[27] Perhaps she wanted to say: having created me, you have acquired glory for yourself. Hers might have been a death of love.

May heaven want this at least in some small way for us too!

Then we will rise to heaven and find our very own Mother, our saint, our model, she who on earth was our Head, Queen, the Mother of us all.

This is the *Via Mariae*, the road each one takes, different for each person, shaped to the individual's personal response and the graces God freely gives to whoever he wants.

Here, very concisely, are some ideas about Mary as she is seen in her Movement, the Work of Mary, which is the living rosary we have been called to form.

Our Movement, this living rosary, since its birth in 1943, has never ceased to be nourished, sustained and given light for its journey through the recitation of the rosary, in its joyful, sorrowful, and glorious mysteries. Now the mysteries of light have been added, making the contemplation of Christ through the eyes of Mary more beautiful, full, and complete.

Thank you, Holy Father, for what you have done for this glorious prayer to Mary.

And to you, Mary, my and our mother, mother of all the men and women of our planet, let me repeat: "If when praying the rosary sometimes a living stream of heaven seems to flow around us, and the world, as beautiful as it is, pales before such enchantment, what will it be like to meet you, Mary?"[28]

A Legacy: Be a Family

Chiara Lubich's message to the Focolare members on 25 December 1973.

Were I to leave this earth today, and were you to ask me for a final word about what our Ideal is, I would have to say, certain that it would be understood in its deepest sense: "Be a family."

Are some among you suffering from spiritual or moral trials? Be understanding to them, as a mother would, and even more. Enlighten them through your words and through your example. Do not allow them to lack the warmth of a family, but rather increase it.

Are any among you in physical pain? May they be our preferred brothers and sisters. Suffer with them. Try to understand their pain completely. Share with them the fruits of your apostolic activities so that they know that, more than anyone else, they have contributed to them.

Are any among you approaching their final moments of life? Imagine you are in their place, and do for them what you would want done for yourself, until their very last breath.

Are any of you rejoicing because of a success, or for any other reason? Rejoice with them, that their consolation may not fade and their hearts not close, so that their joy may belong to everyone.

Are some moving to another place? Do not let them leave without filling their hearts with a single inheritance: the sense of a family, so that they may take it with them wherever they go.

Never place any kind of activity, whether spiritual or apostolic, before the spirit of being a family with the brothers or sisters with whom you are living.

Wherever you go out to bring Christ's ideal, to spread this immense family of the Work of Mary, you will do no better than to try to create, with discretion and prudence, but with solid conviction, the spirit of a family. It is a humble spirit; it wishes the best for everyone; it is not proud… to sum up, it is true, total charity.

So were I to leave this world today, in fact, I would let Jesus in me repeat to you: "Love one another … so that all may be one."[29]

And the Focolare Was Born

> According to a tradition, Loreto contains the House of Nazareth. There in 1939 Chiara Lubich felt called to open a "fourth way" in the Church. This new vocation was to unite three traditional vocations: to form a family, to be consecrated in the midst of the world, and to live for God in community. Chiara's intuition took shape providentially, in the midst of World War II, through the birth of the Focolare Movement. In the image of the Holy Family, consecrated single and married people completely offer themselves to God, though in different ways, by living in community in the midst of the world. The following undated passage, probably from the 60s and previously unpublished, takes us inside the intimate life of the focolare, describing some of its main features.

And the focolare was born: an invention from heaven designed by Mary's motherly care in order to raise children similar to her.

Over the years we often had the intuition that our vocation was particularly "Marian" in nature. Even though we did not actually realize it, the focolare was to become the instrument through which those who entered after they felt called, by following its way of life and by corresponding to grace, would be able to become, if God wanted, other "little Marys."

It is said of St. Teresa that she reached such a high state of sanctity and perfection in such a short time because she placed herself in contact, through prayer, with the One who is Holy, the One who is Perfect.

In the focolare, the calling is different.

Its members grow, as it were, *between two fires.* The ascetic life of the men and women Focolarini, on the one hand, is one of intimate union with God *within self* (listening to the voice of conscience which points to God's will, adoring him in the Holy Eucharist, loving him in moments of meditation, embracing him on the cross whenever occasions arise, living the Word of Life, and practising the teachings of the Church). On the other hand, it is one of union with God *outside of self*, present in the collectivity: Jesus in the midst of two or more, Jesus particularly present in the one responsible for the focolare, who needs to be loved and obeyed as another Jesus, and in one's brothers or sisters who must be loved and served constantly in such a way that the brother par excellence of all, Jesus, be always among all.

Two fires: Jesus within us, Jesus among us. Two aspects of God's kingdom: within us and among us.

This is how the men and women Focolarini live in God, or, as we say, are embraced by God. It is a heavenly reality: a monastery of heaven that keeps them, together with their companions, separate from the world, because the kingdom of God stands in total contrast to the world.

It is an invisible monastery, but real; it is the shield of Christ's soldiers who are separated from while still immersed in the world; it is where they must show daily, through this divine life, that Christ has overcome the world.

In the house of Nazareth, Mary lived "between two fires": the Holy Spirit, "the spiritual director" of her soul, and Jesus, the Word of God.

And when the thoughts of Mary might not have been in unison with those of Jesus, Mary had to silence her way of seeing things, as at the marriage feast of Cana. Nonetheless, of course, Jesus then did what she desired, from which we can deduce that even in making that request Mary must have been inspired by the Holy Spirit.

The Focolarini are asked to live a life similar to Mary's. It is a life both individual and collective, where the plurality of persons who live a life of holiness together increases the holiness of each person, and the holiness of each enriches that of the others.

When the Focolarini, too, have an inspiration, they entrust it to their superior, in a way similar to life in the Church where every charism is entrusted to Peter.

And if the superior does not give weight to their inspiration, the Focolarini must be at peace, happy to have offered that thought out of love. It will be God then who will enlighten the person responsible for the Focolare and conduct things in a way that the inspirations of the other Focolarini may take their course and be carried out.

The Focolarini live in this way because our life requires that we leave *God for God....* * This detachment (one of the many in our life that remind us of Jesus Forsaken) is one of the conditions for unity in the focolare where the members must be of one heart and one soul.

---

* See footnote on p. 34.

Then what occurs, through the grace of state of the superiors (who if they govern well, will not leave fruitless the inspirations they receive, wherever they come from), and after many long years lived "with Jesus in their midst" made present through the love and sacrifices of everyone, the Focolarini acquire a particular sensitivity for all that is supernatural and natural, and can distinguish with greater clarity the voice of God within themselves, and therefore God's will, from other voices.

Not only this, but through the long, constant work of uniting with their brothers or sisters and distinguishing themselves from them in a life similar to nothing so much as to the life, extended in time, of the Holy Trinity, the members of the focolare acquire a sense of the life of the Mystical Body and they learn, often through hard experience, all the guidelines God has given for this spirituality. They learn his devices and his methods to activate always and everywhere, even when they are alone, the life of the Church, according to this ideal, in which this they collaborate with Mary, the founder of this Work, towards bringing about a greater awareness throughout the Church of the Mystical Body of Christ.

The focolare becomes a crucible, a school entered by those called to this vocation in order to love, to struggle, to die to self, and to come out, if everything goes well, mystically "another Mary."

This is sanctity: it is the highest perfection; it is perfection itself.

Between the "two supernatural fires," which in the life of the focolare are one, "the old self" gives its place over to the new self, whose life is this fire. If St. Teresa, in her contact with the One who is Perfect, reached perfection in such a short time, also the Focolarini, even while spending much time in contact with the world, will not be delayed in becoming similar to Jesus.

After all, the life of the focolare is, as we say, the life of "Jesus among us." As the proverb says, "Tell me who your friends are and I will tell you who you are."

This life in contact with God present where there is love and charity gives to the Focolarini a mark, an imprint, a personality that is "the absence of any mark," of any imprint: impersonality, Jesus, Mary.

In its essence, apart from the specific things that the Church asks of the Focolarini, this life can be lived by all Christians, by all religious, by priests and laity, by families and societies, because it is a life lived as a Mystical Body; it is a Marian life, and in Mary all meet and recognize each other.

And Mary is the pattern for a member of the Mystical Body; Mary, in whom all graces have blossomed fully and none have ever gone lost.

She is, as it were, the synthesis of the Mystical Body, a little Church that stands before Jesus who is the head of the Church.

Therefore all those members of the Mystical Body who have allowed their lives to be formed as members of that Body can mirror themselves in her and find in her their most perfect model.

For this reason, the Focolarini, both laypersons and priests, love her as their "form," as their pattern, as a sketch of the Church, as their head, as Mother, Queen, and Leader.

Part Two

A New Look at Faith

The core facts of revelation and of the Christian life
viewed in the light of the spirituality of unity

A God Who Is Love[1]

What is essential today

When Pope Paul VI commented on the *Creed* he said two things that especially echoed in our hearts and provided new insights into many perennial truths.

Speaking of God, he declared: "He is *he who is* ... and he *is Love*."[2] And among the characteristics of Christ, he recalled: "He has given us his new commandment, that we should love one another as he has loved us."[3] Now these truths were there even before the Council, for it was quite clear to people that God is he who is and that Jesus is the one who saved us.

That word love, which expresses the essence of God, and the *commandment of love,* which sums up what Christ asks of us, add further insight into these key points of our faith.

Not only that, but this more explicit statement about who God is and the effect this has on the faith of the Christian people makes a good starting point for a general renewal in the Church.

It is one thing to know we can have recourse to One Who Is, who cares for us, who has redeemed us from our sins, but it is another thing to live with the conviction that we are God's beloved, for this banishes all loneliness, all sense of abandonment, any misgivings or any fear that may restrain us.

When a girl knows she is loved, her life changes: everything around her seems more beautiful and every aspect of life is enhanced. She feels more kindly disposed towards others.

Infinitely more powerful is the experience of the Christian who comes to a more profound understanding of the truth that *God is love*.

Then the boring daily routine suddenly becomes brighter, life's tragedies are eased, the daily melodrama loses its edge and we are ready to trade in our own limited plans for those designed for us in heaven.

We know we are loved and believe with all our heart in this love. We abandon ourselves trustfully to it and are ready to follow.

Life's circumstances, sad or joyful, are illuminated by a love that has willed or permitted it all.

Behind every fact, every circumstance, every meeting, every duty is the will of One who truly loves faithfully and makes all things work together for good.

Thus begins for us weak and vacillating creatures a relationship with the invisible Creator who makes us secure, strong, enlightened and loving.

At once, then, following upon God's revelation and declaration of love, we cannot resist declaring to God our own love.

In this way we begin the ascent towards the goal to which we all are called: to be perfect Christians, to be saints.

God-Love, believing in his love, responding to his love by loving, these are the great imperatives today.

This is the essential thing that today's generation has been waiting for. Without it the world is heading for destruction, like a train off the tracks.

Discovering, or rather, rediscovering that God is Love is today's greatest adventure.[4]

How I met you

When one speaks of love, Lord, people often assume they are thinking of the same thing.

But how many kinds of love there are!

I remember that when I met you I had no anxiety over my love for you. Perhaps because it was you who had met me and you wanted to fill my heart. I remember that sometimes I was all on fire, even while I felt the burden of my humanity as though I were carrying a great weight. But already by that time, your grace enabled me to understand a little who I was and who you were, and I saw that new flame as your gift.

Then you showed me where to find you. "Under the cross," you told me, "under every cross is where I am. Embrace it and you will find me."

You told me many times and I do not remember all the objections I offered. But you finally convinced me.

Then, with each suffering I thought of you, and my will responded with its yes.... But the cross remained; my soul was bathed in darkness, I suffered torments of all kinds ... how many crosses there are in life!

But then you taught me to love you in my neighbour and when suffering came, I did not stop there but accepted it and, forgetful of myself, turned my thoughts to you standing at my side. After a few moments, I would regain my composure and find that my sorrow had vanished.

So it was for years and years: the constant discipline of the cross, the asceticism of love. I underwent many trials and you know all about them, because you have counted the hairs on my head and numbered each one.

Now love is a Someone: it is not just an act of the will.

I knew that God is Love, but I did not believe it was anything like this.[5]

God is within

A letter from 1943 addressed to a group of girls.

My dearest friends,

I would like to be with each of you, to speak to you from my heart about God, and discreetly share with you all that is in my heart.

The almighty has a loving plan for you. You too can live for a grand destiny.

I believe this: God is in you!

When your soul is in grace it is the dwelling place of the Holy Spirit, God the Sanctifier.

Go within yourself and look for God there; he is living in you!

If only you knew what you carry within!

If only you would leave everything for him....

If only you would live for God this life which is so short. It quickly vanishes and fades a bit each day!

Oh! If only God reigned as king in you, and then with all the energy of your body and soul you placed yourself in his divine service as his handmaids!

Oh! If only you loved him with all your heart, mind and strength!

Then ... you would become enamoured of God and go through the world bearing good news!

God exists. Live for him.

God will judge you. Live for him.

God will be everything for you in a few years, as soon as this brief life is over! Entrust yourself to him.

Love him.

Listen to what he is asking of you every moment of your life.

Then do it with all your heart and exert all your energy in his divine service.

Fall in love with God!

There are so many beautiful things on earth! God is even more beautiful!

Don't wait until your youth fades and you end up sobbing over a wasted life and have to say with Saint Augustine: "Too late have I loved you! Too late have I loved you, O beauty ever ancient and ever new!"

No! ... I love you now, my God, my all!

Give me your command and I will do it! Your will is mine! I want what you want!

Loving God on earth means loving his will, so that after a life in his divine service you will see him and be with him forever.[6]

Love the One who is Love

Letter of June 1944 to a young woman

My dear little sister in the Immense Love of God!

Listen, I beg you, to the voice of this tiny heart! You with me have been dazzled by a blazing light, by an Ideal that surpasses all things and encompasses all things:

by the Infinite Love of God!

O my dear little sister: it is he, he who is my God and your God who has established among us a common bond, stronger than death, because it can never be broken, one like the Spirit, immense, infinite, most tender, unyielding, immortal like the Love of God!

It is Love that makes us sisters!

It is Love that has called us to Love!

It is the Love that has spoken deep in our hearts and said to us:

"Look around you: everything in the world passes; every day has its evening, and it comes quickly; every life has its sunset, and the sunset of your life also comes quickly! And yet, do despair: yes, yes, everything passes, because nothing that you see and love is meant to be yours forever! Everything passes and leaves only regret and new hope!"

And yet, do not despair: *your constant Hope, which goes beyond the limits of life,* tells you: "Yes, what you seek exists: in your heart there is an infinite and immortal yearning, a Hope that does not die, a faith that shatters the shadows of death and is light to those who believe. It is not for nothing that you hope, you believe! Not for nothing!"

You hope, you believe — *in order to Love.*

This is your future, your present, your past. All is summed up in this word: Love!

You have always loved. Life is a constant search for the loving desires that are born in the depths of your heart. You have always loved! But too poorly have you loved! You have loved that which dies and is vain and in your heart is left only vanity. *Love that which does not die! Love the One who is Love!* Love Him who in the evening of your life will look only at your tiny heart. You will be alone with him in that moment: dreadfully sad for the one whose heart is filled with vanity, immensely happy for the one whose heart is filled with the infinite love of God!

My dear little sister, I beg you to listen with me to the passing of time, to the beating of your heart that never ceases to knock at the door of your soul. It invites you constantly, everlastingly to *Love*!

Love, love, love! This is the destiny of every human being — Love!

Think on life that slips quickly away! Remember that life is so fleeting! Toss aside what is unworthy of you, of your heart, which is tiny, yes, but noble, precious, powerful: *it can love God!* Why should you waste it? Why?

Go through the world singing to *Love*.

Up! Cover everything with a sea of Flame!

There is no suffering in the world — no joy in the world — no affection in the world — nothing in the world that cannot be drowned in the Love of God! Go through the world and sing to Love!

Yes, there is suffering in the world, but for one who loves, suffering is nothing; even martyrdom is a song! Even the cross is a song. God is Love! And of Love every suffering is the unyielding test; it is the unmistakable seal of God.

Up, up, come with me; let's go Love! Let's run to Love!

Just so: we will let nothing painful pass by our lives without accepting it and desiring it, to show God, who is Immense Love, our tiny but unyielding Love!

Let's leave to our hearts a single desire: to Love!

Let's leave to our minds the measuring of every thought without exception against the infinite and immense love of God.

May God give you Love — a Love of Light and of Flame.[7]

God our brother

Before going up to Calvary, during what were probably the most intimate hours that Jesus spent with his apostles, at the last supper he called them: "children" (Jn 13:33). Indeed, one translation has it as: "My little children." He had become man for them, and now he was about to shed his blood in the way he did, for their salvation. With good reason he could call them "children."

Then he died on the cross, and three days later he appeared to the weeping Magdalene and said: "Go to my brothers and say to them, I am ascending to my Father and your Father, to my God and your God" (Jn 20:17).

It is true and divine love, incarnate love in Jesus, that makes him say "children," not only to the disciples who are present, but also, through them, to all those who were to follow him. But he shows himself to be even more love, when he says to Magdalene: "Go to my brothers."

Perhaps it is possible to think of God as Father, since a father always has a superiority that distinguishes him from his child.

But to think of God as our brother, who together with us in heaven adores his Father and ours, is such a great mystery that we can only begin to perceive it if we bear in mind that God is truly Love. Love which, having deserved, as Man, every title of fatherhood towards the human race (for whom he became incarnate, lived and died), at the end of his earthly life puts himself alongside those others whom he has reunited with the Father, made partakers of his divinity, and made by his Love like him. They say indeed that love makes lovers resemble each other, and this can be seen in Jesus with unique clarity.

What characterizes Jesus the Saviour, then, is that he addresses those brotherly words to a woman who had been a sinner. She is the one he used to give his message to the apostles, those who formed his newly born Church. The purpose of the incarnation and passion of Christ was the salvation of what was lost.

And Jesus always aims at this and is never untrue to himself.

The Church, too, was founded in order to continue this mission. Hence Jesus conveyed the most extraordinary message, the news of the most sublime miracle, to his elect through Mary Magdalene. That death had been particularly for her, for sinners who had been purified and made worthy by the love and the blood of Jesus, made worthy even to the point of announcing to those who, by vocation, would have to transmit to the world the great message of Jesus' resurrection, and of the resurrection through him and with him of all those who love him.[8]

God is powerful; he is the Omnipotent

God is powerful; he is the Omnipotent. Mary has been called the "omnipotent through grace." She too is powerful: she can and she obtains. We are utter wretches. And those of us who believe they are different, are by this very fact the same as the rest of us.

But perhaps our impotence and our poverty — if we love God — can be of use to us. It can help us obtain something.

If our Father in heaven has willed Jesus to be our brother, and if he has prepared an immaculate creature in the human race for his coming, it is because we are in a bad state, with wounded souls, sinners.

Sin is to be hated. But the coming of Jesus on earth through Mary, understood properly, could make us die of joy if God did not sustain us.

Jesus on earth ... who has become our brother ... who says: "If you ask anything of the Father, he will give it to you in my name" (Jn 16:23), just as a well-behaved boy in a family would say to his wild brother who has moved him to pity: "Go and ask father what you want and tell him I sent you," because he is sure that this will ensure him a better hearing.

Jesus on earth ... Jesus our brother ... Jesus who dies between thieves for us: he, the Son of God, sharing a common life with others.

Perhaps we too have a certain power over the heart of the Father, if we go to him as we are: wretched creatures who may well have done every possible wrong, but who, having repented and returned to his love, then say "After all, if you came among us, it was our weakness that attracted you, our wretchedness that moved you to compassion."

Certainly, no earthly mother or father waits more anxiously for their lost child or does more to bring it back, than does our Father in heaven.[9]

No one ever showed such concern for humanity

Jesus died for us. That means Jesus died for me; God died for me.

This is humanity's grandeur: that God died for us. While we may indeed speak of humanism and give it a fully Christian meaning, no one has ever reached such a lofty conclusion. No one has ever had such esteem for humanity as to imagine that God could have loved us to the point of dying for us. But rather than think of a Christian humanism, I prefer to think that Jesus, God, died for me.

How can we not be happy, not enjoy all of life in him, not offer him our sufferings?

If Jesus died for me, he is always thinking of me, always loving me.

And I? I should always be thinking of him, always loving him.[10]

Thoughts: Grant that I may love you

God! Put him first in your life before everything else, for all else is empty and vain. Then you will see everyone and everything through his eyes, the whole world and its history, all its events, major and minor ... and you will love him present throughout nature and throughout the ages.

Finally you will "sense" him in the depths of your heart. You believe by faith that he exists and he will manifest himself to you as *real* with mystical but tangible evidence. You will believe that he is there, really there, in the depths of your soul.[11]

When you adore God present in your heart you do not feel confined or restrained. In fact it will broaden your horizons. Your vista becomes wider than if you were flying through the sky or drifting through the stars of heaven.

The dimensions of the spirit are boundless; the soul falls into an abyss of love where your inadequacy often reduces you to tears on meeting him, though he is closer to you than you are to yourself.[12]

Love God with all your strength and then see all creatures in their relationship to him: this is Christianity.

But sometimes we do not understand that; we misinterpret it and pass on too quickly to the second part.

No, what we must do is: *love God*. We belong entirely to him, with our whole being, all our time, all our labours, all our love and all our intellect.

In order to express that love we must show proper attention, care and love for creatures as well.

We must do it for him and *continue* to love him.

We must become lifelong contemplatives. How short we fall!

What freedom we will find in this one great love! Just thinking about it frees us from the countless snares laid by the society around us.[13]

> If you ask, it is because you do not have.
> If you give, you will have.
> If you want to experience God's bounty, ask him to help you give:
> Grant that I love you, Lord,
> with an immense love
> as immense as your love.
> Grant that I love you, Lord,
> with your own heart.[14]

If your life till now has been aimless, now is the time to take a stand: either for him or against him. Do not be like those half-hearted Christians who by bearing his name bring shame upon Christ and his Church.[15]

Live within

We want to be converted, Lord. Till now we have lived "outside"; from now on we want to live like Mary, "within."

Living "within," being involved with our neighbour and all kinds of activities — even out of love for God — must be replaced by a proper spiritual balance; we need to draw the soul continually down into its depths or we end up in distraction, useless chatter and casting "holy things to the dogs."

Living "within," growing in our inner lives, detached from everything, so as not to be suspended between heaven and earth but "rooted" in heaven, established in the heart of Christ, so that we travel through the heart of Mary on a trinitarian journey, a prelude of the Life to come.

Living "within" means sharing with our neighbour the lifeblood from heaven that flows within us. This is a genuine service. We must not scandalize others by our lack of sanctity.

Living "within" means living like Mary, our exalted Mother, Queen and Guide, who conquers Satan by being anchored in God and not by adopting outward poses, which are as remote from her as earth is from heaven.

Living "within," raised up on the cross by our own hands, so that Christ may continue through us the work of creating unity in this world, confused in all its antics, that suffers, that hopes, that wants to forget, that fears, that gives pain to our hearts today, as the crowds did, in the past, to Jesus.

Living "within" means drawing the world, which lives only "outside," deep into the mysteries of the spirit, where we are elevated and find rest, where we are comforted and strengthened, and we find vigour again to return to the earth and continue the Christian battle till death.[16]

Thoughts: With the Almighty

While you are engaged in life throughout the day, during that half hour of meditation you pause in recollection. Having placed yourself before God, calmly you begin reading a book. If at some point God takes your spirit and stirs you, then you close the book and stay with him, adoring him, loving, asking him for grace, asking him for everything, making the most of the opportunity. If, after a full conversation with Jesus you lose this moment of unity with him, then re-open the book and begin to read again.[17]

To be able to commune with the Almighty, and yet to do it so little, so hurriedly, and often so reluctantly!

At the end of our lives we will be sorry that we have spent so little time in prayer.[18]

God dwells alone within us and we cannot meet him unless we too have the courage to be alone.

If we do not close the shutters of the soul in recollection, then you, Lord, cannot leave your centre and chat with us as sometimes you wish to do.[19]

We are so petty that, not wanting to make the least effort, we turn our soul into a street corner where the whole world goes by, butting in with its chatter. And so you, who have taught us not to give what is holy to dogs, you, the Holy One, cannot give us, even though often you wish to and even though a brief effort by us would be repaid many times over by your love that comforts, sustains, gives us strength so we can live life in the midst of the unending autumn of this world.[20]

We have to work hard, sometimes, to distance ourselves from the affairs and business of the world so as to recollect ourselves and concentrate on God. But as soon as we have done so, we would never turn back, so sweet to the soul is union with God and everything else is worthless and nauseating.[21]

The effect of meditation often is this: to lose interest in the things of this world, even those that are beautiful, even those that are holy. We concentrate our attention on God in intimate conversation with him, as we set our life and our concerns before him, which means before Love and before the Eternal, so that we are then able to return to people and the things of this world with all our intentions made supernatural.[22]

We discover our relationship with you in solitude, we discover our relationship with persons and the things of this world not as slaves but as sons and daughters of God.[23]

Do you know what time of day is most beautiful? It is our prayer time, when we are speaking with the one we love the most.[24]

We have an inner life and an outer life. One is the flowering of the other. One is the root of the other. One for the other brings forth the foliage of the tree of our life.

Our inner life is fed by our outer life. The more I enter into the soul of my brother or sister, the more I enter into God within me. The more I enter into God within me, the more I enter into my brother or sister.

God — myself — my brother or sister: it is all one world, all one kingdom....[25]

You exist. This is how it is.

Those who sincerely love you are often aware of your presence, Lord, in the silence of their room, in the depths of their heart, and every time this feeling moves the soul as if touched to the quick.

They thank you for being so near, for being so Everything, the One who gives meaning to life and to death.

They thank you, but often they know neither how to do it, nor how to say it. They know only that you love them and that they love you and that there is nothing else so sweet here on earth, nothing that can even come close to it. What they feel in their souls when you appear is heaven, and they say: "If heaven is at all like this, oh how beautiful it is!"

They thank you, Lord, for the whole of their lives, for having brought them this far. And if shadows do still exist around them, which could cloud their glimpse of paradise, when you show yourself everything else recedes into the distance: it does not exist.

You exist.

This is how it is.[26]

Our "Yes" to God

Seeing with new eyes

If one morning a man were to wake up and, at first surprised but then fascinated more and more, he were to look upon the world around him transfigured, as if seeing each thing through new eyes, it would be a beautiful day.... The presence, the more-than-human fragrance of an invisible someone has filled the atmosphere.

The faces of familiar friends, of the poor beggar on the street corner, of the workers sweating next to him all day long, of his gravely ill niece, of his grandfather already grown old, the faces of his children, of his wife ... are no longer what they were before: a single light has bathed their features and their gestures and a sublime nobility glows from each one.

The man notices in the air a warm and paternal voice, barely audible but full of love, a love true, sincere, intimate to him who so often has felt overlooked, belittled, alone, useless, an atom of a gargantuan society that oppresses him and makes him anonymous. And he, once unteachable and at times rebellious, does not know how to resist such fascinating commands and he follows their every summons.

He does not even recognize himself anymore. He who was lazy, bored, always tired, finds that a new youth has penetrated his veins and now, with speed and agility, he carries out even the hardest duty.

The ringing of church bells, the radio that informs, the gifts that come, the articles he reads, the news, perhaps sad, he hears from his neighbours, everything, everything that surrounds him acquires new meaning. Details, even though small, open his mind to vast visions of life, to the deep meanings of history; in the chaos of everyday events he begins to discern the thread that seems to link all things, re-ordering them, giving them harmony and, whatever happens, directing each thing towards a good and better end.

And so great is the light illuminating his mind and so strong the urge to love in his will that he has no satisfaction until he communicates to others what he is living and experiencing, so as to understand together, feel together, share together the joy that expands his heart.

Each day will finish with a sunset that seems a dawn and he will see the arrival of each new day as the latest episode in an extraordinary film beyond imagination — where he knows only part of the plot, but the whole is perfectly known and guided by Another.

And he waits, joyful to have discovered and to pursue this divine adventure that has just opened up for his life. He can do it so long as he no longer closes his ears to the inner voice and keeps his heart renewed — a heart once of stone but now of flesh — so that he can love the One who loves him and do whatever pleases him.

This transformation, this transfiguration of persons and of the world is not just a dream, a mere fantasy.

It is the frequent experience of any Christian who one day understands that, if God is Love, and that he or she is the object of this love, it is impossible not to abandon self trustingly to him.

It is the moment in which life changes course and people, disillusioned with their own efforts to shape their own destiny (that never was fully satisfying), decide to conform to the plan God has always had in mind for them. They remember that they have an enormous gift, freedom, and they realize that nothing could be more reasonable for a creature, the child of God, than the act of freely ceding its freedom to the One who gave it.

So they resolve, from that moment on, not to do their own will but the will of God.

This is the great discovery. This is the wise decision true Christians make.

Thérèse of Lisieux said: "I fear one thing only, [clinging to] my own will."[27]

Pope John XXIII wrote: "True greatness consists in doing the will of God totally and perfectly."[28]

Catherine of Siena, who knew from experience the effects produced in the souls of those who joyfully do the will of God, exclaimed: "O sweetest will, which gives life and conquers death, gives light and overwhelms the darkness!"[29]

John of the Cross, referring to those who live a true Christian life, said: "There are no longer two wills, but one, God's, which becomes the will of the soul,"[30] and he explained: "The will of the soul, transformed into God's, does not perish, but becomes his will completely."[31]

This attitude of wanting to do the will of God rather than our own, moreover, is the only and perfect attitude for Christians to have.

Speaking through Isaiah, God says that the Church will receive a new name: "My delight [my will] in you" (see Is 62:4); and Francis de Sales comments: "Among the true children of our Saviour, every one shall forsake his own will, and shall have only one master-will, dominant and universal, which shall animate, govern and direct all souls, hearts and all wills."[32]

In a masterly manner, Pope Paul VI teaches us that this true life of Christians transfers them to a higher sphere, in which greatness, nobility, an atmosphere of paradise reigns, radically transforming an otherwise flat and colourless existence: "The grand designs of God, the undertakings that the Lord's providence proposes for human destinies can coexist with and inhabit the most ordinary conditions of daily life....

"We know that bringing our capricious will into harmony with the will of God is the secret for a *great life*. It means entering into God's design for us and accepting his all-seeing and merciful plans and his great kindness.... We should let ourselves be convinced, then, that a voice from heaven ... provides us with the true and exalted meaning that each one of us has the duty to give to our life.... No life is trivial ... we are predestined to greatness, to the kingdom of God, to be invited by him, to commune with him, to dwell with him and reach perfection in him."[33]

The various ideologies, which deeply influence society today, have their own visions of the world that are promoted very attractively in an attempt to inspire individuals and the masses alike. With them we live in constant hope for a better future.

For the inhabitants of the planet to avoid being taken in, albeit in good faith, by these various interpretations of human history and destiny, we Christians must re-present the gospel message, wherever we happen to live in the world, in the most genuine manner. We must do this with such commitment and conviction that it can again be said of us after twenty centuries that what the soul is to the body, Christians are to the world.[34] Today, furthermore, when individuals and groups are sometimes searching madly for a life different from the one they are leading, where money and comfort have shown themselves to be incapable of satisfying the human spirit and people chase frenetic amusements, senseless eroticism, or drugs to experience a new, hallucinatory vision of things, it is vital to set forth again the true Christian vision of life.

What drives our unfortunate brothers and sisters is not all bad; it is the thirst for happiness, without which human beings would not be human.

Perfect joy is the fruit of Christianity when it is lived as Christ taught: joy in the midst of pain, joy that flowers precisely from pain, from the sacrifice of self, of our own views, of own will, our ego, to leave space for God, for his plans, for his light-filled and wise design for the world and for each one of us.[35]

The only good

"God's will be done" is an expression that, for the most part, is said by Christians in moments of suffering, when there is no other way out; when faith, before the inevitable destruction of what had been thought, desired, wanted, surfaces again and what God has decreed is accepted. But it is not like this, solely, that God's will be done. In Christianity there is more than just "Christian resignation."

The Christian's life is a fact that has roots in heaven, as well as on earth.

The Christian, through his or her faith, can and must be in touch always with Another who knows the Christian's life and destiny. And this Other is not of this earth, but of another world. And he is not a merciless judge or an absolute monarch who only asks for service. He is a Father. One, therefore, who is such because he is in relationship with others, and in this case with his children, children adopted through his only Son, who from all eternity dwells with him.

The Christian's life therefore is not and cannot be decided by that individual's will or personal foresight alone. Unfortunately many Christians wake up in the morning full of the sadness and boredom the coming day will bring. They grumble about lots of things, past and future and present, because it is they themselves who make the plan for their lives. Such a plan, the fruit of human intelligence and narrow expectations, cannot fully satisfy a human being, athirst for the infinite. They substitute themselves for God, at least so far as their own affairs are concerned, and like the prodigal son, having taken their inheritance, they squander it in their own way, without their father's advice, outside the life of their family.

Very often we Christians are blind people who have abdicated our supernatural dignity, for we repeat, maybe every day, in the "Our Father": "Your will be done on earth as it is in heaven." But we neither understand what we say, nor do we do (for our part at least) what we implore.

God sees and knows the course we must follow every instant of our lives. For each of us he has established a celestial orbit in which the star of our freedom ought to turn, if it abandons itself to the One who created it. Our orbit, our life, does not conflict with other orbits or with the paths of myriad other beings, children of the Father like us, but harmonizes with them in a firmament more splendid than that of the stars, because it is spiritual. God must move our life and draw it into a divine adventure, which is unknown to us; one in which, at the same time spectators and actors of the marvellous plans of love, we give moment by moment the contribution of our free will.

We can give! Not: we must give! Or worse: let us resign ourselves to giving!

He is Father and therefore is Love. He is Creator, Redeemer, Sanctifier. Who better than he knows what is good for us?

"Lord, may your will really be done, may it be done now and always! May it be done in me, in my children, in others, in their children, in the whole of humanity.

"Be patient and forgive our blindness, for we do not understand and we force heaven to remain closed and prevent it pouring its gifts upon the earth. For, by shutting our eyes, we say with the way we live that it is night and there is no heaven.

"Draw us into the ray of your light, of our light, decreed by your love when, out of love, you created us.

"And force us to kneel every minute in adoration of your will — the one good, pleasing, holy, rich, fascinating, fruitful will. Thus, when the hour of suffering arrives, we may also see your infinite love beyond it. And we may (being full of you) see with your eyes already on this earth and observe from above the divine pattern that you have woven for us and for our brothers and sisters, in which everything turns out to be a splendid design of love. And may our eyes be spared, at least a little, from seeing the knots lovingly tied by your mercy, tempered by justice, that have been placed where our blindness has broken the thread of your will.

"May your will be done in the world and then peace will certainly descend upon the earth, for the angels said to us: 'On earth peace among those whom he favours!' (Lk 2:14).

"And if you said there is only one who is good, the Father, then there is only one will that is good: your Father's will."[36]

Partnership

The greatest wisdom is to spend our time living the will of God perfectly in the present moment.

Sometimes however we are assailed by an unrelenting attack of thoughts about the past, present or future, or about places, circumstances or persons that we cannot handle directly. It requires our greatest effort to take the helm of our ship and maintain the course by doing what God wills of us in the present moment.

A perfect response on our part requires of us a will, a decision, but above all a *confidence* in God that can border on heroism.

"I can do nothing in that particular case, for that person dear to me who is sick or in danger, for that complicated situation ...

"So I will do what God wants of me in this moment. I will study hard or sweep the house well, and pray well, take good care of my children ...

"And God will tend to unravelling that tangled knot, comforting the sufferer, resolving that unforeseen problem."

This is a partnership of perfect communion. It demands from us great faith in the love of God for his children and this enables God then, by our response, to have faith in us.

This mutual trust works miracles.

We will see that, before we even reach some crisis, Another has arrived there before us and done immensely better than we could.

Our heroic act of confidence will be rewarded. Our life, limited to a single field, will acquire a new dimension. We will feel ourselves in touch with the Infinite, that which we yearn for, and our faith, gaining new vigour, will reinforce our charity, our love.

We will no longer know the meaning of loneliness. It will become clearer than ever, because it is our experience, that we are truly children of a Father who can do all things.[37]

A sanctity of the people

The purpose of a Christian's life on earth is to achieve sanctity.

Paul says this clearly in speaking to the Thessalonians: "For this is the will of God, your sanctification" (1 Thes 4:3).

But for many Christians today, who are such only in name, secularized and devoted to the things of this world, the very word "sanctity" often seems anachronistic. It sounds like something from a time long past, from the age of the monasteries, from some incomprehensible and oppressive medieval world, just a fixation of weak minds who believe in fantasies and indulge them as an escape from the real difficulties of modern life, a flight from this new, dynamic age of ours whose god is now technology and science, diversion and the pursuit of pleasure.

The acceleration of life today leaves no time for people to catch their breath, and modern means of communication absorb all their free time. They have no time left to think and ask the deeper questions. They are entirely indifferent to the idea of sanctity; it has little importance for them. "I don't think about it; there is no problem." There is not enough time; there is no moment of calm, no opportunity for quiet reflection.

Not everyone reaches this point. There are still some who venture on but soon feel unable to continue and finally lose all motivation.

Others never begin the quest. "How do you become a saint? That is only a word! How do you get there? Where do you start? Maybe do penance like the great saints? But that is not for our times, even if it worked at one time. Maybe do a lot of praying? I would do it if I knew that it was the right way for me. Maybe consecrate myself to God? Submit myself in obedience to a superior…. But that does not relate to our modern mentality. Today people are aware of their personal dignity and make their own decisions. What kind of slavery is this? Who are these sluggards who would impose on others the consequences of their own decisions?" With that they give up.

Yet, whether we are in modern times or in times past, sanctity is the only goal for us.

If it seems to be of little concern right now, it will not always be so. Some day we will be examined on this issue because the final judgment is based on love of neighbour, and that does not exist apart from love of God. With love of God comes perfection, sanctity. Moreover, those people (especially Christians) who do not even aim for serious, noble, higher, genuinely human objectives have already lost before they start. And they have lost with regard to humanity because they grow faint at the thought of others now living and who are to come, and in front of eternity where they will not be able to elude the one who has created them and to whom they will return.

Then what is the way to holiness today?

It makes quite an impression on us when we hear a woman, who through contemplation became a great saint and a doctor of the church, tell us that neither time nor solitude is necessary.

That is the conviction of Teresa of Avila, who identified in her extremely rich inner life the essence of prayer, the way of sanctity to which she was called: love.

If you cannot always pray, you can always love.

You may not be alone and able to enter contemplative union with God, but you are always able to love him.

Yes, because to love God means to do his will.

This is something everyone, every Christian, can do.

It is my conviction that doing God's will is the modern way to become a saint.

You do not need to go to a convent, or consecrate yourself to God or become a priest. No, it suffices to do what God wants of you.

"When?" Always.

"But can we know what the will of God is?" Certainly! It means keeping the commandments, fulfilling the duties of your state in life and listening to the voice of conscience through which God speaks to you.

Do it with ever greater perfection.

Then even a mother who has house chores to do, or an office clerk, a worker on the assembly line, someone sick in bed, a child, an elderly person, a businessman, a policeman, an artist, a road builder, a missionary, a writer, a housekeeper, a lawyer, an athlete, anyone at all can become a saint because all can do the will of God.

This way of sanctity is the way for the average person, for everyone.

But remember: it is possible and efficacious when you do the will of God in the present moment.

The present is what counts; it is on the present that we must focus. So the mother will not prepare dinner for her husband and children just because she has to do so, or in order to please them or because she loves her family. She will also do it because she wants to do what God asks of her, that is to say, out of love for God.

So when we do something it has a repercussion in eternal life, which will come. We determine eternal life here on earth. To pass to life eternal the things we do on earth must be done for God, consciously and explicitly.

One who has tried to live this way can be quite certain that God does not let himself be outdone in generosity, and that such a life is beautiful, most beautiful. When Christians do well what they should be doing in the present moment they are making the most of the grace God gives precisely for the present. Living this way moment by moment often brings an inner joy never experienced before. It is no exaggeration to call it a foretaste of heavenly bliss.

This joy urges the soul to live ever more intensely this new life, offering God every action, with the intention from deep within of doing everything for him, and carrying it out perfectly as the inner voice directs.

This is a wonderful, supernatural life, full of joy. It sets us on fire and leaves us no peace when we realize that we are acting for some other intention.

We advance in holiness, aware that the passing moment will never return again; so we are eager to live it perfectly for God alone.

In this way the world, the school, the office, the factory, the streets are filled with saints in process who, by their perseverance, will be saints in eternity. But perseverance is easy: it is enough if we are determined not to think of tomorrow but simply place ourselves in the eternal present of God."[38]

A note of solemnity

If people begin again and again to live well the present moment, you realize with time — even if they have not made a specific intention to do so — that their actions have taken on a note of solemnity. You notice that their lives rest on a single supernatural support: *love of God*. But at the same time this aura of solemnity profoundly affects every activity of theirs and enriches their lives greatly. As a consequence their spiritual features come into focus with ever greater precision.

You can say of them, for example, that they are: *immersed in God* in prayer; *free and happy* in company with others; *precise* in doing their duty; *demanding* of themselves, *like a brother or sister* with everyone; *uncompromising* in disciplining those who depend upon them; *merciful* with the fallen; *convinced* like rock of their own nothingness and God's omnipotence; *dissatisfied* often with their own accomplishments; *ready always* to hope and begin again.

This perpetual beginning again required by a human life traumatized by original sin helps the soul to clothe itself with consistency even amidst a variety of activities. And this will touch it with the fragrance of sanctity, at first a little, then more and more.

Saints are those who live no longer in themselves, within their own will, but transferred into Another.[39]

With feet on the ground

At times "Someone" urges us to live constantly on the *supernatural level,* that is in *absolute uncertainty* about any human situation (plans, journeys, health, the future), in order to live in the *certainty of reality*, which is to live the present moment in a divine manner, knowing and desiring what God wants us to know and desire in the present moment. This is the reason for the soul's imperative to be "watchful" as Jesus recommends (see Mt 25:13), because you know neither the day nor the *hour* of his coming nor, one may add, of any of his comings.

He comes at all times, at every moment, in his will. Whether it is sad or beautiful in human terms, in reality it is him, it is his Love.

This state of soul places, so to speak, our feet on the ground (the promised land of the kingdom of heaven, where we can and should already live here below) and there is no danger of falling: of falling into sin, illusion, delusion or confusion.[40]

Time is fast escaping me

Time is fast escaping me;
accept, O Lord, my life!
In my heart I hold you, the treasure
that must shape every move I make.
Follow me, watch over me; yours
is my loving: rejoicing and suffering.
May no one catch even a sigh.
Hidden in your tabernacle
I live, I work for all.
May the touch of my hand be yours,
only yours be the tone of my voice.
In this rag of myself
may your Love return to this arid world,
with the water that gushes abundantly
from your wound, O Lord!
Let Wisdom divine clear away the gloomy affliction of many,
of all. In this may Mary shine forth.[41]

Thoughts: Improve always

You must never turn back, but forge always ahead.
    Your life has been as it has been. God knows it.
    The important thing is that the present, the only thing in your hands, not escape you. In it love God with all your heart, doing his will.[42]

There are periods in life when time is lived *sip by sip*. With holy trepidation you attend, for example, to every movement, every word, every glance, every breath of a loved one facing eternity. That last stage of life becomes valuable because now we are *standing at the threshold of death;* it is eternity that gives true significance to time.
    Perhaps it would be a good idea to take each instant of our life sip by sip and, grasping the fleeting moment, live it in love for God, and nail it down for eternity.[43]

Begin again always. Improve always.
    Do not rest until each day takes you a step higher, in your union with God, than the one before … make of life an ascent.[44]

One thing alone is beautiful, lovable, attractive, useful, radiant: *what God wants of you in the present moment.*[45]

If everyone did nothing but God's will at every moment without hesitation, not going to extremes, they would see fulfilled before their very eyes God's plan for people and things, for families and nations, for religious groups and for the world; they would share in, as spectators and actors, the unfolding of the mysteries of Providence on earth and their mouths would utter words of wisdom.[46]

In eternity too we will have a *past*, a *present* and a *future*, but they will be in unity.

It will all be concentrated in the present in which, besides the beatific vision, we will have the *recollection* (meaning "to collect again" to oneself[*]) *of the past*, which will not be a recollection but a renewal, and the *dream of the future* which will not be a dream but reality. For this reason eternity will never end, because it is trinitarian, and it will be but a single moment because it is unitary: the Eternal Present.[47]

Not mine but yours be done

"Not my will, but yours, be done" (Lk 22:42).

Strive to remain in his will and that his will should remain in you. When God's will is done on earth as in heaven, the testament of Jesus will be fulfilled.

Look at the sun and its rays.

The sun is a symbol of the will of God, which is God himself. The rays are the will of God for each individual.

Walk towards the sun in the light of your ray, different and distinct from every other ray, and fulfil the particular, wonderful plan God wants from you.

There is an infinite number of rays, all coming from the same sun: a single will, particular for each person.

The closer the rays come to the sun, the closer they come to one another. We too, the closer we come to God, by doing the will of God more and more perfectly, the closer we come to one another.

Until we are all one.[48]

---

[*] "Recollect" is a rendition in English of the original Italian "ricordo." Chiara notes that this word can be explained as: "I give anew to the heart."

The Art of Loving[49]

The little seed

Have you ever seen
how on an abandoned road,
when it is caressed by the spring,
grass grows up and life, without pause, flowers again?
The same thing happens to humanity around you
if you do not bother to see it with an earthly eye
and restore it with the divine ray of charity.
Supernatural love in your soul
is a sun
that allows no respite in the reflowering of life.
It is a life
that makes your corner of life a cornerstone.
Nothing else is needed to uplift the world,
to give it back to God.
Beauty of speech, delicacy of manner,
the weight of culture, the experience of years,
are certainly gifts that should not be neglected.
But for the eternal kingdom
that which has most life has most value.
The sweet-scented slice of an apple
is good to see, tasty, pleasant, and colourful,
but underground, it dies and leaves no trace.
A little seed, unpleasing to the palate,
tasteless and insipid,
underground, yields new apples.
So it is with life in God, the life of a Christian,
the incandescent progress of the Church.
The Church stands, erect and majestic, upon followers of Christ
who the centuries have called senseless and foolish and mad …
against whom the prince of the world has hurled his fury
to destroy their every trace….

They have remained.
The Father cleansed them
so that joined to the vine they might bear abundant fruit
and he raised them up in glory
in the kingdom of life.
You and I, the milkman, the farmer, the doorman,
the fisherman, the labourer, the newsboy ...
And all the others,
disillusioned idealists, mothers weighed down with cares,
lovers near their wedding day,
exhausted old ladies awaiting death,
boys bursting with energy, all ...
All are raw material for God's society:
it is enough that they have a heart that holds high and upright,
fixed in God,
the flame of love.[50]

Our brothers and sisters

We go to God through our brothers and sisters. "Those who do not love a brother or sister whom they have seen, cannot love God whom they have not seen" (1 Jn 4:20).

Today, in a time like ours, this is what Christians must keep in mind above all.

At times, the materialism that surrounds us, with its related temptations, with the chatter and the discussions that attract over-curious ears, the lust for knowledge, the desire to know everything, to read everything, attachments to what is felt legitimate, all take our attention away from what our *brother or sister* needs from us.

Instead everything lies here. "Above all," St. Peter exhorts, "maintain constant love for one another" (1 Pt 4:8).

The scriptures further state: "We have passed from death to life because we love one another" (1 Jn 3:14).

And we are called to live life and to bring *life*, even if fraternal love costs continuous effort. But this is none other than the characteristic cross of the Christian.[51]

The exam

If you were a student and by chance came to know the questions of the school's final exams, you would consider yourself lucky and study the answers thoroughly.

Life is a trial and at the end it, too, has to pass an exam; but the infinite love of God has already told humanity what the questions will be: "For I was hungry and you gave me food, I was thirsty and you gave me drink" (Mt 25:35). The works of mercy will be the subject of the exam, those works in which God sees if you love him truly, having served him in your brothers and sisters.

Perhaps this is why the Pope, the vicar of Christ, often simplifies Christian life by underlining the works of mercy.

And we do the will of Jesus in heaven and of his Church on earth if we transform our life into a continuous work of mercy. In fact, it is not difficult and does not change much what we are already doing. It is a matter of raising every relationship with our neighbour onto a supernatural plane. Whatever our vocation, fathers or mothers, farmers or office staff, elected officials or Heads of State, students or workers, throughout the day there are continuous opportunities, directly or indirectly, to feed the hungry, instruct the ignorant, bear with those who annoy us, give advice to those in doubt, pray for the living and for the dead.

A new intention behind every move we make for the benefit of our neighbour, whoever it may be, and every day of our life will help us to prepare for the eternal day, storing up treasure where moth and rust do not corrupt.[52]

As yourself

Every Word of God contains both the minimum and the maximum that he can ask of you, so when you read, "Love your neighbour as yourself" (Mt 19:19), you have the law of fraternal love at it highest degree.

Your neighbour is another you, and you must love him or her bearing that in mind.

When neighbours cry, you must cry with them, and when they laugh, laugh with them. If they lack knowledge, be ignorant with them. If they have lost a parent, make their suffering your own.

You and they are members of Christ and if one or the other is suffering, it is the same for you.

What has value for you is *God* who is both their Father and yours.

Do not seek to be excused from loving. Your neighbours are those who pass next to you, be they rich or poor, beautiful or not, brilliant or not, holy or sinful, a fellow citizen or a foreigner, a priest or layperson, whoever.

Try to love whoever appears to you in the present moment of your life. You will discover within yourself an energy and strength you did not know you had. It will add flavour to your life, and you will find answers to your thousand questions why.[53]

If your eye is simple

In however many neighbours you meet throughout your day, from morning to night, in all of them see Jesus.

If your eye is simple, the one who looks through it is God. And God is Love, and love seeks to unite by winning over.

How many people, in error, look at creatures and things in order to possess them. It may be a look of selfishness or of envy, but whatever the case, it is one of sin. Or people may look within their own selves, and be possessive of their own souls, their faces lifeless because they are bored or worried.

The soul, because it is an image of God, is love, and love that turns in on itself is like a flame, that because it is not fed, dies out.

Look outside yourself, not in yourself, not in things, not in persons; look at God outside yourself and unite yourself to him.

He lives in the depths of every soul that is alive, and if dead, the soul is the tabernacle of God that awaits him as the joy and expression of its own existence.

Look at every neighbour then with love, and love means to give. A gift, moreover, calls for a gift, and you will be loved in return.

Understood in this way, love is to love and be loved: as in the Trinity.

God in you will ravish hearts, igniting the life of the Trinity in them, which may already rest in them through grace, although extinguished.

You cannot light up a space — even if electricity is available — until the current's two poles are brought together.

The life of God in us is similar. It must circulate in order to radiate outside of us and give witness to Christ, the One who links heaven to earth, and people with one another.

Look, therefore, at every one of your neighbours. Give yourself to them in order to give yourself to Jesus and Jesus will give himself back to you. It is the law of love: "Give, and it will be given to you" (Lk 6:38).

Out of love for Jesus, let your neighbours possess you. Like another Eucharist, let yourself "be eaten" by your neighbours. Put your entire self at their service, which is service to God, and your neighbours will come to you and love you. The fulfilment of God's every desire lies in fraternal love, which is found in his commandment: "I give you a new commandment, that you love one another" (Jn 13:34).[54]

Enlarge our heart

We need to enlarge our heart to the measure of the heart of Jesus. How much work that means! Yet this is the only thing necessary. When this is done, all is done. It means loving everyone we meet as God loves them. And since we live in time, we must love our neighbours one by one, without holding in our heart any left-over affection for the brother or sister met a moment before. It is the same Jesus, after all, whom we love in everyone. If anything left-over remains, it means that the preceding brother or sister was loved for our sake or for theirs … not for Jesus. That is the problem.

Our most important task is to maintain the chastity of God and that is: to keep love in our hearts as Jesus loves. Hence, to be pure we need not deprive our heart and repress the love in it. We need to enlarge our heart to the measure of the heart of Jesus and love everyone. And as one sacred host, from among the millions of hosts on the earth, is enough to nourish us with God, so one brother or sister, the one whom God's will puts next to us, is enough to give us communion with humanity, which is the mystical Jesus.

To have communion with our brother or sister is the second commandment, the one that comes immediately after the love of God, and is the expression of it.[55]

Lord, give me all who are lonely

Lord, give me all who are lonely … I have felt in my heart the passion that fills your heart for all of the forsakenness in which the whole world is drifting.

I love every being that is sick and alone.

Even the suffering of plants causes me pain … even the animals that are alone.

Who consoles their weeping?
Who mourns their slow death?
Who presses to their own heart, the heart in despair?

My God, let me be in this world the tangible sacrament of your Love, of your being Love; let me be your arms that press to themselves and consume in love all the loneliness of the world.[56]

In love what counts is to love

In love what counts is to love. This is what it is like here on earth. Love (I speak of supernatural love which does not exclude natural love) is both so simple and so complex. It demands that you do your part and awaits the other's.

If you try to live only for love, you will realize that here on earth it is worthwhile doing your part. You do not know whether the other part will ever come; and it is not necessary that it should. At times you will be disappointed, but you will never be discouraged if you convince yourself that in love what counts is to love.

And you love Jesus in your neighbour, Jesus who always returns to you, maybe in other ways.

He it is who steels your soul against the storms of the world and who melts it in love for all those who are around you, provided you remember that in love what counts is to love.[57]

Once we have known God

Once we have known God, when we fail to deserve his light because we have not been vigilant in love, and have let ourselves be overwhelmed by the cross without taking advantage of grace, the soul gropes in darkness and in anguish, and it seeks him.

The soul seeks Love, calls for it, cries out to it, screams at times and wails. But it does not find Love. It does not find Love because it does not love.

God does not yield. He has an immutable law. Heaven and earth will pass away … (Mk 13:31) and his words allow no exceptions.

The soul has no right to love before it loves: it receives love when it has love.

God has made it in his image and likeness, and he respects the dignity with which he has clothed it.

It is the soul that must take the initiative and love, almost as if making the first move in response to grace. Then God comes. He manifests himself to the one who loves him, gives to the one who has, and such a one will remain in abundance.

The soul that loves participates in God and feels itself to be lordly. It fears nothing. Everything gains value for it.

We pass from death to life when we love.[58]

Love is what matters

When speaking about love, about charity, Pope Paul VI, in a talk given to the Bishops of Oceania convened in Sydney, remarked: "This is the principal virtue, it seems to us, that is asked of the Catholic Church at this time in the world."[59]

If this is so, and it is, Christians today must moment by moment be "living charity" in order to respond to the needs of the Church, and to the questions the world is raising.

Christians must aim there: on true love, knowing apart from anything that everything has value when it is inspired and conducted by charity and all the rest counts for nothing, at least for the final account of their lives.

This is how Christians must commit their lives so that at the end of each of their actions they can say: *this is a work that will remain.*

This is what they must make of their daily work, of writing letters, of taking care of personal affairs, of educating their children, of engaging in conversation, of taking trips, of choosing clothes, of eating, even of sleeping, down to the smallest of their actions ... when meeting all the unforeseeable things that God will ask of them day by day.

This is how it must be — and it is enormously consoling — for those who can do so little because they are sick or confined in their beds or who remain inactive during an endless convalescence.

This, precisely this is how it must be — how many times have we said it and forgotten it — because what really counts is not our work, our writing, or even our apostolic activities; what counts is the love that must animate our life.

And this is possible for everyone.

For God every action in itself is indifferent. Love is what counts. Love gets the world moving. Even if someone has a mission to fulfil, it will be fruitful to the extent that it is infused with love.

We have to remember, though, that there is love and love. And certainly more powerful is the love distilled from a scrap of life that is consumed like Christ on the cross, than is the love that offers — and everything should be offered — the joy and serenity life can give.

Therefore, so that we Christians do not find ourselves behind the times, we have to try to put love beneath everything we do, being careful that it not be lacking where life proves most difficult and harsh.[60]

Christians' attire

At times, O Lord, amidst the vanity strolling the city streets, frivolous activities, superficiality, sadness and haste in people everywhere, in every person who passes us by, suddenly the rustle of the habit, the silent and angelic passing of a "little sister of Foucald," decidedly humble and unassuming, proclaims to our souls the ideal of her founder who shouted the gospel with his life. And in us is reborn more vehemently the desire that we too should "speak you," we too should "shout you."

But how can we, by our own mere passing by, "give you" to the world, "speak you" to the world, be your witnesses, preach you, when we are dressed like everyone else, lost in the crowd as Jesus and Mary were in their times? How will people be able to recognize you?

Once again I feel bubbling up in my heart the gospel response, your solution to our dilemma: "By this everyone will know that you are my disciples, if you have love for one another" (Jn 13:35). This is the attire that ordinary Christians, old and young, men and women, married or not, adults and children, sick or healthy, can wear in order to shout out always and everywhere with their own lives the One they believe in, the One they want to love.[61]

There are those who do things for love

There are those who do things "for love." There are those who do things trying "to be Love." Those who do things "for love" may do them well, but, thinking they are doing great service for their neighbour, who is sick for instance, they may annoy with their chatter, their advice and with their help. Such charity is burdensome and inappropriate.

They may gain merit, but the other is left with a burden. This is why it is necessary to "be Love."

Our destiny is like that of the planets: if they revolve, they are; if they do not, they are not. We are, in the sense that the life of God, not our life, lives in us, if we do not stop loving for one moment.

Love places us in God and God is Love.

But Love, which is God, is light and with the light we see whether our way of approaching and serving our brother or sister is according to the heart of God, as our brother or sister would wish it to be, as they would dream of it being, if they had beside them not us, but Jesus.[62]

When we have known suffering

When we have known suffering in all shades of its most frightful forms, in the most varied kinds of anguish, and have stretched out our arms to God in mute, heart-rending supplication, uttering subdued cries for help; when we have drunk the chalice to the last drop and have offered to God, for days and years, our own cross mingled with his, which gives it divine value, then God has pity on us and welcomes us into union with him.

This is the moment in which, having experienced the unique value of suffering, having believed in the economy of the cross and seen its beneficial effects, God shows us in a new and higher way something that is worth even more than suffering. *It is love for others in the form of mercy,* the love that stretches our hearts and arms to embrace the wretched, the poor, those whom life has ravaged, repentant sinners.

A love that knows how to welcome back our neighbour who went astray, our friend, brother or a stranger, and pardons an infinite number of times. It is a love that rejoices more over one sinner who comes back than over a thousand of the just, and that puts intelligence and possessions at the service of God, so as to enable him to show the prodigal son the happiness caused by his return.

It is a love that does not measure and will not be measured.

It is charity in bloom, which is more abundant, more universal, more down to earth than the charity the soul had before. Indeed, it senses within itself the birth of feelings similar to those of Jesus, and it notices coming to its lips with reference to all those it meets, the divine words: "I have compassion for the crowd" (Mt 15:32). It starts conversations with sinners who draw near, because it has a certain likeness to Christ, such as those conversations Jesus once had with Mary Magdalene, with the Samaritan woman, or with the adulteress.

Mercy is the ultimate expression of charity, and is that which fulfils it. Charity surpasses suffering, for suffering belongs to this life alone, whereas love continues also to the next. God prefers mercy to sacrifice.[63]

Thoughts: Nothing is small if it is done out of love

The one who loves, reigns. This is the way it is.

It is true also for you, and also for the poor or the sick when they meet the rich and the healthy. The reason is, those who love, give. Always give.

And their giving makes them regal, and they have within a fullness that has no end.

Maybe this is why God commanded us to love: so that he can give us the joy of feeling we are children, not of limited and powerless human beings, but children of God, of the King of kings.[64]

The presence of charity in the world is like the sun's appearance in spring. The barren earth may seem to have nothing to offer, but suddenly all is green again, and flowers are blooming. Their seeds were always there, but the warmth was lacking.

Goodwill and good intentions exist in the world, but we often do not see their fruits. Without the flame of charity, they could not come to the light.[65]

It is the sun's heat that makes flowers, by continuous miracle, bloom even on the most thorny of bushes. It is in their contact with hearts of boundless charity, which know no limits, that the greatest and most repulsive of sinners on this earth will become saints.[66]

Many people in the world burn with the desire to do good. But there is good and then there is good.

There are those who do good for their own families, their relatives, their friends.

Others go beyond and do good for the society of their time, and maybe throughout their whole lives.

But there are those who do good even after their death, for years to come, even for centuries: only saints do this, because it is no longer they who live in them, but God in them.

If today we still feel the desire to do good because we have read the lives of the saints of long ago, it is because they have remained alive in their writings and continue to do good through their words that carry the fragrance of eternal truths.[67]

"Let us love, not in word or speech, but in truth and action" (1 Jn 3:18). Not merely: "Do works and speak the truth."[68]

Charity is not explained through words, but on the cross.[69]

Nothing is small if it is done out of love.[70]

Do you know what you should do when you have loved and loved and loved?
    Love some more![71]

The first Christians are not remembered so much for going into ecstasy but for how much they loved one another: they had grasped, in its first freshness, the testament of Jesus.[72]

The person next to me was created as a gift for me and I was created as a gift for the person next to me. On earth all stands in a relationship of love with all: each thing with each thing. We have to be Love, however, to discover the golden thread among all things that exist.[73]

Jesus Forsaken[74]

There is no thorn without a rose

How painful to think that the lives of many people are simply not lived! They do not live because they do not see. They do not see because they look at the world, at things, at their relatives, at people, with their own eyes. Whereas to see it would be enough to follow every event, everything, every person with the eyes of God. We see if we place ourselves in God and know him as Love, if we believe in his love and think like the saints that "everything that God wills or permits is for my sanctification."

Joy and grief, birth and death, anguish and exultation, failure and triumph, encounters, acquaintances, work, sickness, unemployment, wars and disasters, a child's smile, a mother's love, everything is the raw material for our sanctity.

Around our being moves a world of all sorts of values: a divine world, an angelic world, a world of brothers and sisters, a lovable world and a hostile world, all prepared by God for our divinization, which is our true end.

In this world everyone is a centre, because the law of everything is love.

And if because of the human and divine balance of our life, and by will of the Most High, we must love, always love the Lord and our brothers and sisters, then the will of God, what God allows, and other beings — whether they know it or not — serve us, act out their existence, for love of us. Indeed, for those who love all things work together for good.

With our darkened and unbelieving eyes, we often do not see how each and every one has been created as a gift for us, and we as a gift for others.

But it is so. And a mysterious bond of love links persons and things, guides history, orders the destiny of peoples and of individuals, while respecting their maximum freedom.

But when the soul, which has abandoned itself to God, has for some time made the law of "believing in love" (see 1 Jn 4:16) its own, God shows himself. With newly opened eyes the soul sees that from every trial it gathers new fruit, every fight is followed by victory, every tear flowers in a smile that is new, always new, because God is Life, who allows torture, evil, for a greater good.

The soul understands that the life of Jesus does not culminate in the way of the cross and in death, but in the resurrection and the ascension to heaven.

Then the human way of seeing things fades and becomes meaningless, and bitterness no longer poisons the brief joys of this earthly life. For the soul that proverb so full of melancholy, "There is no rose without a thorn," means nothing. But because of the wave of the revolution of love into which God has drawn the soul, the exact opposite is true: "There is no thorn without a rose."[75]

A paradoxical purpose

In our daily actions and responsibilities, we need to learn how to welcome, moment by moment, that something heavy or oppressive they bring with them. We need to single it out, give value to its heaviness, that particular quotient of fatigue, discomfort, effort, or distress, and we must welcome it all as a precious gift to give to God.

In fact, most important is everything that tastes of suffering. This is not what the world wants to hear, on the one hand because the world is no longer Christian and therefore no longer understands this, and on the other because it is simply natural to not like pain. So the world flees it, and wants to forget it.

Yet, pain has a paradoxical purpose: it is the channel to happiness, if we are speaking of true happiness and lasting happiness, and not a fleeting, or provisional one. We are speaking of that one happiness alone that can satisfy the human heart, the very happiness God enjoys and which human beings, for the transcendent destiny that is theirs, can already share in this life.

Just like Jesus, who through his suffering gave humanity joy here on earth and lasting joy in the next life, we too, by accepting the various kinds of anguish we experience and offering them each day with a supernatural spirit, can acquire happiness for ourselves and for others.[76]

The cross

"Let them take up their cross . . ." (see Mt 16:24).

So strange and unique are these words. Like all the words said by Jesus, they have something in them of a light that this world does not know. They are so bright that the dull eyes of human beings, including those of apathetic Christians, are dazzled and therefore made blind.

There is nothing, perhaps, more puzzling, more difficult to grasp than the cross; it does not penetrate the head and the heart of human beings. It does not penetrate because it is not understood, because often we have become Christians only in name, merely baptized, maybe practising, yet immensely far from being what Jesus would like us to be.

We hear about the cross during Lent, we kiss it on Good Friday and sometimes hang it up in our rooms. It is the sign that seals some of our actions. Yet it is not understood.

And perhaps the whole mistake lies here: in the world, *love* is not understood.

Love is the finest of words, but it is also the most deformed and debased. It is the essence of God, the life of the children of God, the breath of the Christian, yet it has become the heritage, the monopoly of the world. It is on the lips of those who have no right to use it.

Certainly, in the world, not all love is like this. There still exist, for instance, the feelings of mothers which, because they are mingled with suffering, make love noble. There is fraternal love, marital love, filial love, which are good and wholesome. They are traces although perhaps unconscious, of the Love of the Father, Creator of all things.

But what is not understood is love par excellence: which is to understand that God who made us, came on earth as one human being among others, lived with us, and allowed himself to be nailed to a cross: to save us.

It is too high, too beautiful, too divine, too little human, too bloodstained, painful, intense to be understood.

Perhaps maternal love can give us an inkling of it. For the love of a mother is not only hugs and kisses; it is above all sacrifice.

Thus it is with Jesus: love impelled him to the cross, considered foolishness by many.

But only this foolishness has saved humanity and has formed the saints.

Saints, in fact, are people who are able to understand the cross. They are men and women who, following Jesus, the God-Man, have taken up their daily cross as the most precious thing on earth. At times they have brandished it like a weapon, as soldiers of God. They have loved it all their lives, and they have known and experienced that the cross is *the key*, the only key to a treasure, *the* treasure. The cross gradually opens souls to union with God. Then, through human beings, God once more reappears on the scene of this earth. He repeats — although in a way that is infinitely lesser, yet *similar* — the actions that he himself once performed when, as one human being among others, he blessed those who cursed him, forgave those who insulted him, saved, healed, preached the words of heaven, fed the hungry, founded a new society based on the law of love, and revealed the power of the One who sent him.

In short, the cross is the necessary instrument by which the divine penetrates the human, and a human being participates more fully in the life of God, and is raised up from the kingdom of this world to the kingdom of heaven.

But we must "take up our cross ... ," wake up in the morning expecting it, and knowing that only by means of it can we receive those gifts which the world does not know: that peace, that joy, that knowledge of the things of heaven, unknown to most.

The cross. It is such a common thing. It is so faithful that it never misses its appointment every day. To take up this cross is all we need to make us saints.

The cross, the badge of the Christian, is unwanted by the world because it believes that by fleeing it, suffering can be escaped. The world does not know that the cross opens wide the soul of the person who has understood it to the kingdom of Light and of Love: that Love which the world seeks so much, but does not have.[77]

I have found you

I have found you in so many places, Lord!
I have felt you throbbing
in the perfect stillness
of a little Alpine church,
in the shadow of the tabernacle
of an empty cathedral,
in the breathing as one soul
of a crowd who loves you and who fills
the arches of your church
with songs and love.
I have found you in joy.
I have spoken to you
beyond the starry firmament,
when in the evening, in silence,
I was returning home from work.
I seek you and often I find you.
But where I *always* find you
is in suffering. A suffering, any sort of suffering,
is like the sound of a bell
that summons God's bride to prayer.

When the shadow of the cross appears
the soul recollects itself
in the tabernacle of its heart
and forgetting the tinkling of the bell
it "sees" you and speaks to you.
It is you who come to visit me.
It is I who answer you:
"Here I am, Lord, I desire you, I have desired you."
And in this meeting my soul does not feel its suffering,
but is as if inebriated with your love:
suffused with you, imbued with you:
I in you and you in me,
that we may be one.
And then I reopen my eyes to life,
to the life less real,
divinely drilled
to wage your war.[78]

The sun must set

Why is that some people who, though unlettered, even in religious fields, have become saints by reading only one book, that of the crucified Christ?

It is because they did not stop at contemplating him, or at venerating him or at kissing his wounds, but they wanted to *relive him* in themselves. And those who suffer, and are in darkness, see farther than those who do not suffer, precisely because the sun must set before we can see the stars.

Suffering teaches what you cannot learn by any other means. It teaches with the greatest authority. It is the teacher of wisdom, and blessed is the one who has found wisdom (see Prv 3:13). "Blessed are those who mourn, for they will be comforted" (Mt 5:4) not only with the reward of heaven, but also with the contemplation of heavenly things while here on earth.

We have to approach with reverence those who suffer, reverence like that once accorded elderly when their wisdom was sought.[79]

The hour that awaits us

Good Friday: here lies the new value of suffering in our Christian life; the call, I would even say, that is highest among all the vocations of each day, of each hour of our life.

Jesus is "a man of suffering" (Is 53:3). It is the height of his vocation.

In our work and successes, we are tempted at times to see persons who suffer as marginal cases to care for, to visit, and even to help so as to get them back on their feet quickly so they can continue their activity, as if activity were the centre of what we should be.

But instead, no: those among us who suffer, who lie in their sickbed, who are dying, and offer everything to God, are the elect.

They are at the height of the hierarchy of love.

They are the ones who do most, bring about most.

Therefore, let's not be afraid if we learn that suffering awaits us.

It is what we must expect, because Jesus came for the hour of his suffering, and we for ours.[80]

Eli, Eli, lema sabachthani

"Eli, Eli, lema sabachthani" (Mt 27:46). These are the words that Jesus, in his forsakenness, cried out in the language of Mary, his mother.

"How meaningful is that cry of yours in the language of your mother! … When suffering reaches the limit where life itself is suspended … then if a shred of voice remains, we call our mother, because our mother is love.

"But you, being the Son of God, had all your love in God and to God you called out. And, as man, you also had love in your blessed mother; so that, in the impossibility of calling upon both, you called to the Father with the voice of your mother.

"How beautiful you are in that infinite suffering, Jesus forsaken!"[81]

Lament

"We are tired, Lord,
so tired under the cross
and every little cross that appears
makes the larger ones seem impossible to carry.
we are tired, Lord,
so tired under the cross,
our tears tighten our throats,
we drink bitter tears.
We are tired, Lord,
so tired under the cross.
Hasten our time

for there is no more joy for us here,
nothing but desolation.
The good we love
is entirely up there,
while down here
we are tired, oh so tired,
under the cross.
The Virgin is beside us,
beautiful yet mournful creature.
In her solitude
help ours at this hour.[82]

We would die

We would die if we did not look at you, who transformed, as if by magic, every bitterness into sweetness; at you, crying out on the cross, in the greatest suspense, in total inactivity, in a living death, when, sunk in the cold, you hurled your fire upon the earth, and reduced to infinite stillness, you cast your infinite life to us, who now live it in rapture.

   It is enough for us to see that we are like you, at least a little, and unite our suffering to yours and offer it to the Father.
   So that we might have Light, you ceased to see.
   So that we might have union, you experienced separation from the Father.
   So that we might possess wisdom, you made yourself "ignorance."
   So that we might be clothed with innocence, you made yourself "sin."
   So that God might be in us, you felt him far from you.[83]

Where is the slavery?

I have great joy in my heart, Lord, perhaps because in this moment I have given you everything.

   Not to have and not to be: not to have what I believed was mine, and that I knew was yours; not to be in order to be you.

   I know that much awaits me to suffer for you, but you, who are light and joy, life and resurrection, truth and beauty, allow me to see you and to feel you without being veiled by the cross under the veil which is the cross.

   Because I know that the cross bears a God, I know that there is no imaginable emptiness that you cannot fill, I know that your redemption was full and overflowing.

Allow me to express with my life the freedom you paid for and to be your witness of that; as though to say, if, because of you, suffering is now love, the shadow is light, loneliness is peopled and filled with your kingdom, then where is the slavery we deserve, where the chains?[84]

"I know only Christ and Christ crucified"

I have only one Spouse on earth: Jesus forsaken.
I have no other God but him.
In him there is the whole of paradise with the Trinity
    and the whole of the earth with humanity.
Therefore what is *his* is mine, and nothing else.
And *his* is universal suffering, and therefore mine.
I will go through the world seeking it in every instant of my life.
What hurts me is *mine*.
Mine the suffering that grazes me in the present.
Mine the suffering of the souls beside me
(that is my Jesus).
Mine all that is not peace, not joy, not beautiful, not lovable, not serene,
in a word, what is not paradise.
Because I too have *my* paradise,
but it the one in my Spouse's heart.
I know no other.
So it will be for the years I have left: athirst for suffering,
    anguish, despair, separation, exile, forsakenness, torment —
for all that is him,
and he is sin, hell.
In this way
I will dry up the waters of tribulation
in many hearts nearby
and, through communion
with my almighty Spouse,
in many far away.
I shall pass as a fire
that consumes all that must fall
and *leaves standing only* the truth.
But it is necessary to be *like* him:
to be him in the present moment of life.[85]

Thoughts: The foolishness of love

Cold freezes, but if excessive, it burns and chaps the skin. Wine strengthens, but if too much, it saps your strength. Motion is as it is, but if it spins at its greatest speed, it appears still. The Spirit of God gives life, but if there is much of it … it inebriates. Jesus is love because he is God; but his great love for us made him cry out: "My God, my God, why have you forsaken me?" (Mt 27:46) and in this cry he appears merely a man.[86]

The Father, Jesus, Mary, us. The Father permitted that Jesus feel forsaken by him, *for us*. Jesus accepted being forsaken by the Father, and deprived himself of his Mother, *for us*.

Mary shared the forsakenness of Jesus and accepted being deprived of her Son, *for us*. We, therefore, have been put in first place. It is love that does such crazy things.[87]

Suffering may be the most discarded element in the world, but it is the only thing, if taken advantage of, that fills us with God.[88]

It is not so true that those who love the cross because Jesus commanded us to find suffering.

Instead, those who generously cast themselves onto its beams find love; they find God.[89]

Only those who pass through the ice of suffering reach the fire of love.[90]

The grain of wheat develops under the earth, covered by a blanket of snow.

Likewise, the soul matures in its union with God isolated by a layer of forsakenness.[91]

The diameter of a tree's foliage often corresponds to the diameter of its roots.

A soul expands in Christ's charity to the extent of the suffering it has offered for him.[92]

Jesus forsaken, embraced, locked to one's self, wanted as our only all, he consumed in *one with us, we consumed in one* with him, made suffering with him Suffering: here lies everything. Here is how we become (by participation) God, Love.[93]

Love Jesus crucified in yourself, in the infinite details of your sufferings, but love him most of all outside of yourself, in your brothers and sisters, in all your brothers and sisters.

If you could have any preferences among them, love him in the greatest sinners, in the most wretched, the most ragged, the most repugnant, the most forsaken, the rejects of society, in those most tortured by life.[94]

Who is in the Father, having come to him from a long history of sin, out of God's pure mercy is equal in his eyes to the innocent who has arrived there by dint of love.

In fact, the moment you recognize yourself as a sinner, and delight (by loving God more than your own soul, and this is pure love) in being similar to him made sin, you fill the emptiness left by sin.

In this way you arrive in heaven through God's pure mercy (which means having received everything for free) but at the same time out of pure love for God spoken freely by your heart.[95]

I wish to bear witness before the world that Jesus forsaken has filled every void, illuminated every darkness, accompanied every solitude, annulled every suffering, cancelled every sin.[96]

The Dream of a God[97]

Unity, a divine word

Unity: a divine word. If at any moment the Almighty were to pronounce this word, and people everywhere were to apply it in the most varied ways, we would suddenly see the world stop in its tracks, and like a film running backwards, retake its course in the opposite direction. Countless people would reverse their tracks along the wide road to perdition and would convert to God, choosing the narrow road.... Families separated by rifts, their hearts hardened by misunderstandings and hatred, and deadened by divorce, would be recomposed. Children would be born into an atmosphere of human and divine love, and new people would be shaped, giving promise to a more Christian future.

Factories, often a gathering of people who are "slaves" to their work in a bored, if not vulgar, atmosphere, would become places of peace, where all do their share for the good of all.

Schools would break through the limits of their short-lived knowledge, making every discipline a footstool for the contemplation of things eternal, learned in the classroom in a daily revelation of mysteries, intuited from basic formulae, simple laws, or even numbers....

And elected bodies would be transformed into meeting places for people who battle not so much for particular interests, but for the good of all, without deceiving other colleagues or countries.

We would see a world becoming kinder, as if in a dream heaven come down upon earth, and the harmonies of creation become the setting for the unity of hearts.

We would see.... But it is a dream! It seems like a dream!

Yet you asked for nothing less when you prayed: "Your will be done on earth as it is in heaven" (Mt 6:10).[98]

The words of a father

The words of a father are always precious, since we must believe someone who speaks out of love. But when a father utters his final words before leaving this earth, they remain clearly imprinted on the minds of his children. They have as much value as all his other words put together. They are his final testament.

A father's love is nothing when compared with the love of God.

The God become human, Jesus, also spoke and left us a testament: "May they all be one" (Jn 17:21).

Whoever direct their lives towards unity have understood the heart of God.

In this world we are all brothers and sisters and yet we pass each other as if we were strangers. And this happens even among baptized Christians.

The Communion of Saints, the Mystical Body exists. But this Body is like a network of darkened tunnels.

The power to illuminate them exists; in many individuals there is the life of grace, but Jesus did not want only this when he turned to the Father, calling upon him. He wanted a heaven on earth: the unity of all with God and with one another; the network of tunnels to be illuminated; the presence of Jesus to be in every relationship with others, as well as in the soul of each.

This is his final testament, the most precious desire of God who gave his life for us.[99]

He wants to give us heaven

"Father, I desire that those also, whom you have given me, may be with me where I am, to see my glory, which you have given me because you loved me before the foundation of the world.

"Righteous Father, the world does not know you, but I know you; and these know that you have sent me. I made your name known to them, and I will make it known, so that the love with which you have loved me may be in them, and I in them" (Jn 17:24-26).

He wants to give us heaven. Where he will be, so too will we; he wants us to see his eternal glory.

Calling upon the Father, and reminding him that he is "righteous," he asks, in contrast to the world that did not know him, that, indeed, we should have the very love with which the Father loved him.

It is fathomless. In his testament Jesus reveals himself more than ever as "God."

There appears to be nothing of the human in these words so completely trinitarian. Yet, at the same time we feel the heart of a friend, a brother, a loving master, a father who gives us all that he can: to share in his divinity.[100]

Love generates communion

The Christian is called to live life, to swim in the light, to plunge into crosses, but not to pine away. At times our life is exhausted, our intelligence is clouded and our will undecided, because educated in this world, we have been used to living an individualistic life, which stands in contradiction to the Christian life.

Christ is love and a Christian must be love. Love generates communion: communion as the basis of the Christian life and as its summit.

In this communion a person no longer goes to God alone, but travels in company. This is a fact of incomparable beauty that makes our soul repeat the words of the Scripture: "How very good and pleasant it is when kindred live together in unity!" (Ps 133:1).

Fraternal communion is not, however, a beatific stillness; it is a perennial conquest with the continual result not only of preserving communion, but also of expanding it among many people, because the communion spoken of here is love, is charity, and charity spreads by its very nature.

How often, between those who have decided to go united to God, unity begins to weaken, dust creeps in between one soul and another and the enchantment is broken, because the light that had emerged among them all slowly goes out! This dust is a thought, an attachment of the heart to oneself or to others; love of self for self and not for God, or of a neighbour or neighbours for themselves and not for God. At other times, it is withdrawal of the soul that had previously given itself to others, a concentration upon one's own self, one's own will and not on God, on our brother or sister for God, on the will of God.

And very often it is through a faulty judgment of someone who lives with us.

We had said we wanted to see only Jesus in our neighbour, to deal with Jesus in our neighbour, to love Jesus in our neighbour, but now we recall that a neighbour has this or that defect, has this or that imperfection.

Our eye becomes complicated and our being is no longer lit up. As a consequence, erring, we break unity.

Perhaps that particular neighbour, like all of us, has made mistakes, but how does God view him or her? What really is that person's condition, the truth of his or her state? If our neighbour is reconciled with God, then God no longer remembers anything, he has wiped out everything with his blood. So, why should we go on remembering?

Who is in error at that moment?

I who judge or my neighbour?

I am.

Therefore I must make myself see things from God's viewpoint, in the truth, and treat my neighbour accordingly, so that if, by some mishap, he or she has not yet sorted things out with the Lord, the warmth of my love, which is Christ in me, will bring my neighbour to repentance, in the same way that the sun dries and heals over many wounds.

Charity is preserved by truth, and truth is pure mercy with which we ought to be clothed from head to foot in order to be able to call ourselves Christians.

And if my neighbour returns?

I must see that person new, as though nothing had happened, and I must begin life together with him or her in the unity of Christ, as the first time, because nothing remains. This trust will safeguard my neighbour from other falls, and I too, if I use this measure, may hope to be judged by God one day with the same measure.[101]

When unity is complete

When unity with our brothers and sisters is complete, when it has flowered anew and more fully from difficulties, then, as night fades into day, tears into light, often, I find you, Lord.

Going back into the temple of my soul, I meet you; or as soon as circumstances leave me alone, you invite me, you draw me, gently but firmly, into your divine presence.

Then you alone rule within me and outside me, and the house you have given me to use for the pilgrimage of life, feels to me, and I call it, the dwelling place of my God.

This presence of yours is love, but a love that the world does not know.... The soul is immersed as if in some delicious nectar and the heart seems to have become the chalice that contains it.

The soul is all a silent song known only to you: a melody that reaches you because it comes from you and is made of you.

These are the moments when peace seems something substantial, in which the certainty of salvation is absolute, in which, though still on earth, the soul seems to be swimming in heaven.

And ... strangely — strange to the human way of thinking — we have gone out to our brothers and sisters all the day long and, in the evening, we have found the Lord, who has dissolved every trace, every memory of creatures.

It seems unnecessary in these moments to have faith, faith in his existence.

He, sweetly permeating our house, having become our portion and our inheritance, he himself tells us of his existence.[102]

If we are united, Jesus is among us

If we are united, Jesus is among us. And this has value. It is worth more than any other treasure that our heart may possess; more than mother, father, brothers, sisters, children. It is worth more than our house, our work, or our property; more than the works of art in a great city like Rome; more than our business deals; more than nature which surrounds us with flowers and fields, the sea and the stars; more than our own soul.

It is he who, inspiring his saints with his eternal truths, leaves his mark upon every age.

This too is his hour. Not so much the hour of a saint but of him, of *him among us*, of him living in us as we build up — in the unity of love — his Mystical Body.

But we must enlarge Christ, make him grow in other members, become like him bearers of Fire.

Make one of all and in all the One.

It is then that we live the life that he gives us, moment by moment, in charity.

The basic commandment is brotherly love. Everything is of value if it expresses sincere fraternal charity. Nothing we do is of value, if there is not the feeling of love for our brothers and sisters in it. For God is a Father and in his heart he has always and only his children.[103]

Christ will be my cloister

I believe there is no man's heart, still less a woman's, that has not at least once, especially in youth, felt the attraction of the cloister.

It is not the attraction of a cloistered way of life, but of something that seems to be concentrated there, between those four walls, something that makes itself felt, resounding deeply, even from a distance.

In these communities, with which the world, thank God, is strewn like a dark night dotted with constellations, there is the light of the presence of God. A presence that stands out strongly, because it blossoms on the background of persons who, for God, have wished to immolate in the shadows their own poor appearance.

Though sunken in silence, these houses of brothers or sisters united in God, through the mysterious power of celestial things, speak to the hearts of human beings and utter a voice unknown to the world: a blessedness of union with God that humanity longs for.

Yet also my own home can have the fragrance of the cloister; also the walls of my dwelling can become a kingdom of peace, God's fortress in the midst of the world.

It is not so much the external din of the radio turned on at full blast by the tenant next door, or the roar of the traffic, or the yelling of the newspaper boys, that take away the enchantment from my house. It is rather every noise within me that makes my dwelling become an open square unprotected by walls, because unprotected by love.

The Lord is within me. He would like to move my actions, permeate my thoughts with his light, stir up my will, give me, in short, the law of my stillness and of my movement.

But there is my ego which, at times, does not let him live in me. If it stops interfering, God himself will take possession of all my being and he will know how to give these walls the importance of an abbey, and this room the sacredness of a church, my sitting at table the sweetness of liturgy, my clothes the perfume of a blessed habit, the sound of the doorbell or the telephone the joyous note of a meeting with my brothers and sisters, which interrupts, yet continues, my conversation with God.

Then, upon the silence of me, Another will speak and, upon my extinguishing myself, a light will be lit. And it will shine afar, passing beyond and almost consecrating these walls that protect a member of Christ, a temple of the Holy Spirit. And other people will come to my house to seek the Lord with me, and in our shared, loving search, the flame will grow, the divine melody will rise a tone. And my heart, though in the midst of the world, will ask for nothing more.

Christ will be my cloister, the Christ of my heart, Christ in the midst of our hearts.[104]

If a city were set on fire

If a city were set alight at various points, even by small fires, but they managed to resist being put out, soon the city would be aflame. If a city, in the most different places, were lit up by the fire that Jesus brought on earth, and this fire, through the goodwill of the people who lived there, managed to resist the ice of the world, we would soon have the city aflame with the love of God.

The fire that Jesus brought to earth is himself. It is charity: love which not only binds the soul to God, but also souls to one another.

In fact, a lighted supernatural fire means the continual triumph of God in souls who have given themselves to him and, because they are united to him, united among themselves.

Two or more people fused in the name of Christ, who are not afraid or ashamed to declare explicitly to one another their desire to love God, but who actually make of this unity in Christ their Ideal, are a divine power in the world.

And in every city these souls could spring up in families: father and mother, son and father, mother and mother-in-law. They could meet in parishes, in associations, in social bodies, in schools, in offices, everywhere.

It is not necessary for them to be saints already, or Jesus would have said so. It is enough for them to be united in the name of Christ and that they never go back on this unity.

Naturally, they will not remain two or three for very long, for charity spreads of itself and grows by enormous proportions.

Every small cell, set alight by God in any point of the earth, will necessarily spread, and Providence will distribute these flames, these souls on fire, wherever it thinks fit, so that the world in many places may be restored to the warmth of the love of God, and hope again.

But there is a secret by which this lighted cell may grow and become a tissue of cells and give life to the parts of the Mystical Body. It is that those who make up the Body should throw themselves into the Christian adventure, which means *making a spring-board of every obstacle*. They should not just "put up" with the cross in whatever guise it presents itself, but should wait for it and embrace it, minute by minute, as the saints do.

It is a matter of saying, whenever the cross comes: "This is what I wanted, Lord! I know I belong to the Church Militant, where struggle is necessary. I know the Church Triumphant awaits me, where I shall see you for all eternity. While I am still here on earth, I prefer suffering to everything else, because with your life you have told me that only in suffering is there true value."

And having said "yes" to the Lord, the soul must live fully the moment that follows, not thinking of itself, of its own pain. But it must think of the suffering of others, or of the joys of others that it must share, or the burdens

The Dream of a God

of others that it must bear with them. Or it must think of the fulfilment of its duties to which, because God wills it and in order to lift them up as a continuous prayer, it must give the attention of all its mind, the affection of all its heart and all the vigour of its strength.

This is the little secret that builds, brick by brick, the city of God within us and among us. And already on this earth, it places us within the divine will, which is God, the eternal present.[105]

One city is not enough

If you want to win over a city to the love of Christ,
if you want to transform a town
into the kingdom of God,
first make your plans.
Gather round you friends who share your feelings.
Unite yourself with them in the name of Christ
and ask them to put God before anything else.
Then make a pact with them:
promise one another constant and perpetual love,
so that the Conqueror of the world
may be always among you
and be your leader;
that when your ego has been destroyed in love,
your every step may be sustained, your every tear be dried,
by the Mother of Fair Love.

Then size up the city.
Seek out its spiritual head.
Go with your friends to see him.
Present your plans to him, and if he does not consent
do not take even a step, for otherwise you will ruin everything.
If he advises you and offers you some guidelines
accept them as a command
and make them a watchword for you and for your friends.
Assure him of your loyalty
for Christ has commanded it,
and offer to help him
— with your spiritual contribution —
in his heavy responsibility.

Then look for the poorest, the destitute,
the forsaken, the orphans, the prisoners.
Without pause in your action
run with your friends to visit Christ in them, to comfort them,
to reveal to them that the love of God is close to them
and watches over them.
If someone is hungry, take food,
if naked, take clothing.
If you have neither clothes nor food,
ask for them from the Eternal Father with faith,
because they are necessary for his Son Christ,
who you wish to serve in every human person.
And he will hear you.
Loaded with all these goods go through the streets,
go up into attics and down into cellars,
seek out Christ in public and private places,
at the stations, along the railways, in the slums,
and caress him above all with your smile.
Then promise him eternal love
so that the places you are unable to go
may be reached by your prayers and your sufferings,
united to the Sacrifice of the altar.
Leave no one alone,
and do not be sparing in your promises,
because you go in the name of the Almighty.
While you are gladdening the Lord in your brothers and sisters,
God will concern himself with filling you and your friends
with heavenly gifts.
Share these with one another,
so that the light may not grow dim and love go out.
If your action is determined
and your speech filled with wisdom,
many will follow you.
Divide these people into groups
so that with them you may leaven the city
that you wish to undermine with your love.
Keep going.
If others, having got to know your life

and having seen with their own eyes the gifts you have,
ask you to talk, then speak,
but let the core of your speech be the things
you have learned from life.
Base what you say
on the teaching of the Church and on Scripture
from which you and your group have drunk
as your first source, safe, inexhaustible, eternal.
So that, if the Shepherd speaks
you may be his living word.
Having consoled, helped, enlightened, made happy
those who were the dregs of society,
you have laid the foundations
to build the new city.
Then gather your friends together and repeat the beatitudes to them,
so that they may never lose the spirit of Christ
and of his preferences.
After that look further afield and tell everyone
that every neighbour,
rich or poor, beautiful or ugly, gifted or not,
is Christ who passes by.
Let your ranks, the ranks of Jesus, of Mary,
be at his service and each of you weep with those who weep,
rejoice with those who rejoice,
constantly share sufferings and joys
with any sacrifice, without ever ceasing.
Alternate your action
with the deepest prayer,
lifted up by your army in perfect unity,
so that — through Christ —
there may be won the greatest glory from that place.
And if the struggle costs,
know that there lies the secret of success,
and that he who urges you on has paid with his blood.
Forgive and pray for those who think ill of you,
for if you do not forgive, you will not find mercy.
And if suffering consumes you, sing out:
"Behold my spouse, my friend, my brother,"

so that in the hour of your death
the Lord may say to your soul:
*"Arise, and hurry, my friend, my dove,
my fair one, and come away"* (see Sg 2:10).

Do this for a city until victory,
to the point, that is, that good overcomes evil
and Christ through us can repeat:
"I have conquered the world" (Jn 16:33).

But with a God who visits you every morning, if you wish,
one city is too little.
He is the one who has made the stars,
who guides the destiny of the ages.
Come to an agreement with him, and aim further:
at your country, at everyone's country, at the world.
Let your every breath be for this;
for this your every action;
for this your resting and your moving.

Having reached the other side, you will see that which has most value,
and you will find a reward proportionate to your love.
Act in such a way that in that hour you need not be sorry
for having loved too little.[106]

Thoughts: Bend but never break

Unity! Who would dare speak of it?
It is ineffable as God.
You feel it, see it, rejoice over it but ... it is ineffable!
All enjoy its presence, all suffer its absence.
It is peace, joy, love, ardour, and the spirit of heroism, of boundless generosity.
It is Jesus among us.[107]

Only if we have the mark of unity among us can we really call ourselves Christians.[108]

When unity among us becomes difficult, we must not break, but bend, until love makes the miracle of one heart and one soul.[109]

Better what is less perfect, but in unity with our brothers and sisters, than what is more perfect, but in disunity with them, because perfection does not lie in ideas or in wisdom, but in charity.[110]

Nothing is more organized than what love orders and nothing is more free than what love unites.[111]

Whoever lives in God is one with everyone and with everything, yet distinct from them.[112]

When two souls meet each other they are two Heavens that unite, which gives to the two souls joy, peace, serenity, light and ardour — as in the Trinity.[113]

The more we are perfected in unity, the more we acquire the virtue of the other *("All that is yours is mine")*, in such a way that we are all *one*, each the other, each Jesus. We are many equal persons, but distinct, because the virtues in us are dressed in the characteristic virtue that forms our own personality.

    We mirror the life of the Trinity where the Father is distinct from the Son and the Spirit, while still containing in himself the Son and the Spirit.

    The same is true of the Spirit, who contains in himself both the Father and the Son, and the Son, who contains in himself both the Father and the Holy Spirit.[114]

Whoever lives unity, lives Jesus, and lives in the Father. He or she lives in heaven, in paradise always: the earthly here, made paradise through the hundredfold, and the heavenly on high, through life eternal.[115]

Church as Communion[116]

A myriad of shining pearls

I picture a city of gold,
where the divine stands out in relief, resplendent with light,
and the human forms its background,
having withdrawn into the shade,
to give greater stress to the splendour.
Every church, every tabernacle,
glows more brightly than the sun,
because in them has remained
the Love of loves.
In the soul of those who represent the Church,
in the hierarchy that gives structure to the divine society,
brought down on earth from heaven, I find a myriad of shining pearls:
they are the graces deposited by God,
through the hands of the Virgin,
in that channel, which has the one purpose
of quenching my thirst for light,
and of nourishing me with honey from heaven,
as a more than heavenly mother who feeds her child.
And if, recollected in God,
I open the book of life and read the eternal Words,
I hear a harmony full of light
sing in my soul,
and the Spirit of God shines through me with his gifts.
When I meet anyone,
noble or wretched,
I see each face transfigured
into the most beautiful face
of the Word incarnate,
Light from Light.
When I go into the homes of people who love one another,
or families united in Christ,

I see a divine reflection of the Trinity,
and I hear expressed by the community
the Word that is life:
God.
God is the gold of my city,
before whom the sun itself is dimmed,
the sky dwindles,
all the beauty and majesty of nature
recedes, happy to encircle, to serve,
simply a frame.
And this city is in every city
and everyone may see it,
provided that our soul extinguishes itself in God,
forgetting itself,
and lit in it is the fire of love divine.[117]

The Mother

The Church entombs in her heart living creatures — the contemplatives — who, dead to the world but alive to the inner life, the life more true, offer themselves, almost as lightning rods, in reparation for the sins that we have committed.

The Church gathers the most beautiful flowers of the earth that God has already chosen and sets them out in order — as spare parts in a workshop — to go where there is need, spiritual or material, to support and encourage and give counsel and suffer and die, if necessary.

The Church, Mother most pure, has grafted us into her family, opening to us the doors of the true paradise by means of priests and sacraments.

She has forged us into soldiers of Christ.

She has pardoned us and cancelled our sins seventy times seven.

She has nourished us with the Body of Christ; and has placed the divine seal on the love of our father and our mother.

She has raised to the highest dignity poor human beings, people like us, and invested them with the priesthood.

And in the end she will give us the final goodbye: God be with you. She will give us God. If our heart does not sing of her it is a spent instrument. If our mind does not see her and admire her, it is blind and dark. If it does not speak of her, better that the words dry up in our mouth.[118]

Laity like us

Today a lot is said about the role of the laity. The layperson is "the Church" and perhaps the figure of the laity would come into greater prominence if some aspects of Mary were explained more fully and more clearly. From our point of view Mary, even though one of a kind, exceptional, is the model of the layperson.

Catholics do not make a deity of Mary as we are often accused of doing, even though, led by our love and faith to discover all that makes her *special*, we often relegate her to a place far from us, a sphere that does belong to her but does not encompass all that can be said of her.

We extol her as the Mother of God, conceived without sin, assumed to heaven, our Queen, rather than just the *perfect Christian*, fiancée, spouse, mother, widow, virgin, the model of every Christian, one who — like us laity — could not offer Christ sacramentally to the world, because — like us — she was not of the hierarchy; yet she is always very active in the Church, because as a mother, urged by the charity in her heart, she offered her sacrifice with which she participated in the sacrifice of her Son.

Mary is a layperson like us who demonstrates that the essence of Christianity is love and that even priests and bishops, before being priests and bishops must first be true Christians, living crucifixes as Jesus was, who founded his Church on the cross.

Mary, by highlighting in the Church the fundamental quality of love which makes it one, presents to the world the Bride of Christ as Jesus wanted it to be and every person today awaits: ordered charity, organized charity. Only by emphasizing this fundamental quality can the Church today fulfil properly its function of contact and dialogue with the world, which often finds the hierarchy less interesting, but is sensitive to the witness of love in the Church, the soul of the world.[119]

Passion for the Church

The "passion for the Church" about which Pope Paul VI once spoke,[120] reigns in the hearts of true Christians. This passion should move from the level of feeling to that of practical action, where love for the whole Church, just as she is — with her institutions, the fruit of numerous charisms the Holy Spirit has lavished and continues to lavish upon her — invites us to be aware of what the Church is and awareness invites us to even greater love.

What Christianity teaches about relationships between individuals — loving, getting to know one another, making ourselves one with others to the point of sharing the gifts God has given — should be translated into the social sphere, so that we come to know, admire and love the other Movements and associations in the Church, and bring about or foster a sharing of spiritual goods among all.

This would lead to working together, desired by our hearts and wills, and in this way we would serve of the Church we love. If we do not do this, our "passion for the church" would be pure rhetoric and we would put ourselves in the condition of finding ourselves closed and isolated. Furthermore, our love for the Pope would be reduced to fleeting enthusiasm and sentimentality, if we do not share with him that which he loves: the life of the whole Church of God.[121]

Christ through the centuries

Jesus is the Word of God incarnate.

The church is the gospel incarnate: for this reason she is the Bride of Christ.

Many religious orders have flourished through the centuries.

Every family or order is the "incarnation," so to speak, of an expression of Jesus, of an attitude of his, of an event of his life, of a suffering of his, of a word of his.

There are Franciscans who continue to proclaim to the world through their very existence: "Blessed are the poor in spirit, for theirs is the kingdom of heaven" (Mt 5:3).

There are the Dominicans who contemplate the Logos, the Word, under the aspect of Light and Truth, and make it their mission to explain and defend that Truth.

Monks have linked work to contemplation (Martha and Mary). The Carmelites adore God on Tabor, ready to come down to preach and face passion and death. Missionaries carry out the command: "Go therefore and make disciples of all nations" (Mt 28:19).

Orders, congregations and institutes of charity imitate the Good Samaritan.

Saint Thérèse and the followers of the "little way" take for their motto: "Unless you change and become like children, you will never enter the kingdom of heaven" (Mt 18:3).

The sisters of Bethlehem, of Nazareth, of Bethany, etc., are concrete expressions of some point in the life of Jesus. St. Catherine of the Blood of Christ, Saint Margaret Mary Alacoque of the Sacred Heart, the missionaries and adorers of the Precious Blood devote themselves to meditating on the price of our redemption.

To sum up, the church is Christ majestically unfolding through the centuries.

Just as water is transformed into snow crystals, so in Christ love has assumed its form par excellence, the beauty of beauties. Love has taken on various expressions, which are the religious orders and communities in the church.

In the splendid garden of the Church all the virtues have flowered and still flower. The founders of the religious orders each exemplify a particular virtue; they are all making their way to heaven, transfigured by great love and suffering like a "word of God."

By fulfilling God's plan for them they bear out the words: "Heaven and earth will pass away, but my words will not pass away" (Mt 24:35).

The saints were and still are like a word that God said to the world and, because they are identified with it, they will not pass away.

All these orders with their particular spiritualities for each time and place find their true meaning and source in Jesus who lives on in his Church throughout all time.

He unites with a single spirit. But it is up to the religious to allow it be manifested, this harmony, this highest unity in all its fullness, so that the Spouse of Christ may shine in that unique beauty that is "hers" and, to greatest extent possible, witness to the world her divinity.

So that religious orders may shine with the true spirituality for which they were born and have their reason for existence, their followers must see their founders as God sees them. God sees in St. Francis the idea of poverty, which in God is love; in St. Thérèse the idea of "the little way" which in God is love; in St. Catherine the blood of Christ which in God is Love.

God loves every order insofar as it reflects his Son, the Idea of himself made human, Love "made flesh."

The gospel proclaimed by Jesus was good news, Love made word.

For twenty centuries this Love has taken tangible form in his Church, which prolongs the incarnation in a certain sense. The Church has Christ for her head and repeats in a way the incarnation of Christ her spouse.

The best way to serve the Church is to proclaim that Love, especially by putting it into practice and making it circulate among the various religious orders. There will be an order based on meekness, just as there are the Jesuits who emphasize evangelical violence, "acting against."

Since all the founders acted in various ways but were driven by a single love, in the fulfilment of this love we will rediscover their different supernatural faces and understand their words and their rules.

They are truly holy because their love is not restricted to one particular aspect of the Church; they see the Church and embrace it in its entirety. If they emphasized one aspect, it was because they saw in it an instrument of God for the benefit of the whole.

Just as a pedestrian cannot see a whole city, region or country all at once by walking through the streets and squares and climbing the stairs, but must fly in a plane and see it from above, so the Church and our religious founders cannot be understood and appreciated unless they are viewed from above from Jesus' perspective or, to put it more concretely, from the viewpoint of our holy father, the vicar of Christ, who is right at the heart of the Bride of Christ, distant from everyone and thus closer to her than anyone else. The Pope witnesses to the unity of the Church and in his own person reveals the presence of Jesus always in her through the centuries.[122]

The lives of the saints

The lives of the saints are identical even though they vary greatly. Once they have given themselves to God, he takes them under his special care, and as supreme artist and supreme Love, he makes them into divine masterpieces. Angelic spirits or the eyes of other saints can understand them, or the insight, illuminated by a singular grace, of those in the Church who have to give judgment concerning them. To others, for the most part, their intimate selves are hidden and incomprehensible, because in the saint God lives more than human nature, and only the pure of heart see God.

The saint's life is made up of abysses and peaks: bottomless abysses, nights black as hell, dark tunnels where the soul, invaded by an absolutely superior light, is dazzled in a dark contemplation and submerged in a sea of anguish or near desperation due to its clear awareness of its own nothingness and wretchedness. Saints live through months, years, during which their only yearning is to die into the bosom of God from whom at times they feel hopelessly separated. Life is a cruel death and sleep a relief, a respite, almost a caress for the wounded soul. A long time passes in which saints cry out, calling for pardon, for salvation with no longer anything in their hearts but God, their God....

Then, after a long time of being worked upon in a crucible comparable to purgatory, the souls of the saints are slowly drawn by their divine Craftsman into a life that is serene, full, radiant, active and immune to any blow. But *now* in the soul it is no longer itself that lives. In it glorious and strong, honoured and heeded, there lives the Creator and Lord of every human heart.

This is the hour when an unknown, unique, divine strength flourishes in the saints which fuses together the most contrasting virtues in the soul: meekness and strength, mercy and justice, simplicity and prudence. They rejoice in their life in God and offer to their Lord "sacrifices of joy" (see Ps 27:6) with a joy that the world does not know. They are forced to admit that no dream is comparable to the Life they possess, a Life which is divine and extraordinary (because it is a life of love), full of harmony and fruits.

Then God uses them for his great works that make up and adorn the heavenly city, the Church, which is destined to ascend to God as the spotless and worthy *Bride of Christ* who founded it.

Human beings are only given one life. It would be in the interest of each one to place his or her life in the hands of God who gave it. This, in a rational and free person, would be the highest possible act of intelligence, the most effective way of maintaining and extending personal freedom to a divine level. It would mean the deification of one's own poor being in the name of the One who said: "You are gods, children of the Most High, all of you" (Ps 82:6).[123]

Launched to infinity

The saints are great men and women
who, having seen their greatness in the Lord,
risk for God, as his children,
everything that is theirs.
They give, demanding nothing.
They give their life, their soul, their joy,
every earthly bond, every richness.
Free and alone,
launched to infinity,
they wait for Love to bring them
into the eternal kingdom; but, already in this life,
they feel their hearts fill with love,
true love, the only love
that satisfies, that consoles,

that love which shatters
the eyelids of the soul and gives
new tears.
Ah, no one knows who a saint is!
He or she has given and now receives,
and an endless flow
passes between heaven and earth,
joins earth to heaven,
and filters from the depths
rare ecstasy, celestial sap
that does not stop at the saint,
but flows over the tired, the mortal,
the blind and paralyzed in soul,
and breaks through and refreshes,
comforts and attracts and saves.
If you want to know about love, ask a saint.[124]

To become saints as Church

How easy it is to notice a profound desire beginning to take hold in Christians; I would even call it an urgency. They show a desire to serve the Church not so much and not only in outward, material ways but in a different manner, more in tune with their faith, more essential.

One sees, especially among laity, that the way people used to think about becoming saints is not much appreciated; indeed at times they consider it outdated. The style of sanctity for today's Christian goes beyond that of perfection sought individually, and they often express it like this: we want to become saints together, we desire a collective sanctity.

So here and there we see committed Christians forming groups who, in unity, go towards God.

In fact it seems to us that this is what God really wants, so long as it all has the stamp of openness, the pulse of the entire Church, a loving unity with the hierarchy.

The face of the Church, with its lights and shadows, ought to be in every Christian, in every group of Christians. This means that we must feel as our own not only the Church's joys, her hopes, her constantly new forms of growth, her victories, but above all we must feel as our own all of her sorrows: the lack of full unity among the Churches, negative disputes, the threat of discarding age-old treasures, the anguish that many deny or refuse the message God speaks to the world for its salvation.

In all these afflictions, above all in the spiritual ones, the suffering Church appears as the Crucified Christ of today who cries out: "My God, my God, why have you forsaken me?" (Mt 27:46).

Not long ago I was at Mount La Verna. There I meditated on the exceptional gift of the stigmata that God gave Francis as a seal of his imitation of Christ, of his discipleship.

I was thinking that all true Christians should be stigmatics, not in an extraordinary, outward sense but spiritually.

I seemed to understand that the stigmata of today's Christians are the mysterious but real sufferings of the contemporary Church.

If the charity of Christ is not wide enough in us to feel in ourselves the pain of these wounds, we are not how God want us to be today.

In these times, only an individual sanctity is not enough, nor one that is communitarian but closed. We must feel within ourselves the sorrow and also joy that Christ experiences today in his Bride.

We need to become saints as Church.[125]

Thoughts: Like the angels

Virginity is so beautiful and sublime because, through it, human beings give to God the best thing they have: the possibility of extending their earthly lives through children (a need for humans, who *feel* the need *live on*). The virgin detaches self from the earth like a flower that does not wish to develop into fruit here below but continues to carry the seed. Instead, a virgin ascends to heaven in order to be planted and bloom permanently there.

The virgin gives witness to *God* just by the gift of virginity, because there is no earthly reason to remain a virgin; it makes sense only in the light of heaven.[126]

To the world the virgin appears absurd, an enigma to indifferent Christians, but in reality a supernatural masterpiece.

Virgins are only such if their life is God alone. Only God explains the virgin.

True virgins are replicas of Jesus and Mary: "divine" human beings. The woman is strong in herself and does not seek to lean upon a man and the man is complete in himself … "like angels in heaven" (Mt 22:30).[127]

At the café a husband and wife are speaking to each other very intimately. It is Saturday and families are leaving joyfully for the weekend.

In a plane three friends share impressions and comments.

Having been to the countryside, everyone looks forward to the moment they get home.

And the spouse of God? The one consecrated to the Lord? She works all day serving him in others, she adores and loves him at prayer time when, communing with him, she finds comfort and strength to continue her ascent to the heights of sanctity.[128]

Virgins! They have no human spouse, but God. They do not have few children, but many, all those the Lord has placed on their path. Like a natural mother and even more, they bless these children, encourage, help, instruct and sustain them when they are near, and when they are far away, awaiting their return, hoping all things with the charity that is their nature, praying to their omnipotent and ever present Spouse.

Being a virgin, while it releases a person from physical maternity, always implies a spiritual maternity, as wide as the network of society, which benefits from her personal love for Christ. Being a virgin means placing oneself in the midst of a crowd, pointing with one hand to heaven and with the other giving it support in life's trials.

Being a virgin means, without exaggeration, to fulfil in our own corner of the world the role of Mary, the Mother of everyone on earth, really, concretely, silently and supernaturally. As Jesus has remained on earth in priests, in whom, priest and victim, he continues to offer himself to the Father mysteriously and divinely for all humanity, Mary has remained on earth in virgins who continue her mission of motherhood, of service to humanity and co-operation with the sacrifice.[129]

There are the foolish virgins and there are the wise.

The oil is love.

Whoever has love is virgin, so, looking at things as God sees them, Mary Magdalene is more a virgin than many virgins who are proud of their virginity or who just do not love.

Jesus cannot know them, for Love knows only Love. The Bridegroom recognizes as his bride she who bears his name, something of himself, almost himself transferred into her, one with him.

Now God is Charity; nothing is more his than charity, since it is his essence.[130]

The Word That Gives Life

Nourished on the Word

Speaking of the word of God, Pope Paul VI said: " … one form of his presence among us is the word.… How is Jesus present in our souls? By means of the vehicle, the communication of the word, which is so normal in human communication, but which here becomes sublime and mysterious: the divine thought is given, the Word itself is given, the Son of God become man.…"[131]

At various times when I have some inner preoccupation or sorrow, I turn to the word of God. I am nourished by it and it satisfies my soul.

And so I think that this kind of communion with Jesus, in his word, is something I can have at any moment; at any moment I can be nourished by him.

This experience has given me great joy. The gospel is not a book of consolation that we turn to only in times of sadness when we are seeking quiet refuge and an answer. It is the handbook of the laws of life, of its every circumstance. These laws are not meant merely to be read, but to be "eaten" by the soul, thereby making us like Christ in every moment.

The aspects of life (the joys, the sorrows, whether ordinary or exceptional) lose their significance and come to nothing. When we compare one with another, none appears to matter more, while only Christ seems to matter, who fills them and in them lives.[132]

The truth makes us free

Some days things seem to go well, humanly speaking, and there are those days when things go less well. And then you happily repeat the experience in this present life that what counts is not whether the day goes better or worse, but *how* you live this life, because in the *how* is charity, which alone gives value to all things. The one who loves God is the one who keeps his word (see Jn 14:23).

Each day we should recall that in paradise we will bring with us neither our joys nor our sorrows. Even if we hand over our bodies to be burned, without charity it amounts to nothing (see 1 Cor 13:3). Neither do apostolic works have value. Not even the ability to speak in angelic tongues, without charity, counts for anything (see 1 Cor 13:1).

Nor do the works of mercy. Even giving away all we have to the poor, without charity, counts for nothing (see 1 Cor 13:3).

We will carry to paradise how we have lived all this: whether we have lived in accord with the word of God, which gives us means to express our charity.

So, let us get up cheerfully each day be it stormy or sunny, and let us remember that our day will be worthwhile to the extent that during it we have "assimilated" the word of God. Living like this during that day, Christ will have been living in us and he will have given value to everything we have done by our direct action or by our contribution of prayer and suffering. And these, in the end, will follow us (see Rev 14:13).

In summary, we can admire how the word of God, the Truth, makes us free ... (see Jn 8:32, 36), free from circumstances, free from this body of death (see Rom 7:24), free from trials of the spirit, free from the world that as it surrounds us seeks to spoil the beauty and fullness of the reign of God in us.[133]

The Golden Rule

"In everything do to others as you would have them do to you; for this is the law and the prophets" (Mt 7:12).

Have you thirsted for the infinite? Have you ever felt in your heart an all-consuming desire to embrace immensity?

Or perhaps you have sensed in your heart of hearts a dissatisfaction with what you do, with what you are?

If so, you will be happy to find a formula that will give you the fullness you long for: something that does not leave regret for days that drift away half empty....

There is a word of the gospel that sets us thinking and, once we understand it a bit, makes us jump for joy. It sums up all that we should do in life. It recapitulates all the laws that God has inscribed in the depths of every human heart.

Listen to it: "Do to others as you would have them do to you; for this is the law and the prophets."

This is the "Golden Rule."

It was brought by Christ, even though it was already universally known. The Old Testament included it. It was known to Seneca and in the Orient the Chinese thinker Confucius said it. And others too. And this says how close it is to God's heart: how he wants all people to make it the basic rule of their lives.

It pleases the ear, and it sounds like a slogan.

Listen to it again: "Do to others as you would have them do to you."

Let us love every neighbour we meet during the day like this.

Let us imagine we are in others' situations, treating them as we would want to be treated in their place.

The voice of God within us will suggest how to express the love appropriate to every situation.

Are they hungry? I myself am hungry, let us think. And we give them something to eat.

Are they being unjustly treated? So am I.

Are they in darkness and doubt? I am too. And we speak words of comfort and share their suffering; we do not rest until they find light and relief. We would want to be treated like this.

Do they have a disability? I will love them till I can feel in my own heart and body the same infirmity. Love will suggest to me how I can help them feel equal to others, indeed that they have an extra grace, because as Christians we know the value of suffering.

And so on without any distinction between those who we find pleasant and those we do not, between young and old, friend or enemy, fellow citizen or stranger, beautiful or ugly.... The gospel includes everyone.

I think I hear whispers of dissent....

I understand ... perhaps my words seem simplistic, but what a change they demand! How far they are from our usual way of thinking and acting!

So take courage! Let's try it.

One day spent like this is worth a lifetime. At the end of the day we will no longer recognize ourselves. A joy we have never felt before will flood over us. A new power will fill us. God will be with us, because he is with those who love.

The days that follow will be full.

We may slacken from time to time, or be tempted by discouragement and want to stop. We may want to go back to living as before....

But no! Courage! God gives us the grace.

Let us always begin again.

The Word That Gives Life

Persevering we will see the world around us slowly change.

We will understand that the gospel brings a more interesting life, lights up the world, gives flavour to our existence and bears within itself the principle for resolving all our problems.

We will not be satisfied until we have communicated our extraordinary experience to others: to our friends who can understand, to our relatives, to anybody we feel the urge to tell.

Hope will be born anew.

"Do to others as you would have them do to you."[134]

A divine balance

"In patientia vestra possedebitis animas vestras" ("By patience you will possess your souls") (Lk 21:19).*

With these words Jesus teaches us to live well the present moment of our life: to live it profoundly, perfectly and fully. This is what counts in Christianity: doing things well.

Indeed, proverbial human wisdom says, "A job well begun is a job half done." It is good, but does not apply to everyone. Instead, divine wisdom says: "The one who endures to the end will be saved" (Mt 10:22).

The Lord knows that everyone, except Mary, had a bad beginning as a result of original sin. He had good reasons to become man to save us. What is important, though, is that we finish well, that we prepare ourselves for that moment on which our eternity depends.

The Lord teaches us to conduct our affairs well, to apply ourselves to all that we must do in life, with that patient love which knows how to suffer well, that maintains control of our soul, so much that we possess it. God is in our soul, and we, possessing it, always being its master in this present life, guard in ourselves, as in tabernacles, the presence of God there.

This word of life helps us to stay mindful and to live the presence of God in us. This happens directly when we pray, when we meditate, when we are alone. It happens indirectly when we do the will of God in something which requires us to concentrate all our attention outside of ourselves, as when there is a neighbour to love or some task to accomplish.

Many times being with others and applying our faculties to activities, such as study, our job, etc., interrupts our intimacy with God and we do not feel his peace and the sweetness that the presence of God brings.

---

* Chiara Lubich's commentary in the 1950s on this passage from Luke was based on the Vulgate, which differs slightly from more modern translations.

Likewise when we have started some work for him or are in contact with religious people, after a while we find ourselves distracted. Our ego takes the place of Jesus in us, so much so that any change in the will of God for us is difficult and the very work in which we are caught up becomes boring.

All of this comes from the fact that we have lost control of our soul, we do not possess it. And this happens because we have not known how to have the patience with which we stay in possession of our soul. Living this word of life, our life changes. Useless words fall away; everything in us and around us falls into place; our work becomes productive; we acquire a stable peace; we no longer fail by omission; we listen to the voice of God; we avoid a continuous stream of actions that are human rather than supernatural, that empty the soul and put out the light; and the soul is constantly illuminated by God.

Given that this word applies above all to recollection, concentrating our thought on possessing our soul, it can be misinterpreted — not taken as Jesus meant. In contact with their neighbours, those who recollect themselves with an excessive love for their own soul as opposed to the souls of others, stay closed, lifeless, with nothing to say. It means that there is some attachment to self and not much love for the Love within us that urges us to love.

In these souls can be discerned something artificial and dead. Like everything Jesus said, this word asks us to be balanced; we must not exaggerate in one sense or the other.

Every exaggeration does not allow Jesus to show himself in us.

The soul that loves well — and therefore puts Jesus' words into practice — knows where to find God. If it is an exterior will of God, for example a job, it throws itself completely into it, to be God's living will. But the soul does not forget that God is in itself and in every brother or sister. The soul knows that God is present everywhere and always sees it. And despite having projected itself into the divine will where God primarily wants it, the soul loves him everywhere and knows how to leave him in one place, if the will of God changes, to meet him in another.

It is possible at the same time to love God in ourselves and outside ourselves. For example consider a mother's love, so completely beautiful, even with its limits; it is such that it allows her to love all of her children, while attending to just one.

Supernatural love in us must have something of the height, breadth, depth, universality and particularity of God's love: "Love one another as I have loved you."

Our balance is found not just in quietude, nor only in action, nor in a blend of the two. It is like a string pulled and stretched in two directions with equal strength. If through impatience someone neglects the presence of God within the soul, his or her life, even though it seems to be made up of fraternal charity, is a charity that is frivolous, lightweight, superficial and dangerous, because it does not rest on the Rock: therefore it is not charity. This soul seems like a spinning top. If on the other hand a person is shrunk in on self, without love, he or she is dead.

The soul that has true love is like Mary, our heavenly mother, totally taken up with her God, with God alone. She found him within herself in recollection before the Annunciation, in the will of God revealed by the angel, in the child Jesus, in the cross, in St. John and in her final summons when she was assumed into heaven. God was her all, because she always possessed her soul in patience.[135]

Watch

"Watch ..." (see Lk 12:35). The gospel speaks of watching with our loins girt and a lamp in our hand, and it promises the watchful servant that, on his arrival, the master will gird himself and serve him. Only love is watchful. To watch is characteristic of love. When we love a person, our heart always watches and waits for them, and every moment away from them is lived for them and is spent watching. Jesus wants love: so he asks us to watch.

If we are afraid, we are also watchful. Indeed, Jesus speaks of thieves....

We watch because we fear, and we fear because we love someone that we do not wish to lose.

Jesus demands love, but since he too loves, as long as it means he can save us, he stirs up fear. He acts like a mother who promises her children a reward or a punishment according to how they behave. Jesus does not ask just for pure love, which gives without thinking of being repaid.

As long as it means he will see us saved, he also offers reward and punishment.[136]

If we were to live the beatitudes

We have to admit that, except in rare cases, we are not Christians as Jesus would wish.

If we were to live the beatitudes, for example, we would not find ourselves constrained so often to put up with people and to repress rebellious feelings, but we would discover the meekness in the hearts of God's children peacefully conquering the earth.

We would not experience bitter resignation in times of sorrow but, as is possible in the midst of our tears, we would sing songs of thanksgiving to the Lord. We would not find souls ravaged by ugliness in the world, but eyes that, while being in the world, view people and events in God.

We would not encounter poverty as the mother of spiritual destitution, but as the fountainhead of the kingdom of God.

We would not experience hatred, revenge, lack of forgiveness, because all human relationships would be permeated by mercy.

Instead the world is full of continuous sadness and the places of sorrow are of never-ending sorrow, and places of the dead are, even though the dead are alive to life everlasting, places where they are forgotten.[137]

They do not pass

"It is easier for a camel to go through the eye of a needle than for someone who is rich to enter the kingdom of God" (Mt 19:24). The rich person who does not act as Jesus wants gambles with eternity. Yet all of us are rich, until such time as Jesus lives in us in all his fullness.

Even a poor man who carries a chunk of bread in his bag and curses if anyone touches it is as rich as others. His heart is attached to something that is not God. Unless he becomes poor, poor in the gospel sense, he cannot enter the kingdom of heaven.

The way there is narrow and only that which is nothing can pass through.

There are those who are rich in knowledge, and being puffed up by this impedes their passage into the kingdom and the passage of the kingdom into them, so that the Spirit of God's Wisdom finds no room in their soul.

There are those who are rich in presumption, arrogance, or human affections, and until they cut themselves off from everything, they are not with God. All things must be removed from the heart so as to put God there and all of creation according to God's order.

There are those who are rich in worries and do not know how to unload them into the heart of God, and live in torment. They do not have the joy and the peace and the charity that belong to the kingdom of heaven.

They do not pass.

There are those who are rich in their own sins, weeping over them and torturing themselves, instead of burning them in God's mercy and looking ahead, loving God and their neighbour, to make up for the time when they did not love.[138]

Thoughts: To be re-evangelized

When Jesus taught he spoke with authority and what he says is a series of assertions made by Truth personified.

That is why it is good "to be re-evangelized," assimilating his teachings one by one until they penetrate the depths of our souls and become almost the substance of our being, the new mindset of the "new self" in us.

And doing this is the deepest, most intimate, well-founded revolution needed today as always.[139]

Lord, we are aware that we have many shortcomings. But we have the joy of knowing with certainty that "being your living word" removes all the dross, so that we emerge anew moment by moment, like a nut from its shell.

"Being your word" means being in another, acting as Another who lives in us, finding our freedom in freedom from ourselves, from our shortcomings, from our non-being.[140]

Have you noticed that if you fail to learn the alphabet and the basic rules of grammar in primary school, you remain illiterate all your life, unable to read or write despite having intelligence and will?

In the same way if we do not learn to assimilate one by one the words of life that Jesus has pronounced in the gospel, even though we are "good Christians," we remain "gospel illiterates," unable to write with our lives: Christ.[141]

Just as the entire Jesus is in the sacred host and in every single particle, so the entire Jesus is in the gospel and in every one of his words.[142]

One who hears the word of God and *puts it into practice* is like a house built on rock.

Only Christians who put the word of God into practice will know how to triumph in time of persecution. Winds and storms may come, but they will not be shaken.[143]

All my life should be a love affair with my Spouse. All else is vanity. All that is not the word lived is vanity.[144]

We are in God, in God's most intimate self because each one of us is word of God, a word of God and, as a word exists in the word, likewise we are so much in God as to be in God's innermost self.

He has seen us, he sees us and will see us in the Word, in the heart of the Word, in the innermost self of the Trinity.[145]

And I realize more and more that "heaven and earth will pass away ..." (Mt 24:35; Mk 13:31), but God's plan for us does not pass.

The only thing that *fully* satisfies us is to see that we are at every moment where God, *from all eternity*, meant us to be.

And there we shall remain eternally.[146]

In heaven we shall be only Word of God.[147]

Jesus in the Eucharist

In the bosom of the Father

The Eucharist does not only bear good and beautiful fruits of love and sanctity; nor is its primary purpose to increase our unity with God and with one another (as unity is commonly understood) and thus serving to nourish the presence of Jesus in our midst. Yes, this too.

But the task of the Eucharist is something else.

This is the purpose of the Eucharist: to make us God (by participation). By mixing our flesh with Christ's life-giving flesh, which is given life by the Holy Spirit, the Eucharist divinizes us in soul and body. Therefore it makes us God.

Now God can only stay in God. This is why the Eucharist makes the human being, who is fed with it worthily, enter the bosom of the Father; it places the human being in the Trinity in Jesus.

At the same time the Eucharist does not do this only for the individual person, but for many persons who, all being God, are not many, but one. They are God and they are all together in God. They are one with him, lost in him.

Now this reality, which the Eucharist brings about, is the Church.

What is the Church? It is the "one" called forth by the mutual love of Christians and by the Eucharist. The Church is made up of divinized people, made God, united to Christ who is God and to each other. If we wish to look at the whole thing from a rather human standpoint, that is, expressed in human terms, we can use an example from Scripture: the Church is a body, whose head is the glorious Christ.

But as Christ is in the bosom of the Trinity, so is the Church called to be. And it is, already here on earth, in the bosom of the Father in its members in whom the Eucharist is at work. If in part this is not yet so, it is on the way there.

Humanity thus brings with it all of creation, because it is its synthesis.

Everything that came from God will return, therefore, through the Eucharist, into the Trinity.[148]

When you are offering your gift

"So when you are offering your gift at the altar, if you remember that your brother or sister has something against you, leave your gift there before the altar and go; first be reconciled to your brother or sister, and then come and offer your gift" (Mt 5:23-24).

Divine worship and the love between brothers and sisters that composes and recomposes unity among them absolutely cannot be separated from one another.

If a community is not "realized" in Christ, in full communion, it is evangelically unsuited to offer to God befitting worship.

The Second Vatican Council has reawakened this sense of the united community; and the Holy Spirit, prompting in various ways, has brought about a rediscovery of the gospel of charity.

How much we Christians needed it!

This is why we often felt that we did not fully comprehend the value of the liturgy.

For the most part, we are heirs of an individual religiosity that did not give much attention to mutual charity in the community. While a certain sense of mystery still surrounds the great liturgical events, many people still experience a void in them, an incomprehension; they see them as forms that have lost their substance.

All this because Christianity's true strength, charity, frequently has been enfeebled.

What richness of liturgical experience we could expect from a people of God truly united! The face of the Church would turn out to be beautiful in its full splendour and would attract the world as once Jesus attracted the crowds.[149]

His, and our Mass

If you suffer and your suffering is such
that it prevents any activity,
remember the Mass.
Jesus in the Mass,
today as once before,
does not work, does not preach:
Jesus sacrifices himself out of love.
In life

Jesus in the Eucharist

we can do many things, say many words,
but the voice of suffering,
maybe unheard and unknown to others,
is the most powerful word,
the one that pierces heaven.
If you suffer,
immerse your pain in his:
say your Mass;
and if the world does not understand
do not worry
all that matters
is that you are understood by Jesus, Mary, the saints.
Live with them,
and let your blood pour out
for the good of humanity —
like him!
The Mass!
It is too great to understand!
His Mass, our Mass.[150]

Inconceivable

Inconceivable, extraordinary,
something that cuts an ever deeper impression on my soul
is your stillness there,
in silence, in the tabernacle.
I come to church in the morning, and I find you there.
I run to church when I love you, and I find you there.
I drop in out of chance or habit or respect, and I find you there.
And each time
you say a word to me
or you make straight a feeling.
In reality you are composing from different notes a single song,
a song that my heart has learned by heart
and that repeats to me one word alone:
eternal love.
Oh! God, you could not invent anything better!
That silence of yours
in which the din of our life is hushed,

that silent heartbeat
which absorbs every tear;
that silence ...
that silence, more sonorous than the song of angels;
that silence
which communicates the Word to the mind
and gives the divine balm to the heart;
that silence
in which every voice finds itself channelled
and every prayer feels transformed;
that mysterious presence of yours ...
Life is there, expectation is there;
our little heart rests
before continuing, without pause,
on its way.[151]

Gratitude

I love you
not because I learned to tell you so,
not because my heart suggests these words to me,
not so much because faith
makes me believe that you are love,
not even for the sole reason that
you died for me.

I love you
because you entered into my life
more than the air in my lungs,
more than the blood in my veins.
You entered
where no one could enter
when no one could help me
every single time no one
could console me.

Each day I have spoken to you.
Each hour I have looked to you
and in your face
I read the answer,

in your words
the explanation,
in your love
the solution.
I love you
because for so many years
you have lived with me
and I
have lived of You.
I drank from your law
and I did not realize it.

I nourished myself on it,
gathered strength,
I was restored,
but I was unaware
like a child suckling at its mother's breast
but not yet knowing how to call her
with that sweet name.

Let me be grateful
— at least a little —
in the time that is left to me
for the love
you have poured upon me
and that has compelled me
to tell you:
I love you.[152]

Thoughts: Heaven on earth

No, the earth has not remained cold: You have remained with us! What would our life be like if tabernacles did not bear your presence?

You once married humanity, and you remained faithful to her.

We adore You, Lord, in all the tabernacles of the world. Yes! They are with us, for us. They are not far away like the stars in the sky, which you have also given us. We can meet you everywhere: King of the stars and of all creation!

Thank you, Lord, for this immeasurable gift. Heaven has poured itself onto the earth. The starry sky is small. The earth is big, because it is dotted everywhere with the Eucharist: God with us, God among us, God for us.[153]

The most important moment of the day, without compare, is when You come into our hearts. This is our audience with the Almighty.

It is there, while we tell and retell you of our own and humanity's thousand needs, while thanking you for both your supernatural and natural gifts, while adoring you and asking you to greet your Mother for us, that we feel we reach the high point of our day, and we realize that very often we have not been able to grasp in whose presence we really were, and what we could achieve, during our one-to-one talk with God, in the innermost room of our soul.[154]

Jesus did not remain on earth, so that he could remain in all points of the earth in the Eucharist. He was God, and as a divine seed, he bore fruit, multiplying himself.

In the same way, we must die in order to multiply.[155]

Mary, the Flower of Humanity[156]

As a heavenly plane sloping

Mary is not easily understood even though she is greatly loved. In a heart that is far from God, one is more likely to find devotion to her than to Jesus.

She is universally loved.

And the reason is this: it is Mary's nature to be *Mother*.

Mothers, in general, are not "understood," especially by younger children; they are "loved." And not infrequently, indeed often, one hears that an eighty-year-old man dies saying as his last word: "mother."

A mother is more the object of the heart's intuition than of the mind's speculation. She is more poetry than philosophy, because she is too real and profound, close to the human heart.

So it is with Mary, the Mother of mothers, who the sum of all the affection, goodness, and mercy of all the mothers in the world cannot manage to equal.

Jesus, in a certain sense, *confronts* us more: his divine and splendid words are too different from ours to be confused with them. Indeed they are a sign of contradiction.

Mary is peaceful like nature, pure, serene, clear, temperate, beautiful — that nature which is distant from the world, in the mountains, in the open countryside, by the sea, in the blue sky or the starry heavens. She is strong, vigorous, harmonious, consistent, unyielding, rich in hope, for in nature it is life that springs up perennially generous, adorned with the fragrant beauty of flowers, kind in the abundance of its fruits.

Mary is too simple and too close to us to be "contemplated."

She is "sung" by hearts that are pure and in love, who express like this what is best in them. She brings the divine to earth as gently as a heavenly plane sloping from the dizzy heights of heaven to the infinite smallness of creatures. She is the Mother of all and of each human being, who alone knows how to burble and smile at her child in such a way that, even though it is small, each knows how to enjoy her caress and respond with its love to *that love*.

Mary is not understood because she is too close to us. She, who was destined from Eternity to bring graces, the divine jewels of her Son, to humanity, is there, near to us, and waits, always hoping for us to notice her gaze and accept her gifts.

If anyone is fortunate enough to understand her, she carries them off to her kingdom of peace, where Jesus is King and the Holy Spirit is the life-breath of that heaven.

There, purified of our dross and illuminated in our darkness, we will contemplate her and enjoy her, an added paradise, a paradise apart.

Here, let us be found worthy of being called along "her way" to avoid staying always immature in spirit, with a love that does not go beyond supplication, petition, request and self-interest, but knowing her a little, may we glorify her.[157]

"Explanation" of God

A mother never ceases to love her wayward son; she never ceases to await his return when he has gone afar. She desires nothing but to see him again, to forgive him, to embrace him again: because a mother's love fills everything with the scent of mercy. A mother's love is something that is always above any painful or difficult situation in which her son finds himself.

Hers is a love that never fades in the face of moral, ideological or any other kind of turmoil that may overwhelm her son.

Her love, because it rises above all things, wants to cover over everything, to hide his mistakes.

If a mother sees her son in danger she does not hesitate to risk everything, to throw herself onto the train tracks if her son is about to be crushed, or into the waves of the sea if he is in danger of drowning. A mother's love is naturally stronger than death. I heard that recently a mother threw herself out of the window in the attempt to save a child who had fallen from her arms: a useless act, and a desperate one, but it shows how great a mother's love is.

If this is what a normal mother's love is like, we can well imagine what it is like in Mary, the human-divine Mother of a child who was God, and the spiritual mother of us all!

Mary is the Mother, par excellence, the prototype of maternity, and therefore of love.

Since God is *Love*, she appears as an "explanation" of God, an open book that explains who God is.

God's love was so great that for us he died a most atrocious death.

And he did that to save us, with a love like a mother's that seeks the good of her children.

Mary, because she is the divine mother, is the creature that most copies God; she is the one who most shows us who he is.

We must revive our faith in Mary's love for us; we must believe that this is how she loves us. And we need to imitate her, because she is the model of every Christian; she is the direct road to God.[158]

My soul magnifies the Lord

We do not see Mary, the Mother, so much inclined towards her brothers and sisters, her children, as towards God. In her we see "my God and my all."

All of her spiritual energy and her physical powers are consumed, moment by moment, by the Holy Spirit who lives in her. She is like a candle that, consuming itself, feeds the life of God that burns in her. She lives of God, God lives in her, she who makes herself completely nothing, moment by moment, to give life to him. His voice, which is his will, speaks strongly in the depths of her soul, because she always listens to it. She is the handmaid totally at his service: the handmaid of the Lord. In this way she makes him great, because her life shows him to be such: shows him as the all. Drawing herself completely back, she gives space completely to him, and he fills her, because her love calls for his.

But I too can be her. I will offer my being moment by moment to the light, to magnify the Lord and to glorify him. Being a little Mary: a perpetual nothingness, a silence, a service of love to Love. Then the Spirit in me will repeat those same words (as they burst from the Mother's heart): "My soul magnifies the Lord" (Lk 1:46).[159]

How beautiful the Mother

Our Mother is so beautiful in her continuous recollection as shown us by the gospel: "But Mary treasured all these words and pondered them in her heart" (Lk 2:19).

That full silence fascinates the soul who loves.

How can I live like Mary in her mystical silence when our vocation at times is to speak in order to evangelize, always exposed in every kind of place, rich and poor, from cellars to streets, to schools, everywhere?

Our Mother also spoke. *And she gave Jesus.* There has never been a greater apostle in the world. No one ever spoke such words as she, who gave the *Word.*

Our Mother is truly and deservedly called the Queen of the Apostles.

And she kept silent. She kept silent because the two could not speak at once. The word must always rest against a silence, like a painting against a background.

She kept silent because she was a creature. For nothingness does not speak. But upon that nothingness Jesus spoke and said: himself.

God, Creator and All, spoke upon the nothingness of the creature.

How then can I live Mary, how can my life be perfumed by her beauty?

By silencing the creature in me, and upon this silence letting the Spirit of the Lord speak.

In this way I live Mary and I live Jesus. I live Jesus upon Mary. I live Jesus by living Mary.[160]

Two hearts of flesh, clothed in virginity

The relationship on earth between Jesus and Mary is ineffable, belonging to a plan far above any other, the most beautiful relationship after the Trinity.

It is the relationship between the Mother of a son who is God and the child of an immaculate mother, and which carries all the most tender and exquisite expressions that nature provided in both, with an ever more perfect obedience of her will to the will of Love Most High.

She had him in her heart; she raised him as a child and adolescent. She was at his side in the fullness of his youth, when every young boy who is becoming a man discloses his most secret aspirations to the pure love of a mother who becomes at that moment his first friend.

He stayed with her in his maturity until the age of thirty, and almost nothing is known of what they told each other.

He then spent three years with others to found the Church and to accomplish his mission, sealing it with his blood on the wood of the cursed.

Three years in contrast to thirty. Three of which we know something. Thirty of which we know almost nothing.

It is a mystery.

The mystery of love.

The mystery of love divine and human between two hearts of flesh, clothed in virginity. No one ever knew.

We will know something of it in heaven to the extent that we loved and followed them on earth.[161]

Thoughts: The Desolate

We do not think enough about Mary's "passion," about the swords that pierced her Heart, about the terrible forsakenness she felt on Golgotha when Jesus entrusted her to others….

Perhaps the reason for this is that Mary knew all too well how to cover her living, tormented agony with sweetness, with light, and with silence.

And yet, there is no suffering similar to hers….

If one day our sufferings reach such depths that make everything inside us rebel because the fruit of our "passion" seems to be taken out of our hands and, moreover, from our heart, let's remember her.

It will be this coldness that will make us a bit similar to her, and which will shape better in our souls the figure of Mary, the All-Beautiful, the Mother of all because by divine will she was detached from everyone, most of all, from her divine Son.[162]

The Desolate is the Saint par excellence.

I would want to relive her in her mortification.

I would want to be capable of being alone with God like her, in the sense that, even in the midst of others, I feel drawn to make the whole of my life an intimate dialogue between my soul and God.

I must mortify words, thoughts, and actions that are outside the *moment* of God, in order to place them into the instant reserved for them.

The Desolate is certainty of sanctification, the perennial font of union with God, a cup overflowing with joy. The Desolate!

This is my "eureka!" Yes, I have found it. I have found the way.[163]

I have only one mother on earth

I have only one mother on earth:
Mary Desolate.
I have no mother but her.
In her is the whole Church for eternity,
and the whole Work of Mary in unity.
In her design is mine.

I will go through the world reliving her.
Every separation will be mine.
Every detachment from the good I have done
will contribute to building up Mary.
In her "staying" (at the foot of the cross), my "staying"
In her "staying," my "going."
Hortus conclusus, enclosed garden,
Sealed fountain (see Sg 4:12);
I will cultivate her most loved virtues,
so that on the silent nothingness of myself
her wisdom may shine.
That many, all her chosen children,
those most in need of her mercy,
may always find her maternal presence
in another little Mary.[164]

Because I want to see her again in you

I went into church one day,
and with my heart full of trust, I asked:
"Why did you wish to remain on earth,
on every point of the earth,
in the most sweet Eucharist,
and you, you who are God,
have not found
also a way to bring here and to leave here
Mary, the mother of all of us who journey?"
In the silence he seemed to reply:
"I have not left her because I want to see her again in you.
Even if you are not immaculate, my love will virginize you,
and you, all of you,
will open your arms and hearts as mothers of humanity,
which, as in times past, thirsts for God
and for his mother.
It is you who now must soothe pains, soothe wounds,
dry tears.
Sing her litanies
and strive to mirror yourself in them."[165]

The All-Beautiful

When we look at nature, it seems that Jesus gives it his new commandment too.

I observed two plants and I thought about pollination. Before this happens the plants grow upward, as if they were loving God with all their being. Then they unite, almost as if they were loving one another as the Persons of the Trinity love one another. From two they become one. They love one another to the point of abandonment, to the point of losing their personalities, so to speak, like Jesus in his forsakenness.

Then from the flower that blossoms, a fruit is born and life, therefore, continues. It is like God's eternal Life imprinted in nature.

The Old and the New Testaments form a single tree.

Its flowering happened in the fullness of time, and its only flower was Mary.

The fruit which followed was Jesus.

The tree of humanity was also created in the image of God.

When, in the fullness of time, it blossomed, unity was made between heaven and earth, and the Holy Spirit espoused Mary.

Therefore, there is one flower: Mary. And there is one fruit: Jesus. And Mary, though alone, is nevertheless the synthesis of the entire creation in the culminating moment of its beauty when it presents itself as spouse to its Creator.

Jesus, instead, is creation and the uncreated made one: the Marriage consummated. And he contains Mary within himself just as the fruit contains the flower. Once the flower has served its purpose, it falls and the fruit matures.

Even so, if there had never been a flower, then neither would the fruit have ripened.

Just as Mary is daughter of her Son, similarly, the flower is child of the fruit which is its child.

Yet the time span between the flower and the fruit is so short that it is almost annulled, since fruit is the result of the flower.

Whereas the flower, following a long duration, is born by the tree, generated by the seed contained within the fruit.

Likewise, Mary is the flower blossoming on the tree of humanity, born of God who created the first seed in Adam. She is daughter of God her Son.

As I watched a small geranium breaking into a flower of red, I wondered to myself and asked it: "Why are you flowering in red? Why do you change from green to red?" It seemed such a strange thing to me!

Today I understood that all of humanity flowers in Mary. Mary is the flower of humanity. She, the Unstained, is the flower of the stained.

Sinful humanity flowered in Mary, the All-Beautiful!

And just as the red flower is grateful to the small green plant, with its dirt-covered roots, which made her flower, so too is Mary grateful to sinners like us who constrained God into thinking of Mary.

We owe our salvation to her; she owes her life to us.

How beautiful Mary is! She is creation in flower, creation turned beautiful. Mary is all of creation in flower, like the foliage covering the tree. From his heavenly heights, God fell in love with this flower of flowers. He pollinated her with the Holy Spirit and Mary gives to heaven and earth the fruit of fruits: Jesus.

In order to descend, the Lord God of heaven had to find Mary. He could not descend into sin, and, therefore, he "invented" Mary, who, gathering in herself all of the beauty of creation, "tricked" God and drew him to earth.

Yet she is the flower of humanity, and calling God to herself, she calls him *for* humanity, because she is grateful to humanity for having given her life.[166]

The Holy Spirit, the Unknown God

Mary and the Holy Spirit

When the little boat of our life is taking on water and the waves of the storm threaten, we utter a name that comes to the lips of those who suffer, even in their dying breath: Mother.

This does not always refer to mothers on earth; indeed, for a soul a bit familiar with eternal things, it means "Mary."

And this is so true that in moments of trial "Mother" is often the cry of those whose hearts belong to God: "Mother."

And here is the second miracle of love after the redemption: a God incarnate and a Mother for all.

In her every hope for the Christian.

Frequently it occurs to us to ask how Mary, during the long agonies that pierced her heart, managed to live on earth without being able to call upon a mother, the Mother. The direct grafting of her soul into God shows her unique splendour, her greatness, her uniqueness that is "high above all other creatures." Without doubt, God, as he is for us, and so much more for her, was her heart's rest.

But could it not be that she loved someone who, as Mary herself does for us, represented more specifically for her the personification of love? I think she did find something similar, and infinitely more than we find in her, during her earthly struggle in the Father's service as she brought up her Son; she found rest and refreshment, strength and boldness, the ability to live when many deaths would have crushed her, in the One who sustained the Church in her times and in all times: the *Holy Spirit*. The Holy Spirit: this unknown God whom at our final judgment we will realize with infinite regret that we perhaps have not sufficiently loved and honoured and thanked.

He,
the soul of the Mystical Body of Christ,
the strength of the martyrs throughout history,
the flowing of living water in all the wise,
the light of those sent by God,
the certainty of the Popes,

the teacher of bishops,
the friend of all ministers,
the fragrance of consecrated virgins:
he lived with the Immaculate,
finding his delight in shaping,
in overshadowing
the Flower of flowers,
and Mary
in him and for him
brought that yearning expressed by the human heart
through the sweet name of "Mother"
to the very height of God.[167]

You sanctify

O Holy Spirit, how much we ought to be grateful to you yet how little we are! That you are totally one with Jesus and the Father, to whom we more often turn, consoles us, but it is no excuse.

We want to be with you who are "of comforters the best; … the soul's most welcome guest; sweet refreshment here below."[168]

You are light, joy, beauty.

You seize and captivate souls, you inflame hearts, you inspire deep and decisive thoughts of sanctity with unexpected personal commitments.

You work what many sermons cannot teach.

You sanctify.

Especially, O Holy Spirit, you who are so discreet, though impetuous and overwhelming, yet blow like a soft wind that few know how to hear and perceive, look upon our rough-edged coarseness, and make us your faithful followers. May no day pass without our invoking you, thanking you, adoring you, loving you, without our living as your diligent disciples. We ask of you this grace. Envelop us in your great light of love, above all in our darkest hour, when the present vision of life comes to a close, dissolving into the one that is eternal.[169]

Often love is not love

Since in the world often love is not love, the saying is true: love is blind. But if a soul begins to love in the way God teaches (God who is love), it will very soon see that love is light.

Anyway, Jesus said it: "Those who love me will be loved by my Father, and I will love them and manifest myself to them" (Jn 14:21).

A whirl of voices from the most varied sources often floods our soul, especially when it does not know what it means to love God. They are soundless voices but strong: voices of the heart, voices of the intellect, voices of remorse, voices of regret, voices of the passions ... and we follow now one, now another, filling our day with acts that express, or are at least in some way determined by, these voices.

That is why sometimes, despite living in the grace of God, our life has only brief patches of sunshine and the rest of it is immersed in a boredom which one voice, stronger than the others, often rises to condemn — as if to say this is not the true life, the full life.

If instead the soul turns to God and begins to love him, and its love is true, practical, active in every moment, then among the many voices that accompany life, it notices, from time to time, one voice.

More than a voice, it is a light that gently finds its way into the intricate concert of the soul. It is an almost imperceptible thought that offers itself to the soul, which is perhaps more delicate, more subtle, than the others.

This is, at times, the voice of God.

Then the soul that has decided to follow the Lord, that does not bargain with him but wants to give everything to him, draws off this clear and serene spring from the marshland: it is a sapphire among so many stones, it is gold amidst dust.

It takes it, it cleans it, it puts it in light, it translates it into life.

And if it happens that the soul has decided to go to God with other souls, so that the Father may rejoice in the family-like love of his children, the soul (having taken advice from the person who represents God on earth for it) communicates with discretion its treasure to others. It does this so that the treasure may become a common possession, that the divine may circulate and, as in a competition, one soul may learn from another how to love the Lord better.

In this way the soul has loved twice: it has loved by putting God's will into practice, and it has loved by communicating with its brothers and sisters. And God, faithful to his eternal words, will continue step by step to manifest himself.

All of this is highly desirable, so that all day long our heart may be immersed solely in thoughts of heaven, to the point of overflowing, and our life, nourished by the sacraments, will be deified.

You give God if you have him; and you have God if you love him.

Then in the world which is dark and dull there can be lit tiny suns which will point out the path to many. Suns which will give warmth, in the utter humility of their lives that are completely sacrificed to the Lord, where they do not speak, but he speaks, where they do not live, but he lives.[170]

Thoughts: The inner Master

I must never forget that Reality lives in me and that I must give to my brothers and sisters, above all, the vital fluid that rises from the depths of my soul, which is the subtle voice of God that urges and enlightens.

We have to silence everything in us in order to discover his voice. And we have to extract this voice, as we would take a diamond out of the mud, clean it, place it in view and give it when opportune, because it is love, and love must be given. Like a fire fed with straw, love blazes when it is communicated, otherwise it will die out. Let's run because the light remains lit only in the soul where love is in motion, is alive.[171]

We often make resolutions. We are not always successful at keeping them.

But in some rare cases you realize it is not you making them. It is Another who is calling you sweetly, but decisively, from within. It then seems you cannot but keep those resolutions. We have to thank God for these divine moments in which he calls us to Another life that lives inside of us, where every note is in harmony, every darkness is enlightened, every distortion is straightened, every emptiness is filled with him. And this can happen at any moment of the day.

We feel there are two of us: he in me and I in him. Yet we are one: I, water from this source, a flower from this divine seed, the witness of his reality that fills my being.

This indeed is living.

God alone knows how to shape himself in us. We know only how to ruin it.[172]

Who knows how many saints the Holy Spirit in the divine workshops of the Mystical Body is shaping. We will see them one day; God will decide when.[173]

Laypersons are in the condition of necessarily having to listen to the voice of the Holy Spirit; they do not have superiors who express God's will to them.[174]

In unity, "we feel, we see, we enjoy" the presence of Jesus. "All enjoy his presence, all suffer his absence. It is peace, joy, love, spirit of heroism, of the highest generosity...."

This atmosphere and its effects are the fruits of the Spirit of Jesus, which is the Holy Spirit himself. And the Spirit of the Risen Jesus in our midst makes us Jesus, which makes us appear to others as his continuation, the Body of Christ, the Church. Those who build unity through mutual love live Christ's death and his resurrection; they "experience" the life of the Risen One, who they have in themselves through grace. They live, therefore, the life that does not die. Jesus says: "Everyone who lives and believes in me will never die" (Jn 11:26).[175]

The abyss inside me

The Trinity inside me!
The abyss inside me!
Immensity inside me!
The chasm of love inside me!
The Father who Jesus announced
inside me!
The Word!
The Holy Spirit, who I always
want to have in order to serve the Work of Mary,
inside me!
I ask for nothing less.
I want to live in this abyss,
lose myself in this sun,
live together with Eternal Life.
What should I do then? Prune the life outside
and live the one inside.
The more I cut communications
with the external
the more I speak with the Trinity
inside me.[176]

Thoughts: With Mary

And when the disciples were present with Mary, the Holy Spirit descended.

"With Mary" ... born immaculate, visited by an angel and already "experienced" in descents of the Holy Spirit; the Mother of Jesus ... for a thousand reasons chosen and super chosen!

> The Apostles knew it, and for this reason they were glad to have her with them as a guarantee of the Eternal.
>
> At the Second Vatican Council the successors of the Apostles, gathered together in a new Cenacle, also wanted her spiritually present among them: "*Cum Marie Matre Jesu orantes*" (praying with Mary the mother of Jesus), a document of the Council Fathers says, addressing all peoples of the earth.
>
> And today too it will be she who prepares the ground, rendering easier the work of the Holy Spirit, for the new Pentecost that the world awaits.[177]

We do not know whether Mary chose to take care of other people during Jesus' life. It was in her desolation and after her detachment from Jesus that a new maternity was born in her for the Apostles and for all people.

We see her on a level unusual for her, placing herself at the heart of the newborn Church, awaiting a new descent of the Holy Spirit who, if he had worked such wonders in the disciples that they could not be recognized from before, will have established in her a new fullness not yet completely known to us. Perhaps it is the task of this Marian age to explore the effects of Pentecost on Mary and to intuit the marvellous new things that happened to her, she who had already been made "sharer in Christ the redeemer" and heavenly leader of the battles of the Church.[178]

It is the conviction of the saints that when the Holy Spirit, Mary's Spouse, finds her in other persons, he penetrates them and communicates himself to them as abundantly as they have given place in their souls to his Spouse.[179]

We have to have the nothingness of Jesus forsaken, which is infinite nothingness. The Holy Spirit will then rest within us.[180]

Love must be distilled to the point of being only the Holy Spirit. It is distilled when it passes through Jesus forsaken.

Jesus forsaken is the nothingness, the point, and through the point (= Love reduced to the extreme, that which has given everything) there passes only the simplicity of God: Love.[181]

Like an empty chalice

O Holy Spirit, we do not ask of you anything but God for God. Given that soon, perhaps within a decade or so, we must come to adore you where your kingdom triumphs and everything works for you, grant that we may live the rest of our lives — we implore you — only and always and in every instant

The Holy Spirit, the Unknown God　　　　　　　　　　　　　　　　　149

for you alone, who alone we wish to love and serve. God! God, pure spirit, for whom our humanity can be an empty chalice to be filled....

God, who must shine through our being, our hearts, our faces, our words, our actions, our silence, our living, our dying, our appearing when we leave this earth (where we can, we must leave only a luminous streak of his presence, of him present in us, amidst the material and muddle of this world [whether it live or collapse], in the praise or the vanity of all things that can be a footstool or a stumbling block for everything), leaving for the place of the All, the Alone, Love.[182]

Living Life[183]

Life

Joys and sorrows,
hopes,
dreams fulfilled.
Maturity in life and thought.
Solidity.
A sense of duty
and a call of love from on high,
answered by
the integrity of our life.
Weariness.
Fire and conquest.
Storms.
Trust in God:
God alone.
Up. Down.
Torrential rain,
deep roots.
Fruit, fruit, fruit …
Darkening of the soul:
"My God, my God …"
Then, sweet music from heaven,
distant.
Then closer.
Drum roll:
victory!
Long is life,
different the paths,
near is the goal.
All,
everything,
always,

has,
has had,
a single destiny:
union with you.[184]

Whatever happened to boredom?

Are you bored with getting up in the morning, going to school, always taking the same route and attending the same tedious lessons? ...

Are you bored because the week begins in the dismal gloom of a dark office where you carry out again and again the same dusty routine, just to earn enough to live on?...

Are you bored with heading for the market every morning, picking out the same fruit and the same vegetables, cheered only by the smell of some fresh gossip?...

Are you bored of being a rich woman with too much time on your hands, while envy is gnawing at your heart because of friends prettier than you who get more attention and, as much as you try, you cannot give any sparkle to your life?...

Many are bored. Boredom is part of human life.

It cannot be otherwise as long as we persist in not wanting to see; as long as we push aside that which gives light: the One who is Light.

Whether we want to or not, one day we must make the choice: God or mammon, meaning wealth, though not always money and not always lots of it.

If God were our lamp in this night of our days, we would not know the word: "boredom."

Indeed not! He colours the dawn of the gray morning of every unhappy woman.

He shares in the life of those who love him and sows along their path a thousand opportunities to link their flat earthly life to a divine design.

And you see. You see because the Light gives light. And you respond to his call in faith, at first just a little, then more and more.

There are unusual circumstances and they have a meaning; and you understand it, and you follow the God of your heart along paths of thorns or roses. But you do not worry; they are the paths of God.

And unexpected horizons open before you, and behind you, you trail tapestries of heaven.

The swiftness of rockets and satellites around the earth, the speed of modern communications are slow compared to the redemption you bring about: you continue in your hour, Christ's hour, inscribed in the ages, and you free the world which is still in sadness and fill it with love.

Try it. And you will ask: "Whatever happened to boredom?"[185]

The light of a candle in the sun

Human beings thirst for companionship. They seek friendship, sometimes any friendship at all. Even someone diseased with the dislike of other people seeks company, whether with themselves, or with their books, or with their room, or with their own solitude, because the human spirit is made for love. People seek friends, bind themselves to others, and among them are some who are less likely to deceive: the love of a mother, a father, of children, of a spouse. But often they cling to them and seek in their comfort a crutch for their life's journey.

But then there comes, for almost everyone, the moment of detachment.

The supreme providence of God who loves without deception carves out empty spaces that seem cruel to clouded human eyes: we lose our dearest friend or closest relative to death. Then, under the shock, we re-examine ourselves. We shift the focus of our souls, at least for the moment, and introduce God into our scale of values; we banish vanities, forget about amusements, and bring ourselves back into balance. Suffering has drawn the soul into the awesome but beautiful vortex of truth: irresistible, sublime and consoling for those brave enough to face it. Everything crumbles. Everything is vanity. And, while journeying on this earth, we understand soon and well that the spectacle of this world slips quickly away….

Only the one who looks beyond all things and turns to you, Lord, and who, keeping your words, seeks you behind the cross will not be deceived.

You are a God of love and you have offered a platter of suffering to those who wish to follow you. It was not possible that such bitterness would not contain nectar, because it is unthinkable that the One who is pure goodness would be able serve up cruelty. And those who follow you with complete hearts, without reservations in mind or soul, know this. They have measured time against eternity and decided to sacrifice time, to reserve eternity for the bliss you wish to share with us.

Those who know you a little realize the emptiness of the world's vainglory and how bare is the house built by human hands.

They experience in fact, after passing through the anteroom of the cross, your most sweet presence that can be touched and heard by the senses of the soul.

Our soul, the whole of our being, despite expending itself in activity without pause, asks to remain in you, in whom it rests as in its proper element, because it has found in you the vital substance that is the life of its life, principle of every kind of life in it: human and spiritual and divine.

Then every other desire for companionship disappears, because the highest desire for friendship that the human soul can conceive is engulfed — as the light of a candle in the sun — in the love that God-Love has prepared for us.[186]

If a soul gives itself to God sincerely

If a soul gives itself to God sincerely, he works on it. And love and suffering are the raw materials of his divine game — suffering to dig abysses in the soul, love to soothe the suffering and still more love that fills the soul, giving it the equilibrium of peace.

The soul realizes that it is under the powerful hand of God and waits in silent suspense as it watches, despite its tears, the work of the Beloved.

But at times God works the soul to such a point that it is ground down in agonies sharper than death. It no longer feels the help or spiritual support of anyone. For it the whole earth has become an endless desert.

Then the new miracle is born: a boundless trust, a desperate confidence in God who, to prepare it for heaven, permits its sufferings and its nights. And between God and the soul begins a new dialogue, one known only to them. The soul says, "Lord, you see how I am surrounded by the shadows of death. You are aware of the extreme uncertainty of my spirit, and you know that no one seems able to calm me. You take care of me. I trust in you. And while waiting to come to Life, I'll work for you, in the interests of heaven."

The soul is like the bloom of a flower which has opened itself to the love of God and which, detached from its stem, rises in the sun, always closer to its light and its heat. Until, in the hour that God has established, the two merge and it is no longer uncertain, no longer alone, but peaceful now forever in the infinite sea of peace which is God.[187]

You are everything, I am nothing

With one accord saints, great saints, when touched by the grace of God, express a profound truth; nearly prostrate on the ground, as dust in the dust, they cry out to God, at first with their voices, but then with the immolation of the whole of their being: "You are everything, I am nothing."

While some see the footprints of God in creation and use nature as a stairway to the Creator, others take a different path. They fly without propellers, like a modern jet plane compared with the flying machines of the past.

There, at the point where nature is extinguished, where creation makes itself nothing, they take flight, and making themselves nothing along with creation, sharing with love in that death, they sing the glory of God.

Just so. For a star shining in the heavens proclaims that God has made it, but a star being extinguished in the heavens announces its nothingness, reminding the saints who know how to perceive the pleasing harmonies and silences of all things, through the silent Word living in them, that Another is the All, Another is light eternal.

And so at evening, a time of sadness for people, the setting sun gives rise in the hearts of the saints to a dawn, and the evening that falls is the voice that makes increase the eternal day that is God.

And suffering, which gnaws the bodies of the saints or rends their souls, in the decomposition of the organic unity that is health and of the earthly tranquillity that is peace, is taken by them as the voice of the One who is and who is Bliss.

If God is everything, to say that God is *everything* it is necessary that mortal beings sing their own death, glorify him with their own nothingness.

And this process, terrifying for most people, is intoxicating for saints because at the centre of their lives is Life, which like a flame lit by the Lord can shed its light better when what surrounds it is reduced, as it must be reduced, to complete darkness.

Mary glorifies the Lord because she has made of her soul and her body a candle to be consumed to his glory.

And in God she found, though certainly she never sought it, her own glory, the greatest glory that earth knows after that of the Trinity.[188]

What really matters

There are moments in life when everything seems to be destroyed by a hurricane that sweeps away what had been built up patiently for years ... in the process, however, mixing the good cement of the love of God with the sand of self love.

Everything collapses and we find ourselves flat on the ground in an ocean of emptiness, grateful at least to have saved our lives.

These are times in which it becomes apparent that what matters is God and God cannot be deceived. They are moments, unfortunately only moments, when we see where to place our feet so as not to plunge to the bottom. We stay on the lowest step so that, if God permits another hurricane, we shall not have to fall because we are already on the ground.

And we are humble and equal to the lowest person we meet, with whom we exchange words and smiles in our common misfortune.

But then, unhappily, we rise up a bit in our self-pride, in what we think of ourselves. And it is up to God to cast us into the depths again and again, until there is rooted in us the awareness of the nothingness that we are and of All that is God.[189]

But you not pass ...

Yes, Lord, we are happy,
when the wing of an angel
reveals for us the horizons of heaven
once brusquely wiped away
by a trial.
We are happy, Lord,
because your love
shows itself in those moments to be so omnipotent
that our soul
opens into adoration and exultation
to the point of silence.
May the trial which grips our soul in agony pass, Lord;
but may there be no sunset, ever,
of your splendid, luminous figure
in the dark night,
when,
in the desert of all,
you alone have flowered for us,
and, in the silence of each thing,
you alone have spoken,
and, in the absence of everyone,

you alone have kept us company,
gently repeating the truths,
which must not grow faint
in our souls:
that we are here only as visitors
and our destination is elsewhere;
that all things are shadow
and you alone are reality.
May the trial pass, Lord,
but you not pass,
and enclose us,
enchanted by suffering,
in the heart of the Trinity.
Lord,
may the deceit of the world
not overtake us again,
even through the holiest things
that it possesses,
but may only the Holy One be with us and in us,
and the Holy Virgin, your Mother,
be the garment
that covers us
for ever.[190]

The Final Hour[191]

Still more beautiful

The War-horse
He paws the valley, and exults in his strength;
he goes out to meet the weapons.
He laughs at fear, and is not dismayed;
he does not turn back from the sword.
Upon him rattle the quiver,
the flashing spear and the javelin.
With fierceness and rage he swallows the ground;
he cannot stand still at the sound of the trumpet.
When the trumpet sounds, he says, "Aha!"
He smells the battlefront afar,
the thunder of the captains, and the shouting. (Jb 39:21-25)

If we open the Scriptures and read in the Old Testament how God describes some of the animals, we realize that no poet or painter has ever sung of them or painted them in such a vivid or wonderful way.

The eye of the One who created them was needed to inspire such majestic descriptions. Perhaps our own eye is not trained to see beauty, or it only sees beauty in a certain sector of human, and natural, life. For *we have not trained the soul.*

When a young country girl goes to town, even though she is always in touch with nature which is rich with traces of God, she dresses in the strangest of colours, with a disharmony that offends the eye. For her this is beauty, and the greatest works of art have little value, or none at all, *because she does not understand them.*

But in God's sight, where is the greatest beauty: in the child who looks at you with innocent little eyes, so like the clarity of nature and so lively; or in the young girl who glistens with the freshness of a newly-opened flower; or in the wizened and white-haired old man, bent double, almost unable to do anything, perhaps only waiting for death?

The grain of wheat contains such promise when, more slender than a wisp of grass, and bunched together with fellow grains that surround and form the ear, it awaits the time when it will ripen and be free, alone and independent, in the hand of the farmer or in the womb of the earth: it is beautiful and full of hope!

It is, however, also beautiful when, ripe at last, it is chosen from among the others because it is better than they, and then, having been buried, it gives life to other ears of wheat — this grain that now contains life itself. It is beautiful; it is the one chosen for future generations of harvests.

But when, shrivelling underground, it reduces its being almost to nothing, grows concentrated, and slowly dies, decaying, to give life to a tiny plant that is distinct from it and yet contains the life of the grain, then, perhaps, it is still more beautiful.

All various beauties.

Yet one more beautiful than the other.

And the last is the most beautiful of all.

Does God see things in this way?

Those wrinkles that furrow the little old woman's forehead, that stooped and shaky gait, those brief words full of experience and wisdom, that gentle look at once of a child and of a woman, but better than both, *is a beauty we do not know.*

It is the grain of wheat which, being extinguished, is about to burst into a new life, different from before, in new heavens.

I think God sees like this and that the approach to heaven is far more attractive than the various stages of the long journey of life, which basically serve only to open that door.[192]

Thoughts of gold

It is not to have black thoughts, but golden ones, that we think about death. Even in the midst of an abundance of graces, sometimes we are so assailed by the feeling of loneliness in our exile here below that the desire comes to us to say with Paul: "My desire is to depart and be with Christ, for that is far better" (Phil 1:23), or also "We would rather be away from the body and at home with the Lord" (2 Cor 5:8).

The more we recognize and weigh the value of suffering, the more we understand that death is the final offering of our "royal priesthood" here on earth and therefore the fulfilment of our life. And for those who love and who know what love means, it is the moment they long for.

But I would like to make myself clear: I mean "long for" truly, as one would wish for gold and not smoke. It is a time that God has kissed, as one kisses Jesus on the cross. Our Christian brothers and sisters who have died, who have really lived what death means, know what it is. How many times have we wished that someone would come back and tell us something about that "passage"!...

But perhaps — indeed certainly, because this too is love — it is better that each of us should experience this unique event in our lives: it has greater value and ... for a little bit of suffering, for the little bit of faith we have in God's love for us in those moments, afterwards the whole of eternity will be with him.[193]

Stars alight in heaven eternally

If on All Souls Day you go to the cemetery of Verano,
you see an endless line of tombs.
And towards evening, as night begins to pulse,
a tiny light is lit for each.
A common tomb gathers up a number without number of the dead
and for each of the dead a spark.
A number without number of these lights,
like a fragment of the Milky Way fallen to earth.
Days pass
and each day marks thousands of those who are no more.
There is a day set for each.
And the day will come for me, for you, for everyone.
One tiny light more beside the others.
A day of tears and sorrow for those who were close,
then life returns to what it was before.
And next to the sound of weeping for you
the frenetic jazz from a bar;
a white bow on the front of a house;
the howl of the siren from the ambulance, announcing danger,
and the pop of champagne proclaiming a wedding.
Old tramps leaning on worm-eaten gates,
rouged ladies, symbols of vanity.
Such is life.
But, though the stars have each a name,
few of the Verano lights speak to anyone.
They are dead! Dead ... already nameless.

They are dead because they wanted to live.
They are dead because in life they did not die.
But indeed there are courageous ones who confronted death
and were ready in their nothingness to let the Lord live.
They live in eternal glory
and in the unperishing memory of mortals.
How may contemporaries were there of a Teresa of Avila,
a Francis, a Vincent!
But who remembers their names?
They passed away and no trace remains.
The saints are bolts of lightning
who lit up the nights of their times and those that followed,
because as empty lamps, they glowed with eternal Light.
They lost their lives for God
and swore never to desert him.
So he, the divine craftsman,
worked them, filed them, planed them, broke them down
with such harsh trials that leave a person almost spent:
alive only to sorrow, alive to love.
So that once purified in heart and soul and mind,
God gives the saints a heavenly task.
They work and work
but it is no longer they who work.
God works in them
and the world is converted.
Hearts drawn by the brightness so much longed for, dreamt of,
almost unconsciously, in multitudes
follow the light,
and with the saints find the same God.
In them is the law that works a revolution
and from below upholds and creates a divine society,
humanity Christified.
The saints are not lights at Verano;
they are stars alight in heaven eternally.[194]

Death which is the beginning of Life

God, making himself human, and therefore mortal, was born on this earth to die.

And this is the meaning of life: to live like a grain of wheat, whose destiny is to die and rot for the sake of life true and eternal.

It is a good idea to have this awareness as we walk the earth, where every day we grow older to arrive at death which is the beginning of Life. We should look upon the illnesses that befall us as steps prepared by the love of God for our to climb to the summit: trial runs for the "trial"; small hosts, not yet fully consumed, for the consummation that awaits us all: "It is finished" (see Jn 19:30).

It is like this: mortal with the Mortal One, to rise with him to begin a new Life which has no end.

Lord, may our doing your will be the incense we offer in this "Mass" we are preparing.

Lord, may we run without reluctance towards the Goal that soon we have to reach.

Give us the chance to give you all that we are, before death has a chance to rob us like a thief. May we offer you the very best we have, as the Father gave his Only Begotten, as Mary gave her Son, as every saint offered their life's work. That way nothing will change when you call, and death will be a passage, almost unnoticed and splendid in unity with you, dying and good God, who chose to assume our flesh in order to go before us in death and in Life.[195]

Towards our homeland

Today a lot is spoken about Christianity as a social message. It is a good thing and it is right that this aspect come to the fore. Since God became man it is clear that he is interested in all our affairs. Christ's life itself is a model of social relationships.

But we must remember that what he announced is also and above all a spiritual message.

We Christians do great damage to our faith.

We have the courage occasionally to love God and other people, to be fairly good and honest. Not infrequently we pray. Basically we lead lives that have an undeniably Christian flavour.

But there are some truths we think about all too seldom, indeed — let us admit it — hardly ever, unless we are *forced to*....

From time to time my eyes are opened — I consider it a real grace — and I become aware of a truth so beautiful, that my mind can only skim across the surface, can barely grasp it; it is too much for me.

And yet it stirs me, rouses me, encourages me and gives me great joy.

I realize where I am going. I remember hearing it proclaimed — and I believe it with my whole being — that, if I manage to do the duties God has assigned to me, *I will go ... to Paradise.*

Paradise!

But do we think about it? Do we realize that this earth is not the place where we make ourselves ever more comfortable, in an existence as free as possible from disturbances, but that every instant of our life is a step towards another kingdom, another land, another country in which the pure and complete happiness for which we yearn will be ours forever?

What will it be like? It would be better not to risk speaking about it. Too much vain fantasizing only distorts the reality. It will be ... it will be ... Paradise!

Today, part of society is in protest. Today we toss the masks aside. Stereotypes and systems are falling apart. The "pseudo" does not hold up. There is a general demythologizing of everything or of every person that until yesterday was held to be an idol.

People demand authenticity, truth.

And if we let the providence of God act in our history and in our generation, we will see the contention of Boros verified.

This modern writer, in a penetrating and stark but realistic analysis of today's thought processes and its human aspirations, said: "People today cannot claim to be modern if they do not encounter Christ."[196]

This is so. Authenticity means truth and Christ is the truth, with all that he brought us, commanded us and promised, along with the *place* he is preparing for us in *his* kingdom.

This is reality.

Now, if that is how things are, how inconsistent are our lives and how inverted our values! We behave as if it were not true that, for anyone on a long voyage towards their beloved home, the closer they get the faster their hearts will beat.

But who is more fortunate and, consequently, the happier? The child or youth who have yet to face all the many trials of life, with its joys, yes, but its unavoidable sorrows, or the mature person and still more the elderly approaching the threshold of Love's full embrace, which here is always sought in some confused way but there will soon be found, face to face, and possessed eternally?

When the first white hairs appear, when our limbs grow tired and threaten not to work as they used to, when one ages and the number of years increases, why should that cause, in us Christians as well, a sense of melancholy and sadness?

It would make sense if these were preliminary signs of life ebbing away.

But if it is not so, since the grand adventure for which we were born into this world is about to begin, how can we justify such attitudes? What has happened to our faith?

Have we not become like materialists who believe in only what they can see and touch? "My kingdom is *not* of this world" (Jn 18:36), Jesus said to Pilate precisely to let him know he need not fear that Jesus had come to take away his earthly throne.

No! Death comes, but then follows Life, a fullness of life that will never end.

And if to arrive at that point we have to pay a small price, or even a heavy price, how great the reward! St. Francis, who saw things clearly, speaking in the style of his times put it this way: "So great the good I have in sight that in every pain I take delight."[197]

During its transformation the chrysalis is an ugly thing, but it is followed by the butterfly.

It is the same with us human beings. As much as something seems to speak of ending and death — we must remember this — still more it announces life.

This is pure truth.

I think many of us still need to be converted to that way of thinking, so we can joyfully and cheerfully spread through the world good sense and wisdom, the fruit of our experience.

When our departure, the "day of our birth into heaven," draws near and we can repeat only the words of the apostle John in his venerable old age: "Let us love one another" (see 1 Jn 4:7), we will have spoken more eloquently and said much more than in all the passionate discourses of our life, when we were young and strong. We will have rendered to the rest of humanity still on its journey a great and splendid service.[198]

A love that continues

When friends or relatives leave for the hereafter, we say they have passed away, we think they are gone.

But it is not true. If we think like this, where is our faith in the communion of saints?

No one who enters into God is lost: because if anything remains in a brother or sister for whom "life is changed not taken away,"[199] it is charity. Yes, because everything passes. Even faith and hope pass away with the rest of the world as we know it. Only charity remains (see 1 Cor 13:8).

Now, what remains is the love that our brother or sister had for us, if it was a true love, rooted in God. And God is not so miserly with us that he takes away what he has given us in them.

But now he gives it to us in another way. Our departed brother or sister continues to love us in their new state with a charity that does not waver.

We, on the other hand, should believe in this love our brother or sister has for us and *ask* them for graces for our journey, while we do our part for them by praying for the dead, which is one of the works of mercy.

No, our brothers and sisters are not lost. They have moved on, as though they had left home for another place.

They are in the heavenly homeland, living in God, and we can continue to love one another as the gospel teaches.[200]

Thoughts: The rehearsal

If God were to show a soul all the suffering that life has in store for it, the soul would die on the spot. If God were to show a soul all the joys it would experience in life, the soul would die on the spot.

God knows this, and he measures things accordingly.

The soul does not know, but it abandons itself in God who loves it.[201]

Life is an important passage: *here* is our place of rehearsal! Indeed, the amount of Jesus that I will have allowed to be constructed in me, will be the amount established forever in the next life. Each act of mine, every moment, every breath will have an eternal consequence! Every minute of my life here below influences the Life to come! "Paradise is a house you construct now, but live in hereafter."

Why are we afraid to tell everyone that here below things pass, but hereafter we will remain forever?[202]

My God, what a mystery is this life you have given us and what a trial (death) it must undergo to reach its final goal, its home!

Thank you for coming down on earth to show us the Way, to make yourself the Way. When we are lost in you, we will always be in the light even if immersed in the deepest darkness.

Thank you for being born, for having lived and "died for us" (Rom 5:8), for me.

Died! Yes, died. If you had not died, how could we face death? Instead, even in that supreme act, we will think of you and die with you. We should make an ideal of Jesus who dies. This could produce for many a new and unexpected jet of life.[203]

Here below everything is like a play: a rehearsal for the life to come. Play the part that you will have up above (of Jesus in your place, in your vocation), then your life will be a divine adventure that will be fulfilled and perpetuated up there. If you play a bad part, to suit your own desires, then the sham and dead charade will continue in the place below with nothing left for you but the vanities you have clung to.[204]

Part Three

Reflections of Light upon the World

Basic notions of the charism of unity and their practical applications in the Church and the world

The Attraction of Modern Times

Alongside others

This is the great attraction
of modern times:
to penetrate to the highest contemplation
while mingling with everyone,
one person alongside others.
I would say even more:
to lose oneself in the crowd
in order to fill it with the divine,
like a piece of bread
dipped in wine.
I would say even more:
made sharers in God's plans
for humanity,
to embroider patterns of light on the crowd,
and at the same time to share with our neighbour
shame, hunger, troubles, brief joys.
Because the attraction
of our times, as of all times,
is the highest conceivable expression
of the human and the divine,
Jesus and Mary:
the Word of God, a carpenter's son;
the Seat of Wisdom, a mother at home.[1]

"Have faith, I have conquered the world"

We do not have to look far to find remedies or solutions for the fumes that infect the air we breathe. The gospel is eternal well-being. Also today, those who live for the gospel and act in its name, though they may die and disappear — perhaps ignored by all — live.

Because they have loved and forgiven and defended and because they have never given up, they are winners and as such are welcomed into eternal glory.

But the gospel should not only be the model of our dying, it should be the daily bread of our life.

Walking along the streets of traditionally Catholic cities, you are inclined to question the faith of many. In fact, we know how many, even in a Catholic country like Italy, have lost their sense of God. We see it, we feel it, we know it. It is enough to look at the newspapers, films and the theatre, television and fashion, art and music.

Sometimes certain situations take our breath away and a feeling of discouragement could overwhelm us at seeing not only adults but also innocent children immersed in a world so devoid of Christian values…. But then faith, if it is still alive in our hearts, invokes one of Jesus' eternal words and suddenly you are convinced and you understand. Above all you are certain that that word is as relevant today as ever and you are filled with the hope that if nourished on it not only will we be filled with peace, but we will pass from the defensive to the offensive, prepared to take on the evils that surround us for the good of those we love and that we hope to see saved.

"Take courage, I have conquered the world!" (Jn 16:33).

When boredom, listlessness, or a spirit of rebellion threatens to weaken our resolve in carrying out God's will, we must persevere. With Jesus it is possible for the "new self" to live in us constantly and to dissipate the fumes of the world that stifle our soul.

When feelings of dislike and hatred would have us judge or detest one of our brothers or sisters, we need to let Christ live in us. If we love and do not judge, but forgive, we will win out.

And when situations in the family or at work that drag on for years — of mistrust, jealousy, envy, tyranny — weigh us down, we must play the part of peacemakers. We can be mediators among opposing sides, re-establishing unity between brothers and sisters in the name of Jesus, who brought this idea on earth as the truth, the precious gem of his gospel.

And if we find ourselves surrounded by a world hardened by passions and worldly ambitions, stripped of ideals, of justice and of hope — as is often seen in politics and government — we should not feel suffocated. We need to trust and above all not abandon our post and our commitment. With the One who has conquered death, we can hope against all hope.[2]

Invasion of love

The world is made up of unhappy people because humankind has not recognized the source of its happiness. The stars shine in the sky and the earth stays in existence because they are in motion: movement is the life of the universe. People are truly happy only if they turn on the motor of their lives, love, and keep it running.

Even those who are considered happy because they are happily married, or perhaps because they have received an inheritance, or because they live in luxury and enjoy sports and entertainment, sooner or later experience moments of inescapable emptiness in their souls. Instead, the unfortunates who apparently have received a poor lot in life, if they set out to love, possess more than the rich and can experience the fullness of the kingdom of heaven here on earth.

This is the truth. It is reality.

Humanity pines for peace; it waits and it struggles to reach enjoyment. But when that moment finally arrives, the prospect of death makes people feel dejected, and they wish it would never come.

The children of God are children of love! They fight with a weapon, which is the very life of humankind. Their struggle is to restore order to individuals and society, so that the former may shine brighter than the stars and the latter form constellations that will live on in the eternal mansions of the God of the living.

If men and women were to see themselves as God sees them, they would be horrified.

Because even the best among them, those who raised themselves above the level of the majority through art or science, have developed only a part of their spirit, leaving the rest atrophied.

Only love in a soul, only God in a soul, can radiate splendour through it with balance in every part. A soul that loves is a little sun in the world, passing on God. A soul that does not love vegetates and has little of the Church, nothing of Mary and is the antithesis of Christ.

The world needs an invasion of love and this depends on each one of us. Men and women (those in the grace of God) are the reservoirs of this precious element. Every day countless people die, even the great, and little remains of them. When saints pass on to eternal life they reawaken when the Lord calls them to the same life as before yet transformed, and everyone talks about them. Their memory passes on from generation to generation and many follow their example. On that bed where lies the body of the saint but not the soul, no one manages to understand death, but all realize what Life is. Love does not die and, because it serves, it makes those who love into kings and queens.[3]

We have a great responsibility

We certainly have a great responsibility. We Christians must give witness to Christ and from the way we act people should be able to grasp the message that Christ brought on earth.

But at times the witness we give of Christ is weak — if not non-existent — or deformed in one way or another.

Various personalities and minds averse to the action of grace project an image of Jesus that is often in their own image and likeness. Therefore, those looking on deduce what they can from the data they have: for example, that deep down, religion simply bends people's necks but not their will. And this is because those Christians, who call themselves Christ's disciples, since it is they who live and not Christ in them, cast a shadow that veils in their own person the religion they profess. As a result, the separation tragically continues and is perpetuated between those who are far from Christ and those who, if they were to relive the love that is God, should attract the world and bring it to the Lord.

Basically, it is a religion that is not attractive because it has been distorted. And yet, there is a fascination or at least an unspoken respect, even among the people most deeply agnostic, for a missionary who ventures to the ends of the earth leaving everything behind for God, or for the martyrs who shed their blood for their faith.

And all this because Christianity is either genuine and radical, or it leaves much to be desired.

This holds true for the many cases that are obvious at first glance but also on a higher level in more subtle cases. For example, getting to know those who have given themselves to God with real generosity, it is not uncommon to find errors, perhaps practical, that disturb and obscure the beauty of our faith.

At times the journey on this earth is so arduous and this "vale" so full of tears, that people, finding solace only in the cross, cling to it, make it their banner, offer it to others, help them to love it, but … they stop there. They stop there because, although they love with all their heart and love in deeds, *they do not believe enough in God's love for them and for all*.

The Easter mystery bears witness to the fact that Jesus is life that conquers death, light that shatters the shadows, fullness that annuls the void.

This, in the final analysis, is Christianity: the cross is essential, but as a means to an end; tears are a harbinger to consolation, and poverty to possessing the kingdom; purity opens the veil of heaven, and persecution and meekness announce in advance the victory of eternal life and guarantee the Church's progress in the world.

Among the fifteen mysteries that adorn the rosary, the church has established five joyful, five sorrowful and five glorious. And this helps us Christians to understand that we should always hope and sing like the first Christians did, even at the threshold of martyrdom. Because *our* heritage is the fullness of joy that Jesus promised and invoked for those who would follow him.

Let us help one another — in our own small way — to be authentic witnesses to that Jesus who fascinated our hearts, in that Church that we too can help beautify, so that upon seeing her the world's pilgrims will recognize her.[4]

The resurrection of Rome

If I look at this city of Rome as it is, my Ideal seems far away. It appears to me as distant as the days in which the saints and martyrs illuminated everything around them with that eternal light which reached even the walls of these monuments that still stand in witness of the love that united the first Christians.

In blatant contrast, today's world, with all its filth and vanities, dominates this city's streets and even more so the hidden recesses of every home where anger, every kind of sin and uneasiness lurk.

I would say my Ideal was a utopia if I did not think of Him, who also saw a world like this one. He was surrounded by it and at the end of his life appeared to be swept up by it, overcome by evil.

He too gazed upon the crowds around him whom he loved as himself, whom he created. He wanted to forge the bonds that would unite them to him, like children to a father, and unite them to one another as brothers and sisters.

He came down from heaven to reunite us as family: to make us all one.

He came with words filled with Fire and Truth that burned through the accumulation of vanities that cover the life of the Eternal that lives in every person and that passes among them. And yet, notwithstanding, people, many people, though understanding, did not want to understand and remained with lifeless eyes because their souls were in darkness.

And all this because he made them free.

He who descended from heaven to earth could have resurrected them all with a single glance. But, because they had been created in the image and likeness of God, he had to let them experience the joy of freely conquering heaven. Eternity was at stake. They would have the opportunity to live as children of God for all eternity, like God, creators of their own happiness (because participants in the omnipotence of God).

He looked at the world as I see it now, but he did not doubt.

Unsatisfied and sad as he watched everything going to ruin, he responded by praying at night to the heavens above and the heaven within, there where the Trinity lived, the true being, everything, while outside along the streets there was only emptiness that passes.

And I too follow his example so as never to separate myself from the Eternal, from the Uncreated, which is the root of creation and therefore the Life of all, in order to believe in the ultimate victory of Light over darkness.

I pass through Rome and I do not want to look at it. I look at the world within me and I cling to all that has being and value. I become completely one with the Trinity that lives in my soul, allowing myself to be enlightened by its eternal Light and filled with its heaven. I live in that heaven populated by the angels and saints who, not being constrained by the limits of time and space, can all convene in a unity of love with the Three in my humble being.

And I make contact with the Fire, that having invaded the depths of my humanity given to me by God, makes me another Christ, another God-Man by participation. Thus, my humanity merges with the divine and my eyes are no longer lifeless. Instead, through the pupil, which is the emptiness of my soul through which all the Light within me passes (if I let God live in me), I look at the world and everything in it. But it is no longer I; it is Christ in me who looks at the world and desires to make the blind see, the mute speak, and the crippled walk. They are those blinded to the vision of God living within them and outside them; mute to the Word of God that also speaks within them and that could be communicated in turn to others, reawakening the Truth in them. They are the crippled who are unable to move, because they ignore the divine will that from the depths of their hearts spurs them on to an eternal motion that is eternal Love, for when we transmit Fire we are set ablaze.

Therefore, opening my eyes once again to the world outside, I see humanity with the eyes of God who believes all things because he is Love.

I see and I discover my same Light in others, the true Reality of myself, my true self in them (perhaps hidden or secretly camouflaged out of shame). And, having found myself, I reunite myself to me, resurrecting myself in my brother or sister — because Love is Life.

Jesus is resurrected in them; another Christ, another God-Man, manifestation here on earth of the Father's goodness and the Eye of God on humanity. Thus, I extend the Christ in me to my brother or sister and I form a living and complete cell of the Mystical Body of Christ: a living cell, a hearth of God that possesses Fire and Light, which must be communicated.

It is God who makes two persons one by placing himself third, as the relationship between them: Jesus among us.

Thus, love circulates and naturally carries with it (because of its innate law of communion), like a blazing river, all that the two possess to the point that all their material and spiritual goods are held in common.

All this gives concrete and outward witness to a love that is unitive, to true love, the love that comes from the Trinity.

Therefore, the complete Christ truly lives again in both persons, in each one and among us.

He, the God-Man, in the most varied human expressions imbued with the divine, placed at the service of the eternal design: God concerned with his kingdom, ruler of all, distributor of every good thing to all his children like a father who shows no preferences.

And I think that if I allow God to live in me and if I allow him to love himself in those around me, he would discover himself in many of them and many eyes would light up with his Light: a tangible sign that he reigns in them.

And his Fire, which destroys everything in the service of eternal Love, would spread like lightning throughout Rome resurrecting Christians and making this era, cold because atheistic, the era of Fire, the era of God.

But it is important that we have the courage not to waste too much time in other activities that simply reawaken a little Christianity, trying to echo past glories; or at least we should not give them the same priority.

We need to allow God to be reborn within us and keep him alive. We need to make him overflow onto others like torrents of Life and resurrect the dead.

And keep him alive among us by loving one another (and to love it is not necessary to make a lot of noise: love is dying to ourselves — and death is silence — and life in God — and God is the silence that speaks).

So everything is renewed: politics and art, school and religion, private life and entertainment. Everything.

The presence of God in us is not like a crucifix that hangs on the wall of a classroom as nothing more than a talisman. He is alive in us — if we let him live — as the legislator of every human and divine law, since he made them all. And from the most intimate recesses of our being he dictates them one by one. He, the eternal Teacher, teaches us what is eternal and what is passing and gives value to everything.

But only those who let Christ live in them, and therefore they themselves live in those around them, can understand this. Because life is love and if it does not circulate it does not live.

Jesus needs to be resurrected in the Eternal City and introduced everywhere. He is Life, the fullness of Life. He is not just a religious event....* This attempt to separate him from the entirety of our lives is a practical heresy of today's world. It subjects men and women to something that is beneath them and relegates God the Father far from his children.†

No, he is the Man, the perfect man, who sums up and contains all men and women and every truth and inspiration that they may feel in order to raise themselves to their proper place.

Therefore, the one who has found this man has found the solution to every problem, be it human or divine. It is enough to love him.[5]

---

* It is sometimes thought that the gospel does not resolve all human problems and that it brings about the kingdom of God understood solely in a religious sense. But this is not so. Certainly it is not the historical Jesus or Jesus as Head of the Mystical Body who resolves all problems. This is done by Jesus-us, Jesus-me, Jesus-you.... It is Jesus in human beings, in each particular human being, when his grace is in them, who builds a bridge, opens the road. Jesus is the true, deepest personality of each individual. Every human being (every Christian), in fact, is more a child of God (=another Jesus) than a child of his or her own parents. It is as another Christ, member of his Mystical Body, that each person makes a specific and personal contribution in every field: science, art, politics.... It is the incarnation that continues, a full incarnation that involves all of the Jesuses of the Mystical Body of Christ. *(Author's note)*

† Humanity, in all of its human dimensions and capacities, is not to be mortified but elevated. Next to a renewed theology, "new" (because it is based on the trinitarian life lived in the Mystical Body of Christ) there also needs to be new science, new sociology, new art, new politics — new because they are of Christ, renewed by his Spirit. We need to set in motion a new humanism, where humanity is really at the centre, that humanity which before all else is Christ and Christ in human beings. *(Author's note)*

Like a rainbow

The Lord, through the charism of unity, did not intend only to bring about a spirituality in the Church, but also a Movement that was later given the name Focolare or Work of Mary.

Of course, a Movement necessarily needs a soul (the spirituality of communion), but it also needs to be organized, it needs a structure, a rule.

And the Lord thought of this as well.

As I recall, it was in 1954. The spirituality at this point was more or less complete. And one thing was clear to us: we had to be another Jesus.

Already in 1946 I had written in some notes: "The soul must aim at being another Jesus as soon as possible...."

"We must play the part of Jesus here on earth. We need to lend God our humanity so that he may use it to have his beloved Son live once again."[6]

But how could this come to pass? ... Certainly by loving. Love sums up Christian law. If we love we are another Jesus; and we are Jesus in everything we do. Therefore, our life had to be love. Had we wanted to define who we were meant to be, we would have had to say: "We are love," just as God is Love. And if love was our life, love had to be the rule of our life.

And then an idea, perhaps an inspiration:

Love is light. It is like a ray of light that upon passing through a raindrop opens up into a rainbow of seven colours. They are all colours of light, which in turn are made up of an infinite number of shades.

And just as the rainbow is red, orange, yellow, green, blue, indigo and violet, love, the life of Jesus in us, would have different colours and would express itself in different ways, each one different from the other.

Love, for example, is communion; it leads to communion. Because he is love Jesus in us would lead us to live communion.

Love is not closed in on itself; it is its nature to spread. Jesus in us, love, would radiate love.

Love lifts up the soul. Jesus in us would raise our soul up to God. Thus prayer.

Love heals. Jesus, love in our hearts, would be our soul's health.

Love gathers people together in assembly. Jesus in us, because he is love, would bring hearts together.

Love is a fount of wisdom. Jesus in us, love, would enlighten us.

Love is unity; it makes many one. Jesus in us would fuse us into one.

These are the seven main expressions of love that we proposed to live. They, however, represent an infinite number.

Thus, these seven expressions of love immediately became the norm of our personal life and would also make up the guidelines of our Movement as a whole and later on of its various branches.

And since love is at the basis of each expression, of each aspect, and since it is Jesus that is always living in us in every manifestation of our life, our life would be integrated in a wonderful unity.

Everything would be born from love, everything would be rooted in love and everything would be an expression of the life of Jesus in us. No longer would our life be unsatisfying, boring and flat, made up of unrelated events merely set one next to the other: perhaps with time set aside for lunch that has nothing to do with the time for prayer, or the time for apostolate relegated to a predetermined hour, etc. Instead, life would become attractive and fascinating.

No, here it would always be Jesus who lives the apostolate, who works, who eats, etc. Everything would be an expression of him.

We can see now that we were being presented with a rule suited to our human nature that had, at the same time, both an earthly and a heavenly flavour.

These various expressions of love, of the life of Jesus in us, have been included in the Statutes of the Work of Mary and the regulations of its various branches as our rule.[*]

And as such the Church has approved them.[7]

---

[*] See the section *Structure* below 396.

The Family: Treasure Chest of Love[8]

A living cell

Today, in a world where for an idea many are willing to sacrifice human and material resources, putting the lives of others and even of the whole human race at risk, it is necessary that every individual Christian and every society, large or small, should live for the only idea worth saving: faith in God. It is the only faith that must survive for the sake of all humanity. It is true that "the gates of Hades will not prevail against it" (Mt 16:18), but how many fewer victims there could be, how much suffering could be avoided....

So today, perhaps even more than in the past, the Christian family must feel itself to be a living cell of the Church.

Mothers and fathers, husbands and wives with their children must love one another, recognizing one another also as brothers and sisters in Christ and thus giving "supernatural" value to their "natural" love. If they love one another in this way, as Jesus commanded, Christ cannot fail to fulfil his promise and be present among those united in his name.

Thus every family nucleus can better reflect the family of Nazareth that God composed and endowed with the most exquisite sense of family and the most angelic natural affections. It is a family that is less centred on itself, but rather wide open to the world of yesterday, today and tomorrow and created for the highest and most supernatural purpose: redemption. The redemption that the son carried out, in which the mother participated and for which the adoptive father gave his contribution in sacrifice, reverence, work and candid, selfless love.

Christian families that are open and united according to that example become fortresses that prevent the infiltration of the poisonous waters of atheism and, because of their location in the midst of the world, safeguard the most precious human and Christian values.[9]

Family and love

> From an address to the first large public event of the New Families Movement, a branch of the Focolare, Palaeur sports stadium, Rome, 3 May 1981.

What is the family? Sociologists, moral theologians, educators, politicians, psychologists could offer a wide variety of definitions. However, I am convinced that all of you present here today are interested above all in one particular point of view on the family: God's point of view.

How does God see the family? ...

Let's begin from a simple statement of fact.

When God created the world he formed a family. When he became man he surrounded himself by a family. When Jesus embarked on his mission and manifested his glory, he was celebrating the birth of a new family. This should be enough to understand how God sees the family....

The family is nothing but a mechanism, a treasure chest, a mystery of love: nuptial, maternal, paternal, filial, among brothers and sisters, the love of a grandmother for her grandchildren, of grandchildren for their grandfather, for their aunt or cousins.... Nothing constitutes and binds a family like love. And if the family has failed in the world, it is because love has grown less. Wherever love dies out the family falls apart. That is why families must draw from the very source of love. God who is love knows what the family is. He designed it as a masterpiece of love: sign, symbol and prototype of all his other designs. If he made the family, shaping it with love, he can restore the family once again with love.

The "you" of God — We know that men and women are truly such if they behave in accord with who they are: the image of God; therefore, if they are in communion with God and place themselves as the "you" of God. And so love, that love that unites the family, is true love if it nourishes itself, sustains itself, confronts itself and communicates with the love that is in God, with love that is a gift of God. That is why the Church encourages regular reception of the sacraments, which are channels of grace that enrich us with supernatural love. It also invites us to pray together, to participate in the liturgy, to nourish ourselves on the Word of God, to feed ourselves on old and new devotions, especially to the Virgin; all of which are valuable tools in fostering the growth of the life of grace.[10]

When this love burns in the hearts of the members of a family and is truly alive, there are no problems that cannot be solved, no obstacles that cannot be overcome and no one complains of failures that cannot be remedied. The family returns to being beautiful, united and healthy, just as God imagined it.

A new type of family — Today the family needs a potent injection of that love....

Our Movement is called to bring the family, every family it meets, to make this resolution: revitalize the love that is inherent in every family with that love which is a pure gift from God. In other words, love must reawaken love. And it will, because everything cooperates towards the good of those who love. Even the hardships that can cause families to cry out in today's world will bear fruit. They will give life to a new type of family, one demanded by our times and heralded by the signs of the times. The love that comes down from on high will give the most effective contribution to helping the conventional middle class family — so criticized these days for being closed in on itself — open itself up to all of society. That love, more than anything else, will have us revaluate the role of women, giving them their proper place in society. That powerful love will increase in men the awareness of their duty to participate more fully in the life of the family, sharing equally with women in all its aspects. And that love will consolidate all the good that today is emerging in the family, such as the need for sincerity and directness, and less tension among young men and women, a result of the by now normal tendency to grow up together from an early age, helping to dissipate any sense of artificiality, lack of communication and complexes among them.

True values — It will be the love of God in people's hearts that will lead them to a true rediscovery of the body; no longer to be viewed as something to be exploited, but rather positively as a creation of God. Thus, this love will speed up the process that leads us to hope in a certain rejection and reappraisal of the eroticism promoted by popular culture in favour of other aspects of life such as interest in society, politics and culture. And only the love that comes from God will be able to offer a sure standard for responsible motherhood and fatherhood. Our world, despite everything, is searching for and is undergoing major transformations. In times like these we cannot think about turning back. All those who are in a position to propose true values can have a big influence. For example: those who offer models of united families that are built on authentic relationships and that are not oppressive; that are open to the society around them and that make clear choices in favour of life and of children; that have healed wounded relationships between generations and that have rediscovered the role of the elderly....

The model — It seems to me that in order for the family to regain its true countenance, to return it to its true splendour, besides discourses, warnings, directives, expositions of experiences, it needs to look to that luminous and universal example invented by eternal wisdom: the family of Nazareth. All families of the world, both of today and tomorrow, can look to that family as their role model. And not only families: each family member can draw inspiration there in understanding how to behave, what attitudes to assume, what relationships to pursue and what virtues to cultivate.

Every husband and father on earth will always be able to find a source of light, encouragement and inspiration in Joseph, Mary's husband and Jesus' foster father. From him he will learn faithfulness in times of trial, heroic chastity, strength, respect and veneration. He can imitate his silent hardworking nature, his dedication to protecting the mother of his child and his full participation in the concerns of the family. And every wife and mother will be able to look to Mary and discover in her what she should be, her equality with men and her true identity. There, in Joseph's wife, she will find how she too can have a leading role. And thanks to Mary she will understand how to go beyond the family circle in order to share her unique gifts for the good of many: the ability to give of herself, her interior life that gives her self-assurance, her typical religiosity and her innate need always to rise above and lift up others with her radiant beauty, purity and candour.

In the same way the children will be able to identify with Jesus, in particular in the life of the family with Mary and Joseph. There they will discover how to bring together in an effective unity two tendencies that at times can torment them: the need to affirm themselves as a distinct generation destined to open a new chapter in history and at the same time the desire to be sheltered in the shadow of love and obedience to their parents. Yes, the Holy Family is the jewel of human social relationships that reflects the life of the Trinity where love makes God one. May it always be before us and may it remain with us for the good of families in the world, of families in the church and for the glory of God.[11]

As in the family, so in society

> From "Seeds of communion for the family of the third millennium," an address to the New Families Movement, Palaeur sports stadium, Rome, 5-6 June 1993.

We are on the threshold of the third millennium. The family, every family can take a lead in shaping this era. Devised by God as a masterpiece of love, the family is able to inspire the guidelines that can contribute to changing tomorrow's world.

In fact, if we look at the family, if we were to take an X-ray of it, we would discover enormous and precious values, which if projected and applied to all of humanity have the potential to transform it into one big family.

The family is founded on love, a bond that has many dimensions: love between spouses, among parents and their children, between grandparents, uncles and aunts with nieces and nephews, among brothers and sisters. It is a love that grows continuously, always going beyond itself. In the same way, the love among spouses generates new life and the relation among brothers and sisters becomes friendship. And because authority and the various roles are expressions of love, they are accepted naturally.

In the family it comes spontaneously to put everything in common, to share everything and to have a single economy. Savings are not hoarding but rather prudent foresight. It is normal to provide for the needs of those who are not yet productive or of those who no longer are.

In the family people of all ages live together. It is natural to live for the other, to love one another.

Even education occurs in a spontaneous way: it is enough to think of a baby's first steps or his or her first words. Punishment and forgiveness are given only for the good of the person.

The sense of justice is normal in the family just as it is normal to feel the other's guilt and shame. It is natural to suffer and to sacrifice oneself for the family, to carry one another's burdens. Solidarity and faithfulness to one's family are spontaneous.

In the family the other's life is just as precious as one's own, at times even more so; one feels concerned about everyone's health and takes care of those that are not well.

The family is the place where life naturally begins and ends and where the handicapped, the elderly and the terminally ill find acceptance, affection and care.

In the family each member is clothed and nourished according to his or her needs.

The home is built and taken care of together with everyone's participation.

In the family everyone teaches and everyone learns: everything serves for the maturation of its members. Its members may have different cultural values but all these diversities become enrichment for all.

In the family communication is also spontaneous; everyone participates in everything and shares everything.

And so the task of every family is to live its vocation with such perfection that it becomes a model for the entire human family and passes on to it all of its values by example.

In this way the family will become … a seed of communion for the world of the third millennium.

Is it natural for a family to put everything in common? This could be the seed from which an economic system at the service of humankind can spring forth, a seed of a culture of giving, of an economy of communion.

Is it spontaneous in the family to live one for the other, to live the other? This is the seed of acceptance among groups, peoples, traditions, races and societies that opens the door to reciprocal enculturation.

Does the passing on of values from generation to generation come spontaneously in the family? It could then be an incentive for placing new emphasis on education in society. What is more, the example of correction and forgiveness in the life of the family can be a model for the justice system.

Is another member's life valued as one's own in the family? This is the seed of the culture of life that must enlighten the laws and the structures of society.

Does the family take care of its home and try to make it reflect the harmony among its members? This is the seed of a renewed awareness of the environment and of ecology.

In the family, are studies aimed at the development of the person? This is the seed that can lead to cultural, scientific and technological research aimed at discovering little by little the mysterious design of God for humanity and to working for the common good.

In the family, is communication impartial and constructive? This is the seed for a social communication system at the service of humankind; one that highlights and transmits the positive and that seeks to be an instrument of world peace and unity.

Is love the natural bond among the members of the family? This is the seed of structures and institutions that work for the good of the community and of individuals that aspire to universal brotherhood, giving value to each individual nation....

God created the family as a model for every other human coexistence. This therefore is the task of families: always to keep the fire of love burning in every home and to reawaken those values that God entrusted to the family in order to bring them generously and without rest to every sector of society.[12]

The family is our future

> Address to 19th International Congress for the Family, Lucerne, Switzerland, 16 May 1999.

I would like to stop for a moment to reflect on the family as seen in the mind of God. Certainly it is a bold proposal but not an impossible one. It is enough to look for the answer in the Bible, the book that relates his words and the history of his relationship with humankind. It is also not a useless proposal, because besides shedding light on the often confusing and contradictory state of affairs of the family today, such a study might also help us to understand what the family is meant to be.

The family's natural beauty — The Bible is interwoven with nuptial analogies and familial symbols. It is as if the Spirit could not find another way to express the ardour, faithfulness, gratuitousness and universality of the love of God. And it is also a confirmation that also natural marriage, as God imagined it, has in some way a sacred character.[13]

At the beginning of creation there is a man and a woman. God entrusts them with the commandment of mutual love and he invites them to multiply and to use all created things. It is a beautiful image; it is the discovery of the existence of the other and the birth of the family.

Human beings are called to live in relationship with one another. It is how they fulfil themselves. *"Amo ergo sum"* (I love therefore I am), writes Emmanuel Mounier.[14]

It is a "relational" dimension that encompasses all aspects of human life: family, surroundings, and history. And in this "being in relationship" we find yet another confirmation that the family is an intrinsic part of the human person, it is part of our very nature. It is not a form of living together based on a given social model or invented by a dominant group.

Conjugal communion is based on the natural complementarity between a man and a woman, which in matrimony is expressed in the total giving of self.

It is a gift exclusive to and typical of conjugal union, in which the two do not simply give something of themselves, they give themselves, to the point of becoming one. It is a course mapped out by the laws of nature, but that also evokes and expresses divine laws.

Moreover, in matrimony the man and the woman, each urged by love one for the other, adhere to the universal vocation to unity. According to the bishop and theologian Klaus Hemmerle, in the union of the two spouses that are made one while being open to the possibility of welcoming children, there is a simultaneous encounter with and penetration into the world by man and woman. And in this relationship between the world and humankind we can also understand each one's specific role: man's role in dedicating himself to building the world, and woman's, to the process of making it more human, which, in fact, is her typical characteristic.[15]

But there is more.

Its Trinitarian roots — The family is indissolubly intertwined with the very mystery of the life of God that is Unity and Trinity: "God created humankind in his image, in the image of God he created them; male and female he created them. God blessed them, and God said to them, 'Be fruitful and multiply, and fill the earth …' " (Gn 1:27-28).

And when someone asked Jesus to speak about marriage he quoted precisely this passage from Genesis and he recommended that they go back to how it was "in the beginning" if they wanted to understand something about the mystery of married love.

Therefore, when God created humankind, he formed a family. He created a man and a woman called to live in communion, in the image of the mystery of love of his very being. He called them to be fertile and to make use of all created things in the image of God's inexhaustible paternity.

John Paul II affirms: "In the light of the New Testament it is possible to discern how the primordial model of the family is to be sought in God himself, in the Trinitarian mystery of his life. The divine 'We' is the eternal pattern of the human 'we,' especially of that 'we' formed by the man and the woman created in the divine image and likeness."[16]

It is precisely here that the family plants its roots.

Certainly, the mystery of love encompasses all of creation. The laws of nature are the laws of love and human love sums up and refines this continuous dynamic of unity and distinction.

Protector of life and treasure chest of relationships of love — Human love has its seasons. It begins when the couple falls in love. It is like a spark of the love of God that ignites the life of a family. Or like a bolt of lightning that lights up the persons loved with a new light, a novelty that changes their lives, that gives joy and enthusiasm as they set out together on a journey with no end in sight. It is almost a couple's genetic inheritance.

Then comes the fruit-bearing season, a time of growth and consolidation. Situations change, people themselves over time change and evolve. Love experiences other moments, other flavours, and other expressions and so our capacity to love must continuously be renewed.

Precisely is this dynamic, which makes them into a one that cannot be dissolved, is contained the couple's entire future. And it is a future that leads them beyond themselves, in particular through the birth of children.

In fact, fecundity among spouses has multiple expressions, the most typical being the blossoming of new human life.

In procreation the spouses cooperate with the creative action of God who through them extends his earthly family. Bonhoeffer writes: "He (God) allows men and women to participate in his continuous creative act. Parents welcome children as gifts from God and must lead them back to him."[17] In a certain sense, the birth of a baby is the typical way for a married couple to give God to the world.

Parenthood is an important stage of a family's development. It is the birth and multiplication of new relationships, a phenomenon that will increase as the life of the family progresses. The family will become a treasure chest, a wonderful interweaving of relationships of love, of intimacy and of friendship: nuptial love among the spouses, maternal and paternal love towards the children, filial love towards the parents, brotherly and sisterly love among the children, love on the part of grandparents for their grandchildren and vice versa, for aunts and uncles, for cousins, for friends of the family, for neighbours.... God truly created the family as a mysterious jewel interlaced with love.

Its social dimension and influence on society — In this process the family is transformed from being a single couple, a man and a woman, into a community of persons. It is similar to a spring that starts out as a fresh and generous gush of water and that little by little becomes a stream nourishing an ever-wider area.

In this way families become generators of social relationships. In fact, Cicero had called the family "the origin of the city and almost the seedbed of the state."[18] Because it sustains its members throughout the various stages of life and having been created by God in the image of his mystery of love, the family is the ideal model for every human society.

In 1993 I shared this conviction during a conference held in Rome in preparation for the International Year of the Family. On that occasion I emphasized the wealth of values inherent in a family when it is in harmony with the design of God; values that when projected towards and applied to society can transform it into one big family. These values, such as communion, solidarity, the spirit of service and reciprocity, appear "normal" in a family setting, but could be striking innovations for atrophied institutional structures and reference points for a new social order.

Structures and organizations aimed at the common good already exist in society. What is needed is to humanize these structures. We need to give them a soul so that the spirit of service reaches the same intensity and has the same spontaneity and the same drive of love for every person that one experiences in the family.[19]

Bringing about this genuine and profound social revolution would not require great upheavals. It would be enough that every family be truly itself and that it respond to the heartfelt invitation of Baden-Powell, founder of the World Scout Movement: "Families, become who you are!"[20]

The current situation of the family — If we observe the situation of the society that surrounds us, no matter what country we come from, our brief reflections on what the family is and should be may appear to be a naive utopia.

The Western world is permeated by an individualistic culture that is particularly set on categorizing and promoting men and women according to their needs and what they consume. As a result, sexuality, rather than being a divine gift of relationship, becomes an idol, an enemy of human integrity that is progressively separated from love and openness to life. We live off emotions that play games with individuals, joining couples, separating them and joining them again, destroying that fundamental trust in the stability of feelings that is indispensable in family life.[21] The bishops' conferences of the European Union admonish that family life "no longer plays any role in the life of society. Men and women are too often treated solely in their capacity as individuals. The duties carried out in the context of the family are considered as their private business. Thus, we forget how important families are for the unity of society. In a cultural context marked by individualism and the pursuit of profit, the family has become very fragile. And those that are socially marginalized are the ones that most often break up."[22]

Children are the first victims. Deprived as they are of the reference point of family unity, they are put in difficulty by its fragmentation into a series of pseudo-parents coming one after another.

"The family," Bovet writes, "is like an 'organism' and its members are like its organs. Just as every organism has a head, heart and cells, so every family has a father, mother and children. Children must be able to experience a profound, full relationship with their father and mother in order to be able to honour and love them."[23]

And yet today the bond of a stable marriage appears almost to be in contradiction to personal freedom. Rather than stressing "relational" values, emphasis is placed on conflicts and differences.

On a political level, institutions and governments draft these "matters of fact" into laws that are contrary to the overall well being of the person. As a result, divorce, abortion, euthanasia, biogenetic experiments enter into people's consciousness as things that are possible and therefore legitimate. The decline in the birthrate, living together before marriage and sexual anarchy become normal and even fashionable.

In other parts of the planet characterized by a marked disparity in the distribution of wealth, the family is faced with extreme poverty and underdevelopment, obstacles that are difficult to overcome.

What is more, in the poorest countries globalization relentlessly proliferates, as do the myths of consumerism and sick social models based on Western culture that have devastating effects on the local cultures.

Horace's admonishment to the Roman senate rings true also today: "The massacre that destroys nations and peoples is rooted in the family, which you have succeeded in corrupting."[24]

The crisis of the family institution can be seen as a social phenomenon, but it is more than just that. We recently celebrated the 50th anniversary of the Declaration of Human Rights, a fundamental document for civil coexistence and an important step in the process of society's humanization. Nevertheless, blatant and hidden violations of these rights are countless, they continuously occupy the media and they invade us with a profound sadness. And they are all injustices that in the end fall on the smallest and most defenceless sector of society: the family unit.

In a certain sense, the family today is the "container" of humanity's suffering. There is no planetary statistical agency that can estimate the extent of this phenomenon. We can only ask ourselves: how many separated and frustrated couples are there? How many children deprived of one or the other parent? How many children with addiction problems? How many caught in the spiral of delinquency and prostitution? How many spouses and children ravished by wars? How many elderly people abandoned? How many babies die of hunger every day? How many terminally ill whose lives slowly extinguish amidst cold indifference? And what of those with incurable illnesses and the handicapped?

We could create a graphic representation of the contemporary family by way of an image: a wounded and desolate mother who clutches the sufferings of humanity to her breast while crying out "Why?" to the heavens.

It is a situation that takes your breath away. It makes us wonder: what is the family's future? Or even worse: does the family have a future?

Jesus forsaken — Faced with the overwhelming mystery of suffering we often find ourselves lost.

In the Bible we read of a culminating moment of suffering that is expressed with a "Why" cried out to heaven. In the evangelist Matthew's account of Jesus' death, we read: "At about three o'clock Jesus cried with a loud voice … 'My God, my God, why have you forsaken me?' " (Mt 27:46).

Christ reached that moment passing through a devastating range of sufferings: fear, anguish, betrayal and abandonment by his friends, an unjust and engineered trial, torture, humiliation and then being condemned to death by crucifixion, a form of capital punishment reserved for slaves. Perhaps today we cannot fully grasp how gruesome a death it was, how it attempted to destroy the person totally and all memory of him.

And finally, that unexpected cry, "Why have you forsaken me?" that allows us a glimpse into the drama lived by the God-Man. It is the culminating point of his sufferings, his inner passion, his darkest night. He who had said: "The Father and I are one" lives the tragic experience of disunity, of separation from God. And all of this because, out of love for us, he took upon himself all that is negative, all the sins of humankind.

In his forsakenness, the last and greatest sign of his love, Christ reaches the point of total annihilation of self. He reopens the path to unity for all persons with God and with one another. In that "why," to which he received no answer, every man and woman finds an answer to his or her own cry. Is not the distressed person perhaps similar to him, the lonely, the failure, the condemned? Is not every division within the family and among groups and peoples, a reflection of him? Can we not make out his countenance in those who have lost the sense of who God is and of his design for humanity, in those who no longer believe in love and instead accept whatever surrogate comes their way? There is no human tragedy or failure within a family that is not contained in the night of the God-Man. With his death he has already paid for everything; he signed a blank cheque capable of containing the suffering and sins of every man and woman that was, that is and that will be.

He is like a divine grain of wheat that decomposes and dies in order to give us back life. In that terrible experience he also reveals to us what it really means to love: to be capable of giving of oneself completely, to make oneself nothing for the others. "The sign of God who annihilates himself," writes von Balthasar, "becoming man and dying in the most complete abandonment, explains why God had accepted ... all of that: revealing himself to be love that knows no limits was part of his very nature."[25]

Through that emptiness, that nothingness, grace and the life of God flowed back to humanity. Christ re-established the unity between God and creation, he restored the design, he made new men and women and therefore new families.

The family can reacquire its original beauty — The great event of the suffering and abandonment of the God-Man, can therefore become the reference point and the secret wellspring capable of transforming death into resurrection, shortcomings into opportunities to love and family crisis into stages of growth. How so?

If we look at suffering from a purely human perspective there are two choices: we either end up in an analysis that has no way out, because suffering and love are part of the mystery of human life; or we try to rid ourselves of this uncomfortable obstacle by running in the opposite direction.

But if we believe that behind the events of our lives there is God with his love, and if strengthened by this faith we can recognize in big and small daily sufferings, our own and those of others, a shadow of the crucified and forsaken Christ and our participation in the suffering that redeemed the world, it will be possible to understand the meaning of the most absurd situations and put them in perspective.

In the face of whatever suffering may come our way, big or small, and in the face of contradictions and problems that have no solutions, let's try to enter within ourselves and look head on at the absurdity, injustice, innocent suffering, humiliation, alienation or desperation before us. It is there that we will recognize one of the many countenances of the "Man of Sorrows."

It is our meeting with him, the "divine person" who became an individual without relationships. The God of contemporary humanity that transforms nothingness into being, suffering into love. It will be our "yes" to him and our readiness to love him and welcome him into our lives that will cause our individualistic attitudes to crumble and turn us into new men and women who through love are capable of healing and giving new life to the most desperate situations. But is all this really possible?

I would like to call to mind two real-life examples that illustrate that it is.

Claudette was a young French woman abandoned by her husband. She had a one-year-old son. The narrow-minded environment of the province she lived in and of her family convinced her to ask for a divorce. In the meantime she came to know a couple that spoke to her of God who is especially close to those who suffer: "Jesus loves you," they told her. "He, like you, was also betrayed and abandoned. In him you can find the strength to love and to forgive." Little by little her feelings of resentment yielded and she began to behave differently. Her attitude also had an effect on her husband. In fact, when Claudette and Laurent presented themselves before the judge for their first hearing they looked at one another in a new way and agreed to put off their decision for six months. Having reopened the lines of communication between them, when they were called back to court to finalize the divorce, they said: "No!" and descended the steps of the courthouse hand in hand. The birth of two more daughters has given joy to a love that through suffering has now established deep roots.

And another. A beautiful Swiss family one evening learned from their son that he was addicted to drugs. They tried in vain to cure him of the addiction. One day he did not come home. They were invaded by feelings of guilt, fear, impotence and shame. It was the encounter with Jesus Forsaken in a suffering typical of our society. Embracing him in this suffering they seemed to comprehend: "True love makes itself one with others, it enters into the reality that they are living…." In a spirit of solidarity the parents opened themselves towards those that are suffering. They organized a group of families to bring sandwiches and tea to the youth of the Platzpitz, which at the time was known as the "hell of drug addicts" in Zurich. One day they found their son there, ravaged and exhausted. Together with other families they were able to help him embark on and complete his long road to freedom.

And we could go on….

These are not dreams. They are the experiences of many families who by recognizing more and more the forsakenness of the God-Man in their daily lives, have transformed their flood of pain into new life.

Sometimes the traumas are resolved and families are reunited; but at times they are not: externally the situations may remain as they were, but the pain is illuminated, the anguish is eased and the fracture is overcome. At times the physical or spiritual suffering lingers on but it acquires meaning when we unite our "passion" to the passion of Christ who continues to redeem and to save the family and all of humanity. And the burden becomes lighter.

Therefore, the family can attempt to reacquire its original beauty according to its creator's design by drawing from the source of love that Christ brought on earth.

I believe that from that wellspring married couples and families can quench their thirst for authenticity, for continuous and limitless communion, and for values that are transcendent, lasting and always new. God himself can be present in their homes and share his life with them. Jesus said: "Where two or three are gathered in my name (= in my love), I am there among them" (Mt 18:20). Families are being offered an incredible opportunity: to be the dwelling place of God's presence.

For families that live in this way, nothing that happens around them is alien to them. Just by being themselves, they have the potential to witness to, to announce and to restore the surrounding social fabric, since life speaks and acts for itself. I have seen firsthand that a family is capable of opening house and heart to the pressing needs and dramas that effect society, to its lonely and marginalized. It knows how to incarnate the spirit of solidarity and organize concrete activities that have an ever-greater influence on the society around them: promoting initiatives that can influence institutions, block the passage of misguided laws and regulations, and offer politicians guidance.

Due to the presence and activity of its members in the various sectors of society, these families also know how to establish a dialogue with institutions and bring together resources and material needs. They know how to create a collective consciousness and lay the foundations of adequate family policies and trends in public opinion that are based on values. I believe that this kind of family is the most beautiful gift offered to the world today. But why, we might ask; what is humanity searching for? Happiness. And where is it looking? In love and in beauty, and in order to obtain it is willing to do anything. There, in those families, there exists the fullness of human love and the beauty of supernatural love.

I have seen families like this; they are wonderful and they draw many to themselves. On the outside they appear to be families like any other but they hold a secret, a secret rooted in love. Having embraced suffering they are united to Christ. He lives in their homes, drawn there by their bond of mutual love. And with them, with these families, the world is changing.

Conclusion — I wanted to share these reflections with you. I gathered them from the depths of my heart and from the experience of many, many families. I would like to ask that we all commit ourselves to practical action with all the means at our disposal for the true well-being of the family. The health of this first cell of society is critical for the future of all humanity.

"In saving the family," writes the great Catholic writer Igino Giordani, "we are saving civilization. Our country is made up of families. If they perish society too will falter."[26] And he adds: "Married couples become co-workers with God; they give humanity life and love…. Love emanates from the family spreading to the workplace, the city, the nation, and to all humanity like an infinite wave of concentric circles. A revolutionary restlessness has been burning for the past twenty centuries. It was lit by the gospel and calls out for love"[27, 28]

The Talents and Gifts of Women

Address at the Day of Peace, Trent, 1 January 1995.

"Woman educator for peace." This is the title chosen by the Pope for today's gathering. It reveals his fervent, heart-felt desire to give women of the world their due importance. It is a continuation of his many proclamations in favour of women and especially his wonderful letter: *Mulieris Dignitatem,* which besides being the most authoritative, is the most significant document on the dignity and vocation of women.

In giving this title to the Day of Peace, the Pope has in mind all the women of the world, of all continents, of all races: white, yellow, black ... and not only Christians, but of all religions, and not only women of faith, but women of other convictions as well.

Think of the priceless gift that women are in humanity. It is enough to imagine them just as they are: in all their femininity, in their uniqueness, in their natural amiability and goodness, in their innate capacity to be a source of joy and peace for those around them and in all their grace. This is why women have been authoritatively called: "Perhaps the masterpiece of creation." And we know that those women who appear in certain television programmes or are displayed on many billboards are not representative of the women of the world today. In reality those women are a small minority in comparison with the millions and billions of women who are spouses, mothers, virgins, widows and who, unknown to many, silently give life to our society, springing up like lightning rods in the face of many calamities. The Pope is referring in particular to these women. And it is these women that today we want to honour and remember.

Still, I would like to stop for a moment to consider a new type of woman beginning to appear on the horizon of today's world. I do so because it seems to me that the title "educator and peace builder" (true peace) is attributable to her as to no other.

But let's proceed in order.

"Woman educator for peace."

First of all we might ask, who is woman and what should her characteristics be?

For many centuries now women have been asking this very question of themselves as they struggle to be what they are meant to be and reach self-fulfilment.

In recent times they have waged an all-out war in order to have their dignity recognized and to affirm their rights, which all too often have been trampled upon. And though their actions may have perplexed some, they have made progress. Of course, we are no longer in such sad times for women as were the days when Teresa of Avila — "the most saintly of women and the most womanly of saints" — asked the Lord for justice for women. She found it utterly ridiculous that "virtuous and strong hearts be disdained simply because that they belonged to women."[29]

Yes, the plight of women in the world has changed significantly and there are many signs that indicate new developments.

In contrast with times past, today there are women who are aware of their identity and who are ready to give their unique and irreplaceable contribution, in solidarity, not only among themselves, but also with men, for the future of our planet.

This of course is true for our Western culture, which, like it or not, has been deeply influenced by the Christian culture it is rooted in.

Unfortunately, we know of women in other countries and continents where Christianity has not yet arrived, whose situation in terms of self-fulfilment is pitiful, not to mention those who still live in slavery.

But we might also ask ourselves: When women have reached all their legitimate goals, will they feel truly fulfilled?

Personally, I believe that something much deeper is needed. In my opinion, in order to give a valid and honest answer to this question we need to go to the cause of this dramatic problem and find the true solution. It is useless for us women to look elsewhere. The whole question surrounding the position of women has its roots in that terrible prophecy announced in Genesis. After the event of original sin and the announcing of the punishment meted out to the man and the woman (to work by the sweat of his brow and to bring forth children in pain), the prophecy says: "He (the man) shall rule over you" (Gn 3:16).

Therefore, women will find their true fulfilment only in Christ, who by redeeming men and women returned all things to their proper order. And it is Christ who gives back the harmony that was lost in their relationship; Christ, who while here on earth, demonstrated a great love for women and thus gave back woman her true dignity.

In fact, in all his teachings and all his actions there is not a single sign of the discrimination towards women prevalent in his day. On the contrary, his words and actions always expressed the respect and honour owed to women.[30]

In order for women to truly be themselves, they need to reconsider where they stand in relation to Jesus. Today too they need to make the experience of a profound encounter with him, to discover him, just as those fortunate women of Palestine did in their day.

Today, too, it is only Jesus who can truly fulfil their longings, as it was only he who fulfilled them throughout the centuries.

Who, in fact, can deny that Catherine of Siena, Rita of Cascia, Rose of Lima, Clare of Assisi, Joan of Arc ... were successful women and totally fulfilled?

Therefore, to discover Jesus!

He, the son of God-Love, will reveal himself to women as the one who came on earth to live and die out of love and to restore everything and every creature through love. Christ came to teach love to everyone because love is the heart of his doctrine. He came to call each and every person to love: a vocation to which women are particularly inclined.

This does not mean that men are not. History offers countless examples of men who were giants in love, in divine charity. It is just that women are particularly adept in loving.

In fact, the charity that Christ brought has very specific qualities: it is concrete and it involves sacrifice.

We know that charity is not a love that is limited to feelings or even to compassion. Christian charity is authentic not when it is theoretical, but rather when it is concrete, when it becomes service, when it pours itself out to others at every opportunity. Jesus showed us what charity is when he washed the feet of his disciples. In fact, the Pope writes in *Mulieris Dignitatem* "it is commonly thought that women are more capable than men of paying attention to another person."[31]

What is more, charity is primarily sacrifice, living for others and forgetting oneself. Thus, the Pope continues in *Mulieris Dignitatem*, affirming that a woman "often succeeds in resisting suffering better than a man."[32]

But where is it possible for women today to encounter Jesus and his message once again?

We all know that the topic of women in today's world is a sign of the times. And this means that it is a sign of God's will. But God, who is Providence, does not limit himself simply to giving signs. He opens the way, gives answers, offers possibilities. And he generally does so, although not exclusively, through his Church.

In fact, the Church, which includes its leaders at the highest levels, has undertaken the task of providing an answer.

The current Pope, as well as Paul VI and previous Popes and bishops of all countries, are luminous examples. At the Synod of Bishops on the Laity I experienced personally how they raised their voices in the defence of women.*

We are also aware of the fact that there are entire episcopal conferences working, offering ideas, and doing all they can to come up with answers and make sure that answers are found.

Therefore, there are possibilities in the Church today — which also existed in the past — for women once again to experience Jesus' concern for them, to hear once more the echo of his words, to be touched by the rays of his love. In other words, it is possible for them to encounter him again and in so doing better understand themselves.

But Jesus is not present and does not show his concern for us all — and in particular today, for women — only through the channels of the hierarchy of the Church.

He is alive and can be found, for example, in the numerous Orders and Congregations founded in the Church throughout the centuries and renewed and updated after the Second Vatican Council.

He can also be found in the more recent groups, Associations and Movements that have sprung up before, during and after the Second Vatican Council, both in Italy and abroad, all of them an expression of, and a great source of hope for, the Church.

The spiritualities of these new groups in the Church have points in common to which women are particularly sensitive. Certainly, they are of interest to everyone, men and women of every social class and vocation, but they are particularly suited to laypeople and, in a special way, to women.

Coming into contact with these ecclesial realities is truly an encounter with the Lord. We come face to face with a charism of the Church, in other words, with an action of the Holy Spirit whose primary task is to remind us of what Jesus said and did.

And as a result of these gifts, people are invaded by an absolute certainty, an eternal novelty of the Good News: "God, the God revealed by Jesus, is love. He is my father and he loves me immensely."

---

* The synod took place in 1987. Chiara Lubich participated as an observer.

Through these new urgings of the Spirit, the words of the gospel and the scriptures take on a new light and we are encouraged to put them into practice.

In a special way those words relating to love, the heart of Christianity, are highlighted. For example: Jesus' new commandment, that brings peace; the words on unity in Christ, which are the summary of all his wishes, his testament, another expression for true peace; those on the need for communion; those on love for the cross, discovered as the key to understand and bring about unity and peace, because it was the price he paid to restore peace by restoring unity between human beings and God and with each another.

These charisms help us to grasp the sublime and incomparable value of the sacrifice of the Mass and the importance of the Eucharist as it relates to the unity and peace of humanity with God and among us. We love the Church not only because we understand it and obey it, but also because we live it in the deepest communion of hearts and souls, just as it was among the first Christians.

In essence, the Holy Spirit has been forging new spiritualities that meet the most modern aspirations and demands of men and women and that respond to the expectations of the Second Vatican Council.

And it is also through these charisms, which underline in such a strong way the elements of love and suffering — the cross — that women find their complete fulfilment.

Coming into contact with these Movements, as well as with other parts of the renewed Church, women today, of every country and race, can and do discover a Jesus who is alive. And just as in the times when he was physically present, they feel that his love and his message makes them new and whole.

These women can be found everywhere: at home, at work, in schools, in congresses, in theatres, in hospitals, in the structures of the Church....

On the basis of a rediscovered awareness of the equality among men and women and the dignity they both share, also in marriage, they dedicate themselves to ensuring that Jesus is always present in the family. They do this by fostering a spirit of "living one for the other" that is alive and constant among every member of the family. They resolve problems with the peaceful and unifying quality typically theirs, ironing out differences, knowing how to forgive, and sharing harmoniously tasks and responsibilities, so opening the family to all humanity.

These women also work in all areas of society. Just as in their daily lives they are accustomed to being at the service of others and attentive to those around them, in society they give a new soul to the various forms of public intervention, making structures more human and giving them new vitality.

What is more, they dedicate themselves to the most crucial humanitarian issues such as a more equitable distribution of wealth and basic human necessities, international solidarity, and the protection of the environment.

Christ living in them conquers hearts, works conversions, eliminates barriers and brings peace among people of different races and nations, among rich and poor. They work towards bringing a greater unity and collaboration among all the members of the Church.

They are also capable of initiating fruitful dialogues with Christians of other Churches, with the faithful of other religions and with people of goodwill.

They understand that the history of humanity is a slow and arduous discovery of universal brotherhood in Christ, and they work in order to see it fulfilled on all levels.

In this commitment to living love, the greatest of all charisms, these women feel especially close to Mary, whom they see as their model.

In the apostolic letter *Mulieris Dignitatem*, the Pope speaking of women, recalls the figure of Mary, the mother of God, the *Theotokos*[33] and tells of the extraordinary dignity to which God raises women in Mary.

He points out that although all men and women are called to union with God, Mary fulfils this call in a way that is unparalleled. That is why Mary is "the woman"; she represents the entire human race, the prototype of every man and every woman. On the other hand, he continues, in the *Theotokos* there exists "a form of union with the living God which can only belong to the 'woman'… the union between mother and son."[34] Therefore, Mary reaches the fullness of perfection also in "what is characteristic of woman."[35] She is, therefore, in a special way, the prototype of women.

Thus, women who live their vocation out to the fullest, with the faith, nobility and love of Mary, can reveal to the Church the "Marian dimension of the life of Christ's disciples."[36] They can give their contribution to manifesting and keeping alive that Marian profile of the Church which the Pope speaks of from time and which he has declared to be "just as fundamental and characteristic, if not more so … as the apostolic and Petrine profile."[37]

Therefore, there are women who are a real hope and example for many, because the Holy Spirit is at work in their favour. And who knows what surprises he is still preparing in the heart of the Church and beyond?

As we enter the third millennium may Mary help women know how to love and how to suffer. Both are unlimited sources of joy. Both are conditions for becoming builders of unity and peace.[38]

In the School of Jesus: Philosophy and Theology

> From two talks given during the conferral of honorary doctorate degrees in philosophy (Jean-Baptiste de La Salle University, Mexico City, 6 June 1997) and in theology (University of Santo Tomas, Manila, 14 January, 1997).

I thought to begin by recounting very simply some episodes of my life when I was a young woman, in the times when my studies, and in particular philosophy, were the ideal of my life.

I could think of nothing that satisfied my heart and mind more than to study with ancient and contemporary philosophers in search of the truth.

But having been brought up as a Christian and perhaps also driven by an impulse of the Spirit, I realized very early on that I was attracted most of all by one very profound longing: to know God.

I was convinced therefore that if I attended a Catholic university I would have satisfied this yearning.

Since I was unable to afford the tuition due to my family's precarious financial situation, I decided to take part in a competitive scholarship examination that offered student grants to a limited number of Italian girls.

When I learned that I had not qualified for a grant I was terribly disappointed and cried inconsolably.

Then, all of a sudden, as my mother was trying to comfort me, something odd happened. I seemed to perceive in the depths of my soul something like a subtle voice that said to me: "I will be your teacher!" And immediately I was at peace.

I was a practicing Catholic and a daily communicant.

One day I had an intuition.

"How can this be?" I asked myself, "You are looking for the truth? Isn't there a person who claimed to be the truth in person? Didn't Jesus say of himself: 'I am the truth'?"

This was one of the first things that made me seek the truth not so much in books, but in Jesus. And I resolved to follow him.

Following that, in 1943, God's providence gave life to what would later be known as the Focolare Movement.

I went on to attend a state university, but because of the growing demands of the Movement that was coming to life, I was forced to suspend my studies on fourteen different occasions. Until one day I decided to put aside my beloved books and store them in the attic once and for all.

But I did keep one book: the gospel.

In the midst of the raging war I carried it with me into the bomb shelters and read it together with my friends.

And it was amazing! Those words, which we had heard so many times before, took on a profound meaning, a singular beauty; they shone out as if a bright light were illuminating each one.

They were different from other words, even from those found in the best spiritual books. They were universal and therefore spoke to everyone: young people, adults, men, women, Italians, Koreans, Ecuadorians, Nigerians.... They were eternal words and therefore suited to all times, including ours. And they could be put into practice. They were written with divine artistry. They impelled people to translate them into life.

While the entire gospel attracted us, to the point of considering it to be the rule of the newly born Movement, that light (now we can say, that charism) led us to emphasize, and especially make our own, those words which, like links in a chain, would become the key ideas of a new spirituality of the Church: the spirituality of unity.

These main ideas are:
- God, the new ideal of our life who in midst of the horrors of the war, the fruit of hatred, revealed himself to us for what he truly is: love;
- to do God's will, putting into practice his words and thus giving us the opportunity to respond to his love with our love;
- to commit ourselves to love our neighbours, especially the needy, as the commandment that sums up all the law and the prophets;
- to live mutual love in a radical way, putting into practice the "new" commandment characteristic of Jesus;
- as a consequence to reach unity with him and with our brothers and sisters, as we understand from his prayer for unity;
- to live with Jesus among us. For he promised to be present among those, even if just two or three, who unite in his name, that is, in his love;
- to love the cross, keeping the gaze of our soul fixed on Jesus crucified in that moment of his terrible forsakenness. In him, as I will say later, we discovered the key to unity.

We do all of this, nourishing ourselves daily with the Eucharist, the bond of unity; living the Church, especially as "communion"; imitating Mary, "Mother of unity," in her desolation; allowing ourselves to be guided by the Holy Spirit, the personification of love in the Trinity as well as bond of unity among the members of the Mystical Body of Christ....

And if we look closely we will discover, perhaps for the first time in the history of the Church, the birth of a spirituality that is more communitarian than individual in nature. In other words, one that leads not only individuals, but also many, in fact, a whole people to a life of perfection. This kind of holiness, we realize more and more, is surprisingly suited to our times....[39]

We have always been aware and it has been our conviction that what is born in the Church must be in full communion with its tradition and Magisterium. Therefore, a few decades after the Movement's birth, towards the seventies, we wished to compare the main points of our spirituality, as they were understood and lived out, with what had been said by the Fathers of the Church, the Ecumenical Councils, saints, Popes and great theologians.

We were overjoyed in finding a remarkable consonance with the Church's teachings and also in being able to confirm that, while having our own characteristic way of thinking and acting, we were one and the same with our Mother: the Church.

Consequently, we acquired a deeper and more enlightened understanding of all of the Church's doctrine. Steeping ourselves in that doctrine has helped each of us — we hope — to be formed and to grow as souls who are Church.

In recent years, however, we have come to realize that a unique doctrine is emerging from this new way of life, this experience of ours. While it remains anchored in the eternal truth of revelation, it also develops and renews theological tradition.

After all, it is not the first time that this has happened in the history of the Church.

Did not the Holy Spirit draw out a new doctrine from the experience of St. Francis, entrusting it specifically to St. Bonaventure, Blessed Duns Scotus, etc.?

And besides being the *doctor communis* [the universal theologian], is not St. Thomas Aquinas also the theologian of the order founded by St. Dominic?

Likewise, we too (although it is not so much we but God who is at work), after almost fifty years of life, have seen a similar possibility present itself.

The presence of the late Bishop Klaus Hemmerle, a well-known, profound and modern German theologian and philosopher together with Focolarini who are scholars in their various fields has given rise to the so-called Abba School.

The members of the Abba School study, among other things, the intuitions or illuminations regarding the range and depth of faith that the Holy Spirit suggested to us in 1949, not long after the birth of the Movement.

And we need to give thanks to God, for when we dedicate ourselves to study these intuitions with the presence of Jesus among us, as is characteristic in the Movement, we often find ourselves immersed in a light that comes from above. It is an expression of the wisdom that Jesus spoke of in thanking the Father for having hidden it from the wise and revealing it to the little ones.[40]

The charism of unity and theology

A new theology and, at the same time, a new philosophy are emerging from the life of the charism of unity. What are the main points of this theology?

Today I would like to recall some of them even if they certainly do not exhaust all the areas of studies and research that are in process.

I am referring to God who is love, unity, Jesus crucified and forsaken, and Mary.

First of all, God who is love. Pope John Paul II affirmed that love was the inspiring spark of the spirituality that God has given us.[41] The same can be said of for our theology.

Obviously, it is not just any love, but *agape*, God's love, love that is God. Therefore, we could say that the origin of our experience of life and of the theology that emerges from it is the same as that of the Christian faith: "We have known and believe the love that God has for us. God is love" (1 Jn 4:16).

God is Love. The novelty of the Christian revelation is summed up in this confession of faith from the New Testament. It reveals in an unprecedented way the depth of the self-revelation of God in the Old Testament: "I am who I am" (Ex 3:14), and, at the same time, brings those seeds of the Word scattered in the various religions to their unexpected fruition.

Love: not only one of God's attributes, rather his very being. And because he is love, God is one and triune at the same time: Father, Son and Holy Spirit.

Jesus reveals that the essence of the Trinity is love and he does so in particular in the moment of his passion. In his passion Jesus arrives at the point of absolute self-annihilation and even death, which then bears fruit in the resurrection and the outpouring of the Spirit.

The Father generates the Son out of love; he "loses himself" in him, he lives in him. In a certain sense he makes himself "non-being" out of love and in so doing he is, he is Father. The Son, who is the echo of the Father, returns to the Father out of love, he "loses himself" in him, he lives in him. In a certain sense he makes himself "non-being" out of love and in so doing he is; he is Son. The Holy Spirit who is the love that circulates between the Father and the Son, their bond of unity, also in a certain sense makes himself "non-being" out of love and thus is; he is the Holy Spirit.

Very closely linked to the first essential point of this new theology is the second: unity.

Since the early days of the Movement Jesus' words in his prayer for unity struck like a bolt of lightning: "that they may all be one. As you, Father, are in me and I am in you, may they also be in us, so that the world may believe that you have sent" (Jn 17:21).

In attempting to put them into practice, we discovered that these words unleashed a light that illuminated God's design of love for humanity.

As we understood it, Jesus is the Word of God made man in order to teach us to live according to the model of trinitarian life, the same life he lives in the bosom of the Father.

He was not content with simply underlining and linking to one another the two fundamental commandments of the Old Testament: "You shall love the Lord, your God, with all your heart, with all your soul, and with all your mind…. You shall love your neighbour as yourself" (Mt 22:37-39). Instead, he teaches us the commandment which he himself does not hesitate to call "his" and "new," and by means of which we can live the life of the Trinity here on earth: "Love one another as I have loved you" (see Jn 13:34; 15:12).

The commandment of mutual love lived according to the example of Jesus' love for us, to the point of forsakenness that makes us one in him, defines — as the Second Vatican Council also emphasizes[42] — the very vision of humankind that Jesus reveals to us and that is the heart of Christian anthropology.

Therefore, when we live the new commandment, striving to welcome the Father's gift of unity in Jesus, the life of the Trinity is no longer lived only in the inner life of the individual but flows freely among the members of the Mystical Body of Christ.

In this way, the Mystical Body can become in all its fullness what it already is by the grace of faith and the sacraments, in particular the Eucharist: the presence of the risen Christ in history who lives in each one of his disciples and among them (see Mt 18:20).

And now the third point: Jesus crucified and forsaken.

It was the Holy Spirit, we believe, before leading us into the mystery of unity, who concentrated our faith and all of our love in Jesus who ... in an insuperable climax of love and suffering, cries out from the cross: "My God, my God, why have you forsaken me?" (Mk 15:34; Mt 27:46).

In that moment he experienced the most profound separation that can ever be imagined; in a sense, he experienced being separated from his Father with whom he was and remained one. At the same time, he gives all humankind a new and fuller unity than the one lost through sin: he reunites all with one another and with God in a new unity, which is a participation in his unity with the Father and with us. Therefore, Jesus forsaken is the key to understanding and living out unity.

In fact, those who wish to bring about unity must keep in mind and love Jesus forsaken (right from the very beginning this was the name we gave to Jesus in this mystery that sums up and is central to his redemptive mission). We must love him in a radical way, just as St Paul who affirmed: "For I resolved to know nothing while I was with you except Jesus Christ, and him crucified" (1 Cor 2:2).

Scripture tells us that in his forsakenness Jesus made himself "sin" (see 2 Cor 5:21), "cursed" (see Gal 3:13) in order to make himself one with those who are far from God.

This is why Jesus forsaken seems to be the God of our times. He is heaven's response to the terrible chasm of sufferings and trials cut deep into the hearts of men and women by the atheism permeating many aspects of our modern culture; by the extreme poverty of millions of displaced people; by the quest for meaning and ideals of the disillusioned and confused new generations.

Jesus forsaken is the God of our times also because he is a reflection of the division that exists between the Churches, a division that today we are more conscious of than ever.

But precisely discovering his face in these divisions gives us the hope that we can make a vital contribution to the process of reunification.

In particular we have the sense that Jesus forsaken "who, though he was in the form of God ... emptied himself," as Paul writes (Phil 2:6-7), has opened a providential way for dialogue with the faithful of the religious traditions of the East, one of the more difficult and pressing frontiers at the dawn of the third millennium.

And finally, Mary. We feel that she cannot be considered merely as one point of our theology among many, even if an important one.

For many reasons: perhaps because our Movement is her work, the Work of Mary; perhaps because many signs of the times and official statements by the Magisterium indicate the emerging "Marian profile" of the Church; perhaps because we are witnessing the surprising phenomenon of the figure of Mary being recognized by other religious traditions, we foresee the heralding of a new and original season of reflection on the person of Mary.

And we believe that this reflection should explore Mary's role in the context of God's universal design of salvation for all of humanity and the cosmos. In fact, as John Paul II recently said, Mary is "an integral part of the economy of communicating the Trinity to mankind."[43]

She is the mother of the Word of God made man, which places her in a unique and extraordinary relationship with all the persons of the Holy Trinity (see Lk 1:35).

This, above all else, is Mary's true greatness, which "magnifies" the greatness of God and his works.

But Mary is also the mother of the Church. She generated the Son of God in the flesh by the power of the Holy Spirit. Likewise, sharing as no one else in the redemption through her desolation at the foot of the cross (see Jn 19:25-27), she shares in a real way in the regeneration of the children of God that the Holy Spirit has brought about in the womb of the Church.

Having fully carried out God's design for her, Mary now lives in heaven. She is the flower and the first fruit of the Church and of creation, which in her is already Christified and divinized. In a certain way, we can think of her as being set into the Trinity, through grace, the icon and expression of all creation.

In fact, since in God there is a perfect perichoresis* among the three divine Persons, and because, through Christ, in the Spirit, there is also a perichoresis brought about between the Trinity and humanity, apex and synthesis of creation: "You ... loved them even as you loved me" (Jn 17:23) — all creation, recapitulated in Christ, is also destined to be, as Mary already is, eternally set into the Trinity: that is, to live and rejoice infinitely in the intimate life of God, in the ever new and unending dynamism of the trinitarian relationships.

We have the impression that, as I hope to have shown, the doctrine that emerges from this charism of unity sheds a new light on the core of revelation.

Our theologians, in fact, quoting von Balthasar, recall that: "Charisms such as those of Augustine, Francis, Ignatius can receive, as gifts of the

---

* The mutual indwelling of the Persons of the Trinity.

Spirit, glimpses into the centre of revelation that enrich the Church in very unexpected and yet everlasting ways. They are always charisms in which intelligence, love and discipleship are inseparable. Here we realize that the Holy Spirit is at once divine wisdom and divine love, and is never simply pure theory but must be lived out in practice."[44]

Above all, these theologians point out that those who study this doctrine have the possibility of participating in Jesus, or as St Augustine says,[45] of becoming one with him. And this is perhaps because in constantly striving to live according to this charism of unity, they remain united in the name of Jesus, and therefore he is present among them; and also because they are nourished daily by Jesus-Eucharist.

Therefore, one of the novelties that seems to emerge from this charism lived out in this way is that the theology derived from it is not just a theology regarding Jesus, but rather a theology of Jesus: of Jesus present in and among theologians.

In fact, they point out that up until now in Christian reflection the predominant approach has been to look at Jesus as the "object" of theological study. Obviously, there was always the awareness that such an "object" — the Son of God made man — required an adequate knowing subject, that is, reason illuminated by faith, a Christified reason.

In the past, nonetheless, particularly in the recent past, the theology elaborated by most theologians of Western cultures was thought of primarily as a reflection on God and on Jesus rather than as a participation, through faith and love, in Jesus' knowledge of the Father. Of course there are, just to take Western examples, some exceptions among theologians who had gifts of the Spirit and often were saints, such as Anselm of Canterbury, Bernard of Clairveaux, Thomas Aquinas, Bonaventure, and even earlier, in both the East and West, the Fathers of the Church. But in general it was a knowledge sought almost "from outside" rather than from within the mystery being considered. Instead, as Jesus said: "No one knows the Son except the Father, and no one knows the Father except the Son and anyone to whom the Son chooses to reveal him" (Mt 11:27).

Jesus gives this knowledge to his Mystical Body by way of the Spirit. And it is received in all its fullness when we are "one" in him (see Gal 3:28), almost one "mystical person."[46]

Thus, through this charism of unity, the necessary condition is present for the rebirth of a great theology of Jesus: clearly not the Jesus of 2000 years ago, but the Jesus who lives today in the Church.

And from this discovery comes a second novelty. Given that this theology is a theology *of* Jesus, who has ascended to the bosom of the Father and who lives today in unity which is the Church, it sees things from a new perspective: the viewpoint of the *One*, in other words, from God, where everything is in its true reality.

Therefore it is "one" perspective, side by side with others and so not excluding them; on the contrary it presupposes them and gives them value. But at the same time it could also offer them a unique contribution. It could integrate them and lead them to unity, thus opening new horizons for them.

Furthermore, since in a certain sense, as we already mentioned, it is a theology of Jesus, in whom all created realities are recapitulated, it could also shed light on the various sciences, making them truer and more genuine.

In fact, we could hope to see theology return to being the mother of all sciences and even their queen — different from the sense this had in the Middle Ages — not destroying their legitimate autonomy, but leading them back to their true root and their true purpose....[47]

The charism of unity and philosophy

There is also a new philosophy that emerges from the life of the charism of unity.

Philosophy sometimes is called the science of the question "why" in the sense that it seeks to explore in depth whatever men and women ask about and, as much as possible, to give an answer.

After years of intense spiritual life, living this new spirituality, we realized that there is a moment in Jesus' life that is pregnant with answers to all our "whys."

It is the moment before he dies, when Jesus addresses his immense "why" to the Father and unleashes that mysterious cry: "My God, my God, why have you forsaken me?"

Initially, however, when we decided to follow him in this way, we did not feel prompted so much to meditate on or to formulate the doctrine that may lie beneath his being forsaken. Instead, we immediately discovered his forsakenness as the key to recomposing every unity....

It was placing Jesus forsaken as the ideal of our life that gave us the courage to run wherever he was most present and, by loving him, by consuming him in ourselves, we worked to relieve sufferings and to build unity. But Jesus forsaken did not present himself to us only as the answer to the existential questions of humanity.

He is God who asks God "why," who asks the reason for a severed relationship that seems to touch the very unity of God! He is certainly the question, so to speak, carried to its deepest, most radical expression, where no human question dares to go. Thus, he seems to be the one who best represents human intelligence in the face of mystery.

At the same time, he cries out his great "why" precisely in order to give us the answer to the many "whys" which are more properly the object of philosophical reflection, as the Abba School seeks to point out.

I will give two examples of this reflection, briefly and simply.

Let us consider the first: the mystery of being.

What answer does he give us?

Though there may be a number of ways of defining it according to various cultures, in essence, the fundamental affirmation of human thought is: being is. It is the acknowledgment of that great ocean of existence in which human beings are immersed in communion with everyone and everything.

This is the simplest, single, and primordial certainty from which we can then begin to penetrate the multiple and complex layers of reality.

Everything can be negated, except being.

We find being in whatever is near us, beside us (all the various realities) and within us (our inner life).

The existence itself of things, from the smallest to the greatest things, tells us that being is.

This being — which all things have in common and for which they are not simply a nothingness — reveals, in a natural manifestation, that Being which none of them is, but which they all announce. Their becoming, their limits, their very ceasing to exist is the language in which it is stated that the being of all that exists is rooted in a Being that simply and absolutely *IS*.

Referring to the sun, St. Francis said, with the language of a poet and the profundity of a mystic: "Bearing thy likeness, O Most High, he points to thee."

This can be an analogy for our inner life. The awareness human beings have had of themselves from the very beginnings of philosophical reflection, especially if enlightened by faith, is the acknowledgement of being. This being is a light and, at the same time, a confession of the Absolute Being, of the most pure Light which knows neither shadow nor error, and which is invoked and sought by the very light that shines forth in the consciousness of human beings, as its guarantee, certainty, and final destination.

So for human beings to say "I" is equivalent to opening oneself to being able to say, in communion with the being of all things, that the Absolute Being is.

And yet, the course of philosophy in the West has witnessed the clouding over of these initial certainties. Consciousness of self has been — and is — lived as negating the objectivity of being. And it has closed itself off from the Absolute Being.

This has led to the great crisis that has marked recent centuries.

Now we could ask ourselves: is it true that consciousness of self and being — as the affirmation of reality in itself to the point of acknowledging the Absolute Being — cannot co-exist?

Or rather, are we not called by this very crisis to examine in-depth both the concept of the conscious subject and that of being in all its breadth? And in this way to understand that ultimately the difficulty of our times lies in a reluctance to call upon a new, more fully developed solution, in which the specific gift of Christianity shines forth in all its power?

And precisely here Jesus forsaken presents himself as the master of light, of thought, and — I would dare to say — of *philosophy*.

There may be those who think that to affirm self implies a struggle against all that is not self, because what is not self is perceived as a limit and, what is more, as a threat to the integrity of self. But in that terrible moment of his passion, Jesus forsaken tells us that though the consciousness of his subjectivity appears to be diminishing as he is, as it were, made nothing, in that very moment it reaches its fullness.

With his being reduced to nothing, accepted out of love for the Father to whom he re-abandons himself ("Into your hands I commend my spirit" [Lk 23:46]), Jesus shows us that I am myself, not when I close myself off from the other, but rather when I give myself, when out of love I lose myself in the other. If, for example, I have a flower and I give it to someone, certainly I deprive myself of it, and in depriving myself, I am losing something of myself (non-being); in reality, precisely because I give that flower, love grows in me (i.e., being). Therefore, my subjectivity is when it is not, out of love; that is, when out of love it is completely transferred into the other.

Jesus forsaken is the greatest revelation of consciousness, understood as self-affirmation, precisely when he gives himself to the other, to an otherness that, at its greatest extent, in fact, is being. Genuine consciousness of self is born from the communion with being: a communion in which consciousness seems to lose itself but, in reality, it finds itself, it is.

Jesus forsaken thus enlightens being, revealing it as love. And with this he reveals to us that the Absolute Being is itself love, as affirmed in the first letter of John (see 1 Jn 4:8,12).

It is love precisely in the dynamic relationship that exists among the three divine Persons, One with the Other, One for the Other, One in the Other.

There are three Persons in the most Holy Trinity, and yet they are One because love is not and is at the same time.

In the relationship of the three divine Persons, each one is love, each one is completely, by not being: because each one is, perichoretically, in the other Person, in eternal self-giving.

In the light of the Trinity, being reveals itself, if we can say this, as guarding deep within itself the non-being that is gift of self: not the non-being that negates being, rather the non-being that reveals being as love: *being that is the three divine Persons*.

In the light of Jesus forsaken the subject, the being of all created things and the Absolute Being itself, find a new explanation that can serve as the basis for a new philosophy of being.

This was the hope of great thinkers of our times, like Maritain and Przywara, who foresaw the possibility of progressing in the search for the truth precisely on the basis of the understanding of being as love, as is revealed in the cross of Christ.[48]

A second point I would like to touch on concerns the significance of creation.

In Hebrew-Christian revelation the world is seen as the creation of God, of a personal God, and therefore destined to have a lasting relationship with him.

Thus, the world has a value in and of itself as well as its own autonomy, which becomes effective in the history of that personal subject which is the human being who has been endowed with the gift of dialoguing directly with God and with other human beings. What is more, the world finds its eschatological fulfilment in the person of the Word incarnate and risen, the only *You* of the Father, who recapitulates all in himself.

Then, according to Revelation, the world should be seen as filled with the presence of God in his Word, through the Spirit.

In the history of Western society, this Christian concept of the world has gradually replaced the mythological vision. In the process, however, the Christian conception has been marked by a cultural crisis that in these times has given rise to various phenomena such as secularism, post-modernism, and the loss of the sacred.

Consequently, we no longer understand how God can fill the world with himself. For people of Western societies, the world has gradually become empty of meaning. And the same holds true, according to some schools of thought, for time and history.

Gone is the intelligence of love capable of grasping the truth and beauty of creation *from its origins*, from God who contains it and nourishes it with himself. Instead, it has been replaced by a sceptical and cold rationality that moves *among* things without penetrating into their deepest roots.

The groaning of creation, of which St. Paul speaks (Rm 8:22), seems no longer to be heard. It has been covered by what Heidegger called the "idle chatter of existence," and therefore of an "inauthentic" culture.[49]

Are we up against an irreversible crisis?

Or rather the slow coming to birth of a new world?

Here, too, Jesus forsaken provides a light for understanding and living the meaning of this drama.

Jesus forsaken experienced in himself and took upon himself the non-being of all those separated from the source of being: he took upon himself the "vanity of vanities" (Eccl 1:2).

Out of love, he made his own this non-being that we can call negative and transformed it into himself, into the positive non-being that is love, as revealed in the resurrection. Jesus forsaken made the Holy Spirit overflow into creation, thus becoming "mother" of the new creation.

Certainly, this event is *still* in the process of developing: but in the risen Christ, and in Mary assumed into heaven with him, it is already accomplished. In a certain sense, it is already a reality for the Church, his Mystical Body.

If we live in mutual love, which brings Christ among us, and we are nourished by the Eucharist, which makes us become Christ as a community and as individuals, and therefore Church, we can perceive the penetration of the Spirit of God into the heart of all beings, into each one and into the entire cosmos.

And through the Holy Spirit we intuit the existence of a nuptial relationship between the Uncreated and created because in becoming incarnate, the Word aligned himself with creation thereby divinizing it and recapitulating it in himself.

This wide and majestic vision makes us think of the entrance of all creation one day into the bosom of the Father.

And we can already see several signs.

For example, when we die and our body is consigned to the earth, if it has been nourished by the Eucharist and therefore Christified, can it not be considered Eucharist for nature? This being the case, our body, although apparently transformed into earth, in reality acts mysteriously as a seed for the transfiguration of the cosmos into "new heavens and new earth" (Is 66:22; 2 Pt 3:13).

Certainly, these new heavens and new earth are still far from their full realization, but we can already see them developing in the heart of creation if we look at it with the eyes of the Risen Jesus who lives in us and among us.

This sheds a new light upon and opens up the relationship between people and the world, of which the capacity to transform things through work and technology is just one aspect.

As a result of our experience we feel confident in affirming that the most profound intuitions (whether in the fields of thought, art, science, or of practical projects), when understood in the light of that unity among us by which the presence of the Risen Jesus in our midst makes us participate in his thought (see 1 Cor 2:16), can offer a glimpse into this overflowing of the Spirit of God into all things.

Your Excellencies, Ladies and Gentlemen, here are a few words about my passionate journey towards Jesus, Word of the Father, and how he, especially in his forsakenness, can be a light for us all.[50]

Persons in Communion

Jesus the teacher

> From "The Family and Education," an address to the New Families Movement, Castel Gandolfo, Italy, 2 May 1987.

When speaking of education, we naturally find ourselves before two subjects: the educator or teacher who must teach and educate, and the student to be educated.

Regarding educators or teachers, there is a statement made by Jesus in the gospel that causes us to stop and think and that can shed light on education in the family. It says: "You have one teacher, and you are all students" (Mt 23:8).

For Jesus there is only one teacher: he himself.

This does not mean that Jesus is denying the authority of parents. He is saying that this role should be carried out as a service and not as means to domineer or exert power. Because in serving, which is the same as loving, it is not only the human being who acts; rather it is Christ, and therefore Christ is truly the first teacher.

If Jesus is the teacher then Christian parents have the duty to look to him in order to learn how to educate.

But what kind of teacher was Jesus?

There are several important characteristics that come to mind when looking at Jesus in his role as teacher.

First of all, Jesus teaches by example. He incarnates his doctrine in his very person. He does not impose burdens on others that he has not carried first: "Woe also to you lawyers! For you load people with burdens hard to bear, and you yourselves do not lift a finger to ease them" (Lk 11:46). Jesus puts into practice what he then asks of others.

With Jesus as our model we realize that the first method in educating, also for parents, should not simply be setting out to instruct or correct, but to live out one's Christianity radically. Parents must first put into practice themselves what they ask of their children. Do they ask for sincerity, commitment, loyalty, obedience, charity towards their brothers and sisters, chastity, patience, forgiveness? Then their children should be able to find all these qualities first of all in them.

Mothers and fathers must be indisputable models that their children can always refer to.

Another characteristic of Jesus' way of educating is that he concretely comes to the aid of his friends as, for example, when he calmed the storm on the lake (see Lk 8:24).

Parents, who already by nature do all they can for their children, could do much more, and above all much better, if they engrafted supernatural love onto their human love, if they loved with the love that comes from God, a love that takes the initiative, without expecting anything in return. This kind of love never leaves people indifferent.

Jesus puts faith in those he teaches. It is evident in his words to the woman taken in adultery: "Go …" he says, "and from now on do not sin again" (Jn 8:11). He believes that it is possible for that woman to begin a morally upright life.

Jesus leaves us free to take responsibility and make decisions. We see this in his encounter with the rich young man (see Mt 19:16 ff.).

We must never impose our ideas, but rather offer them with love, as an expression of love.

Children are first of all sons and daughters of God and not ours. Therefore, they should not be treated as our possessions, but as people who have been entrusted to our care.

When necessary, Jesus does not hesitate to rebuke with firmness and strength. To Peter, who wanted to stop him from facing his passion, he says: "Get behind me, Satan! … You are setting your mind not on divine things but on human things" (Mt 16:23).

Yes, discipline is also necessary. It is an integral part of education. In fact, in the book of Proverbs (13:24) it is written: "Those who love them [their children] are diligent to discipline them." God, father and teacher, formed the Jewish people and educated them using instruction and discipline.

Woe to those who do not exert discipline! What an omission they will be responsible for!

A statement made by the prophet Ezekiel is quite strong in this regard: "If … you do not speak to warn the wicked to turn from their ways, the wicked shall die in their iniquity, but their blood I will require at your hand" (Ez 33:8).

Therefore, it is the parents' duty to discipline their children. If admonishment is given with peace, calm, and detachment it will make an impression upon the children's sense of responsibility and they will remember it.

In the marvellous parable of the prodigal son, Jesus shows us the Father's mercy — and therefore also his — towards those who repent and return to doing good.

Parents should treat their children as God treats us.

In a family, the mercy shown by the mother and father must reach the point of knowing how to forget and to "bear all things" (1 Cor 13:7), in conformity with God's love.

Reiterated comments about past mistakes are not in line with Jesus' teaching. We can understand, therefore, why they are not accepted.

Jesus teaches in the synagogues, on the mountaintop, along the streets of Galilee and of Judea, in the Temple in Jerusalem.

Therefore, any place is appropriate for parents to teach their children.

Jesus' way of expressing himself, even though using the style of his times, is new: he speaks in a way that is alive, imaginative, concrete, to the point, precise. He avoids being verbose and often states in a single sentence all that needs to be said on a topic.

The family must do the same. Young people do not want to hear long "sermons." It is enough to say a few words inspired by a true, pure and disinterested love.

Jesus also makes use of dialogue, alternating questions and answers; he uses proverbs and, with the scribes and Pharisees, he argues.

The dialogue between parents and children of all ages must never be interrupted. It should be open, peaceful and constructive, as among friends.

It often happens that, despite having grown up in a family where the parents give witness to a life lived according to the gospel, one or another of the children drift away from the family and at times even from their faith. Even in such cases we should never sever the relationship, no matter what path in life they may have chosen to take: perhaps adopting belief systems that have nothing to do with God, perhaps a life of drugs, or of experiences that are in sweeping contrast to the moral teaching they had received in the family.

The fact is that, especially in our Western world, we are immersed in a secularized society in which traditional values are no longer given the same importance they once were.

At the same time, other values are emerging, such as a greater consciousness of personal freedom, the thrill of scientific and technological progress, the overcoming of cultural and national barriers, a new understanding of the role of women in society, etc. Therefore, in order to dialogue with their children, parents need a great capacity for discernment that takes into account the new context in which their children live and that is able to recognize the "signs of the times" manifested by some of their new demands.

Jesus, in educating the people around him, does not hesitate in turning the existing value system upside down. This is evident when he announces the Beatitudes (see Mt 5:2 ff.). In fact, he calls blessed those who do not appear to be so. He presents a path that is difficult to travel and that goes against the current of the one offered by the world.

We too must have the courage to proclaim what really matters in life.

We should not fool ourselves into thinking that if we present a feeble Christianity, a Christ that does not exist, our proposals will be more readily accepted. God makes himself known in the hearts of our children. They react positively only to the truth. But it must be presented in a way that is both accessible and acceptable, presented by parents who, before teaching, have made the effort to understand and share the true needs and desires of the new generations.

The gospel shows us a Jesus who speaks "as one having authority" (Mt 7:29).

Parents need to trust in the grace they have been given as parents and should never shrink from their task as educators. Deep down this is what their children ask of them. In fact, it often happens that children will judge their parents, at times mercilessly, for not having had the courage to tell them the truth.

Jesus educates his disciples by passing on to them "his" typical teaching: "This is my commandment, that you love one another as I have loved you" (Jn 15:12). By specifying that "as I have loved you," he indicates that he is the "teacher" of this love.

It is the teaching par excellence, the gospel in a nutshell, which parents must pass on to their children.

In putting this teaching into practice, parents must imitate Jesus so well that they can repeat to their children that commandment as if it were their own: My little children, love one another as I have loved you.

Therefore, imitate Jesus.

Imitate him as teacher.

Imitate Jesus, or better still, allow him to live in us.

Yes, it would be best that he himself take his place within us.

If he lives in us, our performance as teachers will be irreproachable. If we introduce him as educator into our families, we will have carried out our mission perfectly.[51]

The charism of unity and education

> From an address during the conferral of an honorary doctorate in Education, The Catholic University of America, Washington, D.C., 10 November 2000.

As I have said on other occasions, our Movement can also be viewed from a theological, philosophical, cultural, social, economic or pedagogical perspective, as well as from an ecumenical or inter-religious one. Let me share with you now some of the ways that the more significant points of this spirituality have had an impact in the area of education.

In fact, our Movement and the various stages of its development can be viewed as one continuous, extraordinary educational event. All the necessary factors are present, including an educational theory and a well-defined teaching method that underlies our efforts to educate.

But first let us ask ourselves: what is education? Education can be defined as the itinerary that a subject (either singly or as a community) pursues with the help of one or more educators, moving towards a goal considered worthwhile both for the individual and for humanity.

What then are the characteristic elements of our educational method, which emerge from the main points of the spirituality we live?

Let us consider the first point: the "revelation" — if I may use this term — of God as Love. We see that from the beginning of our Movement there has been only one *educator*, the Educator par excellence: God who is Love, God who is our Father. It was he who took the initiative. *With the intentionality* characteristic of a true educator, he has accompanied us, renewed us and given us new life along an intensely rich itinerary of formation, both personal and communal.

He has enabled us and countless others to rediscover the true meaning of the greatest Fatherhood there is: a discovery of enormous importance, considering the various attempts in Western culture to affirm — on theoretical and practical levels — that "God is dead." There has been an eclipse of God's Fatherhood that has also contributed to an eclipse of the father figure, causing a loss of authority on the level of human and educational relationships. This has led to a moral relativism and an absence of rules in the life of the individual, as well as in interpersonal and social relationships. This often leads to grave consequences such as violence and the like, as if to agree with Dostoyevsky that "killing God is the most horrific form of suicide" … and "If God does not exist, then everything is permitted."

We have had the grace to come to know God. God is Love, and certainly not a distant judge, or a jealous enemy who uses his power to destroy us, or who does not take care of us. On the contrary, he is an educator who acknowledges each person's unique and distinctive identity, extolling the human being. He loves human beings, and this is why he is also demanding. As an authentic educator he demands and educates people in responsibility and commitment. God is love. For this reason he freed us from the greatest slavery of all, and re-opened the doors of his home to us. And we know the price his Son paid for our ransom. No educator has ever considered human beings as highly as a God who died for them. God who is love has raised each and every human person to the highest possible dignity: the dignity of being his child and heir. Each and every person!

It was precisely upon this understanding that we are all children of the same father that Comenius,* that great figure in modern educational theory, based his core idea: we must "teach everything to everyone."

Another key point of our spirituality is the Word of God.

"Teach everything to everyone." But in order to do so, one must use — as Comenius himself said — the educational principle of proceeding step by step. Thinking about it now, it seems that the Father suggested this method to us from the very first days of the Movement. He prompted us to live his word, choosing one sentence at a time from the gospel each month to be put it into practice in our daily lives.

But this immediately gave us "everything," because Jesus is present in his entirety in each word of the gospel (and when we live his word, he lives in us). At the same time, we were like children being nourished on his word and the more we were clothed in it, the more we grew into adults in faith and in life.

Through this very simple educational technique, which combines proceeding step by step with imparting knowledge in full, the light of this Ideal of life has spread and continues to spread far beyond the Movement as a powerful spiritual and educational experience that is constantly expanding.

---

* Comenius (1592-1670), an important figure in the Reformation, was from Moravia (in the present-day Czech Republic). Among his interests was education, and he attempted the first systematic understanding of pedagogy as a science.

The uniqueness of the word of God lies in its being *the word of life*, a word that becomes experience in a world frequently tarnished, even in education, by an abundance of empty words.

And we have experienced the power to educate, to offer alternatives, to challenge carried by this word, which is always alive and always new. Bit by bit, as it was impressed upon our lives, it gave them (and this is the tremendous task of education) an *existential unity*. This unity helped us overcome the fracturing and fragmentation that people often experience in relation to themselves, to others, to society, to God, while at the same time drawing out the originality, the unrepeatable uniqueness of each person.

Precisely because of this *existential unity* between word and life, between saying and doing, many people have found our experience credible and convincing. This experience provokes profound changes in people on an existential level, thereby setting in motion a true educational process.

The will of God is another point of our spirituality.

Faithfulness to the word of God also taught us to "put aside our base will," all those desires that still tie us to the narrow behavioural patterns of the self-centred "I." It helped us instead to follow the will of God, which leads us to transcend ourselves continually, in a movement beyond "I" to "you" that enriches us and makes us free.

As a rule, in the moral education of a person, one gradually moves from a necessary initial phase of dependency (*heteronomous morality*) to the *autonomous morality* that should characterize a mature adult subject. In our experience, too, we observe a movement from an initial adherence to the will of another and to his law (manifested in many ways) — which we grab on to like a *child* trusting completely in the guidance of an adult — to a powerful sense of freedom, the result of having made this Law *our own*. We then feel that it has become our law, that it has become so much a part of us that we feel *adult* precisely because we are able to say: "It is no longer I who live, but Christ who lives in me" (Gal 2:20).

And then another point: Jesus who cries out, "My God, my God, why have you forsaken me?" (Mt 27:46; Mk 15:34).

Jesus forsaken is our secret, our key idea, in education as well. He points to the "limit without limits" that should characterize our educational work, demonstrating the extent and intensity it must have.

But who is this Jesus forsaken whom we have decided to love in a preferential way? He is the figure of those who are ignorant (his ignorance is the most tragic, his question the most dramatic). He is the figure of all who are needy, or maladjusted, or disabled; of those who are unloved, neglected, or excluded. He personifies all those human and social situations, which more than any others cry out for education in a special way. Jesus forsaken is the paradigm of those who, lacking everything, need someone to give them everything and do everything for them. Therefore, he is the perfect example, the ultimate measure of the learning subject, who manifests the educator's responsibility. He indicates to us the "limit without limits" of the need for education, and at the same time, the "limit without limits" of our responsibility to help and to educate.

However, Jesus forsaken — who went beyond his own infinite suffering and prayed: "Father, into your hands I commend my spirit" (Lk 23:46) — also teaches us to see difficulties, obstacles, trials, hard work, error, failure and suffering as something that must be faced, loved and overcome. Generally we humans, whatever our field of endeavour, seek to avoid such experiences in every way possible. In the field of education, as well, there is often a tendency to be over-protective with young people, shielding them from all that is difficult, teaching them to view the road of life as smooth and comfortable. In reality, this leaves them extremely unprepared to face the inevitable trials of life. In particular, it fosters passivity and a reluctance to accept the responsibility for oneself, one's neighbour and society that every human being must assume.

For us, instead, precisely because of our choice of Jesus forsaken, every difficulty is to be faced and loved. And thus *educating to face difficulty* — which involves commitment on the part of both the educator and the one being educated — is another key idea of our educational method.

There are two other points that I would like to consider: unity and Jesus in our midst.

In order to do so we should ask ourselves the following question: what is the aim of this educational process?

We share the same goal as Jesus. We could define it as his goal in educating: "May they all be one": therefore, unity — a profound, heartfelt unity, of all human beings with God and with one another.

Unity is a very timely aspiration. Despite the countless tensions present in our world today, the entire planet, almost paradoxically, is striving towards unity. Unity is a sign and a need of our times.

However, this drive towards unity within people — as the etymology of the word "education" (Latin *e-ducere:* "draw forth") indicates — must be drawn out in a positive way. This implies, on all levels of human endeavour, an educative process consistent with the demands of unity, so that our world will not become a Babel without a soul, but an experience of Emmaus, of God with us, capable of embracing the whole of humanity. This might seem a utopia. But every authentic educational approach includes a utopian thrust, that is, a guiding principle that stimulates people to build together a world which is not yet a reality, but ought to be. In this perspective, education can be viewed as a means for drawing nearer to this utopian goal.

In our approach to education, in which the spiritual and the human penetrate one another and become one (through the Incarnation), this Utopia is not a dream, nor an illusion, nor an unattainable goal. It is already present here among us, and we see its fruits when we live out Jesus' words: "Where two or three are gathered in my name, I am there among them" (Mt 18:20). Education's goal, its highest aim, becomes a reality.

In this we experience the fullness of God's life, which Jesus has given us, a trinitarian relationship, the most genuine form of social relationship, in which a wonderful synthesis is achieved between the two goals of education: to teach the individual and to build the community. We believe that our experience of this trinitarian, communitarian spirituality brings to fulfilment many ideas held by outstanding men and women throughout the history of education, whose initial premises were often different from ours, but who insisted on the importance of education in building a society founded on truly democratic relationships. One example among many would be the great contribution offered by John Dewey to education throughout the world, beginning with the United States. We also find many similarities in the recent concept of "service-learning," which affirms that the formation of the person should also involve a formation in and for the community.

Of course, our experience of community life is based on Jesus' invitation: "Love one another as I have loved you…. Be one" (see Jn 15:12; 17:21). This motivation is religious in nature, but it has extraordinary effects in the field of education.

The goal that has always been assigned to education (*to form the human person*, so as to render him or her independent) is implemented, almost paradoxically, by *forming the person-in-relationship*, which for us means *the human person in the image of the Trinity*, one who is capable of continually transcending self in the context of the presence of Jesus in our midst. It is through this spiritual and educational practice *of mutual love*, to the point of becoming completely one — a practice followed by all the members of the Movement, since all are called to live this communitarian experience in small groups — that we work towards the achievement of the *goal of all goals*, expressed in Jesus' prayer and testament: "May they all be one." As instruments under his guidance, we want to spend our lives for the fulfilment of this goal, which is at one and the same time a utopia, and a reality.

It is through this educational process that we as individuals and as community become capable of meeting with, entering into dialogue with, and working together with other persons, other Movements, and so on. And it is also through this in-depth educational process that, with God's grace, we can aspire to personal and communal sanctity.

Mary is an exceptional example of one who has put all the educational points I have mentioned into practice in her life.

Of course, Jesus is the one who fully lived out this pedagogical itinerary, in the dynamics of an experience that fully included both the life of the Trinity and his forsakenness on the cross. In his earthly experience, he lived interpersonal relationships with exceptional intensity, expressing empathy, acceptance and hope, and experiencing the struggle involved in educating, as well as a life of unity with the Father and with "his own." Clearly he is the most genuine and demanding witness of what it means to be an educator.[52]

Every life calls for love

> From an address to a conference of the Movement for Life, Florence, 17 May 1986.

The human person needs love in every stage and in every situation of his or her existence.

Consequently, every child that is born also needs love.

Children brought up in a loving environment, even while being the centre of attention, acquire an inner disposition that develops and grows towards a life of communion. And this disposition is fundamental for establishing healthy interpersonal relationships with others.

Then, when these children enter adolescence they need love as well. We know that the rapid process of sexual development that characterizes young people at this age brings them face to face with a new awareness of their bodies, never-before experienced emotions, a new attraction towards the opposite sex....

It is a difficult time, one in which they can find themselves in dangerous situations, surrounded by an environment that today offers cheap freedoms and a false vision of sexuality, considered only as a source of pleasure.

It is a time in their lives when adolescents are beginning to acquire a sense of their own autonomy; at the same time, though they may try to hide it, it is also a time when they need a lot of love.

In fact, at this point a sensitive love is needed on the part of parents and of those involved in the child's upbringing in order to understand the struggles they are going through, to encourage dialogue, which perhaps has become difficult and to know how to appreciate the positive aspects of this stage in their development.

In many cases parents must endure moments of terrible concern and suffering that, in a certain sense, are a continuation of the childbearing process. But it is precisely this love, steeped in suffering, that will act within their children and remind them of the greatness that lies in giving oneself to others, in the value of sacrifice, of respecting their friends with whom they work and study.

Engaged couples also need love. Husbands and wives become collaborators with the creator when they bring about new life on earth. Therefore, people preparing for marriage must learn how to cultivate what sustains life: love. But, as Igino Giordani used to say: "If one engaged person wishes to love the other truly, he or she must give God (divine love) to the other," because supernatural love purifies and strengthens human love, rendering it long lasting and imperishable.[53]

The charism of unity and psychology

> From an address during the conferral of an honorary doctorate in Psychology, University of Malta, 26 February 1999.

Our Movement can be considered from a psychological perspective as well as from theological, philosophical, and educational points of view.

In order to understand the contribution that it brings to the field of psychology, we need to refer back to the main points of our spirituality.

The first point is God who is love.

Psychology tells us that every person has a basic need to be recognized as a unique individual with one's own identity and to not be considered as simply a number or an object.

Under normal circumstances, this sense of security comes from parents, from family, from personal talents, or from education, which establish a sense of identity, of being distinct from others. But all of these things can be compromised. Others may not acknowledge one's identity, or may not understand or appreciate it, leading a person into feelings of insignificance and into depression....

But each person's discovery of and achieving certainty that he or she has been wanted and is loved by God — not abandoned to chance or blind fate — is the basis for having that psychological stability which gives a meaning to life and a purpose in the world.

Only the awareness that God is love-for-the-person-too, gives him or her the strength to continue going outside self, to live, to love and to create communion in society.

Another point of this spirituality is doing God's will.

We know that the psychic development of a person (of the self) begins in the early stages of "narcissism" in which one is concentrated exclusively on self and on one's own needs and pleasures. Then, little by little, the person's field of relationships opens up to include members of the family, and later on, the school environment and society. According to Igor Caruso, eventually these relationships should open up to a transcendental "You," after overcoming the final obstacle that stands in the way of reaching full maturity: one's own self.

In other words, freeing the self from all internal and external conditioning and, in the end, recognizing the inherent relativity of the self (which implies ceasing to defend it and to place it in opposition to God and to others) means accepting oneself without masks, in order to bring the individual will into conformity with a transcendent will.

In this lies human perfection as well. Because if God's will is to love one's neighbour, "to make yourself one" with a neighbour means to give up defending the self in order to go beyond self into the other and, ultimately, into the Other ("You did it to me").

It has been said: "Those people who have reached self-fulfilment, basically, are capable of deeper interpersonal relationships than are others.... They are more capable of losing themselves in others, of a greater love, of identifying themselves more perfectly with others, of eliminating the obstacles set up by one's ego than other people find possible."[54]

Then there is love and mutual love.

The affirmation that God is love, and that his will coincides with love, in other words, with loving one's neighbour, is confirmed not only by Jesus' teachings but also by the psychological experience of interpersonal relationships. Only relationships that are not violent or controlling but instead recognize and respect the other's "person" as a transcendent being are relationships that "love the other as oneself." Not only does my love acknowledge the other person as a being who is distinct from me, equal to me, and transcendent like me, but this same love also affirms my own "existence."

Only love takes into account our diversity (or distinction) while, at the same time, safeguarding our equality, and therefore making unity possible.

The novelty of the culture brought by Jesus lies precisely in the fact that he revolutionized interpersonal relationships. Before his coming, relationships among people were governed by family ties, social class, particular interests, or merely external goals. With Jesus, all these motivations become less important because one becomes aware that one has an intrinsic transcendent value, in fact, that one represents God himself for others: "Just as you did it to one of the least of these who are members of my family, you did it to me" (Mt 25:40).

The psychological relevance of this dynamic is obvious. For example, if we take it to its extreme consequences, then I am most fully a person when I freely and consciously affirm the other even at the cost of my own life. This dynamic is expressed by Jesus in these words: "No one has greater love than this, to lay down one's life for one's friends" (Jn 15:13).

Said in another way: no one affirms the self, is so truly a person, as does the one who denies self and thus transcends self in order to save the transcendence of the other (and we have luminous examples in Jesus, Father Maximilian Kolbe, Mother Teresa ...). This is the most authentic "humanism" imaginable and achievable.

Jesus crucified and forsaken.

The psychological law of personal development is also defined by the spiritual law that Jesus announced: "Those who love their life lose it, and those who hate their life in this world will keep it for eternal life" (Jn 12:25).

In fact, in the process of growing to maturity, one cannot reach a new stage without becoming detached from and renouncing the one reached previously. For example, weaning is a painful passage for a child, but it is essential for progressing towards adulthood; accepting the arrival of a new sibling is another painful passage, from the egotistical position of being the centre of attention to a stage of socialization, the relativity of self, to become integrated with others, transcending self in the "we."

It is generally accepted that all psychological illnesses actually are born from the refusal of the suffering inherent in this passage (because a person would rather remain comfortable in a familiar situation), for fear of all that is "new" or of the "others" who are seen as enemies who can limit or even take away my identity.

When, in fact, in order to safeguard the self we refuse to enter into communion — because we are afraid of being made a thing subject to someone else's will, exploited, objectified, squeezed dry, swallowed-up by others, as psychologists say — psychologically (and also spiritually) we are already dead.

According to Carl Jung, the one who expressed the highest point in the achievement of personhood was Jesus, who cried out on the cross: "My God, my God, why have you forsaken me?" (Mt 27:46; Mk 15:34). In the very moment when God experiences human mortality, his human nature reaches the divine....

Living the word and imitating Mary are two other key points of the spirituality of unity.

Those who live the word give witness to the fact that the authentic person is simple and because simple, he or she is also free. All forms of attachment, whether to self or to things destroy the self, fragment it, both because attachments nurture pride and self-satisfaction and because they fabricate that "false self" which psychologists call the ego.

The problem people face today is the need to rebuild an integrated self, freeing it from the propensities of the ego, that is to say, freeing it from all forms of greed and possessiveness. For the one who has an integrated self knows how to empty the self, to strip self of everything in order to be enriched by communion with others.

And this is precisely what the gospel teaches.

Mary is the icon of this self-emptying, above all in her desolation at the feet of her crucified son whom she loses. But into that immense emptiness enter all the children of God.

And at the end, unity.

Psychologically speaking, it impossible for individuals to have a "sense of identity" if there are not others who recognize them as subject.

Psychologists of all schools agree that human beings need to reaffirm one another in their individuality through genuine interactions and contacts.

In fact, in order to be able to be a gift for the others, first one must feel and be recognized as being "different" from the others.

But in order to be a personal gift it is necessary to enter into communion with others.

And herein lies the difference between so-called "interest groups" and the Christian community as Jesus intended. An interest group is made up of individuals who come together with a particular goal in mind (athletic clubs, civic, political or religious associations, trade unions, schools, study groups ...) and whose interaction is limited to carrying out those common interests. As for all that falls outside the realm of such common interests, these individuals remain closed in on themselves.

The Christian community, instead, is not formed for reasons that are external to the nature of community, but as a result of the very character of love which creates communion.

And experience confirms that this type of community is possible. Clearly that the motivation to bring about such a community comes from Jesus' invitation: "Love one another as I have loved you ... that they may all be one" (see Jn 15:12; 17:21). Obviously this is religious in nature. But the psychological effects are extraordinary: each one, being a relationship of love with others, as a consequence becomes fulfilled as an authentic person. This, briefly, is our spirituality of unity seen from a psychological perspective.[55]

The Charism of Unity and Politics

> The first four texts in this section date back to the 1950s and '60s. They reveal the political potential present in the charism of unity when it first started. Beginning with *The Movement for Unity in Politics,* the passages that follow show the subsequent development of those first intuitions.

People of God

This is the era of the Mystical Body, as Pope Pius XII has said.

Therefore, if this era's characteristic were really put into effect, the impact on society would soon be unmistakable.

And one of these effects would be a mutual esteem among countries and peoples.

This is not usual. In fact, it is much more common to find strongly enforced borders between one people and another, to fear the might of the other or, at best, to forge alliances for each nation's own advantage.

But it is difficult to think of acting solely out of love for another nation; popular morality has not reached such heights.

When, however, the life of the Mystical Body among individuals has been developed to the point that all truly *love* their neighbours — be they black or white, red or yellow — *as themselves*, it will be easy to transplant this law to the relationship among nations.

And something new will happen. For love brings us to find similarities or to make them. Each nation will learn the best of the other and each one's virtues will be made to circulate for the enrichment of all.

Then, there will truly be unity and variety. A people will rise up that, even though a child of this world, is guided by the laws of heaven. It will be able to call itself "people of God."[56]

Mary, bond of unity among nations

> Address to an audience including people from twenty-seven different countries, Fiera di Primero, a town in the Dolomite Mountains, Italy, summer 1959.

If one day all people, not as individuals but as nations, would learn to put themselves aside, to put aside the ideas they have about their own countries, their kingdoms, and offer them as incense to the Lord, the king of a kingdom not of this world, the guide of history, and if they would do this as the expression of the mutual love between states that God asks for, just as he asks for mutual love among individuals, that day would mark the beginning of a new era. For on that day, just as Jesus is present among two who love each other in Christ, Jesus will be alive and present among peoples, given finally his proper place as the one king, not only of individual hearts but of nations: he will be Christ the King.

Christian peoples, or their representatives, must learn how to immolate their "collective" egos. This is the price. Nothing less is asked of each us in order for our souls to be consumed in unity. Now is the time for every people to go beyond its own borders, to look farther. Now is the time to love the other countries as our own, to acquire a new purity of vision. To be Christians it is not enough to be detached from ourselves. The times we live in demand from the followers of Christ something more: the awareness of Christianity's social dimension, which not only builds up one's own country according to the law of Christ, but assists in the building up of all other countries as well, through the universal action of the Church, and through the supernatural vision given to us by God the Father, who from heaven sees things quite differently from the way we do. We need to live the Mystical Body of Christ in such an excellent way as to translate it into the mystical body of society.

History speaks almost exclusively of wars, and as children in school we are practically made to learn that wars are good and holy, almost the safeguard of our homelands. This may be so and sometimes it was so.

But if we hear echoing in our souls the appeals of the Popes, like Pope Pius XII, we will recognize how, for the sake of humanity, they dreaded war and how they reached out to government leaders, whether they were asked to or not. They strove to appease anger and overcome vested interests in order to avoid the disaster of war that destroys everything, while with peace everything is gained.

For history is a series of fratricidal conflicts among peoples who are members of one world-family, whose lands were given to them by the one Master of the world, to live on and to cultivate.

He blesses peace because he is peace in himself. We see how one by one the Lord is conquering the hearts of his children of all nations and tongues, transforming them into children of love, joy, peace, ardour, and strength. And we hope that the Lord may have mercy on this divided and confused world, on peoples closed within their shells contemplating their own beauty — the only beauty that exists for them (though it is both limiting and unsatisfying). They strain to hold on to their treasures against all odds, the very treasures that could help other peoples who are dying of hunger. May the Lord cause all barriers to fall, and allow love to run uninterrupted through all lands, flooding them with spiritual and material goods.

Let us hope that the Lord brings about a new order in the world. Only he can make humanity a family and cultivate the unique characteristics of each people so that the splendour of each, placed at the service of others, may shine with the one light of life. This light of life in making beautiful each earthly country will make it the antechamber of the Eternal Country.

It may seem like a dream. But even now — apart from the fact that if the relationship among Christians is one of mutual love, then the relationship among Christian peoples cannot but be one of mutual love, because of the unchanging logic of the gospel — there exists a bond that powerfully unites peoples to one another. It has already been proclaimed by the voice of the people, by every people, in the voice of the people that is often the voice of God. This hidden bond, cherished in the heart of every nation, is Mary.

Who can take away from the Brazilians the idea that Mary is the Queen of their land?

And who can tell the Portuguese that Mary is not "Our Lady of Fatima"?

Who does not acknowledge to the French the beautiful Lady of Lourdes?

And to the Polish the Madonna of Czestochowa?

To the English, that their country is "Mary's Dowry"?

Who can deny that Mary is the "Châtelaine of Italy"?

How often in history have nations taken refuge at their Marian strongholds, her basilicas or shrines, as though seeking protection under Mary's mantle when other peoples, their own brothers and sisters, attacked them. All Christian peoples have proclaimed her Queen, for themselves and for their children.

But one thing is missing, something Mary cannot do. We have to help her: what is missing is our collaboration so that Catholic* peoples, united as brothers and sisters, go to her and acknowledge her as both Mother and Queen. We can crown her as such only if, through our conversion, through our prayers, and through our actions, we take away the veil that still covers her crown, even though the crown was given to her by the Pope long ago when he proclaimed her Queen of the world and of the universe. We must each place at her feet the piece of the world that is in our hands.

If today it is non-Christian laws that have almost made some of the boundaries disappear among peoples who are yet still very Christian, perhaps God is permitting this so that the progress of Mary in the world, which must come, be less obstructed. In this way everything can become her "footstool" (see Mt 5:35), footstool of the greatest Queen known to heaven and earth: Queen of all Humanity, Queen of Saints, Queen of Angels — all because on earth she knew how to immolate herself totally, becoming the handmaid of the Lord, and is thus able to teach her children the way of unity, of the universal embrace of all human beings, so that everything may be "on earth as it is in heaven."[57]

Divine diplomacy

When someone weeps, we must weep too. And if someone laughs, we too rejoice too. Thus the cross is divided and borne by many shoulders, and joy is multiplied and shared by many hearts.

Making ourselves one with our neighbour is a way, the way par excellence, to make ourselves one with God. Because when we love in this way, the first two and most important commandments are fused into one. Making ourselves one with our neighbour for love of Jesus, with the love of Jesus, so that our neighbour, sweetly wounded by the love of God in us, will want to make himself or herself one with us, in a mutual exchange of help, of ideals, of projects, of affections. Do this to the point of establishing between the two of us those essential elements so the Lord can say, "Where two or three are gathered in my name, I am there among them" (Mt 18:20). Until, that is, as far as it depends on us, the presence of Jesus is guaranteed, so that we walk through life, always, as a little Church on the move — Church whether we are at home, at school, in a garage or in Parliament, walking through life like the disciples of

---

* This reflection was written before Chiara Lubich had discovered the ecumenical vocation of her work. As can be seen in other writings in this section, her thoughts apply not just to Catholics but all Christians.

Emmaus with that Third among them, who gives divine value to all our actions.

Then we are not the ones acting in our life, we who are miserable and limited, lonely and suffering. The Almighty walks with us. And whoever remains united with him bears much fruit.

From one cell come more cells, from one tissue many tissues. Making ourselves one with our neighbour in that complete self-forgetfulness which those possess (without realizing it or specifically trying to do it) who think of the other, their neighbour.

This is the diplomacy of charity, which has many of the expressions and features of ordinary diplomacy; hence it does not say all that it could say, for this would displease others and would be disagreeable to God. It knows how to wait, how to speak, how to reach its goal. It is the divine diplomacy of the Word who becomes flesh to make us divine.

This diplomacy, however, has an essential and characteristic mark that differentiates it from the diplomacy spoken about by the world, where "diplomatic" is often synonymous with reticence or even falsehood.

Divine diplomacy has this greatness and this property, perhaps a property of it alone: it is moved by the good of the other and is therefore devoid of any shadow of selfishness.

This rule of life ought to inform all of diplomacy, and with God it can be done because he is not only the master of individuals, but king of the nations and of every society.

If all diplomats in the exercise of their duty were inspired in their actions by charity towards the other State as towards their own, they would be enlightened to such an extent by the help of God as to share in establishing relationships among States as they ought to exist among human beings. Charity is a light and a guide, and the one who is sent as an emissary has all the graces to be a good emissary.

May God help us and may we co-operate, so that from heaven the Lord may see this new sight: his last will and testament brought to life among the nations.

It may seem like a dream to us, but for God it is the norm, the only one that guarantees peace in the world, the fulfilment of individuals in the unity of a humanity that by that point would know Jesus.[58]

More wisdom in government

Today, politics is a weapon that serves Satan, but it could also be put to the service of God.

It is necessary that many embrace this instrument again as a cross, without the fear of getting dirty, without sluggishness.

The Catholics* in the world involved in politics are many, but they lack a recognizable bond that makes them brothers and sisters: they lack "Jesus among them" who could make them a powerful army at his service in the world.

Whether missionaries live in Thailand or in Tierra del Fuego, our religious sensibilities move us to recognize them as brothers or sisters, and we help them.

But if a Catholic is fighting for a political cause in another country, to safeguard a Christian law, we do not feel, as we ought, that struggle to be our own.

We need to put more religion into politics, more mysticism into practice, more wisdom into government, more unity among all.[59]

Reflections: Universal brotherhood

We need to be aware as we take part in the day-to-day life going on around us. And not only in our private lives, in our relationships shoulder to shoulder with others, but also fully and consciously aware of all the vast developments unfolding before our eyes.

We need to find our role in all of these developments so as to serve the Church through them, bringing to struggle and victory, defeat and discouragement, a breath of Christian inspiration. We must suffuse time and society with the perfume of heaven, and, where needed and possible, take the lead in defending the Church against those eternal enemies who bedeck it with blood and with glory.[60]

This is the equilibrium of Christian love: to love the individual soul nearby, and to work for the entire community of the Church and of all humankind wherever we may be.[61]

---

* As said in the previous footnote, this thought is couched in language that expresses the culture of its time. It applies to all Christians.

Keep your heart open to all of humanity and teach those for whom you are responsible to do the same. May it not be that Jesus came on earth in vain to preach the universal family.[62]

The one who is close to other people, serving them in their minutest needs — as Jesus commanded — easily understands also the huge problems that trouble the human race. But the one who, lacking charity, sits at a desk from dawn till dusk dealing with and discussing the great problems of the world, ends up not understanding those few problems that weigh down the brother or sister nearby.[63]

The Movement for Unity in Politics

> Address to the first conference of the Movement for Unity in Politics of the Focolare Movement, Castel Gandolfo, Italy, 9 June 2000. This text puts those that precede it in this volume in their historical context.

We are here today to open the International Congress of the Movement for Unity in Politics: an important step towards defining its identity, the ideals it pursues, its methods and its goals.

It is a fairly new Movement. In fact, its origins date back to 2 May 1996, on the occasion of a meeting I had with a group of politicians in Naples, Italy. But its roots sink deep into the history, spirituality and doctrine of the Focolare Movement that promotes it. Indeed, we have always given special attention to the world of politics because it offers us the possibility of loving our neighbour in a crescendo of charity: from interpersonal love to an ever-greater love towards the *polis*. Many of our people have committed themselves in politics on various levels, often holding positions of responsibility.

Today, I would like to go over with you those events in our history that have had the greatest influence on the formation of our political thought, underlining in each of them what retains lasting value and, from my viewpoint, what it might contribute to the heritage of the Movement for Unity in Politics.

In 1948, in the Chamber of Deputies,* we first met the Honourable Igino Giordani, a prominent person with extensive cultural, social and political experience. He was an active figure during the first years of the difficult postwar period, a scholar and a reference point for the generations that longed for freedom during the years of dictatorship. Giordani was a co-founder of the Focolare Movement and for us, he has always represented,

---

* The Chamber of Deputies is the legislative house of the Italian Parliament. The title "Honourable" indicates that Igino Giordani was a member of Parliament.

due to a special plan of God, the dimension of humanity, with its history, its sufferings, its achievements, its quest for an authentic ideal.

He opened our heart to humanity, to its problems and concerns: the rebuilding of Italy and the rest of Europe in the wake of World War II, the rise of democracy, the division between East and West. In turn, from the spirit of the Movement Giordani received a new stimulus for his own political activity. We can see this in an address he made on universal peace, applauded by the entire Italian Parliament; the first bill on conscientious objection, presented together with the Socialist, Calosso; his dialogue on peace with the Communist, Laiolo.

Within a short time, a small but significant group of politicians began to gather around Giordani. They shared our ideal of life and sought to live it in Parliament.

There, for the first time in a political setting, they experienced the "art of loving" that I spoke about a few months ago on a special occasion in Campidoglio.*

It is an art that requires that we love *everyone*, without exception, regardless of their party affiliation; that we be *the first to love*; that we *make ourselves one* with them in order to welcome them, emptying ourselves of all our worries and thoughts.

Christians are the first, but not the only ones, called to live this art of loving: *everyone can and must love*. It is a law for believers of all traditions of faith. In fact, it is written in the DNA of every human being.

Consequently, if love becomes mutual, according to Jesus' commandment, "Love one another as I have loved you" (see Jn 13:34), Jesus himself is present among us. In fact, Jesus promised us: "For where two or three are gathered together in my name [in my love], I am there among them" (Mt 18:20). It is a presence of Jesus that transforms people individually and creates unity among them. It is not simply an agreement of opinions or choice to follow a certain course of action based on the same political choice. Instead, this human-divine unity bonds people in a deeper way, beyond differences of culture and political affiliation. On the foundation of unity, differences acquire their true meaning, and in mutuality, they become enrichment for one another.

Therefore, the basic principle is to live first of all as true Christians and then as people engaged in politics.

---

* When Chiara Lubich was made an honorary citizen of the city of Rome on 22 January 2000.

In view of the fact that people of other religions and cultures also participate in the Movement for Unity in Politics, the same commitment can be formulated as follows: first, be people who believe in profound and lasting human values, and then take political action.

Just as the presence of Jesus among us, the effect of unity, is the heart of all our communities, it is likewise the heart of our political communities. Already in 1962, Tommaso Sorgi, a Member of Parliament, sensed the urgent need for this presence.

He wrote to me from the Chamber of Deputies: "Those of us who live at the very core of this 'blessed' public life continually experience that, on a purely human level — even on the level of the most noble ethical values — there is not the slightest hope of redemption for this narrow-minded world full of insincerity, conflicts, and power struggles. And, unfortunately, we find that not even religious values are able to change the *homo politicus*, who accepts them only as long as they are expedient, and then sets them aside when they no longer serve his or her purposes.... Individual efforts alone ... seem to be insufficient. We need a lightning bolt of wisdom to reawaken all of humanity...." [64]

And we can receive this light of wisdom especially from God present in Jesus who is drawn by our mutual love. He himself comes among us wherever we are engaged, and through us, takes political action.

This was the purpose of the group of politicians in our "parliamentary cell." Its members, who after a while came from different parties, have changed since 1950, but not its goal: *since our unity makes it possible, to bring Jesus into Parliament.*

The presence of Alcide De Gasperi was also noteworthy because it underlined the political significance that our Movement could have. De Gasperi, like the first men and women Focolarini, was originally from Trent and was very close to the Movement.

He knew the spirituality of unity quite well. In fact, it fascinated him and reinforced his vocation to unity, that same vocation which eventually made him, together with Adenauer and Schuman, a founder of the European Union.

In fact, a documentary on the life of De Gasperi points out how, especially in the final years of his life, all of his thoughts seemed to come together in Jesus' testament: "May they all be one" — the same Jesus whose name he invoked three times before dying.

Our contacts with De Gasperi made us realize how much a politician who loves his country can accomplish and how much that love can cost him.

At a certain point, we began to correspond with one another. In one of my letters to him from 1950, I had written: "You are as important to us as is Jesus among us, because we are convinced that all authority comes from God....

"You have all the grace of state necessary to govern Italy.... You should be the best and brightest expression of your own party and of the parties of others."

This letter provides an opportunity for me to speak about the view that we have had of authority from the early years of the Movement.

We know that it is God who gives authority to human beings as his delegates in the world, an authority that should be used as an instrument of truth and love (see Jn 19:11). For this reason we have always had *the highest respect for authority.*

However, it is an authority given by a God who is Love and is Trinity and therefore takes on a meaning not always easily found in political theories and codes of law. For us, authority participates in the love of the Creator for each created being. It is the love of a Father for each and every person, even the weakest and most insignificant, who nevertheless bear in themselves the undeniable dignity of being children of God.

This authority given by God to every human being (see Gen 2:28-29) is then the source of the specific partaking in this authority conferred upon political leadership for the government of the "city of Man."

However, it is important to keep in mind the great, the tremendous responsibility that those who govern have before God and before the people. We must never forget that citizens are the first partakers in God's love for the city. They have a role to carry out in conscience and each one possesses inalienable rights and duties. Each citizen is an active subject in the political community, not simply a passive object, and is called therefore to behave accordingly. Political power must put itself at the service of the citizen, as we hear so often from all sides.

But in order that this may be accomplished ever more fully, the political activity carried out by those who govern, as a service of truth and love, must be met by an ever-growing participation of its citizens in public affairs as an expression of the authority they have received from God. Only in this mutuality is it possible to build the well-being of the whole community.

This dynamic of mutuality reminds us of the Trinitarian relationship of the two parts, a harmonious relationship of unity in multiplicity.

In the Movement we certainly do not want to confuse religion and politics, as has happened and happens as a result of the extremist tendencies of some

Christians and also non-Christians. It is necessary to recognize the precise role politics plays in society with its specific expertise.

On the other hand, Jesus is Life and he is Life in all its fullness. He is not only a religious fact. To separate Jesus from the wholeness of the life of human beings is a real modern-day heresy. It makes people slaves to something beneath them, relegating God the Father to a place far from his children.

No, he is *the Man*, the perfect Man who sums up in his person all men and women and every truth and drive that they may feel, in order to be raised to their rightful place.

At times it is thought that the gospel does not resolve all human problems and that, instead, it simply brings about the kingdom of God understood in a strictly religious sense. But it is not so. Certainly, it is not the historical Jesus who resolves today's problems. It is Jesus-us, members of his Mystical Body, Jesus-me, Jesus-you.... It is Jesus present in each person, in that given person — when his grace and love live in him or her — who constructs a bridge or builds a road. It is Jesus, the true and most profound personality of every person. And it is as another Christ that the Christian brings his or her characteristic contribution to all fields, whether in science, in art, in politics.

Our politicians' sense of commitment took this direction and in 1959 the *St. Catherine Centre* was founded for them. Renewed in the spirit of unity and reinforced by an ever deeper understanding of the principles of Christian social doctrine, for almost ten years this Centre was the point of convergence for their many aspirations and concerns and the point of departure for their activities.

For the St. Catherine Centre, however, political responsibility was not exhausted simply in the pursuit of the common good of citizens from a purely material point of view, which for the most part is useful. It had to work also towards building a society that is open to achieving more noble goals.

Politics was seen as having the possibility and the duty to encourage all individuals to assume their responsibilities as members of a body, the body of the whole of humanity, and to offer them the opportunity of reaching that self-fulfilment in this world and that happiness which is possible only in the context of universal brotherhood.

In addition, they also emphasized how Christians should never forget that what they accomplish, in common purpose with all those who seek the good of humanity, builds up the earthly city and thus continues the work of God the creator. At the same time, their work brings closer the "new heavens" and the "new earth" (see 2 Pt 3:13) because together with the cosmos, Christ has redeemed all human activity. Therefore, if these works are completed in conformity with the commandment of love, they will endure.

What is more, while broadening the commonly accepted view of political commitment and encouraging its members to set their daily choices in a wider historical perspective, the St. Catherine Centre also examined, in the light of the truth present in the human heart, all the political laws that have withstood the test of time in order to confirm their validity. And our people involved in politics did not feel alone; they sensed the active presence and help of those who throughout the course of history have contributed to accomplishing the same objective. Moreover, they studied new laws inspired by relationships of mutual love among persons, among groups and among peoples.

There has always been a further conviction, confirmed and rediscovered in new forms every day, that the Providence of God is never lacking, but acts in human affairs and also, therefore, in political matters.

These are some of the ideas that the Movement for Unity in Politics has inherited from the St. Catherine Centre.

But one basic idea lies at the foundation of everything and guarantees the success of our politicians as they continually strive to live the ideals they pursue. We offer it to those of you who are Christians, but not only, because Christ died for all people.

We have already affirmed that one must, first of all, be an authentic Christian and on this foundation, carry out one's activity in politics. Very well, to be an authentic Christian means to follow Christ by living what we have called "the art of loving," but also, as he himself said in powerful words, by denying oneself and taking up one's own cross.

One's own cross.

What is the specific cross of those who move and work in the political world today? I think it is often the lack of unity, of harmony, that makes their task heavy and not very fruitful; the rigid and opposed positions between parties without understanding the others' motives; the divisions caused by clashes among ethnic groups within nations, divisions between nations....

We need to find the way to overcome these disunities, to restore unity.

Jesus himself came on earth to restore the unity that had been lost between humanity and God and of men and women with one another. He accomplished this through his passion and death, and above all — this is the conviction of theologians and saints — when he experienced within himself the greatest possible disunity: the disunity between himself and the Father with whom he was one. And he cried out: "My God, my God, why have you forsaken me?" (Mt 27:46).

This mystery is the key that opens the way to unity for the members of the Focolare Movement, and therefore also for that specific expression of the Movement, the Movement for Unity in Politics.

Only those who keep the image of Jesus crucified and forsaken ever before them, who recognize his face in every division, who love him and know how to embrace the cross of division out of love for him, are capable of recomposing unity.

And in loving Jesus crucified and forsaken they receive the gift of a light that the mind does not produce on its own and a strength that is more than common.

Little by little, the Focolare Movement is spreading throughout the world. In 1956 the Volunteers of God were born: men and women radically committed in the life of society. Faced with the invasion of Hungary by the troops of the Warsaw Pact, we felt urged to promote another kind of invasion. It would be an invasion with similar determination but aimed in the opposite direction: to bring a revolution of love into everyday life, into families, into the workplace, and into all cultural, social and political endeavours.

The Volunteers are the moving force behind the so-called New Humanity Movement, which coordinates all the members of the Focolare Movement with regard to their participation in the affairs of society.

Throughout these last decades, this movement has given rise around the world to a people in the true sense of the word. They are the people of unity, which today numbers more than five million members, and which is beginning to offer its original contribution in various fields of human learning and activity: in economics, politics, art, justice, communication, and so on. It is a people made up of adults and young people, even children, people of all cultures, professions, and countries. The academic, civic and political recognitions that prestigious universities and international bodies, such as UNESCO and the Council of Europe, have conferred upon me are, in reality, recognitions given to the life of this people and to its presence in this moment of history.

We have always been aware, since the earliest days of our Movement, that the charism of unity also contains its own culture. On the one hand, it is the offspring of Christian tradition, but at the same time, it is new, because it is enlightened by this charism. But it was the growth of the people of unity, the spreading of their Ideal outside the structures of the Focolare Movement, that highlighted the specific characteristics of this culture and that led to the studying of its doctrine: in theology, philosophy, politics, economics, psychology, art, and so forth. A group we call the Abba School, which in addition to myself is composed of experts in various disciplines, has brought these studies ahead for some ten years now.

And now the latest innovation: the encounter between the people of unity and its doctrine has given rise to what we call "inundations" or "torrents of living water," using an expression taken from St. John Chrysostom. In other words: the development of authentic new movements, particularly in the field of economics, through the Economy of Communion, and in politics, continuing the work of the St. Catherine Centre, through the Movement for Unity in Politics.

Thus the Movement for Unity in Politics is bringing about a new political culture.

But its vision of politics does not give rise to a new party. Instead, it changes the method of political activity: while remaining faithful to his or her own genuine ideals, a politician of unity loves everyone, as we said, and therefore in every circumstance searches for what unites.

Today we would like to present a vision of politics perhaps as it has never before been conceived. We would like to give life — forgive my boldness — to a politics of Jesus, as he considers it and where he acts through each of us, wherever we are: in national and regional governments, in town councils, in political parties, in various civic and political groups, in government coalitions and in the opposition. This unity lived among us, then, must be brought into our political parties, among the parties, into the various political institutions and into every sphere of public life and into the relationships among nations.

Then the people of all nations will be able to rise above their borders and look beyond, loving the others' country as their own. The presence of Jesus will become a reality also among peoples and states, making humanity one universal family. It will be a family that goes beyond a limited concept of international society, because within it relationships among persons, groups, peoples are conceived of in a way that dismantles all types of divisions and barriers.

This is the goal of the Movement for Unity in Politics which is beginning to blossom all over the world. It is a Movement that is capable of giving rise to new political projects and that appeals to politicians at every level and position. Through their profession and social commitments, members of the Focolare Movement are present in it, together with many others who know the Ideal of unity and live it, without necessarily belonging to the Focolare.

Now, in order to have a better understanding of this Movement let us look more closely at what is specifically characteristic of it.

We know that the redemption brought about by Jesus on the cross transforms from within all human bonds, imbuing them with divine love and making us all brothers and sisters.

This has profound meaning for our Movement, if we consider that the great political plan of modernity was the attainment, as summarized in the motto of the French Revolution, of "liberty, equality, fraternity." While the first two principles, however, have been partially achieved in recent centuries, despite numerous formal declarations, fraternity has been all but forgotten in the political arena.

Instead, it is precisely *fraternity* that can be considered as *the hallmark of our Movement*. What is more, by living out fraternity, freedom and equality acquire new meaning and find greater fulfilment.

In order to conclude this part of my talk, I would like to explain now the importance that the figure and role of Mary have had in the history of our Movement.

In 1959, as was customary during those years, all the people of our community spent their summer holiday together. During that time, in the little town of Fiera di Primiero in the Dolomite Mountains, some twelve thousand people from twenty-seven countries came and went. And in a solemn act, representatives of these nations consecrated themselves and their nations to Mary. Members of parliament who were present consecrated also their political commitment to her.

Why this special love for Mary, and why do we consider her as the Queen of all nations and leader of our Movement?

Mary is the one who sings: "The Mighty One has done great things for me" (Lk 1:49). God has placed his plan for humanity in her; in her he reveals his mercy for humankind, destroys the false projects of the proud, casts down the powerful from their thrones and lifts up the lowly, reestablishes justice and redistributes riches.

Who, then, is more a politician than Mary?

The task of the Movement for Unity in Politics is to contribute towards fulfilling in human history what Mary announces as already accomplished in herself.

I will leave to others the task of narrating the many compelling and practical experiences lived by the Movement for Unity in Politics in recent years. But I would like to share one in particular with you myself.

It is an example I was able to witness first-hand a few weeks ago during a two-week trip to Africa. It illustrates how the fraternity characteristic of the Movement for Unity in Politics has political influence on the community that lives it.

For the sake of clarity, I must tell you a short story, which seems almost a fairy tale, about the Bangwa people, in the English-speaking part of Cameroon.

In 1966, we Focolarini were invited to offer our assistance to a native people dwelling in the heart of the forest. They lived in very primitive conditions and were affected by many illnesses, with a ninety percent infant mortality rate.

Desperate because their own assiduous prayers to the god of their traditional religion had obtained no results, they brought an offering to the closest Catholic mission and entrusted themselves to their prayers.

Having been told of these circumstances, Focolarini came to their aid and soon opened a makeshift clinic in a run-down shack, which at times was also visited by snakes.

During one of my first visits there in the sixties, while groups of Bangwa, subjects of their wise and prudent king, Fon Defang of Fontem, took turns performing dances in a large clearing in the forest, I had a strange impression. It seemed to me that God, like a sun, was enveloping all of us, Focolarini and Bangwa together; and that the sun, almost like a divine sign, made me foresee the rising of a city that we would build together, there in the midst of the tropical forest.

In the years that followed, with the help of funds collected by the youth of the Movement around the world, the Focolarini built a modest hospital, opened schools, scaled a mountain to channel a spring of water in order to generate a bit of electricity for the hospital, and with bricks made from *pota-pota*, or wet earth, they were able to erect a few houses. Later on, they built a church.

But first of all, and most importantly, having been formed by the spirituality of the Movement, the Focolarini loved. They set out to love all those brothers and sisters who were in dire need, sick, and illiterate, seeing Christ in them. And they loved one another: they themselves were the living words they could offer to that tribe.

The Bangwa observed them carefully for months; they wanted to see if those white people truly loved them or if their actions were motivated by personal interest. Eventually, convinced of the sincerity and honest openness of their new guests, they worked side by side with them as much as they were able. And thousands converted to the Catholic Church. Thus, Focolarini and Bangwa found themselves together in the Focolare Movement, joined as brothers and sisters by mutual love constantly renewed in the midst of inevitable difficulties.

Years passed and everything grew: the hospital was expanded; the infant mortality rate was reduced to two percent; the plague of sleeping sickness was controlled; a school for children of all ages was built; twelve roads were opened to connect the nearest villages; the Focolarini, with the help of the Bangwa, built sixty houses; the Bangwa, with the help of the Focolarini, built many others. Local Church authorities set up a parish.

Then, more than thirty years later, I returned to Fontem and the attractive, large town is there for everyone to see. I saw what love can do, what fraternity can build when it is lived among people of two different continents who have become one.

In the meantime, the government opened elementary schools and a high school. It installed a long aqueduct…. In 1992 the district that includes Fontem and other locations became a region of local government, and in 1999 power lines for electric light arrived.

It does not matter that many of the Bangwa continue to profess the traditional religion and that the underlying structure of their culture still rests upon an ancestral system regulated by thousands of ancient norms. Fraternity, which in any case is inscribed in the heart of each person like a seed of the divine word, prevails and works miracles.

The new king, Dr. Lucas Njifua Fontem, son of the previous king, saw and understood. All those who follow this way, he told us, are upright and just and they work together for the good of the community. Indeed, during my recent stay there, as head of the Bangwa people and in a determined and fervent manner, he officially invited everyone to adopt the spirit of the Movement, whose statutes provide that among its adherents are included people of every religion as well as non-believers of goodwill.

While the nation of Cameroon is said to be plagued by rampant corruption, the king openly declared that there, in Fontem, the inhabitants who follow the spirit of the Movement never present any problems. They resolve everything among themselves with love; they do not fight over land boundaries but settle them in harmony with one another. They live in absolute peace.

No one steals, they do not harm much less kill one another; they seem to have no need for police. They find solutions to all problems having to do with their families because they uphold the institution of the family with the fullest solidarity. Their children do not cause them serious economic problems. They defend life in all its stages, something that has always been highly valued by the African culture. They respect authority and, again in accordance with their culture, they hold their elders in high esteem. They care for public health meticulously. They are incredibly generous; the "culture of giving," an effect of fraternity, shines out among them. Illiteracy is in decline.

Clearly, brotherhood creates a new style of life. It unites the community but at the same time differentiates the various roles and tasks. In this way, by means of fraternity, individual persons, families, small businesses, traditional and state institutions set out to meet their own goals while respecting and working together with all the others. By doing so, society as a whole is able to achieve its political goal: the common good.

Church and government authorities encourage us there by saying: "What you have done in Fontem, you must do all over Africa and in Madagascar." In observing what has happened, others speak of a kind of miracle: an entire people, including its king, is carrying out a revolution of love similar to what was seen in the times of the Roman Empire. Thoroughly corrupt though it was, the early Christians, "born yesterday," as Tertullian said, quickly invaded the whole known world of that time.

Ladies and Gentlemen, this is what a spirit of fraternity has been able to accomplish and continues to accomplish in an African tribe become a people, a tribe we met before they had come into contact with so-called civilization.

And we ask ourselves, what could this attitude of fraternity do if it were to fill the rest of the world with its spirit?[65]

A united Europe for a united world

> Address to *"One Thousand Cities for Europe,"* a conference for European mayors, Innsbruck, Austria, 9 November 2001, attended by 1300 people of 35 Eastern and Western European countries, representing 700 municipalities.

The talk I have been asked to present to you today is: *The Spirit of Brotherhood in Politics, Key to the Unity of Europe and of the World*.

The spirit of brotherhood!

When this subject was suggested to me last summer, I could never have imagined the terrible events that would take place before the time actually came to deliver this address. Above all, what an extraordinary confirmation these tragic events would bring of the need for brotherhood in the world, and in particular, of the need for brotherhood in politics.

It was September 11th and the Twin Towers of New York had collapsed. A symbol of the world's most powerful nation had been destroyed along with a terrible and significant loss of human life.

There was shock and great consternation, and not only in the United States!

But then, out of the chaos and confusion of suffering, from that night which had descended so abruptly in broad daylight, emerged an unusual phenomenon: a display of solidarity such as had never before been seen. New York was transformed: walls of indifference dissolved into an avalanche of practical help, of gestures of compassion, of comfort, of readiness to do whatever was needed to relieve the pain.

Through one of its cities, the United States, a multireligious, multiethnic, multi-cultural country, offered the world a model of solidarity and unity.

As if the eyes of a nation were suddenly opened, in the span of a few moments, they saw the absolute necessity of establishing universal brotherhood everywhere.

Universal brotherhood, outside of Christianity too, has not been far from the minds of a few rare giants of the spirit. Mahatma Gandhi is reported to have said: "The Golden Rule is to be friends of the world and to consider the whole human family as 'one.' Whoever distinguishes between the faithful of his own religion and those of another, misinforms the members of his own and opens the way to rejection and irreligion."

Universal brotherhood is still present even today in great souls like the Dalai Lama. Concerning what happened in the United States, he is said to have commented:

"To us the reasons [for these events] are clear. We have not learned the most basic human lessons.... We are all one. That is a message the human race has largely ignored. Forgetting this truth is the only cause of hatred and war, and the way to remember is simple: Love, this and every moment."

But the one who brought universal brotherhood on earth as a priceless gift for humanity was Jesus. In fact, before dying he prayed for unity: "Father, may they all be one" (see Jn 17:21). He revealed to us that God is our Father and consequently, that we are all brothers and sisters. He introduced the concept of humanity as a family, of the "human family" that is possible if we put universal brotherhood into action. Consequently, he knocked down the walls separating those who are considered "alike" from those who are "different"; friends from enemies; walls that isolate one city from another. And he loosened all people from the bonds that imprisoned them, from the thousands of forms of domination and slavery, from every unjust relationship, thereby carrying out a genuinely existential, cultural and political revolution.

And so the idea of brotherhood began to make headway in history. We can retrace its presence through the evolution of thought in various eras; its influence, at times obvious, at times more subtle, can be seen at the basis of many fundamental political ideas. It is a brotherhood often practiced, even if in a limited way, each time a people has joined together to fight for their freedom, or when social activists have battled to defend the weak, or whenever people of different convictions have risen above mistrust in order to affirm a human right.

The extent to which the discovery of brotherhood was fundamental to the development of politics is also affirmed by a watershed event between two eras: the French Revolution. Its motto, "liberty, equality, fraternity," sums up modernity's great political project, even if it intended these three principles in a very limited way.

Furthermore, while numerous countries have managed to establish democratic governments and have succeeded in achieving some degree of liberty and equality, fraternity, in particular, has been more proclaimed than lived.

But the French Revolution, despite its contradictions, intuited what later experience would prove true: its three principles stand or fall together. Only the person who sees the other as a brother or sister can recognize the other's full freedom and equality.

Therefore, we can no longer look at brotherhood as something naïve or superfluous, or as an appendage to politics to be tacked on from outside.

The foundations of Europe — To achieve the grand project of European unity it is necessary to live brotherhood, even though it may be difficult.

We must remember, however, that this plan was not born today. It began long ago.

For example, let's consider a handful of saints chosen as the patrons of Europe, because they are its founders. They managed to intervene at crucial moments of history, constructing the framework and outlining the features of what we call Europe today.

Between the fifth and sixth centuries, during one of the most critical periods in the history of the continent, Benedict of Nursia offered his contemporaries a new model of being human, on the one hand completely immersed in God, and on the other, forging tools and working the land.

Monastic fraternity, beginning with Benedict, created a network of spiritual, economic and cultural centres around which Europe was reborn, a rebirth both spiritual and social.

In addition to this movement, expanding it towards the East, there was the work of two brothers, Cyril and Methodius. In the ninth century they left an indelible mark on the Slavic peoples, devising a form of writing that expressed their language. They integrated these peoples much more deeply into the communion of the Church and, at the same time, preserved their cultural identity. In doing so, their work was a practical application of the Christian model of unity in distinction, which is the DNA of Europe and which continues to be the reference point for the journey that lies ahead.

At a time when Europe seemed to have lost the sense of its spiritual unity — having broken with the previous feudal order yet still lacking a new equilibrium — Bridget of Sweden and Catherine of Siena turned to the powers of the time and, with an authority of love, reminded them of their true objective of serving justice.

And then with Edith Stein, nearly our contemporary, holiness descended into depths of the horror that overwhelmed Europe. In her personal sacrifice she gave witness to a dual faithfulness: to her people and to her faith. She died as a Christian nun, but she died because she was Jewish. Thus, she set the cornerstone of a "European home" in which all religions can cooperate in building brotherhood.

There is holiness at the roots of Europe. And this is true not only of the Europe handed down to us by history, but also of the Europe that we are building today, as witnessed by some of those who were founders of the European Union, such as Robert Schuman and Alcide De Gasperi. The process of canonization, witnessing to their holiness, has been started for them both. And through this process it is becoming clear how they lived out in a heroic way not only religious virtue, but also those civic virtues required by their political profession.

If we go back and consider their original inspiration, to the concept they had of European unity, we may find a light to focus better on our goal.

The first step was the founding of the European Coal and Steel Community (ECSC). But the pooling of coal and steel resources was not motivated by the desire for an economic arrangement. Instead, it was said to be about "solidarity in production" that would render impossible any form of war between France, Germany and the other countries taking part in it. The goal, therefore, was peace, preserving brotherhood, and economic activity was the means for achieving it. As Konrad Adenauer declared in front of the Bundestag in June 1950: "The importance of the project is above all political, and economic."

This initial objective, concerning a major component of the industrial sector, was seen as only one step towards the effective economic unification of Europe. This economic union, in turn, was meant — as Robert Schuman underlined, echoing the ideas of Jean Monnet — to be "the leaven from which may grow a wider and deeper community between countries long opposed to one another by sanguinary divisions." Nevertheless, the ultimate goal of this great effort towards communion is not merely European unity. This is clearly pointed out in the project's first official statement, the "Schuman Declaration," which reads: "With increased resources Europe will be able to pursue the achievement of one of its essential tasks, namely, the development of the African continent."[66]

Thus, in the vision of its founders, Europe is a family of sister nations that are not closed in on themselves, but open to a universal mission: Europe wants to achieve its own unity to contribute then to the unity of the human family.

A united Europe, therefore, to build a united world.

A united world?

We may think it a dream, especially at this time in history. Perhaps even a utopia. But it is not necessarily so, especially if we consider the words that Pope John Paul II addressed to the youth of the Focolare Movement a few years ago: "Truly, this seems to be the perspective which emerges from the multiple signs of our times: the perspective of a united world. This is the great expectation of people today ... and at the same time, the great challenge for the future. We are aware that the world is moving towards unity. In fact, it is being propelled towards unity at an exceptional speed."[67]

This acceleration towards unity may also be due to circumstances that seem, and indeed are, contrary to its existence. But paradoxically, today, the idea that everything can cooperate towards the good for those who believe is an idea shared by not just a few.

The Church has also been affirming it for quite some time when it speaks of a new order for the world, a new order for economics, a globalizing of solidarity. The wake-up calls we are hearing today make us realize that such ideals are not simply optional; they are essential for the development of humanity here on earth.

Instruments of unity — But how can we continue the work of those who have built Europe down through the centuries?

We do not lack the necessary tools to promote brotherhood in Europe and give it the soul it needs to generate spiritual unity, the guarantee of unity in politics, economics, and so on. What is needed is to single them out.

One of these tools, whose effectiveness has not yet been completely discovered, is the appearance, in the latter part of the twentieth century, of the dozens and dozens of new ecclesial movements and communities. They have sprung up mainly in Europe (Spain, France, Germany, Italy) and not only in the Catholic Church. And because these Movements were founded by or made up primarily of laypeople, they demonstrate a profound interest in human endeavours and, consequently, in the life of society. For this reason they offer practical contributions in politics, economics, and so forth.

The true colours of these ecclesial realities were seen in the meeting of Pentecost 1998 when the Church re-discovered and re-presented itself to the world as being constituted, not only by the institutional aspect, but also by its co-essential charismatic aspect. This aspect of the Church has enriched the centuries with spiritual movements (for example, the Franciscan Movement), and with the widest variety of currents of thought and spirituality. These movements served to bring Christianity back to the authenticity and radicalism of the gospel when it had strayed, often having been weakened and secularized by its contact with the world.

Authenticity and radicalism, especially in living the extraordinary love that the gospel speaks of, the primary source of brotherhood. It is a love that must be directed towards everyone, therefore, also towards enemies, a love that courageously takes the initiative, a love that is not mere sentimentalism but practical action, that treats everyone as equals. It is a love that, if lived together with others, becomes mutual and generates brotherhood, unity.

These Movements, each following its own charism, make love concrete in many different ways. But above all, many of them manifest the power of the Spirit, who is always attentive to the needs of the moment, through their capacity to open a profound dialogue with all men and women throughout the world. Today four dialogues are truly necessary for building brotherhood in Europe. There is the dialogue within each Christian church, already under way also through the work of the new ecclesial Movements. There is the ecumenical dialogue, working towards recomposing the unity of the one Church. There is the dialogue with people of other religions: Muslims, Jews,

Buddhists, etc., present today in Europe also as a result of widespread immigration and the interaction among nations linked to increasing globalization. This dialogue is possible because of the so-called "Golden Rule," common to all the major religions of the world, which says: "Do not do to others as you would not have them do to you" (see Lk 6:31). Ultimately, the Golden Rule means: to love. And so if we, because we are Christians, love, and they love in return, there is mutual love. Thus, brotherhood is established with them too. Finally, there is the dialogue with those brothers and sisters, perhaps the majority, who do not profess any religious faith, but who have the desire to love also in the DNA of their souls.

Furthermore, John Paul II has lent his authoritative voice to the call to work for brotherhood. In 2001, in his apostolic letter *Novo Millennio Ineunte*, he proposed to all Christians what he called the "spirituality of communion," which makes brotherhood possible.

This spirituality has already been present in the Church for some sixty years in one of its Movements, the Focolare, but has been limited to it. Now that it has been endorsed by the Holy Father, it can and must animate the entire Church and beyond.

The secret to this spirituality lies in fixing one's gaze upon the one who is the author of brotherhood. We are called to imitate him, who gathered all people into unity — unity with God and with one another — the crucified Lord who cries: "My God, my God, why have you forsaken me?" (Mt 27:46).

All of us, men and women, were separated from the Father and divided among ourselves. It was necessary for the Son, in whom we are all represented, to experience separation from the Father, with whom he was one (see Jn 10:30).

But he did not remain in the abyss of that infinite suffering. With immense effort, the abandoned one re-abandoned himself to the Father saying: "Father, into your hands I commend my spirit" (Lk 23:46), and thus brought us back to unity with God and with one another.

It is the mystery of Jesus Forsaken-and-Risen. Imitating him makes it possible for all of us to overcome every division and to engage in dialogue with all.

Political prospects for fraternity — The new Movements usually take an active interest in human endeavours. In the Focolare, living out the "spirituality of unity or of communion" has articulated itself in several ways. These include the one known as the Movement for Unity in Politics, whose specific aim is to promote brotherhood in the political arena.

The Movement for Unity in Politics began in Naples in 1996, building on the experience of Italian politicians who, beginning in the fifties, sought to live this ideal of unity. After years of living this spirituality at various levels of political commitment, from the administration of cities to parliamentary activity, we can now see that it is possible to derive some practical guidelines, which could be developed further and applied throughout the continent.

First of all, we realized that there is a true and proper political vocation. It is a personal calling that emerges from circumstances and is communicated through one's conscience. Those who believe clearly discern God's voice entrusting them with a task. But also those who do not adhere to any particular faith feel the political calling, perhaps inspired by a social need, by a minority group that needs help, by a violated human right, or by the desire to do something good for their city or nation.

Furthermore, the response to a political vocation is before all else an act of brotherhood. In fact, one does not become politically active simply in order to resolve a problem; one acts in response to a public need and deals with questions that concern others, wanting their good as if it were one's own.

By living in this way, politicians are able to give their total attention to citizens, to get to know their needs and their resources. They are able to understand the history of their city, to value the heritage of its culture and its associations, to discern, little by little, its true vocation and to map out with confidence a path to be followed.

In fact, politics seen as love creates and preserves those conditions that allow all the other types of love to flourish: the love of young people who want to get married and who need a house and employment; the love of those who want to study and who need schools and books; the love of those who run their own businesses and who need roads and railways, clear and reliable laws…. Thus, politics is the love of all loves, gathering the resources of people and groups into the unity of a common design so as to provide the means for each one to fulfil in complete freedom his or her specific vocation. But it also encourages people to co-operate, bringing together needs and resources, questions and answers, instilling mutual trust among all. Politics can be compared to the stem of a flower, which supports and nourishes the fresh unfolding of the petals of the community.

We all know that today, too, it would appear that for some "the city" does not even exist, citizens for whom the various government institutions struggle to come up with answers to their needs. Some feel excluded from the fabric of society and separated from the political body because they lack employment, housing, or adequate health care. Every day, such citizens bring these and many other problems before those who govern. The response they get dramatically influences their perception of themselves as full-fledged citizens, and they feel the need and discover the actual possibility to participate in the city's social and political life.

From this point of view, therefore, the town or municipality can be considered the most important institution because it is closest to the people and comes into direct contact with all types of needs. And it is through this relationship with the various expressions of government at the most local level that a citizen develops a sense of gratitude — or resentment — toward political institutions as a whole, including more distant ones, such as national government.

If then we consider the national dimension of politics and the relationships between the main political currents which alternate in governing our countries, we note that living out our political choice as a vocation of love leads us to understand that others, who have made a political choice different from our own, can be motivated by a vocation of love similar to ours. They too — in their own way — are part of the same design, even if they are our political opponents. Brotherhood helps us to recognize their task, to respect it, and to help them to be faithful to it — even through constructive criticism — while we remain faithful to our own.

We should live brotherhood so well that we reach the point of loving the party of the other as we love our own, knowing that neither party was born by chance, but each as the answer to a historical need within the national community. And only by satisfying all the needs, only by harmonizing them in a common design, can politics reach its proper goal. Brotherhood brings out the genuine values of each party and rebuilds the political life of a nation as a whole.

The initiatives of the members of the Movement for Unity in Politics bear witness to this. Seeking to create a spirit of brotherhood between the governing majority and the opposition in Parliament and in the various municipalities, their initiatives have been translated into national laws or into local policies that have brought a greater unity to the cities in which they have been enacted.

Their numerous experiences concerning the welcoming of immigrants also bear witness to this. People pour into the more industrialized countries for many reasons, not only economic but also political. A city or nation does not lose when it opens its doors to others; on the contrary, it gains. Its political stature is raised when it offers citizenship and a country to those who have lost their own.

And because we love our own country we can understand that others feel the same for their own, in which there also exists a plan of love.

Therefore, those who respond to their political vocation by practicing brotherhood enter into a universal dimension that gives them a vision open to all humanity. Because they acknowledge the universal consequences of their choices, they try to discern whether their decisions, even if serving the interests of their nation, might harm others. In this way, each political act, not only that of a national government, but also the most local gesture carried out in the smallest municipality of the most distant province, assumes a universal significance, because the politician who implements it is fully human and fully responsible. Politicians of unity love the country of others as they love their own.

This is the characteristic of the political dimension of being citizens: maintaining a continuous relationship with others; acknowledging the fact that the others are distinct from me, but, at the same time, being convinced that we belong to "the city" together. This is also the characteristic typical of Europe.

In fact, when we began to speak of Europe, we did so in relation to the city.

Throughout the centuries the perception of what Europe is grew deeper at the same time as its borders widened. From the small country of Greece, Europe would eventually see itself extending from the Atlantic Ocean to the Ural Mountains. This was possible mainly because of the penetration of Christianity, which instilled religious principles into the peoples of "geographical" Europe. The eventual development of these religious principles into civic, social and political ones would later build up the "cultural" Europe. And all of this without suffocating the distinct identities of the cities and nations gradually being formed.

We find the same situation at the change of every era: what we thought to be Europe at a given point proved to be too small. Each time Europe was confronted with something different and that put it in cheque, it was challenged to understand this new element, to assimilate it, thereby changing it and changing itself.

In doing so, Europe continued to progress toward its true self, towards the coming to full maturity of that Christian seed which, to be sure, can be expressed no longer in terms of medieval "Christendom," but more deeply in the dynamics of universal brotherhood, which embraces various people and nations.

The vocation of Europe lies in this model of universal brotherhood, which creates unity while respecting distinction. It is a work in process. The wars, the totalitarian regimes, the injustices have left open wounds in need of healing. But to be truly European, we must succeed in looking at the past with mercy, acknowledging as our own the history of my nation as well as the others'. We need to recognize that what we are today is the fruit of a history lived together, of a European destiny that we must fully and knowingly take in our hands.

Today, the unity of Europe asks that European politicians interpret the signs of the times and formulate, as it were, a pact of brotherhood with one another, a pact that commits them to consider themselves as members of Europe, just as they are members of their own nations. It urges them always to seek what unites and to work together towards finding solutions for the problems that still remain as stumbling blocks to the unity of all Europe.

Without a doubt, it is worthwhile dedicating one's life to such a lofty goal.

Ladies and Gentlemen, this is my wish for you.[68]

Politics based on communion

> A previously unpublished address to British politicians, the Palace of Westminster, London, 22 June 2004.

Distinguished Speaker of the House of Commons,
Honourable Members of Parliament,
My Lords, Ladies and Gentlemen,

It is a real honour and a joy for me to address such a distinguished gathering here in London. In thanking you all for coming, it is my heartfelt desire that this meeting will prove to be a moment of peace and calm in the midst of your busy schedules.

I would like to share with you something that has come to life in the political field in these last few years. It has come about as a result of a charism or gift that I myself received many years ago and that has borne fruit in every part of the world, among people of different cultures, religious faiths and social backgrounds. It is an experience and culture founded on unity, something for which humankind has always felt a profound need.

The title proposed for today's meeting is: "Liberty, equality ... whatever happened to fraternity?"

These three: liberty, equality, fraternity, almost sum up the political programme of the modern world, expressing a deep intuition and leading us to a profound reflection today. But what point have we reached in achieving these great aspirations?

The French Revolution announced these three principles but it certainly did not invent them. They had already been elaborated through the centuries, above all through the Christian message, which enlightened the best ancient traditions of the various peoples and drew on the heritage of Jewish revelation, bringing about a true revolution. The new humanism revealed by Christ enabled people to live these principles to the full.

From that announcement onwards, and down the centuries, the richness of these principles has been revealed through the works of men and women.

Much ground has been covered along this journey and the United Kingdom has often paved the way.

Liberty and equality have deeply marked the political history of peoples, resulting in a more civilized society and creating the conditions for the expression of human dignity to grow.

Certainly, the development of these two principles is familiar to a people that produced *Magna Carta* and the *Bill of Rights*, to a people that acted as teacher in the invention of democracy and social politics.

Liberty and equality have become juridical principles and are applied every day as real and true political categories.

But as we know well, if emphasis falls solely on liberty, it can easily become the privilege of the strongest. And as history confirms, emphasis solely on equality can result in mass collectivism. In reality, many peoples still do not benefit from the true meaning of liberty and equality....

How can these be acquired and brought to fruition? How can the history of our countries and of all humankind resume the journey towards its true destiny? We believe that the key lies in universal fraternity, in giving this its proper place among fundamental political categories.

Only if taken together can these three principles give rise to a political model capable of meeting the challenges of today's world.

Rarely has our planet been subject to the suspicion, fear and even terror of our times. We only have to remember September 11, 2001, and more recently in Madrid, March 11, 2004, as well as the hundreds of other attacks which, in the last few years, have riddled our daily news reports.

Terrorism — a disaster just as serious as the dozens of wars that even now bloody our planet!

But what are the causes? There are many. However, we cannot help but recognize that one of the deepest causes is the economic and social imbalance between rich and poor countries. This imbalance generates resentment, hostility and revenge, thus providing a breeding ground for fundamentalism that takes root more easily in such terrain.

Now, if this is how things are, in order to reduce and put an end to terrorism, war is certainly not the answer. We need to pursue the way of dialogue, and therefore, political and diplomatic routes. But this is not enough. We need to promote solidarity among everyone in the world and a more equitable communion of goods.

It goes without saying that there are many more burning issues facing national and international politics. In the Western world the very model for economic development is now undeniably in crisis, a crisis that no longer demands merely minor adjustments, but a global reappraisal in order to overcome the current downturn.

The relentless march of scientific research cannot continue unless it guarantees the integrity and health of humankind and the entire ecosystem. In acknowledging the essential role of the communications media in the modern world, we must establish certain basic rules aimed at promoting values and safeguarding individuals, groups and peoples.

While recognizing the current irreversible process of globalization, a key question arises from the need to defend and appreciate the many riches that come from the different ethnic, religious and cultural groups.

These are some of the major challenges facing the world today that urgently call for the idea and the practice of fraternity, and since this is a worldwide problem, they call for universal fraternity.

But are there signs of fraternity in people's lives today?

The facts are in front of us, but we have to know how to interpret them. The world's longing for unity has never been so alive and evident as it is today. The signs of this are:

- the coming together of separate states and the processes of an economic and political integration — and here we cannot fail to mention Europe — which are gaining strength both on a continental level and in other geopolitical areas.
- The role of international organizations, especially the United Nations, more crucial today than ever in knowing, facing and responding to the key questions affecting the lives of peoples and countries.
- The development of an increasingly wide and fruitful dialogue among people of various Christian traditions, with people of different religious faiths, and also with people who have no particular religious affiliation.
- the growth of social, cultural and religious movements which present themselves as new leading figures in international relations and working together towards worldwide objectives.

Therefore, the means necessary to give the world that fraternity which generates spiritual unity and which guarantees unity in politics, economics, and in social and cultural spheres are not lacking. We need only to recognize them.

One means whose effectiveness has not yet been completely discovered is the existence of dozens and dozens of Movements, which began to appear in the Christian world after the first few decades of the twentieth century. They form many networks that link people who vary in ethnicity, culture or any other way, almost a sign that because in prototype this is already true for them, the world could become a home for the nations.

These Movements are the result not of human plans or projects but of gifts of the Spirit of God who, more than any man or woman on earth, knows the problems of our planet and wants to provide all his support to resolve them.

Because these Movements were founded by or are mostly made up of laypeople, they carry with them a profound concern for human affairs. Consequently, they have effects in civil life, offering practical and achievable projects in the fields of politics, economics, and so forth.

These diverse and wonderful Movements have come to life in various Churches: Catholic, Anglican, Evangelical Lutheran, Orthodox, and others. On 8 May 2004, in Stuttgart, Germany, they presented themselves in a highly successful event that they themselves organized, transmitted via satellite across Europe and beyond. The day was entitled: *Together for Europe*.

They offered to work towards achieving — alongside the Europe of politics or economics, or the Euro — the Europe of the spirit, seeking to give a soul to Europe, a process that would also give a better guarantee to the continent's plurality and cohesion.

To give an example of these movements I would like to present to you the main ideas of our Focolare Movement whose aim is precisely that of unity and universal fraternity.

It came to life while Trent (Northern Italy) was being bombed during the Second World War. Buildings were crumbling and with them our plans for the future, our hopes and certainties.

Everything was collapsing, yet in our young hearts a single truth was emerging with an intensity we had never known before: God is the only Ideal that never dies, God who was revealing himself to us for what he is, Love. And precisely at the height of hatred and division, God who is Love suggested to us that to love him we needed to love one another and bring this love to everyone, a love that spread immediately throughout the city, and later, with the passing of time, across the world to 182 countries.

This call to unity made us prefer those places in the world where there was the most division. As a result, there stood out ever more clearly specific areas of dialogue and sharing: first of all within the individual Churches, where the Movement gives its contribution so that there may be more communion; among Christians of various denominations; then with the faithful of the great religions via numerous respectful and fruitful experiences of the "dialogue of life," the premise for peace; and finally, a dialogue with those who have no particular religious affiliation, which includes a committed working together on various projects.

Although the Focolare is primarily a religious movement, from its beginnings and down through the years it has shown special interest in the many aspects of the life of society, including the political world. As a result of this, the Movement for Unity in Politics was born. Now it too is spreading and establishing itself throughout the world.

I have had several opportunities to speak of the birth and development of the Movement for Unity in Politics, addressing members of Parliament in various European nations as well as in Strasbourg, at the European Centre in Madrid and at the United Nations.

The specific goal of this Movement, the political expression of the Focolare, is to help people and groups involved in politics to rediscover the profound, eternal values of the human person, to put fraternity at the basis of their lives and only then to move on to political action. A consequence of this is that political action goes from interpersonal love to the possibility of a greater love, which reaches out to the entire *polis* (the city). In acquiring a political dimension, this love does not lose its particular characteristics: the involvement of the whole person, with the intelligence and the will to reach everyone; the intuition and the imagination to take the first step; the realism to put oneself in the other person's shoes; the capacity to give oneself without hope of personal gain and to open up new paths to dialogue even when human limitations and failures would seem to block them.

The Movement for Unity in Politics aims to include administrators, members of parliament, party activists — politicians at every level of government and of the most varied political parties — who feel the duty to work together with the one who really has sovereignty, the citizen. In addition, it embraces citizens who want to be involved politically, students and political analysts who want to offer their contribution in expertise and research, and local government officers aware of their particular place in the political system.

This Movement proposes and gives witness to a lifestyle that allows politics in the best way possible to reach its goal: the common good in the unity of the social body.

Indeed, it would be good to invite all those involved in politics to make a pact of fraternity for the benefit of their country, one that puts its good above all partial interests, whether those of individuals, groups, classes or parties.

Yes, fraternity offers surprising possibilities. It helps to bring together and give value to demands that otherwise could develop into insoluble conflicts. It harmonizes the experience of local autonomy with the sense of a shared history. It strengthens our awareness of the importance of international organizations and all those systems that attempt to overcome barriers and take important steps towards the unity of the human family.

Fraternity can give rise to projects and actions in the complex political, economic, cultural and social fabric of our world. Fraternity brings peoples out of their isolation and can offer the opportunity for development to those still excluded from it. It shows us how to resolve differences peacefully and relegates war to history books. Fraternity in action allows us to dream and even to hope for some kind of communion of goods between rich countries and poor countries.

The profound need for peace expressed by humanity today indicates that fraternity is not only a value, not only a method, but also the global paradigm for political development. This is why an increasingly interdependent world needs politicians, entrepreneurs, intellectuals and artists who put fraternity —

an instrument of unity — at the centre of their actions and thoughts. Martin Luther King dreamt that fraternity would become the organizing principle for business people and the principle of organization for people who govern. The politicians of the Movement for Unity in Politics want to make this dream a reality.

But this is only possible if, in political activity, one does not forget the spiritual dimension or at least believe in the profound values that must rule the life of society.

Igino Giordani, an Italian member of parliament and co-founder of the Focolare Movement, wrote in his own unique style: "When we cross the threshold of our home to plunge into the world, we cannot leave our faith hanging on the back of the door like a worn-out hat." And shortly afterwards he added: "Politics is charity in action, handmaid not ruler."

One day I seemed to understand in what sense politics could be considered love. If we were to give a colour to every human activity, to economy, to health, communication, art, culture, the administration of justice ... politics would not have a colour. It would be the background, it would be black so as to highlight all the other colours. For this reason politics should seek to be in constant dialogue with every other aspect of life, in order to provide the conditions for society itself, in all its expressions, to achieve its design completely. Of course, in this constant attention towards dialogue, politics must reserve to itself certain areas: promoting fair, unbiased policies; giving preference to those in need; fostering participation at all times, which means dialogue, mediation, responsibility and practical action.

The politicians I am speaking of choose to seek office as an act of love. It is a response to a genuine vocation, to a personal calling. Those who are believers discern the voice of God calling them through circumstances, while those with no religious affiliation respond to a human call, to a social need, to a city's problems, to the sufferings of their people which speak to their conscience. In both cases, it is love that motivates them to act. And both find their home in the Movement for Unity in Politics.

The politicians for unity, having come to understand that politics at its root is love, realize that others too — even those who at times can be called their political opponents — may have also chosen politics as a vocation to love. They realize that every political group, every political choice can be a response to a social need and therefore is necessary in building up the common good. They are as interested in the others' goals, including their political causes, as they are in their own, and thus criticism becomes constructive. They seek to live out the apparent contradiction of loving the other's party as their own because they realize that the nation's well-being requires everyone's cooperation.

This, in outline, is the ideal of the Movement for Unity in Politics. And in my opinion it is a kind of politics worth living. It forms politicians capable of recognizing and serving the vision for their community, their town and nation, indeed for all humanity, because fraternity is God's vision for the whole human family. This is the kind of genuine, authoritative politics that every country needs. In fact, with power comes strength but only love gives authority.

This type of politics builds works that will last. Future generations will be grateful to politicians not for having retained power but for how they used it.

This is the kind of politics that the Movement for Unity in Politics, with the help of God, wishes to generate and support.

So, then, what is my wish for you, politicians of the United Kingdom?

That this people and in particular its representatives, rich in their noble history of democracy, may find through fraternity the energy necessary to continue along their path with even greater effectiveness and give their contribution as leading figures in the human family's history of unity. We, for our part, promise not to leave you on your own, but to put at your disposal the charism of unity that heaven offers to the whole of humanity.

For an interdependence based on fraternity

> Following the September 11th terrorist attacks Professor Benjamin R. Barber, political scientist and professor at the University of Maryland, proposed what he called a "Day of Interdependence." The first Day of Interdependence was held in Philadelphia on 12 September 2003. On that occasion, a "Declaration of Interdependence" was proposed and signed by 500 political leaders, scholars and artists. Faced with the danger of irreparable divisions in the world between the North and South and with unrestrained globalization, the project hopes to weave a network of relationships and an open dialogue aimed at finding an alternative to the logic of terror and war. On the second Day of Interdependence, held in Rome, 12 September 2004, Chiara Lubich delivered this previously unpublished address.

Dear friends,

I feel extremely comfortable today reflecting with you from various perspectives on the many, many facets of interdependence that together we wish to examine, in order to understand better how to direct them toward the ultimate good of the human family.

For my part, I would like to emphasize an aspect of interdependence that I mentioned in my message for the first World Day of Interdependence held in Philadelphia on 12 September 2003. I am referring to this: the reality of interdependence stirs within many an urgency and a need for an ideal to which people of goodwill worldwide have decided to dedicate their lives. It is the Ideal of helping to bring about universal brotherhood, the basis for the unity of the human family.

Yes, because interdependence implies a mutual relationship between two parties who condition one another. This relationship cannot be lived out perfectly between individuals or among nations if it is not characterized by mutual respect and understanding, by the capacity to embrace the difficulties and issues that each one faces, and by the desire to welcome one another's unique gifts. Practically speaking, it requires mutual love as it is lived out between brothers and sisters.

Interdependence between brothers and sisters presupposes, in fact, the choice of respectful dialogue as opposed to hegemony and the practice of sharing among all as opposed to concentrating resources and expertise exclusively in certain parts of the world.

Interdependence between brothers and sisters is actually "mutual dependence" because it implies that affirming my identity cannot be achieved either by being defensive or by opposing others, but only through communion: of resources, of civic virtues, of cultural riches and of political and institutional experience.

But these are not merely my own words. They are the fruit of the experience of the Focolare Movement, to which I belong and which is the effect of a charism of the Holy Spirit. It is a multi-cultural, multi-ethnic and religiously diverse Movement that has now spread to 182 nations, with millions of adherents whose goal is fraternity, in fact, to bring about universal brotherhood.

It is this same experience that gave rise to a certainty and a renewed confidence in me as I interpreted, for example, what occurred after the Twin Towers were destroyed. While that tragic event was clearly a moment of the greatest breakdown in relationships among individuals and peoples, paradoxically it also appeared to me as an opportunity for the world to take a step forward towards universal brotherhood.

And my feelings were confirmed immediately in the hours following that terrible event by the eyewitness accounts and reactions that I heard from many Focolare members around the world. From the United States, they told me that even in the midst of the tragedy that had shaken the whole nation, the American people was experiencing a perhaps unprecedented sense of solidarity and a willingness to share what they had with those in need. The Christian and African American Muslim communities of our Movement joined together and reacted to the backlash of hatred by visibly demonstrating the deep fraternal bond that exists between them.

I received similar confirmations from Algeria, from the Palestinian territories, from Jerusalem, as well as from South Africa and from all the European nations. Young and old, members of different faiths, all assumed a greater and more conscious sense of responsibility. From that day on, our commitment to build unity among all peoples acquired greater conviction and determination.

For this reason we have given our full support to the principles and the substance of the Interdependence Days. In fact, it is impossible not to recognize that interdependence and brotherhood are two of the stages in humanity's journey towards its complete reconciliation.

As John Paul II wrote on the occasion of the World Day of Peace in 2001, it is precisely the "present reality of global interdependence that helps us to recognize the common destiny of the entire human family."

On the basis of all this, in agreement with Dr Barber — with whom there was an immediate and profound meeting of minds — I would now like to set before you some ideas regarding the principles, both human and supernatural, on which our experience rests.

Some sixty years have passed — we were just a few young women then — but I remember one of my first intuitions as clearly as if it were yesterday. The Second World War was raging and, under a fierce bombardment, we had taken refuge in a cellar. Aided by the faint light of a candle, we read in the gospel — the only reference point for our lives — Jesus' testament where he proposes universal brotherhood: "May they all be one" (Jn 17:21). We understood that our Movement had come to life to fulfil this page of the gospel. That "all" would be our field of action, and unity our reason for being.

Making this, God's dream, our own linked us to heaven. At the same time, it immersed us totally in the history of humanity, in order to uncover the path leading to universal brotherhood.

In the midst of the war, the most painful of divisions, paradoxically we chose the highest form of interdependence: unity.

The possibility of fulfilling this ideal was rooted in what seemed to us a genuine discovery: God is Love, a love that embraces every era and makes all men and women brothers and sisters. This love immediately became mutual among us, thus generating a profound experience of community. That same love urged us to reach out, above all to the most needy, in order to resolve — as we used to say in those days — the social problems of our small city, Trent.

This new inclusive way of looking at our city immediately caught on and within a few months we were more than 500 people of every age, professional and social background.

Unity, therefore, is the specific "sign" of the Focolare Movement's inner nature, but it is also a "vocation," a calling for all people of goodwill.

As the years have passed, certain specific dialogues and forums fostering mutual exchange have emerged. We have found ourselves creating spaces and opportunities for encounter within each of our various churches, so as to foster an ever-greater "communion." What is more, we also have experienced being one Christian people among Christians of different traditions, where in sharing in the specific gifts of each Church we experience a prelude to doctrinal unity.

But in particular there is one front on which we feel called to work, and even more so after September 11th a challenge we already began to face more than twenty years ago. It is dialogue with the faithful of the major world religions.

In a dialogue of life that is respectful and the fruitful, the premise to peace, we aim on both sides to live out the so-called Golden Rule: "Do to others as you would have them do to you," which means to love the others. It is a principle present, with varying nuances, in all the great faith traditions.

Lastly, from the very beginning, we have come together, working actively with those who have no particular religious affiliation. We are united by our love for humanity and for human values.

This constant searching for that which unites, this conviction that union is possible, throughout the years has brought to fruition initiatives both great and small. I will mention two, which express the surprising ability brotherhood demonstrates when applied to the great questions of our times.

The project for an Economy of Communion, born in 1991, today includes 797 businesses throughout the world. They operate in the marketplace and divide their profits into three parts: one is used to assist those in need, giving them the help they require until they find a job; another to develop structures that promote the "culture of giving"; a third for the growth of the firm. In the inspiring idea and the experience that lie at the basis of the Economy of

Communion some economists glimpse a new interpretative tool that could contribute to overcoming the individualistic mentality that prevails today.

In 1996 the Focolare's concern for politics, understood from the start as a vocation essential to the realization of the human family, was consolidated into a particular branch, the Movement for Unity in Politics. Today this movement, is an international political workshop that gathers together citizens, officials, scholars, politicians at various levels representing different political convictions and parties, who have placed at the centre of all that they do the fundamental values of their various political cultures. Several things could be said of them, but their goal is to make fraternity be recognized as a political value.

In my lifetime, I have come to know countless individuals, groups and peoples. I find always that the longing for unity is an unquenchable aspiration in the heart of every human being, of every social group, of every people.

Experience has shown me how to recognize the steps that mark the progress of humanity, to the point of being able to affirm that human history is nothing more than a slow, unstoppable journey towards universal brotherhood. But unity is a journey that needs to be looked after and supported. If there is one gift that we can bring to this second Interdependence Day, it is precisely fraternity. And not only in terms of the real benefits that have come about from its practice in daily life, but also in its meaning as a cultural paradigm.

Animated by fraternity, interdependence, beyond being a simple "fact" or "tool," can become the force that drives the process of positive developments.

It can become a gift for all and a strategy not only for the good of a single people, but for all of humanity.

After thousands of years of history marked by the fruits of violence and hatred, we have every right to ask that humanity may now begin to experience the fruits of love, and not only of love lived out among individuals, but also among peoples.

The Charism of Unity and Economy

> The texts in this section, from the 1960s to 2004, highlight the economic implications of the charism of unity, focusing in particular on what is called the Economy of Communion.

The "Magna Carta"

The Magna Carta of Christian social doctrine begins when Mary sings: "He has brought down the powerful from their thrones, and lifted up the lowly; he has filled the hungry with good things, and sent the rich away empty" (Lk 1:52-53).

The gospel contains the highest and most radical revolution. And perhaps it is in God's plans that also in this era, deeply concerned as it is with social problems, Mary should be the one to lend a hand to all of us Christians in founding, strengthening, raising up and displaying to the world a new society in which the power of the Magnificat resounds.[69]

Underdeveloped Christians

A lot is said about the Third World, and action is taken on its behalf. Hunger, nakedness, homelessness, ignorance, illiteracy, illness and often the resulting immorality in different ways claim their victims in appalling proportions in many countries of the world.

The media have highlighted these ill-omened wounds and to a greater or lesser extent they have left all of us shaken.

The encyclical *Populorum progressio* has been a clarion call, the voice of Christ in the twentieth century, encouraging those organizations, associations and individuals already devoted to improving conditions in developing countries and inviting the world to do more, much more. It is an invitation to progress, which today is synonymous with peace. In fact, much is already being done and much will be done.

Unfortunately, however, our efforts, our hard work and expense of energy and resources, do not always produce a satisfactory result in proportion to what we may have expected. And this can be shown in a thousand ways.

It is proof of the words: "One does not live by bread alone ..." (Mt 4:4).

There is something that stops or slows the efforts of those dedicated to their duty-bound acts of fraternal charity.

There is something we Christians ought to do and have not yet done: a confession we ought to shout out if we do not wish to be and seem to be hypocrites.

It is this: is the Third World materially underdeveloped?

Very well, there is also a world underdeveloped spiritually, Christianly.

In fact, the great majority of us who follow Christ are underdeveloped Christians.

Does this come as a surprise?

And yet it is true. The statistics concerning baptized Catholics who do not go to church make you shudder. But we do not wish to speak here about those who are non-practicing or already secularized. No, let us speak about ourselves and about those who like us are called "the faithful," "church-goers," or even "good Christians...."

It is shocking, even if not dismaying, what many saints thought a true Christian to be. Catherine of Siena and Teresa of Avila, both doctors of the Church, and Thomas Aquinas and Francis de Sales considered that only those who have reached the full development of love could call themselves real Christians, Christians who are, so to speak, "actualized." Indeed, God's commandment to love him with all one's heart, mind and strength, is for all Christians.

Furthermore, this conviction corresponds to the often little-understood words of the Master directed to everyone: "Be perfect, therefore, as your heavenly Father is perfect" (Mt 5:48).

Pope Pius XI, commenting on this exhortation by Jesus and explaining Francis de Sales' idea of Christian life, said: "We cannot accept the belief that this command of Christ concerns only a select and privileged group of souls and that all others may consider themselves pleasing to Him if they have attained a lower degree of holiness.... The law of holiness embraces all men and admits of no exception."[70]

The tiny sac that appears on the blossom when the sepals have swollen and the petals dropped away can be called an apple only with difficulty. And when the fruit finally takes form but is still green and bitter, waiting for new sap and sunshine to be able to fulfil the task for which it was created — that is to nourish human beings — even if it is called an apple, it must be said to be "unripe." It is no use to humans. At most, were it to fall, it could be useful for animals.

The same is true of us Christians.

Until we reach "ripeness" in loving, we cannot take for ourselves the name "Christians" in the fullest sense of the word.

In the beginning we are Christians because we have been baptized. Then, we become, so to speak, "developing" Christians…. But only when Christ's life, his law and his holiness have triumphed in us, can we truly call ourselves Christians.

If this is how things stand, it is no wonder that we feel ourselves to be "underdeveloped Christians."

And the way, the manner, the means to improve our spiritual situation?

The means are not lacking. The Church offers them in abundance. It teaches that if baptism has given us the right to the name "Christian" because we have been incorporated into Christ, the grace of God still requires our cooperation.

We are often so tremendously undernourished to the point that we no longer feel the pangs of hunger. Yet the Eucharist is there, waiting for us to be nourished by very flesh of Christ.

We are frighteningly defenceless and exposed to every sort of spiritual illness, which we frequently transmit to one another. Yet the sacrament of Penance is there to heal us and give us new strength.

We are naked, yet we could be clothed with Christ.

We are homeless, yet even here on earth we could all be in the warmth of the Father's house. We could all be in that foretaste of heaven if we lived in the mystical but true reality we share as blood relations with Christ and with each other, and if we rediscovered ourselves as brothers and sisters and rebuilt the family, where Christ is present among us and where spiritual and material riches flow among everyone.

We walk like those who do not know where they are going, yet we have in our hands the code to life, to every life: the gospel. All we have to do is want it.

We complain that priests today are in crisis and we are scandalized by certain things they ask for, yet we do not realize that priests generally reflect the Christian community.

Third World countries are underdeveloped economically and in other aspects as well.

We Christians foolishly are underdeveloped, because the means of development surround us, yet like the mythological king Midas, we risk dying of hunger in the midst of gold.

The problems of the Third World are no joke. They require a massive shift of goods, an enormous restructuring, a setting things right. Yet we do not know how to do it.

However much we want to help, we lack the skill to design comprehensive projects on a worldwide scale, because to do so requires a love that is universal.

Here must come into play the One who created this world and knows the destinies and penetrates the most hidden thoughts and aspirations of human beings and who knows the spiritual and material potential of every people, the One who knows our humanity because he experienced it firsthand, the One who sums up humanity in himself, because he is not just a man, but the Man. Only he can inspire in us a universal spirit and vision of love. Pope John XXIII, for example, tells us that we should measure the surplus we give to those who do not have according to their needs. But who can better measure the needs of all our brothers and sisters, if not someone who contains in himself the measure of humanity? This is none other than Christ.

And for the most part he wishes to act in the world through Christians. And he can do this through those in whom, because of their charge of love, he lives and acts freely.

Therefore, their projects are enlightened by his wisdom and despite any difficulties are brought to completion.

I think that a true resolution of the Third World's problems urges us to resolve our own, the most serious being our limited Christianity.

To take up again the example mentioned earlier: just as an apple fulfils its purpose only when it is ripe, a Christian can offer true, decisive, competent help to humanity only when perfect as the "heavenly Father is perfect," because when perfect as the Father he or she is another Christ, and therefore another "Son of Man."

And this is wonderful, because it means that only a true Christian turns out to be a "complete" man or woman. But that is not enough. Here it is necessary to draw out all the consequences. The authenticity required by these times demands it: the perfect Christian is also a saint. Therefore, we must conclude that in God's eyes "human being," "Christian" and "saint" are synonyms.

"Holiness! It's just a word ... " say many, very many people.

No. Christ does not ask us the impossible!

Furthermore, we must rid ourselves of a certain idea of holiness inherited from the past. Phenomena such as miracles, ecstasies, visions do not constitute holiness.

Holiness lies in perfect love.

And today, an era when the masses are reawakening — and this is a sign of the times — today, when the peoples as well need to establish fraternal relations with one another and every detail must be seen from a global perspective, what is required is a holiness of the masses, a communitarian holiness, a holiness of the people.[71]

The heavens protest

Our days are overflowing with problems. We can read them on the faces of many we meet on the street. "My son doesn't study and he'll fail his exams...." "My husband is always late...." "My mother is ill...." "Will I be able to buy myself that dress? To save enough to go on holiday?"

We run here, we run there. We make our calculations. We are troubled by many things. And this is true for us and for those around us.

But if we let our gaze turn to other lands and other countries, we see problems much greater and more severe than our own: starvation, disease ... people lacking the minimum for survival. And if we have even a bit of generosity in our hearts we want to do something also for them.

Then, perhaps we come across unusual words, words we realize are not from the earth nor from the crowds that surround us, yet we know them well. They say: "Therefore I tell you, do not worry about your life, what you will eat or what you will drink, or about your body, what you will wear ... it is the Gentiles who strive for all these things.... But strive first for the kingdom of God and his righteousness, and all these things will be given you as well" (Mt 6:25, 32, 33).

It is a gentle protest that heaven makes to earth, that God makes to men and women. He opens their eyes so that they see they have a father who thinks of them.

Is it still necessary to run about, do, work, be concerned, trouble ourselves? ... Yes, but for another reason: not in search of bread or clothing or money, but of the kingdom of God in us, which means striving to carry out not our will, but God's will.

The gospel puts it very well: "All these things will be given you as well." And it really does come true, when you least expect it. Things arrive on your doorstep and you say: "It's providence!" This is the delightful experience of all who are true to their Christianity.

Therefore, you understand from your own life experience that if you have found the answers to your own small problems, the best possible solution to the big problems that plague humanity is to find the most effective method to help the world come to know and live the gospel.

We have been told it, so that we can preach it to everyone: "Is not life more than food and the body more than clothing? ... Consider the lilies of the field, how they grow; they neither toil nor spin, yet I tell you, even Solomon in all his glory was not clothed like one of these" (Mt 6:25; 28-29).

In these times, particularly in the countries where there is need, the main emphasis often is placed on social problems to which, also as an expression of a religious approach to life, we dedicate all our energies.

We do live the gospel when we feed the hungry and clothe the naked. But even such actions, taken on their own, may not give witness to Christ's message in all its beauty. In fact, in a certain way they can even distort it because they may leave those on the receiving end with the complex of being mere "beneficiaries." Instead the gospel raises humankind, all men and women to their highest dignity: to be children of God.

The gospel is a whole; it cannot be understood truly and lived out in its parts if we do not know it and live it in its entirety.

The fundamental solution to the problems — even the earthly ones — of the poor countries is, and always will be, the proclamation of the gospel. It is important that all men and women know Christ and that they strive for the kingdom and his righteousness. Then in addition, the rest, all the rest, will come to them as well.[72]

Towards an Economy of Communion

> From an address during the conferral of an honorary doctorate in Economics, Sacred Heart Catholic University, Piacenza, Italy, 29 January 1999.

Typical of the Focolare Movement is what we call the "Economy of Communion," a unique manifestation of a free economy based on solidarity.

This authentic expression of the spirituality of unity in economic life can be understood in its entirety and its complexity only if viewed within the vision this spirituality has of the human person and social relationships.

It originated in 1991, in Brazil, where the Movement has been present since 1958. It later spread to all of that country's states, attracting people of every social category.

For a number of years, however, I had realized that given the rapid growth of the Movement (in Brazil we have spread to about 250,000 people), despite our communion of goods, it was not possible to meet even the most urgent needs of some of our members.

It seemed to me, then, that God was calling the Movement to something more and something new.

Although I am not an expert in economic issues, I thought that our people could set up businesses that could tap their expertise and resources to produce together wealth for the benefit of those in need. They would have to be managed by competent persons capable of making them function efficiently and deriving profits from them.

These profits would then be put in common.

One part would be used for the same goals as the early Christian community: to help the poor by providing for their needs until they found work. Another part, to develop structures to form "new people" (as the apostle Paul calls them), that is, people formed and animated by love, capable of living out what we call the "culture of giving." The last part, of course, would be used for the growth of the company.

Throughout the world our Movement has more than twenty "little towns" that witness to the gospel. They are modern communities with all the features of modern society, and therefore they need to have businesses alongside schools of formation, homes for families, a church, handicrafts and other activities that have sprung up to provide a livelihood for their inhabitants. With this new development of the Movement, in these towns real industrial areas were to come into being.

This idea was welcomed enthusiastically, not only in Brazil and in the rest of Latin America, but also in Europe and other parts of the world. Many new businesses sprang up and several existing businesses joined in the project, modifying their methods of management.

Today some 654 companies and 91 cottage industries are involved with this project. It includes enterprises operating in different economic sectors, in more than 30 countries: 164 in the tertiary sector, 189 manufacturing firms and 301 providers in the field of social services.

The experience of the Economy of Communion, drawing on the specific characteristics of the spirituality that inspired it, takes its place alongside the numerous initiatives by individuals and groups that have sought and seek to "give a human face to the economic system." It joins those frequently little-known entrepreneurs and workers who envision and live out their business dealings as something more than and different from the pursuit of sheer material gain.

In fact, as in many other economic activities motivated by an aspiration for the ideal, the people involved with this project — entrepreneurs, managers, employees and others connected somehow to the various businesses — take as their primary commitment to focus their attention, in all aspects of their activity, on the needs and aspirations of the person and on advancing the common good. In particular, they strive to:

- establish loyal and considerate relationships based on a sincere spirit of service and cooperation with clients, suppliers, government offices and also with competitors;
- appreciate the employees, keeping them informed and involving them in different ways in the management of the business;
- maintain a way of doing business inspired by a culture of legality;
- pay special attention to the working environment and respect for nature, even if these require considerable added costs;
- work together with other local business and social concerns while keeping in mind the needs of the international community, with whom they feel a sense of solidarity.

The Economy of Communion project also has other characteristics with great significance for us because they are linked more directly to the view of the world that comes from our spirituality. Here are some of them:

1. Those working in Economy of Communion companies strive, while acting in accordance with the practices required by productive organization, to make this aspect of their life consistent with everything else they do. In fact, we are convinced that it is necessary to let the values we believe in shape every aspect of social life, and therefore also economic life, so that it too can become a field of human and spiritual development.

2. The Economy of Communion proposes ways of acting inspired by free service, solidarity, and concern for the most needy — ways of acting usually considered typical of non-profit organizations — to for-profit enterprises as well. The Economy of Communion, therefore, is not so much a new type of enterprise, alternative to those that already exist. Its aim is rather to transform from within usual business structures (be they public ownership, cooperative, or other), establishing all relationships inside and outside the business in the light of a lifestyle of communion. And all this is done respecting in full the genuine values both of business practice and of the

market (those highlighted by the social doctrine of the Church, and in particular, by John Paul II in *Centesimus Annus*).
3. Those in economic difficulty, recipients of one part of the profits, are not viewed merely as dependents or beneficiaries of the enterprise. Instead they are essential members of the project within which they make a gift to the others of their needs. They too live the culture of giving. In reality, many of them choose to give up the help they are receiving as soon as they regain a minimum of financial independence and often they share with others the little they have. All of this reflects the fact that, while promoting a culture of giving, the Economy of Communion is not based upon the philanthropy of a few, but rather upon sharing, where each one gives and receives with equal dignity in the context of a relationship of genuine reciprocity.
4. The enterprises of the Economy of Communion, besides resting upon a profound understanding among the people who run them, feel themselves part of something much larger. They share their profits because they are already experiencing communion. For this reason — as I mentioned earlier — the enterprises develop within small (at least for now) industrial parks near the little towns of the Movement, or if geographically distant, linked "ideally" to them.

Many ask how enterprises can survive in the marketplace when they are so attentive to the needs of all the people they deal with and to the good of the whole of society.

Certainly, the spirit that animates them helps them to overcome those internal conflicts that hinder and in some cases paralyse all human organizations. Furthermore, their way of doing business inspires the trust and goodwill of clients, suppliers and investors.

We must not forget, however, another essential element: Providence. It has constantly accompanied the development of the Economy of Communion throughout the years. Space is left in the enterprises of the Economy of Communion for God's intervention even within the hard facts of economic reality. And every time they choose to go against the trend that commonly accepted business practices would advise, they have experienced that God never fails to supply the hundredfold promised by Jesus: some unexpected revenue, an unforeseen opportunity, the offer of new joint venture, the idea for a successful new product....

This, in a few words, is the Economy of Communion.

In proposing it, I was certainly not thinking about a theory. I see, however, that it has caught the attention of economists, sociologists, philosophers and scholars of other disciplines who find in this new experience and in the ideas and categories that support it, grounds for further study that go beyond the Movement in which it has historically been developed.

Specifically, in the "trinitarian" vision of social and interpersonal relationships that is the foundation of the Economy of Communion, some glimpse a new interpretative tool that might deepen also the understanding of economic interactions and, therefore, contribute to moving beyond the individualistic notion that prevails today in the science of economics.[73]

Fundamental concepts of the Economy of Communion

> In April 2001, ten years after the birth of the Economy of Communion, more than 700 entrepreneurs and others involved in various ways gathered for a conference in Castel Gandolfo, Italy. Chiara Lubich delivered this previously unpublished address.

I would like to offer a few thoughts on something that has been the foundation of the Economy of Communion since it first began in São Paulo, Brazil, the spiritual characteristic that has brought it to life, gives it life still, sustains it, and must continue doing so in order to guarantee its true character.

I feel urged to do this for an inescapable reason: the Economy of Communion is not a merely human activity, fruit of ideas and projects of human beings, however gifted they may be. It is an expression of the Focolare Movement, which is a work *of God*. Yes, a work of God, even if he, the Almighty, is pleased to use as instruments for his ends men and women of this world.

Consequently, if the Economy of Communion is part of a work of God, it is in itself a work of God, at least in its spirit and essential features.

If this is the case then, obviously it would be wise for us to understand and explore how heaven has designed and inspired it, and how on earth we have conceived and shaped it. Practically speaking, this means to see how it has been led by the charism of unity, a gift of God that has inspired, developed, and still brings ahead our Movement throughout the world.

But *what* and *how many* are the suggestions, intuitions and even inspirations that have so far guided the Economy of Communion? It seems to me that there have been some valuable ideas, a significant number of them. If I may, I would now like to highlight four that have become evident during the Economy of Communion's ten years of life.

Here we must consider them together thoroughly, to understand them with precision and carry them out with great fidelity. These four points have to do with: the aim of the Economy of Communion, that is, the purpose for which it came to life; the "culture of giving" which is its hallmark; the "new men and women" who are indispensable for managing it; and the "schools of formation" for these same men and women, which are absolutely necessary and for which we must provide.

The aim of the Economy of Communion is hidden within its very name: it is an economy that has to do with communion among people and with the sharing of goods. And since the Economy of Communion is, in fact, a product of our Ideal, its aim cannot be anything else but a part of the goal of our Movement: to work towards unity and fraternity among the whole human family according to Jesus' prayer to the Father: "May they all be one," to the point of becoming one heart and one soul through mutual charity.

And this unity can be accomplished following our Movement's characteristic "spirituality of unity."

Now, with regard to the indications which seem to have come from Above, we should note that even from its birth in 1991 we were conscious of the aim of the Economy of Communion, as can be seen in this passage: "It was born for the glory of God, to revive the spirit and way of life of the early Christians: 'They were of one heart and soul, and there was not a needy person among them' (see Acts 4:32-34)."

And in 1994 we see the same idea: "If we put the Economy of Communion into practice, in time we will see that marvellous page regarding the early Church fulfilled in our Movement: 'The whole group of those who believed were of one heart and soul ... but everything they owned was held in common.... There was not a needy person among them' (Acts 4: 32-34)."

In fact, 1994 was a year in which we continually called to mind those first steps that had been taken in the Economy of Communion so as to not forget its importance and its aim, lest it lose its lustre. Those words from that year can help us today too:

When the Economy of Communion project was announced in 1991, the whole Movement was thrilled and everyone was convinced and won over by the idea. It was evident to us that there could not be those who are hungry and those who are satisfied living in the same house (the Movement).

Many offered land and houses; they divested themselves of their dearest possessions, such as their family jewels, for example. They thought up many different systems for orienting their businesses towards the goals of the

Economy of Communion. It was an incredible display of love, not only in Italy, but throughout the world.

A year later, with the same intention of coming closer to the aim of the Economy of Communion and encouraging others to do the same, we wanted everyone to know the brothers and sisters benefiting from it:

Who are these brothers and sisters of ours?

I know them and I have seen photographs of some of them: smiling, dignified, and proud to be children of God and of this Movement.

They are not in need of everything, but of certain things.

For example, they need to be relieved of the anxiety that oppresses them night and day. They need to be assured that they and their children will have enough to eat; that their homes, at times nothing more than a shed, will at some point be improved; that their children will be able to continue their education; that the illness, which they have postponed treating because of the cost, will finally be cured; that it will be possible to find work for their father.

Yes, these are our brothers and sisters in need, who quite often, in one way or another, help others in turn. They represent a special face of Jesus who deserves our love and who one day will tell us: "I was hungry, I was naked, I was homeless, or living in ruins ... and you ... " We know what he will say.

Therefore, the aim of the Economy of Communion is clear. But how can we achieve it?

Within the Movement, in our meetings, for example, we often use these words that appear beautiful to us: the "culture of giving." In fact, is it not the antidote to the culture of having so dominant today, particularly in economics? It certainly is.

But at times we might have placed too much trust in the expression "culture of giving," interpreting it in a rather simplistic and limited way. It does not always mean depriving ourselves of something in order to give it away. In reality, these words stand for the characteristic culture our Movement bears within itself and spreads in the world: the culture of love.

The "culture of love." That truly profound and demanding evangelical love, which sums up all the Law and the Prophets and, therefore, all the Scriptures. Consequently, whoever wants to have this love cannot evade living the entire gospel.

But how is it possible? I will come to that in a moment. But first, I would like to read something written in 1991 about the "culture of giving":

Unlike the consumer economy based on a culture of having, the Economy of Communion is the economy of giving.

This could seem difficult, arduous, heroic. But it is not, because the human person, made in the image of God who is love, finds fulfilment precisely in loving, in giving.

This need to love lies in the deepest core of our being, whether we are believers or not.

And the passage concludes: "Precisely in this realization, backed up by our experience, lies the hope that tomorrow the Economy of Communion will spread worldwide."

Thus we foresee the possibility of the Economy of Communion reaching out beyond the boundaries of our Movement.

On the subject of giving, and also with regard to the amazing consequences when we give, we find something written a year later, in 1992:

> Give, give; put "giving" into practice. Create and increase the culture of giving.
>
> Give our surplus or even what we ourselves need, if our heart urges us to do so. Give to those who do not have, knowing that this way of using what we have reaps an infinite return, because our giving opens God's hands, and he, in his providence, fills us superabundantly so that we can give anew and receive anew and thus be able to meet the boundless needs of many.

The project of the Economy of Communion, however, does not ask us to love only the needy, but everyone. The spirituality of unity demands it.

Therefore, it asks that we love all those who in one way or another are involved in the business. For example, I wrote: "Let's give always: give a smile, understanding, forgiveness, our listening; let's give our intelligence, our will and our availability; let's give our experiences and skills. Give: let this be the word that gives us no rest."

In 1995 we clarified the deepest and truest meaning of giving:

> What is this culture of giving?
>
> It is the culture of the gospel; it is the gospel because we understood "giving" from the gospel. "Give," the gospel says, "and it will be given to you. A good measure, pressed down, shaken together, running over, will be put into your lap" (Lk 6:38). And this is what we experience every day.
>
> If everyone lived the gospel, the problems that afflict the world would not exist, because our heavenly father would intervene to fulfil Jesus' promise: "gifts will be given to you."

Furthermore, over the years, certain things have spurred us strongly concerning the basic meaning of giving, of actually giving, especially from particular saints.

St. Basil says: "The bread you store belongs to the hungry; the cloak you put away in your wardrobe belongs to the naked; the money you keep hidden belongs to the needy.

"You commit as many injustices as there are people to whom you could give all these things."

St. Thomas Aquinas says: "When for their personal benefit the rich consume the surplus necessary for the sustenance of the poor, they steal from them."

And since in this meeting today we have men and women who hold positions of responsibility in various businesses, I would like to call to mind another passage:

"A bit of charity, a few works of mercy, a small amount of surplus from individuals is not enough [to reach our goal]; entire companies and businesses must freely put in common their profits."

Finally, in the span of this past decade, between 1991-2001, we see the need for the Economy of Communion to have and to help develop "new men and women."

But who are these "new men and women"?

First of all, they are laypeople, and laypeople today are living a privileged moment in history.

All of us are probably familiar with those wise words of the Old Testament, which say: "For everything there is a season, and a time for every matter under heaven: a time to be born, and a time to die … a time to keep silence, and a time to speak; God … has made everything suitable for its time" (Eccl 3:1-11).

Well then, what time are we living in now? What time is this for the Church?

John Paul II tells us: "In the Church today the hour of the laity has struck."[74]

If this is so, it is our time, your time, the time of the laity.

Now, because the Lord guides the grand history of the world and of the cosmos and, at the same time, the small life-story of each one of us, his sons and daughters, we should ask ourselves: how does he want us laypeople to be in this moment?

The Holy Spirit has already answered this question in two ways: through the Second Vatican Council and through the emergence of the new Movements in the Church.

The Council tells us that the laity must become holy where they are, in the world. Therefore, as workers, employees, teachers, politicians, economists, drivers, housewives, and so forth. Wherever they find themselves they are called to Christianize (renew with the gospel) the various spheres of human society, by their personal witness and by the spoken word, because the Holy Spirit has given laypeople special gifts precisely for this very purpose.

Moreover, the various Movements are ways, each different from the other, to help the laity fulfil what the Council requires of them: that they become holy by their life-giving involvement in everything humans are and do.

They, especially they, can do this. And they do it with the gospel, by living the gospel in its entirety.

In fact, the Movements have this characteristic. Their members are called to live the gospel in a radical way, to live the gospel with authenticity. It is a great vocation, one that enhances their dignity.

Through the laity the gospel can truly penetrate every aspect of the worlds of economy and work, of politics, law, health, education, art, and so on, transforming everything, as we have experienced in our Movement. It can give rise to a new economy, which puts the human person at its centre and sends a considerable portion of profits to the needy; or a new political model, which requires that politicians put love for others, even those belonging to rival parties, at the basis of their lives so that they understand and complement one another. In this way each one, while remaining faithful to his or her own ideals and commitments, can work together in order to safeguard the sacrosanct values of humanity, of the common good.

In 1998, writing elsewhere, it was pointed out that the members of the Movement are laypeople, yes, but special laypeople, called to this task, perhaps, for the first time in history. The ideas in that passage are these:

> When we reflect on the Economy of Communion, we should not forget one of the factors that makes it so beautiful and alive, an example for the world: it was started and developed by laypeople.
>
> I remember that there was a time when it was thought that the only job of the laity was to listen and learn.
>
> As a result, Igino Giordani, because he was a layperson, felt as if he was merely part of the Church's proletariat.
>
> Now, in the wake of the Second Vatican Council, and in view of the new Movements, like ours, which were born from laypeople, we see the layperson coming forward and taking a leading role. Why? To our wonder and not without surprise, we are discovering, with great gratitude to God, that certain laypeople today have something special

about them. They are people who want more than the typical fulfilment found in a job, a career, or in a simple family life. It is no longer enough; they are not satisfied, they do not feel that they are themselves unless they also devote themselves explicitly to humanity.

Therefore, the decision to become involved in the Economy of Communion is not a burden for them; on the contrary, it is a cause of joy because they find a way to fulfil themselves completely.

And it is indeed moving: they could easily put those profits into their own pockets, buy a fur coat for their wife, new gifts for their children, a car for their son.... But they do not. They live for a great ideal and they are consistent with their choices.

And they reach holiness not in spite of politics, economy, and so forth, but precisely in the life of politics, economics, and so forth.
May God bless them and give them the hundredfold in this life and the fullness of life in the next.

What more should we say about these "new men and women"?
First of all, they are people with a strong faith because they have a profound inner life. Again in a passage from 1998 we read:

> If in practicing the Economy of Communion we live the gospel, we seek his kingdom, because we relate to our workers but as Jesus to Jesus; to our clients, but as Jesus to Jesus; to our competitors, but as Jesus to Jesus; if we live in this way, the Eternal Father looks after us.
>
> And we witness small and not-so-small miracles of grace in the world of the Economy of Communion. Companies that began with three workers now have two hundred.... Some industries were ready to close down, but because they continued to hope, said: "We can go ahead for another day." And in the meantime they found all that was needed to overcome the crisis.
>
> In other words, there is Someone else watching over our businesses, funds not kept in our offices, heavenly funds that become available at precisely the right moment.

Then, in 1998 new horizons opened before us. The Economy of Communion constantly requires new commitment, and we see how this ennobles those who work in it, giving them dignity.

> It is important that the Economy of Communion does not limit itself to prototypes upon which new firms are modelled, with a few comments from those who are more or less experts in the field. It must become a

field of study with the input of well-qualified economists capable of outlining both theory and practice, comparing it with other economic systems, and giving rise not only to academic theses, but also to schools that many can come to and learn from. It must become a truly scientific discipline, giving dignity to those called to demonstrate the theory in practice, a true "vocation" for those involved in it in any capacity.

Therefore, in order to bring about an Economy of Communion we need a clear aim, a "culture of giving" and "new people." But these new people are those who live the gospel in the most up-to-date fashion, who make mutual love a reality, who make their own, in actual practice, the spirituality of unity that brings the presence of Jesus in our midst....

The Economy of Communion has been possible because it began in a particular cultural context, the culture of love, which requires communion, unity; a context that helps us think of a new world, create a new people, with a new culture, which contains those values we feel are most important.

Indeed, we read elsewhere: "Why has the Economy of Communion progressed? Because it was promoted by people of the Movement shaped by our Ideal."

And we must add, why is it that today in some parts of the world the Economy of Communion has come to a standstill? For various reasons, certainly valid, but not least because an adequate formation in this culture might have been lacking.

That is why we feel the urgent *need to open schools* for entrepreneurs, economists, teachers and students of economics, for all sectors of business.

Its format could be patterned upon the school for politicians who wish to be part of the Movement for Unity in Politics, a well thought-of school that already meets monthly close to the Italian Parliament.

It involves a spiritual itinerary, a journey, making its various stages our own; an itinerary proposed by an expert member of the Focolare Movement, to be applied in everyday living. It involves, furthermore, understanding this itinerary's implications in the world of economics and confirming them with well-grounded experiences. The whole meeting, which would last about two hours, would conclude with comments and suggestions from the participants.

It is something "simple and feasible," as one of the participating members of parliament said. We hope the entrepreneurs will say the same....

Our charism wants it. The Economy of Communion as it exists in the world requires it.

What kind of work is done by the Economy of Communion?

> From a previously unpublished address to a conference, "New Horizons in
> the Economy of Communion," Castel Gandolfo, Italy, September 2004.[75]

The Economy of Communion is not merely spiritual. On the contrary, even if it is spiritually motivated, it is very concrete. It is a human activity, requiring those who work in it to use their brains and roll up their sleeves. In short, it involves work.

For this reason I would like to review with you how those committed to the Economy of Communion should carry out their work.

Since the Economy of Communion expresses a work of God, we must seek suggestions for its work patterns more in the spiritual and religious realm than in the earthly and human.

We are filled with wonder that the Word of God having become man, during the years of his private life did not only retreat into solitude to meditate and pray, but he chose to be a worker. This choice makes us see how important work is in the mind of God and how much it constitutes the make-up of a human being. Without it a human being would be considered less human.

Thus, human beings are fulfilled precisely through their work.

Therefore, in the Economy of Communion, too, we need to carry out our work in the best way possible. Indeed, we should feel called to transform every hour of our workday into a masterpiece of precision, of order and of harmony. We ought to have a lively awareness that we should make the most of our talents in order to enhance them and strive to better ourselves in this way, also by pursuing the studies relevant to our professions.

Moreover, the Focolare Movement, and consequently the Economy of Communion, had its first inspiration in the place that housed three workers: Jesus, Joseph and Mary (namely, the house of Nazareth, "transported" from the Holy Land to Loreto, Italy). Likewise those who work in the Economy of Communion in the first place must feel, like Jesus, Joseph and Mary, that by working they do God's will. In other words, they work not simply in order to earn money, even for the good of others, but in the first place in order to love God.

They should also remember that behind that pile of paperwork they need to get through, beyond that demanding job they are immersed in, behind the machines they operate, beyond all they make or produce, there are the end recipients of their labour: their brothers and sisters, or better, Jesus, who considers done to him whatever we do for the community or for the individual person.

Furthermore, those who work in the Economy of Communion are called to make themselves one with each individual and with the collectivity they serve; in other words, to work in such a way that everything done by their hands may be love. The voice of their conscience, enlightened by the Holy Spirit, will not fail to admonish them when they do not do things well, or to make them feel approval and consolation when things go as they should.

In the Focolare Movement we also underline the importance of being conscientious in carrying out our work, developing attitudes such as listening, openness, hospitality and attention to others in all relationships, be they with end users, clients, colleagues or those in positions of responsibility. This way of behaving, together with all the paraphernalia of the various professions, acquires the value of real virtue, indeed becomes an instrument for holiness.

The same must hold true for those who work in the Economy of Communion.

In the burden of their tasks, in the difficulties with relationships and in the contradictions they encounter, they will find their typical form of penance, penance that cannot be lacking in the life of a Christian or of anyone who sincerely desires to do good.

But in order to ensure that work is given its proper value, the Economy of Communion promotes a principle that seems to contradict what we have said thus far, but does not: it calls all to labour with a certain detachment from their work.

It is a principle that every human being must put into practice because the words of Christ, at least in their spiritual application, are for all: "And everyone who has left houses or brothers or sisters or father or mother or children or fields, for my name's sake, will receive a hundredfold, and will inherit eternal life" (Mt 19:29).

Therefore, everyone must be detached, at least spiritually, also from their "fields," which means, also from their work. Yes, "fields," work, should be loved, but loved for God, not before God. And what happens? They "will receive a hundredfold, and will inherit eternal life." A "hundredfold," which means an indeterminate number: a hundred times more also in material goods, in economic growth. Thus, for the small detachment asked of us, all the abundance of the Father's Providence springs forth.

And we know that the Economy of Communion businesses have experienced this Providence.

There is another specific dimension of the spirituality we all live that cannot but have important consequences for our way of working and of conducting ourselves in the various areas of economic life. As we know, our "spirituality of unity" is both personal and collective. Conforming to the vision of the Church as communion brought back into fashion by the Second Vatican Council, it gives great emphasis to the principle of fraternity and the communitarian dimension of human and Christian life.

Therefore, for those of us who adhere to it, it is not enough to worry only about our own inner life and our personal commitments. It asks that we also put at the basis of our lives, in every aspect, the same mutual love that St Peter asked of the first Christian community: "*Above all*, maintain constant love for one another" (1 Pt 4:8). Only if we act in this way can we guarantee unity among all and attract the presence of Jesus into the collectivity.

This presence of the Risen One among brothers and sisters united in his name must characterize people working together in enterprises of the Economy of Communion.

Therefore, we must all feel the duty, without which we risk personal and collective failure, of always reviving this presence of Jesus through our mutual love.

This is how we should understand the work of those called to the service of God and neighbour through the Economy of Communion.

So what more could be wished for this conference if not that all working in this field — from entrepreneurs to office staff to manual labourers — carry out their work as has been outlined here?

Mutual love will help everyone not only to understand and esteem one another, to carry one another's burdens and problems, but also to find together new forms of work organization, of ways to participate in companies and of management. Christ in their midst will make their businesses "new" and for many they will become models of communion: "dwelling places of God among men and women," real antechambers of heaven.

Church doctrine states that through work and the fatigue it demands, a human being participates in the work of the Creator and of the Redeemer.[76]

The Second Vatican Council adds: "For after we have obeyed the Lord, and in His Spirit nurtured on earth the values of human dignity, brotherhood and freedom, and indeed all the good fruits of our nature and enterprise, we will find them again, but freed of stain, burnished and transfigured, when Christ hands over to the Father: 'a kingdom eternal and universal, a kingdom of truth and life, of holiness and grace, of justice, love and peace.'"[77]

This is how we should see, how we should understand the Economy of Communion: something built according to the mind of God, a work that will endure not only on this earth but remain in the life to come, where we will have the immense joy of finding it again in the new earth and the new heavens that await us.

The Charism of Unity and the Media

Communication and unity

> Address to the conference, "Communication and Unity," Castel Gandolfo, Italy, 2 June 2000.

The mass media, apart from being the marvellous phenomenon we all know, and that in a certain way mark our times, have a particular resonance and are of fundamental importance in our Movement, both in its development and now. I emphasized this in my presentation at Bangkok, Thailand, in January 1997, when the prestigious St John's University conferred on me, and through me on the Movement I represent, an honorary degree in Social Communications.

The connection between the media and the Focolare Movement — In effect there is a twofold affinity between the Movement and the media that prompts me to say something. First of all, they share similar goals.

The purpose of the Focolare Movement is to share in bringing about what our young people have called the *dream of God*, that is the fulfilment of Jesus' heartfelt request to his Father just before he died: "May they all be one" (see Jn 17:21).

And what is the goal of the mass media? Its collective vocation is obvious: it too works to bring people together.

But it is not just the goal for which the Movement works that links the mass media so closely to our way of living. There is a second kind of affinity, one related to methodology. The *spirituality of unity*, which is characteristic of the Movement, is not practiced on a purely personal dimension; it is communitarian, collective. In the development of mass communication we can see a new step in the evolutionary plan for humanity. This development introduces into it, we could say, an unstoppable movement from complexity to unity, a movement in real time from fragmentation to the search for oneness....

The means of communication and the Focolare Movement: the press — This thirst to feel that we are united is something we have had from the earliest days, when we were linked together by a constant stream of correspondence in which we shared with one another the work God had begun to do in each of us, work that intensified the more it was communicated.

But the Movement's first real form of "media" was a little leaflet with a theological-spiritual commentary on a verse of the gospel, periodically selected for meditation and for putting into practice. Now well known as the *Word of Life*, it continues to nourish the Movement.

Today we print 3,400,000 copies in 90 languages or dialects. It is transmitted by numerous radio and television stations all over the world, reaching an audience of about 14 million people.

In 1956 we began our magazine, *Città Nuova*, first mimeographed and then printed. Its goal and the line it was to follow were spelled out in one of its first editorials: "To help all those with a desire and thirst for unity to achieve this ideal ... to be a popular magazine in which all can write, whether learned or not ... without a flashy appearance and not appealing only to well-known writers ... [because] what is important is the truth spoken out of love for the common good and for individuals."[78]

Città Nuova now has 34 different editions in 22 languages (including the European languages as well as Chinese, Arabic, Urdu, Japanese, and so forth).

Along with it ten or so other magazines little by little have been developed for various sectors of the Movement.

In 1959 came the *publishing house* of the same name. The readers of the magazine insisted on having a collection of the spiritual reflections that had appeared in it. So with the first volume, *Meditations*, the publishing house *Città Nuova* was born. It has spread across various countries so that today the Movement has 26 publishing houses, with a series of books covering spirituality, scripture, patristics, theology, literary essays, experiences of life, domestic, social and cultural topics, catechesis and education.

The "new media" — The beginning and development of our using the so-called "new media" really deserves a separate chapter. Here again, it all started with life. In 1952 we were given a wire recorder and a little later a home movie camera. They were small events.... I remember we said: "The spiritual step we are now taking here should be made at the same time by all our members even to the ends of the earth."

This desire to share everything, this fire of communion, over the years led to two audiovisual centres. Dedicated to Saint Clare (patroness of television), they have multiplied in many other countries. These centres produce audio and video material, two useful means of communication continually updated as technology advances. The *broadcast media* too, with generous help from several public telecommunications entities, are employed more and more by the Movement, especially for large international events.

Familyfest '93* linked various points of reception live from Rome via satellite. Sixty-three national television networks transmitted to thousands of local stations, with a potential audience of 500 million. It was the first television transmission in the history of telecommunication with seven interactive linkups, using 13 satellites simultaneously. *Genfest '95* was transmitted by three intercontinental, 53 national and 288 local networks.

For about two years the Movement has had an official site on the Internet, which presents the ideal, the history and spread of the Focolare with news updates and links to similar sites in other countries.

But the Movement has its own typical way of using the "media" at regular intervals, the so-called *link-up*. As we are spread out over many nations, in 1980 we began speaking with one another every month via conference call to the capitals or other cities where our centres are located.

We are now up to 83 connections with another 79 listening in. It is truly a moment of profound unity, where a family scattered all over the world shares its joys, sorrows and efforts to live the same Ideal.

As I said, our "media" arose from practical circumstances, little things, like the desire to stay in contact or the need to update those not present for events we considered important, or the duty to give spiritual support to those in difficulty.

For many years we did not publicize the Movement and its extraordinary spread, so what we have now has come not so much through the deliberate effort of the Movement as it has happened spontaneously.

What is important for us is that everything continues to develop out of life, even as we are ever more convinced that the media are, so to say, *made especially for us*, since their purpose is to bring people together in unity.

Be that as it may, we realize that the first Christians did not have the media. Their hearts overflowed with the message of Christ and they passed it from mouth to mouth until, as Tertullian said, though they were born "yesterday" they had already encompassed the earth.

Jesus used his voice. He wrote nothing, except in the sand.

---

* An international meeting with personal experiences and talks on various topics to do with family life, seen from the perspective of the gospel-based Ideal that inspires the Focolare Movement. The event includes songs, dances and sketches. The Genfest, mentioned in this paragraph, is a similar event for young people, looking at their life in the world.

A look at worldwide communication today — A rapid overview of modern means of communication, cannot fail to reveal that along with the swift development that day by day renders them more useful and fascinating, they also seem to present a series of major new problems for societies, families and individuals.

It offers a panorama of lights and shadows.

To cite just some of them: *globalization* which risks homogenizing cultures and suffocating the wealth of their diversity; *ethical relativism* which mixes messages of substance with what is biased, partisan or superficial; *turning life into a spectacle* which exploits suffering and private life; an atmosphere of *excessive competition* among the providers of the means of communication; the exaggerated *invasion* of public space.... How to use the media without being used?

Lights and shadows, I said.... The media today are either accepted uncritically or blamed for promoting immorality, violence and superficiality or overvalued as infallible instruments of power, almost new idols for a humanity without other certainties. We know they are simply tools, but let us appreciate all their "enormous untapped potential," to use an apt expression of Pope John Paul II.[79] We would like and would encourage everyone to use them well, faithful to the prophetic message they contain.

The universal movement towards unity — Their message is "unity." Here I would like to offer great thanks to God for the way in which he is not absent even from modern discoveries and new technologies, for the way in which he guides history.

And so it is that at this precise moment when humanity seems to wander in darkness after the collapse of powerful ideologies and the obscuring of so many values, and on the other hand at this precise moment when there is a yearning for a world that is more united, for universal brotherhood, at this precise moment we find in our hands these powerful means of communication, a *sign of the times* that says "unity." Do we not see the finger of God in this?

The apostle Paul, the first Christian who in a hostile culture had the courage to make himself, so to speak, *the means of communication* for the message of Christ, were he alive today, would certainly have used the media. At Athens he took the floor in the Areopagus (see Acts 17:22), which was in some way the TV of the day. As John Paul II has said: "The means of social communication are indeed the new 'Areopagus' of today's world — a great forum which, at its best, makes possible the exchange of truthful information, constructive ideas and sound values, and so creates community." And as he said in the same address: "It is the task of communication to bring people together and enrich their lives."[80]

At the root of communication — One of you asked me a question: "How do we achieve such communication? What is the basis for a communication that enriches and unites humanity?"

I am not an expert in the media, as am I am not in many other fields, but I would reply with St. Paul: "For I decided to know nothing among you except Jesus Christ, and him crucified" (1 Cor 2:2). I would add: "crucified and forsaken," according to the particular aspect of Jesus' passion that has been revealed to our spirituality.

Perhaps in him we can find an answer, even if our hearts waver and our minds are bewildered upon merely touching the remarkable similarities between the Son of God, who is the Word, and the subject of communication.

Jesus was a great communicator: "Never has anyone spoken like this!" (Jn 7:46), "All the people were spellbound by what they heard" (Lk 19:48), his contemporaries acknowledged.

Let us linger for a moment on his final personal experience. Jesus ended his earthly existence by being killed in the most shameful way possible in his day (crucifixion, reserved for slaves), a punishment that also meant separation from the community, rejection, erasing any social and religious belonging for the condemned person.

The *great communicator*, who had captivated the crowds, now found himself alone, betrayed, ignored: "I do not know this man " (Mk 14:71), said his chief disciple. But that was not all. Even God the Father, who he said knows all that is hidden (cf. Jn 5:20) and whose relationship had always supported him, seems to break off all communication. This "forsakenness" is certainly the darkest night, the most dreadful agony. He cries: "My God, my God, why have you forsaken me?" (Mt 27:46).

His cry, which sums up the nothingness of all things, has always accompanied the human story. We can cite here two iconic images that certainly are fixed in our memories. Who does not recall the agony of *The Scream*, the painting by the Norwegian, Edvard Munch, symbol of the isolation of a human being without relationships? Or the terror caught by a reporter's casual snapshot of the little Vietnamese girl, Kim Phuc, wrapped in napalm flames as she fled screaming from her scorched land, the very image of humanity as a child torn from its roots? These appalling signs draw us back to the abyss of forsakenness experienced by Christ the Word who cries out at the silence, at the "absence" of God.

Jesus crucified and forsaken, the mediator (the *medium*) between humanity and God, who, when the last separation has collapsed, when unity has been achieved, disappears and becomes nothing, is a terrible and fascinating mystery. He is an infinite void, almost the pupil of God's eye, window through which God can look at humanity and humanity in a certain way can see God.

He spoke, lived and worked, and taught for three years, and his words, spoken "for all time" were then and will be for all eternity "the way, and the truth, and the life" (Jn 14:6). Yet our faith teaches us that his being "himself" reached fulfilment at the moment of his most total gift, when he offered his life in the way just described.

So we can ask ourselves, was his cry at the ninth hour his fullest expression as the Word? Was it, so to speak, the height of his communication?

Yes. And it is in this self-annihilation in the abyss of individuality, where every relationship is dead, that he gives us the gift of his reality as *person*, capable of meeting God and other creatures. Precisely in giving himself without limit he reveals himself as Word, infinitely communicating himself and introducing us into the mystery of redemption and of the life of God, into the vortex of love among Father, Son and Holy Spirit.

If every human relationship reflects and follows the pattern of the trinitarian relationships, how can communication, another word for human relationship, avoid this dynamic, this law inscribed in its DNA?

New people for a new communication — The things I have said so far are only intuitions prompting further research in communications, which would involve various disciplines, beginning with theology. It is research still to be done, or better, still to be lived.

It is unthinkable that a *new communication* be imposed from above, by some international agency or institution. It will come rather from the experience of communicators who have God-Love as a model for communication and as a paradigm for professional relations.

Guiding principles of our communication — And indeed it is God-Love that those of us who are involved in communication seek to draw upon.

They have developed out of their daily experience an *original way of communicating*. We present it here as a small contribution to the body of research being developed today.

The first thought: for them *communication is essential*. The effort to live the gospel in everyday life, the experience of the *Word of Life*, has always been indissolubly united with communicating it, describing the various steps and the results, since it is a law that we love others as ourselves.

They believe that what is not communicated is lost. So life generates light, both for those who speak and for those who listen, and it seems the experience is fixed in eternity. They have almost a vocation for communication.

The second thought: *to communicate*, we feel the need "*to make ourselves one*" as we say, with the one who is listening. So when we speak or address some topic, we do not stop at merely relating the content of our thoughts. First we feel the need to know who we have before us, to know the listener or the audience, their needs, desires, problems. Likewise, we make ourselves known as well, explaining why we want to give this talk, what has led us to do it, its effects on ourselves, thereby creating a certain mutuality. In this way the message is received not only intellectually but is also shared in and taken to heart by all.

A third thought: *emphasize the positive*. It has always been our way to put what is good into light, out of a conviction that it is infinitely more constructive to point out what is good, dwelling on the good and positive aspects, than to stop at the negative, even though whoever is in a position of responsibility has the duty at the proper moment to point out errors, shortcomings and failures.

Finally: *the person matters, not the media*, which are merely an instrument. Bringing about unity first of all requires the indispensable means, which is the person, St. Paul's *new self*, who has welcomed the mandate of Christ to be leaven, salt, light of the world.

To be that, our communicators always need to keep their gaze turned to Jesus and see how he communicated to us everything the Father had said to him ("the words you gave me I have given to them" [Jn 17:8]). They see how in his forsakenness he gave everything for us, to the point of making himself nothing that we may be enriched. They see how in that cry, extreme expression of the ransom paid for us, like a mother (so theologians affirm) in so to speak a divine begetting, he gave birth to us as children of God.

And they want to take this as the pattern to follow. They know the qualities of a mother, how she is capable of believing all things, of hoping all things for her child, even the most wild, of understanding, of putting up with all the trouble involved.

And they understand how she, illuminated by love, sees further than others. They learn from her how to understand people and events better, to communicate in a way that we do not always know how to achieve, a way that is more truthful, more penetrating, broader, where the negative things about others and circumstances are not kept quiet, but the positive is brought more to light. Because this is how love is: it is aware of reality, but it knows how to transfigure it in order to make good triumph in others.

Many of them have been working actively along this line for some time all over the world. Their experiences are perhaps still limited by circumstances, in areas that are hostile or apparently resistant. Nevertheless new relationships have been built in editorial or production departments, and there are flashes of a new awareness in how to handle and profit from the media. They may seem modest advances, but they are not, because the witness of remaining faithful to our ideals always plants a seed, destined to make a new culture slowly grow.

What is important, however, is that we manage to acquire a common determination to use the media as they should be used: as *instruments for achieving a more united world*.

We alluded before to the evocative mystical image of Jesus crucified and forsaken as, in a manner of speaking, the pupil of God's eye. If the pupil — pardon my analogy — is a void through which the images are reversed (analogously, we enter into Christ as sinners and emerge redeemed), let us try to look through this divine "medium" at the problems we have spoken of, picturing a growing number of people working in communications who love humanity as Christ has loved it. We shall see situations turned upside down, or rather, set right:

— we shall not see the media as *invasive*, but attentive to increasing the socialization of human persons;
— structures of production will not be torn by *competition*, but guided by the search for a genuine relationship with the public;
— information *will not take advantage of* suffering and people's private lives, but respect the presence of God in every creature;
— the media will know how to be clearly committed to *true values that can be shared*, helping people in their search for the truth;
— *globalization* will not suffocate people, but will be transformed into a *worldwide communion among civilizations and cultures*, where all the spiritual and material riches will become a common heritage, without destroying the uniqueness of each but rather emphasizing it, in a unceasing dynamic of unity and distinction.

Conclusion — My dear workers and experts in the world of communication, God calls you to this today and humanity expects it of you, now more than ever.

I ask Mary, whose heart became a space for communication where Love could speak its Word, to make each of you, in this jubilee year, a new person able to begin and make grow a communication in keeping with the heart of God.[81]

Mary and communication

> From an address to a seminar on communication, Castel Gandolfo, Italy, 6 June 2003.

Gathered in this room today are people involved in what we call the "inundations," to use a variation of an expression of St. John Chrysostom, specifically the inundation of communications.

These inundations are the product of a particular dialogue — the dialogue with culture — which the Focolare Movement for some time now has established between the wisdom offered by the charism of unity and the various areas of human life and learning, such as philosophy, education, the human and natural sciences, the arts, health, law, and so on.

Here we deal with communication.

The inundations, it is not difficult to see, remain as inundations only if they are constantly enlivened and flooded by the light issued from God's gift, on pain of falling back into merely human thought and action.

That is why we open this seminar with a spiritual message: "Mary and communication."

Divine providence has ensured that our seminar on the media be held during the year that the Holy Father wished to consecrate to Mary, virgin most sweet, mother of the Word, of the Word brought to life. For months now the Catholic Church has offered a wide of range of initiatives all over the world to honour her. We too in the Focolare Movement, here at this centre, have had the deep joy of lifting up our praise in a completely exceptional way with a congress devoted entirely to her. On this occasion the media showed yet again its extraordinary ability to add good to good through three successive days of live broadcast.

This gave us great joy because, as you probably know, there is a very special bond between Mary and our Movement, which aspires to be, as far as it is possible, a presence of her on earth, almost a continuation of her.

If in the sixty years of the Movement's history she has shown us many facets of the exquisite plan of God for her, a rare creature set, in a unique way, within the Most Holy Trinity, let us hope that she will open to us now a glimmer of light in today's seminar of Net*One*.*

---

* Net*One* gathers people from every country who, guided by the perspective of a united world, work and study in the field of the media. They meet to share their ideas, projects, insights, and life experiences.

Mary desolate — Three years ago we focused on the terrible and fascinating mystery of the cry of Jesus crucified: "My God, my God, why have you forsaken me?" (Mt 27:46).[82]

Like Jesus, Mary too had her culminating moment, her desolation, her forsakenness; she is the Desolate. When from the height of the cross, Jesus, indicating John, who represented all of us, said: "Woman, behold your son!" (Jn 19:26), those words sounded in her like a substitution. Mary underwent the trial of losing Jesus, not just because he was dying, but also because someone else was taking his place. And she accepted it. And with her new fiat at the foot of Calvary she let go of Jesus and thus became the mother of all, taking on the motherhood of countless human beings.

Mary desolate is the Mother par excellence. In her desolation, in the peak of inexpressible sorrow and love, we have always seen God's plan for her completely fulfilled. There at the foot of the cross Mary becomes mother not only of Jesus but of his Body which is the Church. She is the universal mother who holds together, with her love, all human beings, her children; she makes them brothers and sisters in the same way earthly mothers do. She is the mother of unity, the bond of unity for all her children.

And for this reason we have always linked all she represents to this aspect of love which is communication, indispensable for attaining unity, and have taken the Desolate as patroness of our means of communication.

In the preceding conference, thinking of Mary, we noted how communicators inspired by the charism of unity know the qualities of a mother.[83]

And if Jesus forsaken seemed to us to be the pupil of God's eye open onto the world, we can say that Mary desolate seems to us a kind of *camera obscura* taking in all that is negative in the world. But just as from a film negative we develop a positive image, she transforms situations in such a way that in what is negative, we can also see the positive.

Mary is the type and figure of the church and so it is evident that in such a sublime creature all Christians can find a model for themselves; but I think professionals in communication can in a particular way find in Mary desolate the model for their own perfection.

From the beginning Mary appeared to us in two guises: as a monument of virtue and as an icon of the gospel's most profound law: knowing how to lose. "For those who want to save their life will lose it, and those who lose their life for my sake will save it" (Lk 9:24).

Mary desolate: monument of virtue — Mary at the foot of the cross, in her heart-rending *stabat* that makes of her a bitter sea of anguish, is the highest expression in a human creature of heroism in every virtue.

In her is the triumph of the virtues of faith and hope though the charity that enflamed her throughout her life, and here set her ablaze as she participated in such a living way in the Redemption.

The picture of her as mother who bears God dead in her arms yet still believes, hopes and loves, can be the model and support for communicators who, in order to transmit the news, often have to be present at events which in different ways call to mind the forsakenness of the Son of God crucified.

A faith like that of the Desolate and a hope against all hope modelled on hers will allow them to avoid turning away from human tragedies and make them participate more with the greatest respect for the truth, but above all for persons. By being love themselves, as she was, they will be able to find the golden thread that runs through things and to unveil to many the more true and profound vision of reality, one capable of discerning the love of God beyond the complex pattern of human events.

Their word then will be like Mary's, who in the Magnificat saw into events more deeply and prophesied the wonders that God would work through his Son, while at the same time conquering with love injustice and abuse of power.

The Desolate is meekness par excellence, gentle, poor to the point of losing her Son who is God: all qualities absolutely vital for communicators who in a discreet but effective way can often facilitate dialogue and act as "mediators" through their way of reporting the news, as well as doing the same at the various sites to which their work calls them.

Mary Desolate is the righteous one who does not complain when deprived of what was given her purely by election; the pure one in emotional detachment, tested to the utmost, from her Son who is God; the strong one who endured — and remained standing — while seeing Jesus die in the way he did.... Her example will help professionals in communication see events objectively and remain firm in service to the truth even when inconvenient and sometimes at personal cost.

Mary, in the desolation that clothed her with every virtue, furthermore will teach communicators to equip themselves with patience, perseverance, simplicity and silence, so that in the night of what is human in them, there may shine out for the world the light of God dwelling within.

Always, in fact, the word must rest on silence, like a painting on a background. Silencing the creature in them and on this silence letting the Spirit of the Lord speak, professionals in communication will be more like Mary, the transparency of God. Then their word will not be merely word, but the Word with Silence! The Word with Being! It will be Love.

In this way communicators will acquire the prudence necessary to evaluate properly the situations about which they speak and verify the sources of their information.

And even when they are a long time in the limelight, which can easily dazzle them, they will stay humble and know how recognize the limits of their knowledge.

They will have the Wisdom indispensable for those who must comment on news events without distorting reality.

They will be capable of offering good counsel and have the gift of discernment to communicate only what deserves to be passed on, especially at a time like this when the flow of communication is intrusive and turbulent.

The gospel presents Mary as the one who "treasured all these things in her heart" (Lk 2:51), yet no one ever spoke a word like her, who gave birth to the Word incarnate she later lost on Golgotha.

Mary desolate, suspended in the void just like Jesus forsaken, is in some way communication in its pure state, in which the communicator is only a *medium*, so much so as almost to disappear. This is transparency, that is, something which seems not to exist, but does. It is because it is not, like love. Is this not perhaps one of the greatest qualities of the *mediator*, the communicator? Does the media not find perfection when it forgets its own existence?

Icon of knowing how to lose — As I said, in our history Mary did not appear to us only as a monument of virtue, but also an icon of the most profound law of the gospel: she knew how to lose. Gospel love knows how to lose because it knows how to give. Precisely because she gives, she receives.

The Desolate lost, in order to do the will of God, that is, for God, even Jesus: her "Work." But precisely because she lost him, she found him again, many times over. In exchange for Jesus whom she gave it was impossible that she receive many partial Jesuses, but "other Jesuses" who are genuinely so, with his light and with his love. Just like him.

An intense apprenticeship — The "desolation" of Mary, however, did not take place only at the last moment of the life of Jesus. She had an intense apprenticeship during the whole of her life.

At the Annunciation it seemed that she would have to change her own life plan. And she was to be Mother of Jesus while remaining a virgin.

Later she presented Jesus in the Temple, where she heard announced her own way of the cross: "And a sword will pierce your own soul too" (Lk 2:35), words that took away the joy she had received at the birth of her son. She would live her entire life followed by the echo of those words, filling every attitude of hers with an unusual detachment.

When Jesus was twelve years old, she lost him in Jerusalem. With Joseph she sought him anxiously and finally found him in the Temple. But the explanation he gave them, "Why were you searching for me? Did you not know that I must be in my Father's house?" (Lk 2:49), clearly showed that he did not belong to her.

At the wedding in Cana, Jesus treated her with apparent harshness: "O woman, what have you to do with me?" (Jn 2:4 [RSV]), calling her to an even greater love.

Next Mary followed Jesus in the hard struggles of his public life, rich with fruits, studded with glory, made bitter by the gall of human ingratitude.

At the foot of Calvary, as we have seen, she pronounced the final fiat of her "desolation" in an abyss of sorrow beyond human endurance, where in her *stabat* she remained standing by a singular grace granted through her lifelong training for that hour.

And so it is that Mary, who prepared all her life to be *alone*, became Mother to each of us, to the whole of the world.

By looking to her, the icon of the deeper law of the gospel, that is, knowing how to lose, professionals in communication can fulfil their vocation completely.

Truly to welcome other people and events into oneself requires knowing how to lose everything, everything, like Mary desolate, to make oneself empty before everything and before every brother or sister, to be nothing. Only nothingness can gather everything into itself.

The figure of Mary desolate will be our example then, spurring us on to be channels, pure transmitters and true communicators.

Conclusion — Again I ask her, whose heart became a space for communication where Love could speak its Word, to make each of you, in this special Marian year, a new person capable of giving birth to and making grow a communication in keeping with the heart of God.[84]

The Charism of Unity and the Arts

> The texts in this section come from many different periods and shed light upon Beauty as the highest form of unity and upon the place of art in human life.

The Madonna of Michelangelo

You sit, beautiful Madonna of Michelangelo, in the chapel of St. Peter's and every time I look at you, you seem more beautiful. Over the days, the years, the centuries people from all over the world have run to see you and you have left in their hearts something sublime, something most sweet. You give to those who admire you a taste of beatitude; it seems you touch the depths of every human soul, the depths of the soul of humanity, and this heavenly ray, that comes from you, kisses the immortal human core, the core of every man and woman, yesterday, today, always. When the tragedies of life overshadow me, when certain television programmes humanize me but do not lift me up, when the news in the daily paper, always too much the same, saddens me, when sorrow gnaws at my soul and at my body, I look at you and I am refreshed.

There is something in you that does not die.

And it is that something which makes me think.

It is said the artist is one who knows how to express what is within. In the same vein it is also said that the philosopher is one who responds to the question "why." But it is not so: philosophy seeks the truth; it is the science of truth. In the same way I do not think the artist can be defined as one who expresses what is within. There are many things within a person: hatred, rancour, jealousy, longing, love, passions of every sort yet every expression of these cannot be called art, otherwise those who are mad would be the best artists — indeed, they are able to express what they feel better than anyone.

Perhaps art is something else, and you tell me, beautiful Madonna of Michelangelo, that art is the ability to infuse into a painting, a sculpture, a piece of architecture, of music … something of that which in the soul does not die. A work of art is thus rendered eternal by that "something," so that, though years, fashions, techniques pass by, though technology progresses, though discoveries increase, this work remains, because it is stamped with the immortal, with the divine.

Today as I was looking at you, beautiful Madonna, I was thinking: how sublime and divine is the effect of a work of art! It gives witness to the immortality of the soul, because if the sculpted image does not die, but it is art precisely because it is immortal (in the sense that it does not pass away as long as it is cared for), the one who made you cannot die. And it seemed to me that art is elevated to a height never thought of before and that beauty is, like the true and the good, the raw material of the heavenly kingdom awaiting us, and that true artists have, without realizing it, an apostolic mission.

With their masterpieces of art they give us silent, invisible angels that point us to heaven....

I have come to understand that only Beauty is beauty and only Art is art, in the sense that either beauty is universal and eternal or it does not exist.

If a work of art expresses the immortality of the soul, that does not mean that art is religion in the sense that the artist is necessarily religious. Certainly truly religious persons — by the very fact that they are in touch with God, creator of the soul made in his own image — find the way to art opened up to them more easily (and this is demonstrated by the immense number of artistic masterpieces of a religious nature).

It is enough that artists infuse into their work their soul; the soul of an artist, even a nonbeliever or an atheist, is still immortal.

It is immortal, it is spiritual: it is one. Here, I believe, is the first cause of a work of art.

If the content of philosophy is truth, the content art is beauty. And beauty is harmony, and harmony means the "highest unity." Now, who knows how to compose in harmony the colours and shapes of a picture, if not the soul of an artist who is one in the image of the God who created it?

It is the human soul, a reflection of heaven, that artists infuse into their work, and in this "creation," fruit of their genius, artists find a second immortality: the first is in themselves, as for every other human being born on this earth; the second is in their work, through which, in the course of time, they give themselves to humanity.

The artist is perhaps closest to the saint. For if the saint is the miracle of one who knows how to give God to the world, the artist gives, in a certain way, the most beautiful creature of the earth: the human soul.

This was what I meditated on before you, beautiful Madonna of Michelangelo.

And given that I was speaking to you, I asked of you a gift: look upon artists, who contemplate you daily, with the eyes of a mother, and satisfy the world's thirst for beauty. Send great artists, but shape them with great souls, that with their splendour they may set others off on the path towards the most beautiful of the children of men: your own sweet Jesus.[85]

Art, "a new creation"

The purpose of art is somewhat obscure, almost mysterious, perhaps simply unknown. Certainly it does engage reason alone.

Yet art, in a manner equal to science, has always produced more or less beautiful expressions of itself, because the imagination, its mother and origin, is a marvellous human talent and gift like memory, affectivity and reason, and it too has flowered in works: in "works of art," even spontaneously.

The true artist is a *great person*. Everyone says it even though few are art critics, but everyone admires and is fascinated by "beauty."

The artist in a certain way is like the Creator.

True artists possess their skill almost unconsciously and use colours, musical notes, stone as we use our legs to walk. Their point of concentration is in the soul, where they contemplate an impression, an idea that they wish to express outside themselves.

Hence, within the infinite limits of their human littleness before God, and thus within the infinite difference between the two "created" things (if I may speak like that), artists are in some sense those who recreate, create anew: and a true "recreation" for some could be provided by the artistic masterpieces produced by others. Unfortunately, for lack of true artists, people find recreation for the most part through empty fantasies in the cinema, drama, shows, where art has little place.

With his or her masterpieces, playthings in comparison to nature, God's masterpiece, the true artist gives us in some way a sense of who God is and makes us discern in nature the trinitarian traces of the Creator: matter, the law that informs it (what we might call a gospel of nature), life (what we might call a result of the first two). The totality then is something that continuing to "live" presents an image of the unity of God, of the God of the living. The works of great artists do not die and that is the measure of their greatness, because the artist's idea, expressed in some way perfectly on canvas or in stone, composes something that lives.

Today we bemoan the scarcity of great artists. Perhaps that is because in the world there are few great people. We never ought to let our imagination play in detachment from everything else in us; that way it would cease to be a gift and fall into vanity.

We must not consider human beings as they are not, but as they are: as social beings.

For this reason there will never be great and universal art except from artists who love other people and, in the first place, love God.

There will be artists for whom this has little interest, and to an extent some people may enjoy their work. To win the favour and applause of a certain number of people is in itself a good thing and a sign of some natural gifts. Perhaps it would be helpful to artists to listen with mind and heart open to the critique of others and see their way to putting things right accordingly. In that way they would become, in their art, more the expression of *humanity* than of merely one human being.

They would not waste or misuse time and talents, nor feed on some petty passing glory while they could, after death, render perpetual service (insofar as possible) to humanity and give glory to God, by helping reveal, through their masterpieces, the infinite beauties of the masterpiece of God: *creation, one of whose most beautiful works is certainly the soul itself of a great and true artist.*[86]

The Beautiful

Like love, beauty has become the world's possession.

We ought to reclaim beauty for God, to let live in us the One who apart from being the true, the good and the holy, is also the beautiful. Then all around us we will perform deeds and actions and arrange each thing with such superior harmony as to make our corner of the world like nature, which with its mere silent presence, uplifts the soul and leads it to God.[87]

God who is beauty, and the Focolare Movement

> Address to the "First International Conference of Artists," organized by the Focolare Movement. Castel Gandolfo, Italy, 23 April 1999.

The opening of our conference on beauty and art coincides to the day and the hour (23 April 1999, 11 a.m.) with the promulgation of the *Letter to Artists* of John Paul II, under the direction of His Eminence Cardinal Poupard. A wonderful coincidence. We can see in this the hand of God, the Lord of history including the small history, which is also his, of our Movement. This letter is addressed to "All who with passionate dedication seek new 'epiphanies' of beauty to make of them a gift to the world in the creations of art." So to you as well.

Last February some seventy bishop friends of the Focolare Movement visited Loppiano.*

When they returned to the Mariapolis Centre at Castel Gandolfo they wanted, as usual, to ask me some questions: "During our visit to Loppiano we experienced in an overwhelming manner the 'beautiful' which flourishes with great clarity and purity in the Focolare Movement. How do you explain this ever-higher flowering of artistic expressions?"

The question did not surprise me. It confirmed that this little town of ours demonstrates with its artists that art is at home in our Movement. That is as it should be.

That explains the title of my presentation. The title focuses my words on a precise topic.

I do not intend, nor do I have the competence, to speak of art in general, of its various schools throughout the centuries, and so on.

The discussion I wish to have with you about art is limited to its connection with how we are set up as an ecclesial and social entity, including not only the religious, but all the human aspects of life, not excluding the arts.

The work of art as incarnation — Without doubt, for us too absolute Beauty is God, God who is eternal.

Genuine artists participate in some way in this attribute of God. They do this through their works, which — if true works of art — live on after them, after their earthly life, since these works bear within them something of the eternal. This is a clear sign that they are related to the supreme and eternal Beauty, to God, and to the human spirit, created by God to be immortal.

Consequently artworks, with their brushes, chisels, musical notes, verses ... cannot be seen but as a sort of incarnation, a renewed incarnation, as Simone Weil writes in *Gravity and Grace:* "[In true art T]here is as it were an incarnation of God in the world and it is indicated by beauty. The beautiful is the experimental proof that the incarnation is possible."[88]

If that is so, art cannot but elevate, cannot but transport us to that heaven from which it descended.

Plato speaks of this effect in the *Dialogues*, if in some way art and beauty ultimately have the same end. He defines beauty as a ray from the face of God that, as from a glorious sun, is transmitted to created nature, which

---

* Loppiano is the first little town of the Focolare Movement, set up in 1964 near Incisa Valdarno, Florence, Italy.

participates in it. Having made nature beautiful and gracious with its colours, it brings nature back to the same source from which it issued.

I recently had a small experience of the sublime ability of art to elevate, which seems to me fitting to tell you now as an act of love. It is an experience that also clarified for me the function of beauty so strongly felt by us today.

One day in the car I was listening to Gounod's *Ave Maria*. It was performed with consummate skill, bringing to mind a diaphanous veil embroidered here and there with great delicacy.

Listening to it lifted my spirit, such that it opened me to union with God and in him to Mary, extolled by Gounod so sublimely.

It was the feast of her divine maternity and I wondered at her, "utterly beautiful beyond all telling." If God, I thought, had pictured her as his mother in Jesus, the Word incarnate, splendour of the Father, what heights of beauty she must have reached! I could not even imagine it!

And I spoke with her of my eventually meeting her, perhaps in the not too distant future. And I felt that her presence made everything vanish away in me and around me — everything to which I could still be linked, even the beautiful and the good, on this earth.

The thought of her and her beauty was enough to stamp like a seal upon my heart: "You, Lord, are my only good."

And I understood that those virtues I ask her every day to teach me, and which are needed so that those words could become reality, were being given to me by her, not as a list, not as an explanation, not as an inspiration to me for living them, but in her showing herself.

Yes, it is beauty, of which Mary is the divine exemplar, that will save the world.

And I understood all that because a piece of music, listened to, was a work of art.

Beauty and our Movement — But when and how did beauty come to take a rightful place in our Movement?

From the outset, immediately.

Enlightened by the first glimmers of the charism that began to disclose a certain divine plan for the Church and for the human race, the reaction of those who heard what was being said was not: "How true!" "How good!" No! It was: "How beautiful!"

"Beautiful," surely because what was said related to God who is beauty.

Was this wisdom?

And very often, then, it seemed to us that the persons who spoke of our great Ideal appeared beautiful, in truth very beautiful; that was the common impression.

Beauty had found a place in our Movement because the word our charism began to speak to the world was one alone: unity.

And unity means the highest harmony.

And it was this vocation to harmony that characterized even the smallest, most concrete details of the culture that was beginning to flourish as an effect of the charism.

It required, for example, beauty and good taste in the manner of dress; beauty, harmony, a sense of welcome in the interior design of the houses, centres and little towns.

The Son of Man, the Incarnate One par excellence, seemed to be telling us: "Consider the lilies of the field …" (Mt 6:28).

And the beautiful and our regard for the beautiful revealed themselves, from time to time, when, for example, transfixed before something written or a picture or a sculpture, we could not but express enchantment and profound admiration.

And here, to give one example, is a well-known passage about the "Madonna of Michelangelo" that greets anyone who enters St. Peter's. It a passage that emphasizes an idea already mentioned:

It is the human soul, a reflection of heaven, that artists infuse into their work, and in this "creation," fruit of their genius, artists find a second immortality: the first is in themselves, as for every other human being born on this earth; the second is in their work, through which, in the course of time, they give themselves to humanity.

The artist is perhaps closest to the saint. For if the saint is the miracle of one who knows how to give God to the world, the artist gives, in a certain way, the most beautiful creature of the earth: the human soul.

Then, aware of the great value of art, I concluded: "And given that I was speaking to you, I asked of you a gift: look upon artists, who contemplate you daily, with the eyes of a mother, and satisfy the world's thirst for beauty. Send great artists, but shape them with great souls, that with their splendour they may set others off on the path towards the most beautiful of the children of men: your own sweet Jesus."[89]

All of you know, more or less, our Movement's long history of more than fifty years, its goals, its spirituality, the universality of the vocations within it, all that goes to make it up, the way it has spread, its dialogues at 360°,[90] its practical activities.…

And in this last category there are creative works, esteemed to varying degrees, that have emerged here and there from the hands of our artists. Without self-promotion, though expressing themselves in art, in Italy and other European nations as well as in Asia, in South America, in Australia, they have firmly maintained their place in the Movement, their particular vocation within it.

Hence the fervent words of encouragement expressed from time to time: "Thank you ... because with your efforts you help in telling the world that God is beautiful!"

From its beginning this has always been the passion, one of the passions of our Movement: to shout with our lives, with our words, with our art that God is Beauty and not just Truth and not just Goodness.

For this reason too the Movement was born as a peaceful protest against the prevailing mindset of that time.

The three periods — Our movement has a long and rich history. It is marked by three stages.

We know, indeed, that God is not just beautiful. He is also good and true. And beauty is not given, genuine beauty is not given, if it is not also truth and goodness.

In our Movement this conjunction has always been emphasized and our task has been to explore it in an original way.

In a first moment, which lasted some decades, the Holy Spirit urged us to imitate God in his being good, his being love.

Our Ideal, in fact, from the beginning was centred on God-Love.

God, infinite goodness, who we were called in some way to relive, becoming in this way a tiny sun beside the Sun.

In a second period, after this way of life of ours had been clarified and was well-defined, the Spirit called us to another task: to draw forth from how we live, from our spirituality, at once both personal and communitarian, the doctrine that lies within it: its truth.

It was — to use a Franciscan way of speaking — as if "Paris," city of intellectual pursuits, was joined to "Assisi," city of life.

There was never any fear, as suggested by the well-known saying, that "Paris" would overwhelm "Assisi."[*] In fact the experience for almost a decade of our Abba School, dedicated to such pursuits, has confirmed how the light of truth greatly aids life, the life of love.

---

[*] St. Francis of Assisi is reputed to have exclaimed: "Paris, Paris, you destroy Assisi!"

In a third period, the one we live in now, we have become aware that the Holy Spirit is urging us to express not only the goodness of God and of our life, not only truth, but also beauty.

And we have called this era by the name of another city, "Hollywood."

This "Hollywood" does not erase "Assisi" and "Paris" but presupposes them, and it cannot be itself if it is not also the other two.

Jesus in us, in fact, desires to be the Way (Assisi), the Truth (Paris) and the Life (Hollywood).

Many signs have announced this last period and the present conference is one example. It could not have been held before. Our artists, in fact, are not artists if they have not already let ripen in themselves the experience of goodness and truth.

Another indication, among the many, which would not be out of place to mention here, is this. Recently, but not for the first time, about seventy actors, directors, producers, writers and technicians from the city of Hollywood gathered in an atmosphere of enthusiasm and celebration with some members of our Movement at a villa in Los Angeles, desiring to learn about our spirit and take it to Hollywood.

One Jewish photographer who was there ended the meeting by saying: "Let's have the courage to live what we heard today: let's put God in the first place in Hollywood, on the set and in our lives."

Now they look forward to meeting with us again.

On one side, there are artists who have reached God; on the other, there are people who love and know God and aspire to be true artists.

At the root there is no difference: in both ways our third period makes progress.

Who the artist is — But who is an artist? Salvatore Fiume, a contemporary painter, exaggerated when, equating the artistic spirit and the Spirit of God, he claimed that the artist is like a person writing from dictation: as God dictates, the artist paints, sculpts, writes music, poetry, architectural plans, novels and philosophical concepts.

When the work is finished, with ingenuous impertinence he signs it.[91] But that is not too far from the truth, as Vatican Council II urged artists: "Do not close your mind to the breath of the Holy Spirit."[92]

Clearly you cannot be an artist if you do not have real talent. You are not an artist if you do not have artistic inspiration.

But the Holy Spirit too is not far from artists.

As John Paul II has put it: "When we turn over certain wonderful pages of literature and philosophy, justly admire some masterpiece of art or listen to passages of sublime music, we spontaneously recognize in these expressions of human genius a radiant reflection of God's Spirit."[93]

Our artists and modern art — What are our artists like? What is our art like? What is art in the culture of our "people"?

We know that Vatican II said: "The Church acknowledges also new forms of art which are adapted to our age...."[94] This is an imperative valid for us too.

And that is what our artists are trying to do.

Today, as everyone knows, there is modern art. It has its own needs, new and interesting, a rationale of its own that does not fail to fascinate.

Even so, as has happened for all types of art throughout the centuries, there are those who do not interpret it well and are able to use art for ill.

God, as we said, is beautiful, but he is also good and true.

The true artist cannot consider the beautiful apart from the good and the true.

The beautiful, in fact, that does not contain in itself and the true and the good is an emptiness, a void.

"Beauty," Vladimir Soloviev affirms, "without truth and goodness is only an idol."[95]

But if the beautiful contains the good, then nothing sinful, scandalous, or anything evil can be art's prerogative, not even in passing, not even with the intention of making the beautiful triumph. Here too the end does not justify the means.

Certainly art can portray the ugly, the painful, the distressing, the dramatic, the tragic. All of that can be expressed in a work of art, as it always has been. This is affirmed in a statement attributed to a group of expressionist artists, the Blue Rider: "The joys and the sorrows of humankind, of the peoples, lie behind the inscriptions, the paintings, the temples, the cathedrals, the pageants, the works of music, the performances and the dances. Where these do not form the foundation, where forms become empty, without purpose, there is no art."*

Jesus forsaken on the cross was certainly not beautiful.

---

* "Der Blaue Reiter" (the Blue Rider) is a group of expressionist artists founded by the painters Wassily Kandinsky, Franz Marco and others at Munich in 1911.

He, in fact, the Word of God, the Great Artist, in becoming incarnate assumed our human nature, to the point of making himself sin though never a sinner. "He had no form or majesty," says Isaiah, "that we should look at him, nothing in his appearance that we should desire him" (Is 53:2). And yet in him, our faith tells us, there was already present the glory of the resurrection.

Jesus crucified and forsaken is the model of artists and especially of our artists who, like him, will always know how to offer, even in the saddest circumstances, a ray of hope. The Holy Father told artists: "All great artists confront, at times throughout their lives, the problem of suffering and despair. Nonetheless many have let something hopeful shine through their work, something greater than suffering and decadence. Expressing themselves in literature, or in music, in shaping matter, in painting they have evoked the mystery of a new salvation, of a world renewed. In our times too this must be the message of genuine artists, who live with sincerity all that is human, even human tragedy, but know with precision how to reveal in tragedy itself the hope given to us."[96]

Our artists must remember that art, because it is a new incarnation, is mysterious; it cannot be otherwise. Hence it is demure; it does not disclose everything.

Seeing certain deviations in art we turn with nostalgia to the great artists of the past, some long-gone but whose works live on. It is like the tragedy of the nun of Monza in *The Betrothed*, which Manzoni summed up in just a few words: "The unfortunate girl replied."

A new art in a new culture — The Movement, as we have said, brings about a new culture. It is characterized in the most varied fields by new paradigms that come from of a trinitarian view of humanity and the world.

This has been verified in recent years in the fields of theology, philosophy, sociology, economics, politics and, most recently, psychology....

Therefore it cannot be absent from the realm of art.

This new way of looking at human life in its various manifestations is possible because the men and women of the Movement strive always to pursue a way of life at once personal and communal, as our collective spirituality demands.

Therefore also for those who work in the arts, we should be able to say: "Above all, maintain constant love for one another" (1 Pt 4:8).

And, as with every other culture that has appeared on the earth, in ours too the arts will display particular characteristics.

Hence we should look forward to a new art.

And what will its characteristics be? They cannot but be the expression of its personal and of its collective aspects.

It is true, therefore, and I say again now, as I did last summer: it is not always necessary that a new work of art be the product of a group with Jesus in the midst of them. It is necessary that he be in the midst of those individuals at some point so they can become a single soul, because then, when distinct from one another the whole will be in each one.

But what I affirm now is also possible.

Camus says: "And often he who has chosen the fate of the artist because he felt himself to be different soon realizes that he can maintain neither his art nor his difference unless he admits that he is like the others. The artist forges himself to the others, midway between the beauty he cannot do without and the community he cannot tear himself away from."[97]

And so, since the closeness of other people takes nothing away from the artist, indeed is an enrichment, it is possible also to imagine art as the fruit of a group of artists dedicated to the same art form, united in the name of Jesus, expressed in the particular work of one or the other of them.

And we have to ask ourselves: if this way of acting is possible in other fields, why not in the field of art? And is it not possible that this way of acting will be the harbinger of new and unforeseen works of art?

We see this happening in the Abba School.[98] What an advantage for every field is this way of being at the service of knowledge! It is as if the breath of the Holy Spirit already present in each individual were to swell enormously! In the Abba School, in fact, there is a "something more": a something more that is human and divine. The atmosphere there is sacred. Without exaggeration, it often seems like being in Paradise.

But there is a price to pay: the total death of each one's self because another Self, this one with a capital *S*, must triumph in all and in each.

That is what we learned in 1949 when a blaze of light dazzled us.

The intuitions or inspirations of that period have been commented upon from many points of view by the members of the Abba School.

One says: "If you love Jesus forsaken you must detach yourself from your way of thinking, from thinking itself: this is the non-being of the mind. But the same goes for the will, the memory and the imagination (synonymous with artistic expression). We reach these deaths by 'losing' (learning how to put aside even what seems our own inspiration)."

Another put it this way: "We speak also of the imagination, perhaps because in contrast to other spiritualities, we emphasize 'the beautiful'....

The imagination, however, must be lost in unity, but only to have a kind of new 'inspiration,' and be able somehow to see heaven with it, as well as to see (in a new way) all the things of the earth."

A third one says: "One of the effects of our spirituality will be a new art.

"With regard to this new art, many times the members of the Movement involved in art have been free to work on their own, given that, generally, it is very difficult for artists to achieve mutual understanding. Instead, if there were unity among them, we would see the appearance of works of art never before imagined."

Finally one says: "This losing everything and finding everything is a classic teaching of the spiritual life ... (but) we do not readily find in the spiritual authors that it is necessary to lose the imagination to have a new imagination: generally it is only said that we must lose the imagination. Here, instead, we come to find a new imagination. This is easier to understand nowadays, after Vatican II's affirmation that everything human lies within the sphere of Christianity. Imagination is no longer something that distances us from the ascetic life required for holiness. We have anticipated these ideas."

And the same person added: "In addition, there is the root here of a renewed and great new Christian art."

A new art, then, is emerging in our midst. Or perhaps it is here already....
And here comes to mind the "Resurrection of Rome":

We need to allow God to be reborn within us and keep him alive. We need to make him overflow onto others like torrents of Life and resurrect the dead.

And keep him alive among us by loving one another....

So everything is renewed: politics and art, school and religion, private life and entertainment. Everything.[99]

Mary — The Focolare Movement deals with beauty because it must, one by one and all together, in some way reflect Mary.

Mary is the *tota pulchra*, the All-Beautiful.

Mary, in fact, is the fullest expression of Christ's redeeming work. She is the creature who reflects the image of the Creator in a singular manner. That is why she is the object of attention and admiration for artists, who are especially sensitive to beauty and to the call of the supernatural. She is therefore the object of inspiration for painting and sculpture, for music and literature....

In the *Paradiso* Dante says that she has "the face that to Christ is most similar";[100] Boccaccio sings: "Adorn the heavens with your glad countenance";[101] and Petrarch: "Who in the sun arrayed, / And crowned with stars, to a greater Sun didst bring / Such joy that He in thee His light did hide."[102] Tasso sees her as: "Star from which serene light is born, / light of the non-created and highest Sun."[103]

Mary most beautiful, surround our artists with your splendour.

To conclude — Every movement, like ours that has a religious base and that has made a mark on history, has produced new forms of religious art. We truly hope that this will be so for ours as well, if it is true that it is a Work of God. But it is true. A while ago the Pope inscribed the following words on my heart: "Work of Mary?" he said, "Work of God."

Yours then is the honour and duty of being its expression in art.[104]

Artistic vocation — a talent for unity

> From a previously unpublished message to the third conference for young artists of the Focolare Movement, Castel Gandolfo, Italy, 10 September 2004.

Dear young artists,

We meet together again to explore another important aspect of your artistic vocation, lived in the light of our Ideal. It is a talent God has given you for the service of unity, a talent for unity.

For some years we have watched with joy and wonder as new and true vocations have emerged in our Movement. They are modern, secular vocations in society, for persons who are competent in some area of human life (as doctors, engineers, architects, artists, etc.) and who feel the desire to achieve perfection through their hands-on involvement in the things of the world.

This is the triumph of the lay dimension after the Second Vatican Council; it is the triumph of Mary. Politicians, for example, or entrepreneurs who live out this vocation of theirs show that they can become holy not "despite politics and economics," but precisely "by means of them," making use of the commitment they require, of the crosses they obtain.

It was that way for Igino Giordani, whose recently begun process of beatification shows how he lived not just the religious virtues, but also the virtues of secular life.

It should be the same for you in the various fields of the world of art in which the Lord, if it is his will, will call you to work.

Today we often hear the famous line of Dostoyevsky: "Beauty will save the world"[105] and we understand at once how very important beauty is and how it can contribute decisively towards building a united world.

In our times, marked by a spreading relativism and by an always more absurd immorality, it is difficult to make a convincing case by presenting immediately the true and the good. Indeed there is the risk that one may be swiftly accused of presumption and backwardness.

But presenting beauty instead leads to acceptance and success. That is why television and magazines appeal to beauty and they appropriate it for themselves. But we want to claim beauty for God and, if that is what conquers the world, that is what we must present.

But what is true beauty? It is God. God is not only good, that is, the Good, and true, the Truth, he is also Beauty. And beauty presented on its own, without containing in itself the good and the true, would not be true beauty.

We must offer the world true beauty. We have been aware of that calling from the foundation of our Movement.

Our charism always had a close connection with beauty because unity is harmony.

I already said as much in a letter in 1947, when we experienced Jesus in our midst for the first time: "Oh! Unity, unity! What divine beauty! We have no human words to say what it is! It is Jesus!" In the first place, it is with our unity, with our mutual love, which is a small reflection of the trinitarian life lived among human beings, that we give witness to the beauty of God who is Love.

But that is not enough. It must be reflected also in all that clothes and houses us as a people: our clothing, our homes, our centres and our little towns.

There is no unity without beauty and there will be no united world without harmony among individuals and peoples.

The works of our artists contribute to its construction.

From the beginning of the Movement we have had very clear ideas with respect to the arts in the real sense of the word. In the forties I wrote a letter to one of my companions:

It seems to me that every philosopher has spoken some truths. That is undeniable and it is the reason for my attraction to all those who have found some ray of light.

Truths that are truth but not in the Truth that is Christ, therefore, not passing through the gate — in a tomorrow (the tomorrow of disillusionment) — will collapse as illusions.

I think exactly the same thing about love. Human friendship between two persons is love. But if it is not love of Love (and for Love), tomorrow it will be an idol and will shatter.

I think exactly the same thing about Art. Every artist has something of Art and every art is born of the Creator, even if the artist does not recognize it.

But art done for God will remain for the glory of God. That not done for God will fall as vanity....

Like art, so also science, politics, economics, sport, etc. ... are not Religion. Because Religion is the Spirit of God who must shape everything. But all these, including those not mentioned, derive their value and acquire the stamp of immortality if they are: for God — in God — with God.

My dear young artists,

Put your talents at the service of God and his plan of beauty for all humanity: unity. Above all give him the first place in your life. You cannot do anything better or more beautiful!

I know that some of you still have doubts about your vocation.

Pray. Say to Jesus: "Open my eyes, make me understand. Open my heart, make me hear." And then love. God does not speak in noise, in whispers, in the void. God speaks in love.

If you really want to do his will, you will become labourers for Jesus, in whatever vocation he calls you to.

And have no fear. Fear must be cast aside.... I can assure you that with all that happens in life, there is a noticeable grace. You will become saints where God wants you.

That will also be your path for becoming, God willing, artists of value. Your responsibility is great!

360° Dialogue

> While it is deeply rooted in the Catholic Church, the Focolare Movement has opened up and spread out to various Christians of every kind. It has also established deep relations with believers of other religions, many of whom recognize themselves to be a living part of the Movement. In its promotion of human and social values, it has gained the respect of people from a wide variety of cultural backgrounds, not all of whom have a specifically religious form of conviction, but who, sharing its spirit, wish to cooperate in achieving its goals. That is why the Movement has what could be called a 360° dialogue, that is, one that encompasses partners of every kind of belief.

With Movements and various charisms within the Catholic Church

> From a previously unpublished address written by Chiara Lubich for the Catholic Charismatic Conference, Fiuggi, Italy, October 2004.

The title given me for this presentation is: "Communion of the ecclesial Movements in the Third Millennium." This topic, which is very close to my heart, is of great importance. Above all it is an emerging reality in the Church today, and something to which we have been dedicating ourselves with great passion for many years now, together with other founders and persons responsible for ecclesial Movements.

As everyone knows, at the beginning of the third millennium the Holy Father John Paul II specifically directed us to the "the great challenge facing us in the millennium which is now beginning, if we wish to be faithful to God's plan and respond to the world's deepest yearnings," which is "to make the Church *the home and the school of communion*."[106]

In his well-known apostolic letter, *Novo Millennio Ineunte*, he said: "Communion must be cultivated and extended day by day and at every level in the structures of each Church's life. There, relations between Bishops, priests and deacons, between Pastors and the entire People of God, between clergy and Religious, *between associations and ecclesial movements* must all be clearly characterized by communion."[107]

From that moment he has promoted tirelessly throughout the entire church the *spirituality of communion*, the nucleus of which is the "new commandment" of Jesus: "Just as I have loved you, you also should love one another" (Jn 13:34).[108]

Communion (*koinonia*) — writes the Pope — "embodies and reveals the very essence of the mystery of the Church. Communion is the fruit and manifestation of that love which springs from the heart of the Eternal Father and is poured on us through the Spirit which Jesus gives us (cf. Rom 5:5) to make us all one heart and one soul (Acts 4:32)."[109]

With the apostolic letter *Novo Millennio Ineunte* the Holy Father clearly points out to us God's will for the Church at the beginning of the third millennium and indicates the way to achieve it. We have thus a well-founded hope of seeing the marvellous face of the Spouse of Christ, as she presented herself to the world in the documents of the Second Vatican Council, become reality.[110]

At the same time, providential circumstances have brought into existence many ecclesial Movements which have entered into and are developing always more fully among themselves a profound communion. It is a beautiful story that can be briefly summarized.

It all began on the vigil of Pentecost 1998 when the Holy Father gathered the Movements and the new ecclesial communities at Rome. That day St. Peter's Square was filled with people (about 400,000). It looked like a wonderful garden, blooming with every colour because of the handkerchiefs waving in celebration.

The Pope recalled the first Pentecost and said that what happened in Jerusalem two thousand years ago was being renewed that evening there in the square.

He saw in these groups tangible evidence of the new "outpouring" of the Holy Spirit on the Church.[111]

Highlighting, then, that the institutional and the charismatic aspects are co-essential to the constitution of the Church, he defined our Movements and ecclesial communities as "a significant expression" of its *"charismatic dimension."*[112]

Knowing that it was the desire of the Church, I felt impelled on that occasion to make, along with others, an effort towards a fuller communion among the Catholic Movements, while respecting their distinctive characteristics.

This meeting marked a turning point for us. Before, each one tried to develop and organize its own Movement in itself and in relationship to the Church. Afterwards, we made an effort to look beyond ourselves and enter into communion with the other Movements.

So right away in the following months the Focolare Movement developed connections with the Community of St. Egidio, Catholic Charismatic

Renewal, Cursillo, Schönstatt, Regnum Christi, Equipes Notre Dame and others.

We began to live our communion like this. We prayed for each other, encouraged each other in difficulties, got to know each other's central committees, offered practical help for each other's needs, participated in and worked together for some of each other's events, gave space in our own publications to articles about the other Movements, and so on.

These were various ways for us to practise the new commandment of Jesus, to establish a love "which passed back and forth" among our Movements.

What we noticed everywhere was a great enthusiasm for this communion, a stimulus that could only be supernatural. Truly the Holy Spirit had prepared for us a special hour in the Church.

Aided by these encouraging circumstances, in conjunction with dozens and dozens of other Movements and local ecclesial communities, on all continents we planned and held day-long conferences, which at times were truly amazing. So far we have had around 220 and have seen the following marvellous results:

- An increased love for the Pope (who has so generously blessed and assisted us) through the Pontifical Council for the Laity which represents him, and through all our bishops.
- Our hearts opened to the whole Church, since every charism has been given for the entire Church.
- Through all the friendship created, the individual Movements have become aware of something like a new youthfulness.

At the outset of this endeavour I wrote to the Pope, giving him a report on our efforts. I received a personal letter in which he thanked us for the "very comforting" news, which "filled him with joy" because "the indispensable collaboration among the various ecclesial groups will certainly bear much fruit."

One important person in our Church who noticed the results of a joint presentation of two Movements commented: "If the Movements unite, they will be a power in the Church for the kingdom of God."

Despite ourselves in our smallness, that is what we would like to be: a force for God, to sanctify his name and make it fashionable again in our streets, often frozen by materialism and secularism; a force for God in our homes, our schools, our workplaces, our public offices, and above all on the front lines, places where the institutional Church cannot normally gain entry, but where our Movements are often present. That is what the Holy Spirit has called and enabled them to do.

In October 1999, with Andrea Riccardi, founder of the Community of St Egidio, we made contact with many persons responsible for Movements in the evangelical and free Churches. A climate of mutual esteem was established among us and we had the joy of meeting with them many times in Germany and in Rome.

There was a spontaneous exchange of gifts and also of forgiveness, requested and received, for all the prejudices and the sense of superiority that one Church or Movement has had with regard to the others. Love opened the way of communion among the Movements and spiritual groups of various Churches.

In 2001 the conviction was strong that God's hour had arrived for enlarging the circle of communion beyond what had already been experienced. So on 8 December of that year, 800 persons responsible for more than 45 movements in various Churches gathered in the Evangelical Lutheran church of St Matthew in Munich. In a solemn atmosphere they made a "covenant" among themselves as a pact of mutual love. It became clear that if we all love one another by trying to realize that unity which is possible now, in a certain way we will already be one soul, as it were the expression in the present of what is to come.

In the afternoon about 5000 members of the Movements gathered in the cathedral of Munich to deepen their mutual acquaintance, in the presence and to the joy of Cardinal Friedrich Wetter.

The Evangelical Lutheran bishop of Bavaria, Johannes Friedrich, also present, remarked about the meeting that "Anyone who has shared this experience cannot say that the Holy Spirit is any less powerful today than in the days of the apostles."

While this relationship among the Catholics and Evangelicals was growing, there began in Lebanon a friendship between the Mouvement de la Jeuness Orthodoxe and the Focolare, and in Great Britain, between our Movement and the Movements of various Churches.

Later it was not hard for us to see that the Spirit also wanted us to spread this communion among the Movements to the various religious families, such as the Franciscans and Benedictines, for example, born centuries ago of ancient but still living charisms.

We did all this with joy and to our mutual enrichment. We also built up communion with other Associations, some quite important, such as Catholic Action.

We then undertook the great project of an event entitled "Together for Europe," which took place in May 2004 at Stuttgart, Germany. Our Movements and ecclesial communities appeared to us as many networks spread by God throughout Europe, preparing the way — almost a trial run — for European unity. Each of them followed their own charism and practiced gospel love in many different forms. We wanted to make known these good works to give glory to God (see Mt 5:16) and join forces to bring about, next to the political and economic Europe, the "Europe of the spirit."

Before this event, I realized during a meeting organized by the Polish Bishops' Conference that the Movements and new ecclesial communities were our greatest real hope for giving a soul to Europe and for better assuring its cohesion. That could be deduced from the comments that religious and political figures made after hearing the presentations of the founders and the leaders of the Movements.

Indeed, they affirmed that "the new Movements are a living witness to the vitality of the Christian roots of Europe"[113] and that "they can lead it to holiness."[114] They continued, "The continent should not confine itself to mere economic needs, because Europe has many treasures of the Spirit."[115]

They affirmed further that "the development of this 'Europe of the spirit' requires new ideas ... and the Movements ... have the role of producing them."[116] And finally they said, "The founders are witnesses of European unity. It is already a reality between their Movements and within them."[117]

Based on all these consoling premises a highly successful event took place on 8 May 2004 at Stuttgart, and its fruits surpassed all our expectations. It was, according to many, a prophetic and historic event at which something extraordinary occurred.

Overflowing with communion and joy, 9000 members of more than 150 Movements and communities of various Churches, expressions of the Marian profile of the Church, gathered together with bishops and church leaders, expression of the Petrine profile.

Transmitted by satellite to our continent and others, the event was followed live in 163 gatherings taking place at the same time in many other cities of Europe connected with Stuttgart – from the Campidoglio in Rome, to the grand hall of UNESCO in Paris, to the World Council of Churches in Geneva.

The attendance of politicians was highly significant. Speaking at Stuttgart, Romano Prodi affirmed that the great political project of Europe would be sustained over time only if supported by a powerful soul nurtured, decisively, by the Movements.

At the conclusion of the day authoritative voices stated that in the hall they sensed a mix of overwhelming energy, joy, determination, vitality, courage, art, prophecy and an amazing communion of purpose. Archbishop Stanislaw Rylko[118] described the day as "something miraculous," while Cardinal Kasper[119] said he was certain that from a similar spirit the ecumenical movement also would acquire new energy and move ahead with new hope.

But for those who worked for the event, such a marvel of grace was explained by a single word: Jesus, Jesus spiritually present in the midst of all, because all were determined to keep him alive constantly, with well-tested mutual love, and with total love for each person. He, in fact, the risen Jesus, is the primary secret of such richness and beauty. He was the beginning, the middle and the end of all our communion.

With other Christians

> Address to the Second European Ecumenical Assembly, Graz, Austria, 23 June 1997.

"Reconciliation: gift of God and source of new life" is the theme of this Second European Ecumenical Assembly — reconciliation in the widest sense of the word.

In first place, the kind that has priority: reconciliation with God.

Then reconciliation among the Churches in order to reach visible unity; then, further, reconciliation with other religions insofar as it is possible through dialogue; and also reconciliation among cultures, among peoples; and between the human race and nature....

In this talk I want before all else to give thanks to God for his free gift. Without it we could not even speak of unity.

Then I want to consider the reconciliation that the Holy Spirit has inspired among the Churches. He is the one at the origins of the vast ecumenical movement, which has shown thus far an unexpected vitality throughout the world. He has brought about prayer groups, activities of all kinds, new institutions, special structures and Movements in various Churches and ecclesial communities.

But I will dwell on one detail of the whole ecumenical movement.

As you know, Christ founded his Church as one and only one, which all Christians in the world profess in the Nicene-Constantinopolitan creed: "We believe in one, holy, catholic and apostolic Church."[120]

There is only one Church of Christ, therefore. It is entered by baptism, which is "the sacramental bond of unity existing among all who through it are reborn." [121]

We know, however, that it is not enough only to be united spiritually in a common baptism. "The ultimate goal of the ecumenical movement is to re-establish full visible unity among all the baptized." [122]

This seems to me to emphasize the fundamental role of ecclesiology.

Indeed, it is so.

But what kind of ecclesiology do we mean?

Cardinal Willebrands was almost prophetic when he wrote that "a deeper ecclesiology of communion may offer perhaps the great opportunity for the ecumenism of tomorrow. The restoration of the unity of the Church should be sought in the light of this ecclesiology, which is at the same time very ancient ... and very modern." [123]

Today the ecclesiology of communion (*koinonia*) is accepted in the theological dialogues among the Churches as the way to understand the Church and ecclesial unity: "The Church finds its proper model, its proper origin and its proper fulfilment in the mystery of the one God in three persons." [124]

But then we come to the pressing question: is there something that can make these new ecclesiological insights work?

In this regard the World Council of Churches and others are seeking an ecumenical spirituality. [125]

An Italian Waldensian pastor said that "the lack of an ecumenical spirituality renders our task much more difficult and demanding." [126]

An ecumenical spirituality, therefore, a spirituality of communion.

But is such a spirituality within reach today?

We can take into consideration that there exist praiseworthy efforts towards this goal. Perhaps they are known, perhaps they are not, because serious things, the things of God, usually grow in silence.

But if they are the work of the Spirit, then unity is not just a dream or a utopia. It is a real possibility.

We can ask ourselves, however: what are the fixed points, the indispensable principles for an ecumenical spirituality worthy of the name?

Since the Church is not something just human but divine, a first key point cannot but be: God, and, given that this spirituality is a spirituality of communion, God understood as he is, as Love (cf. 1 Jn 4:8).

If now at the dawn of the third millennium we Christians take a new look at our two thousand year history and especially that of the second millennium, we cannot but be saddened by the succession of misunderstandings, struggles and confrontations which often ripped apart the seamless robe of Christ, which is his Church.

Who was at fault? Certainly there were historical, cultural, political, geographical and social circumstances…. But there was also a deterioration among Christians of their characteristic unifying element: love.

Exactly so.

So now, in trying to put right all that was wrong and to find new strength to start again, we must turn our attention to the very source of our common faith, to God-Love, the great revelation of the Christian mystery.

In these times it is God-Love who, in some way, must reveal himself anew to our hearts as individual Christians and to the Church that we compose.

First of all to each one of us. For how could we think of loving others in order to bring about reconciliation, if we do not feel loved profoundly, if we Christians do not have in ourselves the certainty that God loves us?

The fact is that while we know by faith that God is Love, we often do not think of it and live as if we were alone on this earth, as if there did not exist a Father who looks after us in everything and through everything; who counts even the hairs on our head, who knows everything about us; who wants to make everything work together for our good — the good that we do and the very evil he permits.

To begin living a spirituality of reconciliation effectively in the Church and the world today, we need to be able to repeat, with full conviction and in truth, the words of John the evangelist: "We have known and believe the love that God has for us" (1 Jn 4:16).

But he does not love us only as individual Christians, he also loves us as Church. And he loves the Church for when in history it has acted according to God's plan for it. But also — and here is the wonder of God's mercy — he loves it inasmuch as it has not lived up to his plan, in Christians being divided, if however they now seek full communion in his divine will.

It is this extremely consoling conviction that led John Paul II, trusting the One who draws good out of evil, to reply as he did to the question, "Why did the Holy Spirit allow all these divisions?" While admitting that it could have been because of our sins, he said: "Could it not be that these divisions have also been … a path continually leading the Church to discover the untold wealth contained in Christ's gospel and in the redemption accomplished by Christ? Perhaps all this wealth would not have come to light otherwise."[127]

Believing, therefore, in God who is Love for us and for the Church; this is the starting point.

But if God loves us we cannot remain immobile in the face of such divine benevolence. Like true children we must reciprocate his love, and here too both as individuals and as Church.

As individuals by acting as Jesus did: wanting the will of the Father in place of our own, repeating with Jesus: "My food is to do the will of him who sent me" (Jn 4:34) — that divine will which is written, we know, in holy scripture, especially the New Testament.

For those who wish to commit themselves to reconciliation, it is a duty and therefore a key point for any possible ecumenical spirituality, to live the words of the gospel, one by one, to re-evangelize our way of thinking, of seeing, of loving.

Cardinal Bea used to say that the more Christians live the word, the more it makes them similar to Jesus and therefore more similar to one another and more united.

Christians should make the words of holy scripture their own, especially the New Testament, and in particular the one that sums up the law and the prophets: fraternal love.

The only genuine Christian reconciler will be the one who knows how to love others with the very charity of God, which brings Christ to light in each person, which goes out to all (Jesus died for the whole human race), which always takes the initiative; that charity which makes us love each person as ourselves, which makes us one with our brothers and sisters, in suffering, in joy....

And the Churches too should love with this love.

"That the love with which you have loved me may be in them, and I in them" (Jn 17:26), Jesus prayed. And we instead are always ready to forget his testament, to scandalize the world with our divisions, a world we should be winning for him.

Over the centuries every Church, in some way, has turned rigid through waves of indifference and misunderstanding, if not of mutual hatred. What is needed in each Church is a supplement of love. Indeed, the Christian world needs to be overwhelmed by a torrent of love.

Love, therefore, mutual love among Christians, mutual love among Churches. That love which leads to putting everything in common, each a gift to the others, so that we can foresee the future Church with one truth, one truth alone, but expressed in different ways, seen from different perspectives, made beautiful by the variety of interpretations.

In his book *Crossing the Threshold of Hope* John Paul II writes: "It is necessary for humanity to achieve unity through plurality, to learn how to come together in the one Church, even while presenting a plurality of ways of thinking and acting, of cultures and civilizations."[128]

It is not that one Church or another must "die" (as at times it is feared), but that each Church should be born anew in unity.

And living in this Church in full communion will be marvellous, as fascinating as a miracle, and will excite the attention and the interest of the whole world.

Mutual love, however, is true to the gospel and genuine when it is practised in the measure Jesus desired: "Love one another as I have loved you. No one has greater love than this, to lay down one's life for one's friends" (Jn 15:12-13).

But in what way did Jesus die?

In his passion and death he did not suffer only during the agony in the garden, the scourging, the crowning with thorns, the crucifixion, but also in that climax of his suffering when he cried: "My God, my God, why have you forsaken me?" (Mt 27:46). And this suffering, as theologians and mystics affirm, was his greatest trial, his deepest darkness.

Now, it seems that to build communion up to the full in mutual love requires today that we contemplate and mirror in ourselves that particular suffering.

And it makes sense.

If Jesus was called to remedy the sin of the world and therefore the division of people cut off from God and in consequence disunited among themselves, he could not have fulfilled his mission without experiencing in himself the extreme depths of separation: that of himself, God, from God; feeling himself abandoned by the Father.

Jesus, however, re-abandoning himself to the Father ("Into your hands I commend my spirit" [Luke 23:46]), overcame that immense suffering and in this way brought human beings back into the bosom of the Father and into a mutual embrace.

But if this is so, it will not be difficult to see in him, precisely in him, the brightest star that must light up the path of ecumenism; the pearl we must find to bear great fruit.

An ecumenical spirituality will flourish to the degree that those dedicated to it see in the crucified and abandoned Jesus, who re-abandons himself to the Father, the key to understanding every disunity and to recomposing unity.

A productive ecumenism demands hearts touched by him, that do not evade him, but understand him, love him, choose him and know how to see his divine face in every disunity they meet. And they find in him the light and the strength not to stop in trauma, in the fracture of division, but always to go beyond and to find a solution, the complete, achievable solution.

Mutual love leads then to realizing unity.

And unity cannot but be another key point of an ecumenical spirituality.

Jesus, before being crucified, before being forsaken by the Father, prayed a long prayer for unity: "Father, may they all be one" (Jn 17:21).

And unity, lived out, has an effect which is also, so to speak, a *pièce de résistance* for a living ecumenism. We are speaking here about the presence of Jesus among people united in his name. As Jesus said: "Where two or three are gathered in my name, I am there among them" (Mt 18:20).

The Fathers of the Church often based their explanation of Jesus' presence of in the Church on two passages: "Where two or three … " which I have just quoted, and "I am with you always, to the end of the age" (Mt 28:20).

Living with Jesus in our midst, present through mutual love, we enter more fully and livingly into the presence of Jesus in the Church.

And this is already a powerful bond! It is a help on the path to visible unity! Jesus between a Catholic and an Evangelical who love one another, between Anglican and Orthodox, an Armenian and a Reformed…. It is a gift that also makes less painful the time of waiting until we can all share in one Eucharist.

Another key point must be a great love for the Holy Spirit, Love personified.

Jesus gave him to us as he breathed his last on the cross. He filled the Church at its birth with him at Pentecost.

It is the Holy Spirit who binds in unity the Persons of the Holy Trinity, and the Holy Spirit is the bond of the members of the Mystical Body of Christ.

In the reconciliation among us Christians, then, we must not forget Mary, who a Council we share, the Council of Ephesus, proclaimed Mother of God, *Theotokos*.

Mary, precisely because she is Mother, can do much for unity.

And not only under that title; she is the perfect Christian. As infant, fiancée, spouse, virgin, mother and widow, she can be a model for Christians, who are called to become more perfect Christians (see 2 Cor 13:9-11). Clothed in the Word of God, icon of the gospel lived, she is our "form." And under the cross, more than anyone else, she is able to be for us an example of one who can repeat: "In my flesh I am completing what is lacking in Christ's afflictions" (Col 1:24) in the effort to work and suffer for unity.

An ecumenical spirituality lived in this way can produce exceptional fruits.

But we become aware that it will have one effect above all. Since it is communitarian it will bind into one all those who live it, so that they will feel solidarity among them and already be, in a certain way, one. They will be conscious of forming, we might say, a single Christian people which, with all that is happening as a result of the other forces inspired by the Spirit in this ecumenical age, can be leaven for the full communion among the Churches.

It will be in effect the implementation of another dialogue, added to the dialogues of charity, prayer and theology: the dialogue of the people. A people formed not only of laity, but of the whole people of God.

A dialogue more than urgent and timely if it is true, as history shows us, that little is certain in the ecumenical field when the people are not involved.

A dialogue that will lead to our discovering with greater clarity, with greater interest, and to our valuing all the immense heritage already common to Christians, made up of baptism, holy scripture, the first Councils, the Fathers of the Church ... and will make us live it together.

We are waiting to see this people, already appearing here and there, and we wish to wonder at it wherever there is a Church....

As we can readily understand, a spirituality of communion is useful not only to help bring about unity among Christians, but also to open dialogue with people of other religions. This dialogue is one of our most demanding and urgent challenges at the dawn of the third millennium.

By means of this spirituality, in fact, we will be able to offer them the witness of the unity we can already achieve, a witness all the more convincing because it is offered by Christians of different churches.

Furthermore, if we Christians love as this spirituality teaches, we would have greater light to see and discover in other religions the "seeds of the Word."[129] The non-Christian religions "often reflect a ray of that Truth"[130] which Christ revealed. And this discovery can bring us closer together and lead to mutual understanding.

Countless elements unite us to our Jewish and Muslim brothers and sisters, beginning with the revelation of the one God to Abraham, our common father in faith.

If it is true that almost all religions have the so-called Golden Rule, which in different ways states: "Do to others what you would want done to you; do not do to others what you would not want done to you," it is possible to establish also with them a relationship of mutual love.[131]

It is, however, above all the mystery of Jesus crucified and forsaken that offers great possibilities in this field too.

We realize, in fact, that in him "who was God and made himself nothing," as St. Paul says in the letter to the Philippians (see 2:6-8), we can see opening up a providential way for dialogue particularly with the religions of Asia, which are generally centred on detachment from all things and on the annihilation of self.

And this is because, as we too make ourselves nothing, we will be able to understand them and "enter" into them, since it is true to say: "To know the religion of another … involves getting inside the skin of the other … seeing the world in some sense as the other sees it … getting inside the other's sense of 'being a Hindu, Muslim, Jew, Buddhist,' or whatever."[132]

Then there is dialogue with those who do not believe.

Here too, Jesus on the cross, in his cry of forsakenness, is the divine response to the abyss of suffering and of trial hollowed out of human hearts by the profound questions of much contemporary culture.

It is through him and with him that we can approach effectively all these brothers and sisters of ours.

And dialogue among peoples?

The Churches with their members already give the world a witness of unity among persons belonging to many different peoples. But with a communitarian spirituality we could go further down this road — and precisely by looking to him "who has made both groups into one" (Eph 2:14).

And finally, unity between the human race and nature. The entire cosmos awaits the revelation of the children of God (see Rom 8:19).

From all that we have said, living an ecumenical spirituality gives men and women a greater possibility to reveal themselves as sons and daughters of God.

So that, while all of us take great care to protect nature, in a mysterious way nature itself will respond to our love, as all that God gives life to and sustains knows how to do.

A spirituality of communion, then.

Unity is the distinctive feature that sums it all up.

If we put it into practice we will see the world go in reverse, like a film running backwards.

By what dramatic divisions, by what disintegration, by what crises is our planet pervaded, our planet which is immersed even now in indifference, in secularization, in materialism.

With this new life we can turn back, while still going forward. Humanity will find again the unity for which God created it and the Churches will live in full communion in the way that he planned and founded his Church.

It is worth trying, therefore. And may this Second European Ecumenical Assembly be the opportune moment.[133]

With our elder brothers

> From an address to the B'nai B'rith and other members of the Jewish community, Buenos Aires, 20 April 1998.

It gives me great joy to be here with you who are part of one of the largest Jewish communities of the world.

A great joy because as a Christian I have had the honour of speaking to other groups of men and women of religions different from my own as, for example, Muslims in the United States and Buddhists in Japan and Thailand, but I have never had the good fortune of meeting with such a notable number of those who, with the Holy Father John Paul II, I know to be my "elder brothers" and to be able to honour and love them as such.

And what does my heart tell me then in this very precious moment?

First of all there is the desire to get to know you at least a little. And then to begin a relationship with you, precisely as brothers and sisters.

Not just a relationship in the abstract, with fine words and compliments, but concrete, nurtured possibly by mutual gifts. Because this is what happens when, after a long time, brothers meet again and discover they are brothers; they love one another.

To us you are brothers and sisters with whom we share an authentic faith in one God and have the inestimable common heritage of the Bible, in that which we call the Old Testament.

What should we do? What should we think?

If the simple Golden Rule[134] can bring us together as brothers and sisters with the faithful of other religions, if not always in God, at least through faith in a superior being, could it not be that the Lord is beginning to manifest his will clearly that we establish a fraternal relationship also among us, Jews and Christians?

Before coming here I read something about our relationship. I studied it and I share first of all the esteem for you my Church has revealed especially in the document *Nostra Aetate* of the Second Vatican Council.

But I have found light above all in many divine truths, set like stars in your Jewish tradition and which we share — truths that can become a bond between your spiritual life and ours.

Consequently I feel in my heart the desire to tell you about the secret of our Movement's success.

It lies in its spirituality which certainly came from the gospel of Jesus, but which already has its roots in the Old Testament — so that the spirituality could almost be re-expressed using the words of the Old Testament.

Thus I have dreamt of our being able to live these truths together and offering through our profound communion, through our working together, fresh hope to the world.

Our Movement was born from the perception of the reality of things by a group of girls, including myself, under the bombs of the last World War during 1943 and 1944 in Trent, northern Italy.

In the midst of the destruction brought about by the conflict, they experienced firsthand the truth that "everything is vanity of vanities." And already at that point Qoheleth gave us light.

Seeing how everything passes, a grace undeniably of God led them, as everything was crumbling, to choose an ideal for their life that no bomb could destroy: God, and they pledged themselves to love him with all their hearts.

They decided, therefore, as is expected of everyone who wishes to live our Movement's way of life, to put into effect the words of Jesus already present in Deuteronomy, in the Shema (6:4-5): "You shall love the Lord your God with all your heart, and with all your soul, and with all your might."

They understood from the gospel that to love God means to do his will. It says, in fact: "Not everyone who says to me, 'Lord, Lord' will enter the kingdom of heaven, but only the one who does the will of my Father in heaven" (Mt 7:21).

That is what we find wonderfully expressed in the "Sayings of the Fathers," part of the Mishnah, a very important work of the rabbinic tradition: "Be strong as the leopard, swift as the eagle, fleet as the gazelle, and brave as the lion to do the will of your Father in heaven" (Mishnah Avot 5:23).

Central for us Christians then is doing the will of God that requires us to "love your neighbour," in which there is, as Jesus says, all the Law and the Prophets.

Our brothers and sisters are loved because we see Christ, who for us is God, in each one. We know that we will be saved only on the basis of this love. The majestic description of the universal judgment to be made by Jesus expresses it: to the virtuous he will say that all the good done to their brothers and sisters, and even what may have been evil, he takes as done to himself: "You did it to me" (Mt 25:40).

But you also have the rabbinic tradition that love of neighbour is "the great principle of the Torah" (Rabbi Akiva). Since God created human beings in his image, for anything done to any other person it is as if it were done to God himself.

We have, then, the same commandment: "You shall love your neighbour as yourself" (Lv 19-18). And the Talmud demands, just as Jesus does: "The Holy One clothed the naked. As he did for Adam, so do you also clothe the naked. The Holy One, blessed be he, visited the sick, as he did with Abraham, so do you also visit the sick. The Holy One, blessed be he, comforted the mourners, as he did with Isaac, so do also you comfort the mourners. The Holy One, blessed be he, buried the dead, as Moses did, so do you also bury the dead" (see Babylonian Talmud, Tractate Sotah 14a).

Love of neighbour then, if lived by many people, becomes mutual. And here is the heart of the thought of Jesus, who gives us a commandment that is new and completely his own: "I give you a new commandment, that you love one another" (Jn 13:34).

But if we love one another in this way, the gospel assures us that Christ is in our midst: "Where two or three are gathered in my name, I am there among them" (Mt 18:20).

Most studies indicate that this verse is based on a Jewish tradition. We often read in the "Sayings of the Fathers": "When two sit and words of Torah pass between them, the Shekhinah [the dwelling place of the divine] rests between them" (Mishnah Avot 3:3).

Central for us is the mystery of Jesus who cried out on the cross in the words of Psalm 22, "My God, my God, why have you forsaken me?" (Mt 27:46).

We believe he suffered, in addition to all the other agonies of the cross, also being forsaken by the Father, with whom he was one, in order to recompose the unity of human beings with God and with one another, broken by sin.

I was moved by the statement of a contemporary Jewish writer, recently deceased, regarding Psalm 22: "What better can personify the Jewish people than this poor Rabbi from Nazareth?"[135]

This same Jewish author sees in the cry of Jesus also and above all the anguish of the Shoah, and he says: "The words 'My God, my God, why have you forsaken me?' are not just the psalm of David and the prayer of Jesus on the cross, but almost, I would say, the leitmotif of those who were transported to Auschwitz and Maidanek." He continues: "Is not this rabbi, bleeding to death on the cross, the very embodiment of his suffering people, too often murdered on the cross of that anti-Semitic hatred which we too were forced to experience in our youth?"[136]

The abyss of suffering and the feeling of being forsaken by God has been expressed as God hiding his face. Martin Buber, after the Shoah, spoke of the "eclipse of God."

The recent document of the Catholic Church concerning the Shoah is above all an urgent warning not to forget that unprecedented crime and a call to free ourselves once and for all from the toxic residue of anti-Semitism which for centuries has poisoned the relationship between Jews and Christians.[137]

Even those unspeakable sufferings of the Shoah and all the more recent bloody persecutions cannot but bear fruit. We want to share them with you so they become not an abyss separating us but a bridge uniting us. And that becomes a seed of unity. Yes, of unity!

This is the word that sums up our spirituality, based on Jesus' last testament: "May they all be one" (Jn 17:21).

And unity is strongly felt also by the Jewish people. The famous philosopher Abraham Heschel wrote: "Unity of God is power for unity of God with all things. He is one in Himself and striving to be one with the world.... The unity of God is a concern for the unity of the world."[138]

These are the basic points of our spirituality.

They are things found in your Jewish tradition that are similar, though not always identical, to ours.

As we reflect on them before God for a moment can we not think that he wants us to walk together, hand in hand? That he wants us to tell everyone he has made us brothers and sisters? That we should do this in order to give witness to a world given over today to materialism, secularism, hedonism, a witness of the marvellous adventure of spending our lives that his name be proclaimed, faith in him be strengthened, his values be affirmed? That his values of peace, of solidarity, of the defence of human rights, of justice and so forth be restored?

May the Lord inspire us.

May love triumph![139]

With the world religions

> From "What Future for a Multiethnic, Multicultural, Multifaith Society?" a previously unpublished address, Westminster Central Hall, London, 19 June 2004.

In recent years, our European societies are being changed by significant patterns of migration from east to west and from south to north. This phenomenon is having a profound impact on the appearance of our continent, bringing to our cities an ever greater diversity. We see it as we walk down the streets and note the presence of mosques, for instance, but also of many temples in countries which, until a short while ago, were almost exclusively Christian.

At the same time, the communications media bring people and nations, although in reality very distant, close to one another to the point that what takes place in Asia or in Africa can have a decisive impact on the personal choices of Western youth. No one is "foreign" to us any longer because we "see" people, because we know about them.

Furthermore, economic and financial globalization has woven together all our interests. They are no longer separated from one another. Many problems are of interest to humanity as a whole, problems which no nation can face in isolation from all the others. In a word, we live in a world that has truly become, as people say, "a global village": — a new and complex village.

This situation opens up opportunities for knowledge and development previously unknown, even though fears, indifference and intolerance remain, especially due to the ever imminent danger of terrorism.

A great saint and doctor of the Church, Augustine of Hippo, found himself in a situation that, in some ways, was similar to ours. Faced with the fall of the Roman Empire under the pressure of peoples migrating from the North and the East, he had the grace and foresight to help Christians understand that the upheaval taking place in society, which he and his contemporaries were witness to, was not the end of their world but the birth of a new world.[140]

His was a vision that came from the faith and conviction that God is not absent from history. God's love is such that it directs everything towards good. St. Paul himself said this: "We know that all things work together for good for those who love God" (Rom 8:28).

And now it seems to me that this same faith must sustain and guide us in our present-day situation.

This is also the experience that has been lived for the past sixty years by something new in the Church, the Focolare Movement, which I have the joy and honour of serving: a multicultural, multiethnic, multifaith Movement present in 182 nations of the world. Allow me to tell you about this Movement because it may be a light and a stimulus to many.

When it began no one had any projects or plans in mind. The idea for this Movement was in God, the design was in heaven. Even with our most optimistic predictions we never could have imagined that we would see the progressive coming together of this "people," as John Paul II often describes our Movement.

It brings together, like a real family, people of different languages, races, cultures, nations and also faiths, because beside being made up of Christians of numerous Churches, there are also followers of various religions and people who do not have a religious faith but who share with the others great human values such as justice, solidarity, peace, human rights....

The secret of this ability to gather in unity people who are so different lies in the timely and modern gospel spirit that animates our Movement: a spirituality both personal and collective. It is a "spirituality of communion" that generates a new way of life. This spirituality is not the monopoly of our Movement, because it is the fruit of a charism, a gift of God by its nature meant for all those who want to receive it.

What does this spirituality teach with regard to relationships among people of different races, cultures and religions? What is the attitude, truly full of light, it suggests in order to build fraternity among all?

First of all, this spirituality is based on a profound appreciation, for those who have faith, that God is a God of Love, a Father.

How could we consider unity and fraternity in society and in the world without a vision of all humanity as one family? And how can we understand this, unless there is one Father of all?

Therefore, this spirituality calls us to open our hearts to God as Father, who certainly does not abandon his children to their own destiny but who desires to accompany them, to protect them, to help them. God alone, who created them, is able to embrace and unite everyone.

To believe in his love is the first requirement of this new spirituality: to believe that we are personally and immensely loved by God.

He knows each one intimately and cares for each one personally. The gospel says that he counts even the hairs of our head (see Lk 12:7), and the Qur'an says: "We [God] are closer to him [man] than his jugular vein"

(50:16). Therefore, he will not leave the renewal of society to our efforts alone, but will take an active role.

Obviously, however, it is not enough to believe in the love of God, not enough to have chosen him as one's Ideal. The Father's presence and loving care calls each person to be a true daughter or son, loving the Father in return and living, day by day, according to God's loving plan for each one. And we know that a father's first desire is for his children to treat each other as brothers and sisters, care for one another, love one another.

Consequently, our spirituality urges us to love, to live in conformity with the love beating in the depths of every human heart. For the followers of Christ it is the *agape* which is a participation in the very love that is in God; for those of other religious faiths, it is a love that proceeds from the Golden Rule which is so precious to many religions and which says: "Do to others what you would have them do to you" (see Lk 6:31) or "Do not do to others what would not have them do to you" (see Tb 4:15).

For people with no formal faith, love can mean philanthropy, solidarity, non-violence.

With regard to the way to love our neighbour, ever since the beginning of our Movement the Holy Spirit pointed out some qualities that distinguish a simply human love from a gospel-based love.

This way of loving requires us to love everyone: people who are pleasant or unpleasant; beautiful or ugly; fellow-citizen or foreigner; of my culture or of another, of my religion or of another, friend or enemy. In fact, the gospel asks us to be perfect, in the image of the heavenly Father who "makes his sun rise on the evil and on the good, and sends rain on the righteous and on the unrighteous" (Mt 5:45). This love towards everyone is very fruitful. It is the experience of many that it would be enough to live this one quality of gospel-based love in order to bring about a total change in the society around us.

Loving like this, then, requires us to be the first to love, without expecting the other person to love us. It is a love like that of Jesus, who when we were still sinners, and therefore not loving, gave his life for us.

It is a love that makes us consider the other person as ourselves, that makes us see our very own selves in the other person. In the words of Gandhi: "You and I are but one. I cannot injure you without harming myself."[141]

It is a love not made up only of words or feelings; it is practical. It requires that we "make ourselves one" with others, that "we live the others" in a certain way, that we share their sufferings, their joys, in order to understand them, to serve and help them in an effective, practical way. It is a matter of weeping with those who weep, rejoicing with those who rejoice. Making ourselves one: it is the attitude that guided the apostle Paul, who wrote that he made himself a Jew with the Jews, Greek with the Greeks, all things to all (see 1 Cor 9:19-22). It is very important that we follow his example so that we can establish a sincere, friendly dialogue with everyone.

Yes, dialogue — a word especially suited to our times. Dialogue means that people meet together and even though they have different ideas, they speak with serenity and sincere love towards the other person in an effort to find some kind of agreement that can clarify misunderstandings, calm disputes, resolve conflicts, and even at times eliminate hatred. This dialogue, especially among the faithful of different religions, today is more indispensable than ever if we want to avoid the great evils threatening our societies.

It has been written: "To know the religion of another … involves getting inside the skin of the other … seeing the world in some sense as the other sees it … getting inside the other's sense of 'being a Hindu, Muslim, Jew, Buddhist,' or whatever."[142] This is not something simple. It demands that we empty ourselves completely, that we put aside from our minds our ideas, from our hearts our affections, from our wills everything we would want to do, in order to identify with the other person.

It is a matter of momentarily putting aside even the most beautiful and greatest things we have: our own faith, our own convictions, in order to be "nothing" in front of the other person, a "nothingness of love." By doing so we put ourselves in an attitude of learning, and in reality we always do have something to learn.

If we are motivated by this kind of love, other people will be able to express themselves because they feel accepted. They can give themselves because they find someone who listens. So then we become acquainted with their faith, their culture, their way of speaking. We enter their world, in some way we become inculturated in them and we are enriched. This attitude enables us to contribute to making our multicultural societies become intercultural, that is, made up of cultures open to one another and in a profound dialogue of love with one another.

Our complete openness and acceptance then predisposes the other person to listen to us. We have noticed, in fact, that when people see someone dying to self in order to "make him or herself one" with others, they are struck by this and often ask for an explanation.

This leads us then to what the Pope calls "respectful proclamation." "Respect" is the key word in every dialogue. Being true to God, to ourselves, and being sincere with our neighbour, we share what our faith affirms on the subject we are discussing, without imposing anything, without any trace of proselytism, but only out of love.

However, through the Holy Spirit who is always present when we love, our brothers or sisters are struck by something we say, something alive and spiritual which echoes within them. These are the "seeds of the Word" which the love of God has placed in every religion. Or while we are speaking, our brothers or sisters identify some aspect of those purely human values that the Lord, in creating us, planted in the core of every person and in every culture.

And on the basis of these "seeds" or values we can offer — always serving, however, always with gentle and boundless discretion — those aspects of truth we possess which can give greater fullness and completeness to what our neighbour already believes. First he or she gave to us; now we do the same. And in an atmosphere of communion created by this exchange of gifts, the truth is gradually revealed and we feel that it has brought us closer to one another.

We have had many experiences of this fruitful dialogue with people of the most varied cultures and even with large groups of believers of other religions. Precisely because of this practice of "making ourselves one" and the friendship born from it, we consider them as Movements that are supportive of our own, and they know that our Movement is supportive of theirs. With them, we have built up substantial portions of fraternity, as with the Buddhists of the Rissho Kosei-kai, which includes six million members, or the members of the American Muslim Society, which numbers two million, and others.

Real, true, heart-felt fraternity is, in fact, the fruit of a love capable of making itself dialogue, relationship, that is, a love that, far from arrogantly closing itself within its own boundaries, opens itself towards others and works together with all people of goodwill in order to build together unity and peace in the world.

Yes, peace.

But can religions, also as a whole, be partners in the journey to peace?

This, as we all know, is a question of great importance and of the highest relevance today.

Many interpret the spread of terrorism, the wars waged in various parts of the world in response to it, the ongoing tensions in the Middle East as symptoms of a possible "clash of civilizations." They say it is marked and even intensified by the different religious allegiances.

Upon a closer examination of the facts, however, this viewpoint, triggered by various forms of extremism and fanaticism that distort religions, proves very partial.

Never so much as in our present day have believers and leaders of all religions felt the duty to work together for the common good of humanity. Organizations such as the World Conference of Religions and Peace or initiatives such as the day of prayer for peace in Assisi promoted by John Paul II in January 2002 are a confirmation of this.

On that occasion the Pope stressed, in the name of all those present, that "whoever uses religion to foment violence contradicts religion's deepest and truest inspiration" and that "there is no religious goal which can possibly justify the use of violence by man against man" because *"to offend against man is, most certainly, to offend against God."*[143]

On September 11, 2001 humanity discovered, in shock and horror, the nature of the vast, colossal danger that terrorism is. It is not a war like others, which are usually the fruit of hatred, of discontent, of rivalry, of interests either personal or collective.

Terrorism, instead, as affirmed by the Pope, is in addition the fruit of the forces of Evil with a capital "E," the forces of Darkness.

Now, forces of this kind cannot be opposed only by human, diplomatic, political and military means. We need forces of Good with a capital "G." And Good with a capital "G," we know, is God and all that is rooted in him. Therefore, we can combat terrorism with spiritual forces, with prayer, for example, with fasting, as the representatives of the world religions did in Assisi, the city of St. Francis.

But it seems to us that we have to say that prayer is not enough.

We know that the causes of terrorism are many, but one of them, the deepest, is the unbearable suffering of a world half rich and half poor. This has produced and continues to produce resentments that have long brooded in people's hearts, violence and revenge.

More equality is needed, more solidarity, especially a more equal sharing of goods.

We know, though, that goods do not move by themselves, they cannot walk on their own. Hearts must be moved, hearts must be shared.

This is why we need to spread among as many people as possible the idea and practice of fraternity, and — given the vastness of the problem — a universal fraternity. Brothers and sisters know how to look after one another, they know how to help one another, they know how to share what they have.

And to meet this unprecedented challenge, the contribution of religions is decisive.

From whom, if not from the great religious traditions, could a strategy of fraternity begin, a strategy capable of marking a turning point even in international relations?

The enormous spiritual and moral resources of religions, the contribution of ideals, of aspirations to justice, of commitment to the most needy, along with the political leverage of millions of believers, all springing from religious sentiments and channelled into the field of human relations, could undoubtedly be translated into actions that could have a positive influence on the organization among nations.

Much is being done in the field of international solidarity by non-governmental organizations. What is missing is for states in their own right to make political and economic choices that can build a worldwide community of peoples committed to bringing about justice.

In the face of a strategy of death and hatred, the only effective response is to build peace in justice. But there is no peace without fraternity. Only fraternity among individuals and peoples can guarantee a future where there is peaceful coexistence.

Besides, universal fraternity and the peace which follows from it are not new ideas that have emerged today. They have often been present in the minds of deeply spiritual persons because God's plan for humanity is fraternity, and brotherly love is written in the heart of every human being....

Our experience tells us that whoever wants to move the mountains of hatred and violence in today's world faces a task that is enormous. But what is beyond the strength of millions of separated, isolated individuals becomes possible for those who make mutual love, understanding of one another and unity the driving force of their lives.

And for all this there is a reason, a secret key, and a name. When we, of the most various religions, enter into dialogue among ourselves, that is, when we are open to one another in a dialogue of human kindness, of mutual esteem, of respect, of mercy, we are also opening ourselves to God and, in the words of John Paul II, "we let God be present in our midst."[144]

This is the great effect of our mutual love and the hidden strength that gives vitality and success to our efforts to bring unity and universal fraternity everywhere. It is what the gospel proclaims to Christians when it says that if two or more are united in genuine love, Christ himself is present among them and therefore in each one of them.

And what greater guarantee can there be than the presence of God, what greater help can there be for those who want to be instruments of fraternity and peace?

What future therefore for a multicultural, multiethnic, multifaith society?

A future where, let us say it again, all people live as one family made up of brothers and sisters who love one another beneath the gaze of one Father. Or, for those who do not know God, a family united in the name of that voice of truth which speaks out in every human conscience.

There is no alternative if we want to avoid plunging our planet once again into a sea of trouble, fear, hatred, war.

Instead, if we live as we said before, if we love one another, we cannot fail to stir up love around us, and many from different races, cultures and religions will follow us. Then one day in the not-too-distant future, mutual love will come to flourish also among peoples.

A utopia? No, it is God's most heartfelt desire, it is Jesus' last testament, his prayer for unity, and it will become a reality. If he, the Son of God, prayed to the Father for the unity of all, this request cannot but be granted.

The Focolare Movement's experience of interreligious dialogue

> From an address to an interreligious seminar organized by the Initiatives of Change Centre, 29 July 2003, Caux (Switzerland).

The first major experience we had with brothers and sisters of other religious faiths was with the Bangwa, a tribe in Cameroon, which followed a traditional religion. They were almost on the point of extinction from high infant mortality when we began to assist them.

One day their king, the Fon, and thousands of his people were gathered, in a large clearing in the middle of the forest, for a celebration in which they offered us their songs and dances. All at once I had a strong impression of God, like a huge sun, embracing all of us, we and they, with his love. For the first time in my life, I intuited that soon we would be involved also with people of non-Christian traditions.

The event that in some "founded" this dialogue occurred at London in 1977 during a ceremony conferring the Templeton Prize for Progress in Religion. I gave a talk and when I was leaving the hall, the first to greet me were Jews, Muslims, Buddhists, Sikhs, Hindus.... The spirit of Christianity that I spoke of had so impressed them, that it was clear to me that we would have to be involved not just with our own and other Churches, but also with these brothers and sisters of other faiths. So began our interreligious dialogue.

Two years later, in fact, came the meeting with a distinguished Buddhist, the Rev. Nikkyo Niwano, founder of the Rissho Kosei-kai, who invited me to Tokyo to speak about my spiritual experience to ten thousand Buddhists. So began between the Focolarini and followers of the Rissho Kosei-kai a great spirit of fellowship wherever we happen to meet.

But the most surprising meetings with Buddhism were with some eminent representatives of Thai monasticism.

During a long visit to our international little town of Loppiano in Italy, whose 800 residents try to live a life faithful to the gospel, two of them were touched profoundly by the unity among everyone and by a Christian love they had never before experienced.

That reduced the prejudices that were preventing a true dialogue between them as Buddhists and us as Christians.

These monks returned to Thailand and lost no opportunity to tell thousands of the faithful and hundreds of monks about their encounter with the Focolare Movement. So began, if we may call it this, a Focolare-Buddhist Movement, that is, of one of Buddhists and Christians, one part of the relationship of fraternity we are building in the world.

Later we were invited to Thailand to speak at a Buddhist university and in a temple to monks, nuns and many laity.

Their interest was remarkable and we were edified by their asceticism and their detachment from everything, so characteristic of them.

And the dialogue with Islam?

There are now 6,500 Muslim friends who belong to our Movement, and what binds them to us is the spirituality, which gives a spur and an affirmation that leads to a more profound and vital adherence to the essentials of their own Islamic faith. We have had many meetings with our Muslim friends. What characterizes these gatherings above all is the presence of God which one notices when they pray, and which gives much hope.

I saw this hope become a reality in the Malcolm Shabazz Mosque in Harlem (USA) six years ago when I was invited to explain my Christian experience to 3,000 African-American Muslims.

Their welcome, beginning with that of their leader, Imam W.D. Mohammed, was so warm, sincere and enthusiastic that it led us to great expectations for the future.

I returned three years ago to the United States, to Washington, to make a presentation about our working together before a large convention of 7,000 Christians and Muslims. In an atmosphere of the greatest elation and accompanied by endless applause we exchanged a sincere embrace, promising each other we would continue our journey in the fullest union possible and spread it to others. So now there exist yet more portions of fraternity.

I cannot fail to mention the increasingly frequent meetings with Jewish sisters and brothers in the state of Israel and elsewhere. The most recent for me was in Buenos Aires, with one of their larger communities, a meeting then followed up on various occasions by other members of our Movement.

Deeply moved, we exchanged a pact of mutual love. It was so profound and heart-felt that it made us feel we had suddenly overcome centuries of persecution and misunderstanding.

In the last three years we have begun a promising dialogue in India with the Hindus. We have strong fraternal contacts with the Gandhian Movements in the south of this vast country. A profound dialogue has begun at Mumbai with professors from Somaiya University and from the Indian Cultural Institute. More recently a relationship has began with a very large Movement, Swadhyaya, which shares our goals of brotherhood and unity in diversity.

A year ago we had our first Hindu-Christian symposium. The atmosphere was so beautiful and inspiring that we were able to share with them many truths of our faith. We had the impression of a horizon that we never imagined opening before us.

A few months ago I returned to India and we were able to continue this dialogue at a level of spirituality which, in the words of the authorities of the Church I belong to, "is the summit of the various forms of dialogue and responds to the deepest expectations of people of goodwill."[145]

Now we are planning other similar symposia, Buddhist-Christian and Muslim-Christian.[146]

With the expansion of our Movement we are in contact with all the principal religions in the world, and approximately 30,000 members of these religions share, as far as they are able, the spirituality and goals of the Movement.

Our interreligious dialogue has developed so rapidly and fruitfully because the decisive and characteristic element has been the art of loving, of which I spoke previously.[147]

The Golden Rule fosters a climate of mutual love in which you can establish a dialogue with your counterparts. In this dialogue you try to make yourself nothing in order, as it were, to enter into the others.

To "make yourself nothing" means the same as to "make yourself one" with others.

In these two simple expressions, which I already referred to, lies the secret of a dialogue that can build unity.

"Making yourself one" is not a tactic or an external way of behaving. It is not just an attitude of goodwill, openness and respect, or an absence of prejudice. It is all that, but it is something more.

This practice of "making yourself one" requires that we empty the ideas from our mind, the affections from our heart, and everything from our will in order to identify with the other. We cannot enter into the soul of our brothers or sisters to understand them, share their sorrow or joy, if our own spirit is rich with a preoccupation, a judgment, a thought ... with any other thing. "Making yourself one" demands spirits that are poor, poor in spirit in order to be rich in love.

And this most important and indispensable attitude has a double effect. It helps us become inculturated in the world of others, thus getting to know their culture and customs, and disposing them to hear what we have to say.

We have noticed, in fact, that when people see someone dying to self in order to "make him or herself one" with others, they are struck by this and often ask for an explanation.

Then we can pass on to "respectful proclamation."[148] Being true to God, to ourselves, and being sincere with our neighbour, we share what our faith affirms on the subject we are discussing, without imposing anything, without any trace of proselytism, but only out of love. This is the point at which, for us Christians, dialogue opens itself into proclaiming the gospel.

Our work with many brothers and sisters of the major religions and the brotherhood we experience with them has convinced us that the religious pluralism of humanity can lose much of its negative value as an instigator of divisions and war so as to acquire in the awareness of millions of men and women a sense of challenge: that of restoring unity to the human family, because the Holy Spirit is present and active in some way in every religion, and not just in the individual members but also within the religious tradition itself.

Speaking about the remarkable event at Assisi, John Paul II defined it as the "marvellous manifestation of the unity that binds us despite our differences and divisions."[149]

Let us fill our hearts, then, with genuine love. With this we can hope all things for unity among the believers of the world religions and for a brotherhood that is lived out in the whole human race.[150]

With Muslims

> To participants at the first international meeting for Muslim friends of the Focolare Movement, Castel Gandolfo, Italy, May 1992.

Dear friends,

Welcome to this first meeting held especially for our Muslim friends, adherents of the Focolare Movement.

I would have liked to welcome you personally, together with the other members of the Centre of the Movement, but as you may be aware, I am currently in Nairobi, Kenya with other brothers and sisters of our numerous family.

They too wish to extend to you their best wishes and are happy to be united to you in our great Ideal.

But what is it that has made this meeting happen? What urged you, my dear Muslim brothers and sisters, to travel such long distances, to dedicate your time and face such significant expenses to meet here together, to meet with all of us?

We know: a sign of times is that today men and women of goodwill yearn for concord, for harmony, for a world where all live together in peace, even though this is continuously threatened in various points of the earth.

This movement towards unity of many people is a sign of the times.

It is a sign of the times that manifests the intervention in human history of God, the one God, Father of us all, brothers and sisters.

And a manifestation of God's intervention today is the special gift or charism, as it called, that we have had the good fortune to chance upon, that is, our Ideal which has come to us in the most varied ways.

This has fed in all of our hearts a new flame: the faith that is the foundation of our believing, the faith that makes us certain that God is love and that, as such, loves each one of us, looks after us, accompanies us, enlightens us, helps us, saves us.

This faith, for us Christians, is expressed in Holy Scripture, which is permeated with this truth and in particular where John the evangelist writes: "God is love" (1 Jn 4:8).

And also in your Holy Book many of God's attributes reveal him to us as love.

Having received this gift we feel an urgency to reciprocate the infinite and personal love that God has for us. For the Muslim poet Rumi speaks the truth when he says: "God has predestined us eternally for love."

During these days we will learn how to fulfil these words in many ways. We will see how we can respond to what the Lord asks of us, as one of your great thinkers, Ibn Arabi, expresses very well:

"My beloved, love me!

Love only me, love me with a true heart!

No one is closer to you than I.

Others love you for themselves.

But I love you only for you...."

And then, after having loved him, we will also love our brothers and sisters, as God asks of us when he says: "Love your neighbour as yourself" (Lev 19:18) and we will love one another as Jesus teaches us in his principal commandment: "Just as I have loved you, you also should love one another" (Jn 13:34).

And through this love we will contribute to building universal brotherhood in the one Father God.

And with his blessing this brotherhood will grow and will render the world a better place, more peaceful, more united.

With my most heartfelt wishes, I leave you in God.[151]

> In the many meetings between the Muslim friends of the Focolare and Chiara Lubich, there have been moments of both profound and sincere dialogue. The following are answers she has offered to some of the questions raised.

- *"Chiara, we would like to ask you, what has it been like establishing a relationship with the faithful of other religions?"*

I have always felt very comfortable! Because even if our religions are different we have much in common and this unites us. Our diversity attracts us to one another; it makes us curious about one another. Therefore, I am happy for two reasons: because I come to know new things and I enter into another's culture; but also because I come to know brothers and sisters who are the same as me insofar as we believe in so many of the same things.

The most important thing we have in common is the Golden Rule: "Do not do to others what you would not have them do to you." This saying is present in the sacred books of all of the most important religions. It is also in the gospel for Christians.

It means: treat your brothers and sisters well, hold them in high esteem, love them. Thus, when they discover this sentence in their scriptures and I discover it in mine, I love, they love, and in the end we love one another. This is the foundation on which we can begin to live universal brotherhood.

- *"What do you feel when you meet a brother or sister of another religion?"*

I feel a great desire to relate with them as with members of the same family, to enter immediately into a fraternal relationship, to make unity.

- *"When you first began the Focolare Movement it was formed solely by Roman Catholics. Can you tell me how you were able to open the minds of people of other races and religions and unite them among themselves, helping them understand love for others in such a simple way?"*

We began to love because the gospel told us to love. Love is the word that sums up the whole of the Christian religion. Loving: it is all there.

And since we are spread out all over the world, if one of us met a Buddhist, a Muslim or a Hindu, we loved him or her because we must love everyone. And so a contact was established simply by loving.

Then, as I said before, we discovered that there are truths in these religions — especially in the more important ones — that are the same as those that exist in our religion. Therefore, we helped them to discover in their scriptures precisely those truths that corresponded to the main points of our spirituality, because with the passage of time we understood that God had prepared this charism for many.

- *"One would imagine that the process of making your ideal effective in practice has not been lacking in difficulties, as is usually the case with large undertakings at the service of humanity. Could you tell us, even briefly, of the difficulties you have faced?"*

They are the difficulties you too will face. The first is a difficulty within ourselves.

Perhaps there are times when we want to say: "That's enough, I'm tired of loving, I'll live my own life, I'll turn on the television, I'll watch it, I'll go and get a drink...." And this is what Saint Paul calls the "old self." In other words, it is that purely human behaviour which is inclined towards self-centredness and towards our passions. Instead, when we love, when we live our Ideal, we have the "new self."

But we need to train ourselves, to be athletes of the spirit. If we do so, little by little we are able to live as our "new selves" all day long. Of course, not perfectly because we are still sinners, but we will get there. Therefore, you will find the first obstacle within; it comes from our "old self."

We, as a Movement, also found many difficulties from the outside. Since the Movement first began we loved one another completely and like the first Christians we put all that we had in common. As a result we were accused of being Communists. We knew that it was not true, and our bishops knew it as well, but the accusation remained.

Or, because we read the gospel with such fervour and we tried to put it into practice, others said: "They are Protestants."

Therefore, people will accuse you too, and one day you will tell me about it. But what matters is that we keep on going.

- *"I have seen that in the talks that you prepare for us you often cite the Qur'an and this has really touched me. What moved you to take our Holy Book and make a comparison with the gospel?"*

Since Islam is one of the major religions, I was convinced that the Qur'an contained profound truths similar to ours. Therefore, I began to look for those fundamental truths that God had underlined for us in the gospel, so that we might be able to live them together and therefore already in some way be united.

- *"How can we as Muslims face suffering?"*

In order to explain this point well, I must say first that in the spiritual life it is very important always to live the present moment. We cannot live in the past because it is already gone; we must cast it into God's mercy. We cannot live in the future, because it has not yet come. We must live in the present. The skill of the spiritual life tells us: live now, totally and fully in the here and now.

I know, for example, that for us, when someone is close to death, we advise him or her to live in the present, because it is the most reasonable thing to do.

Now, with this as a premise, I will tell you how to approach suffering.

Suffering is very, very precious. It is not something to be discarded. In this regard, the Qur'an made a great impression on me. There is a sentence in it that is almost identical to something that Jesus says: "Unless a grain of wheat falls into the earth and dies, it remains just a single grain; but if it dies, it bears much fruit" (Jn 12:24). It is like saying that if we do not know how to accept suffering, learn to die to ourselves, we do not bear any fruit, we remain sterile all our lives. If instead we accept suffering and we die, we will bear much fruit.

If you were to ask me: "What is it that fuels the Movement?" I would have to respond: "It is suffering accepted."

How many people — even now for your meeting — offer up their sufferings, hardships, even their death? Every day I receive news: "Chiara, today this woman left for heaven, and she offered everything for the Movement and for this moment." "This man discovered that he had a tumour, he accepted it and offered everything for this moment." And this is because we know that suffering is something extremely precious.

Well then, the Qur'an also speaks of a grain of wheat thrown to the ground. Therefore, it also recognizes, although in a slightly different way, how precious suffering is. It says that certain people who appear to be made nothing by suffering, then instead are resurrected with a thousand lives. It is the same thing, the same idea. Thus, suffering is extremely precious. It is a constitutive element of the spiritual life.

So, what do we do when suffering comes?

I repeat, we must live the present moment. And so when suffering comes our way, we go deep within our hearts as we do when we pray. We know that God is everywhere; therefore he is also in the depths of our hearts. And so we say to God: "OK, I accept this suffering and I offer it to you, for you." And then, in the following moment we must continue to do God's will, which, for example, might be to come here and listen or to go and do some shopping, to read, to study…. We must do this will of God immediately. I assure you, it has been our experience for several decades now that many sufferings, in particular spiritual ones, fade way, vanish, we no longer feel them. Try it! It is a challenge, but it is true.

- *"Having come to know the Movement and its members, I have noticed that you and other members do not marry. Since marriage is very important for us, could you explain this choice of yours? Would it not be better to marry in order to pass on this beauty that I have noticed, especially in these people, to their own children?"*

I would preface my response by saying that also in the Church, among Christians, marriage is considered to be a wonderful state of life. And not only from a human point of view but from a supernatural point of view as well. Marriage is even sealed by a sacrament, which for us means that it is something truly from God. Having said this, in the Christian world, especially in the Catholic Church, there are people who, instead, follow God in virginity. Some of us present here today are among those who follow God in this way.

Why have we made this choice? Because God called us; but also because we saw that Jesus was a virgin, Mary was a virgin, even though a mother. Joseph, Mary's husband, was a virgin and also some of the apostles, like Saint Paul, never married. What is more, we also find that due to virginity we can approach many more people.

In fact, Jesus encourages virginity and he speaks very highly of it because he sees it as a possibility to dedicate all of one's time for God's work, to spread the kingdom of God. And this is precisely what happens.

Of course, if we live our virginity well we also become mothers and fathers, spiritually speaking, and we have many children.

Do you know that people all over the world call me "mother"? Just the other day I heard that there is a Buddhist monk who goes around saying: "I am a Buddhist, a Buddhist monk, but I am the son of a Christian mother." He says this to everyone.

Thus, with regard to motherhood, we are not lacking anything. Another kind of maternity takes its place, a spiritual maternity.

- *"Discovering the Focolare Movement has filled me with joy and has opened my eyes, showing me how to be Muslim. What would you advise me to do in order to give this treasure to other Muslims so that they can understand it as I have?"*

This is the way: you must go and love. If you find someone who is suffering, try to help him or her. Love is never made up only of words: "I love you, I love you." Love is always made up of concrete acts. It means giving the hungry something to eat, helping those who suffer…. The Qur'an says it too.

At first we must love without speaking. Beware of speaking, because people will immediately point you out and they will judge you. You have to love for a long time without speaking, until one of these people whom you have loved asks you: "Why are you different? You are not like everyone else, you understand people. Why is that?" Then you can speak up and say: "Well, I live my life differently; I've changed." Tell them that little that you think they can understand. And usually you will win them over to your cause.

Of course, here we have many Imams who must preach, who have to speak. To them I would say that if they must teach, let them teach the right things, and so they can speak right away. But for us laypeople it is better that we take this other path.

In this regard, I heard that two Buddhist nuns, to whom I had spoken while I was in Thailand, participated in one of the meetings of our Movement, a Mariapolis, and that they learned there how to love without speaking. When they went back to their convent they began to love. The others, noticing that they were acting differently, asked them what had caused this change. Now they have begun to speak and little by little other nuns have begun to love.

Just to say that there is room in all the religions; we just need to enter with love, because love and the Golden Rule are present everywhere.

- *"How do you manage to love us Muslims so much as to make us feel this unity so strongly?"*

It comes spontaneously to me. It is not that I have to think about it. It comes spontaneously because you are all so loveable.

But it is not just something human. I think it comes from the fact that there is God in this. Because there is spontaneity and spontaneity. There is human spontaneity, for example of a child who reacts in a certain way, and there is also the spontaneity of a true Christian, of a true Muslim, who is moved by the Holy Spirit. It is, I think, the Spirit of God in me who feels one with the Spirit of God in you.

- *"Chiara, what impression did your experience with your Muslim brothers and sisters make on you?"*

It is as if I had known them all my life. When I am with them I feel as if I am among brothers and sisters. I attribute this to our common faith in God.

I feel that there is a pre-existing bond that was there already. And it is God, the same God that we both love.

- *"How do you foresee the fulfilment of unity among Christians and Muslims in the future?"*

Only God knows that. I could not even begin to imagine. God knows. It will be something very beautiful, but only God knows.

With people of convictions not based in religion

> Statements and answers to questions principally at two meetings: Loppiano, Incisa Valdarno, Florence, May 1955, and Castel Gandolfo, Italy, February 1998.

- *On solidarity with everyone*

Jesus considers as his allies and friends all those who fight evil and work, often without being aware of it, to bring about the kingdom of God.

Jesus asks of us a love capable of becoming dialogue. This is a love that, far from closing itself off arrogantly in its own concerns, knows to open up to others and work with all persons of goodwill in building together peace and unity in the world. Therefore let us try to open our eyes to the neighbours we meet, to appreciate the good they do, whatever their convictions may be, to feel solidarity with them and encourage one another in the way of justice and of love.[152]

- *Why did the Movement start this dialogue? What set it in motion?*

It was not any human planning that brought the Movement to dialogue with people of other convictions; it was the impulse of the Holy Spirit. He steered us down that road.

What set it in motion was the consideration that Jesus is God and Man. Though he is divine he gives value to all that is truly human.

One is not Christian without first being human.

The grace of God that makes us Christians does not supplant nature, but elevates it.

We recognized that people who appreciate and promote humanity, human values are very important.

Not only that, but your presence in the Movement is useful as well as corrective for anyone who would be tempted to limit his or her life to spiritual things. With you there is no such danger; you have your feet on the ground.

- *The proposal to begin dialogue goes far beyond simple tolerance — quite an achievement in its time and still threatened in our society today. Two centuries ago Lord Stanhope said that tolerance was once sought as a favour and then demanded as a right, and that "a time will come when it will be spurned as an insult." He said this because he foresaw the day — hopefully we are there — when we would be ready for a higher value, which is dialogue. It goes beyond just tolerating others. It means profoundly respecting them, welcoming their different ideas and discussing them in the light of our own, and above all building a relationship as in a true family. What do you think about this?*

I think that dialogue certainly is a great advance beyond tolerance, yet I would not entirely disparage tolerance, since it is useful in some places where at least it prevents fighting and quarrelling. Dialogue is an entirely different matter: it is a mutual enrichment, a love for one another, a feeling that we are already brothers and sisters, the creation of a universal brotherhood here on earth.

Naturally dialogue is true if it is animated by true love. But love is true only if it is disinterested; if not, it is not love. It is egoism.

You have asked me a number of questions about whether there might be some self-interest in love, even in dialogue itself.

If there is, it would be a dialogue built without love; hence it would not be a dialogue but something else: proselytism, for example. Proselytism must stay completely out of the picture; it has no place in it. Otherwise there is no dialogue.

Dialogue means loving, giving what is in us out of love for the other, and also receiving and being enriched. It means becoming as our Gen put it, "world people," who have the others within and have also been able to give to others what is theirs.

I recall the early days of the Movement when we were getting started. It was suggested to us that the way we should follow was love. But we were clear in our minds that love has to be disinterested. You must not love in order to win the other person over. You must not love in order to set up your own little group for yourself. You must not love in order to have some sort of influence, it could be anywhere, such as in the position you hold or at your school. No, you must love just to love.

We behaved like this for a spiritual reason, because we had Christian convictions. Therefore people, feeling free, seeing the beauty of this life, followed us.

Now this is the way we can build up true fraternity, achieve universal brotherhood.

• *The Movement promotes dialogue with people of various convictions, accepting their differences. But do not those who have faith always desire that, by means of this dialogue, those who do not believe find God?*

Well, the desire may be there because faith brings such happiness, such joy if it is lived (Jesus promised "the fullness of joy"), that seeing a brother or sister who may not always have the same joy, you naturally want to say: "Why not do what I do?"

But if we have that desire we must erase it, because proselytism is anti-Christian, insofar as it is not love: it is love of self, of our own group or our own Church. Instead what we must have is love for the other.

We also need to erase that desire because you do not know what in the plans of God these persons can bring to you, with what they are in themselves, with the values they hold, with what they believe, and by which perhaps you should be enriched. Maybe you believe yourself to be well informed about Christian doctrine, but you do not know all about justice, you do not know all about fairness, you do not know all about a healthy economy that would bring relief above all to the poorest.

• *We are a group that believes in equality, solidarity, fraternity and in all those primary human values which unite a human being with others. Convinced that unity can be achieved only by recognizing and respecting the cultural identity of each member of society, what does the Focolare Movement offer in the dialogue with these women and men from different cultures?*

We need to open ourselves as widely as possible, but not as an act of charity! We open ourselves as widely as possible in order to be enriched.

Why do we want you to be present? Because we know that you bring values into our Movement that need at least to be emphasized.

We know that to some degree Christianity includes all values, but you too bring values, and call attention to some better received through you.

Therefore, opening ourselves as widely as possible so that we can be enriched by each other. And at the same time, however, this openness must always be mutual, otherwise what kind of dialogue is it? It turns into a monologue and a monologue is no use.

• *You have told us: "Without you the Work of Mary would lose its identity." Can you explain that further?*

It is absolutely true! Because as a new Movement in the Church, we have a universal vocation. Our motto is: "May they all be one." Now, that "all" includes you too. We cannot do without you because you are part of that "all," otherwise we would be cutting away half or at least a third of the world, all the while saying: "May they all be one."

Naturally we should "be one" as far as we can: we will be one in our values, be one in other ideas, be one in doing something practical.

On reasons to share our lives

> A previously unpublished letter to the conference "Reasons for a Shared Life, the Shared Life of Reasons" for people of convictions not based in religion, Castel Gandolfo, Italy, 1 June 2001.

Dear all,

A heartfelt welcome to all of you, our friends, with warmest gratitude for your being here!

This conference that you who hold various convictions are attending is a fine thing and it is very important. You have come out of your interest in the spirit that has bought life and moves the Focolare, in its goals, its life, and its achievements. You have full citizenship in our Movement; you are an essential part of it.

And yet someone might wonder: how can a Movement like the Focolare, arising from a very profound religious conviction, from the choice of God as the ideal of one's life, be of any interest to men and women of other convictions?

Indeed, it can be, and there is an answer to the question.

Indeed, because we Focolarini believe in a religion that is not merely consigned to the heavens, as some might say; it is profoundly human.

We, as all Christians certainly do, believe in a transcendent God, but one who became incarnate on this earth, who made himself man. Hence, if God who is pure spirit, the most Holy Trinity, may be of the greatest interest for us, we know that this God is Love and has shown that fact by not remaining only in heaven delighting in his infinite bliss, but has made himself one of us, one human being alongside others.

He did not keep his greatness, his divinity jealously for himself, but wanted in some way to make us partakers of it, to share it with us, making us too sons and daughters of his Father, sons and daughters in him, the Son of God.

The fact that he took on human flesh is — I would say — the central point of our faith, which our Movement emphasizes to the full.

And here is that great thing which permits us to have a profound bond with you, a communion with you, committed as you are to respecting, to empowering humanity, every human being, cultivating and safeguarding human values. That is what we as well have to and want to do with you.

For us, because of our faith, as we know, Jesus is God and Man together. And we focus particularly on God in Jesus when dealing with, when dialoguing with other Christians or with believers of other religions. But we turn our gaze to Jesus the Man when, together with you, we wish to devote ourselves for the good of humankind and its needs, as well as when we wish to understand humankind's immense potential and its riches.

My friends, that is how things stand. But one can still ask: is there any indication in our common history that assures us we are on the right road? That we are doing what we should? That all we are doing can contribute to the great project before us: universal brotherhood for a world more united, or rather, a world united?

I think that the very development reached in our Movement by your branch, that of our friends who hold various convictions, in many parts of the world already shows its great value; indeed this development demonstrates always more clearly how every genuine form of shared human life, today more than ever, cannot do without the great, common values of humanity, peace, justice, solidarity, liberty and the dignity of every person.

And it is for this reason we hold that dialogue with you is absolutely necessary. And not only dialogue but also active collaboration with you.

In a previous message I wrote about our "economic initiative" based on love for all, on mutual love, which has led to a growth in solidarity and to practical achievements. Many of you have contributed to setting this up and developing it, in order to work toward resolving the problem of marginalization. This year, as you know, apart from our "economic initiative" you will also hear about our "political initiative," which is also aimed at fulfilling some of our great ideals.

We are already planning and have begun other activities in various areas of human need: for example, education, law, health....

My dearest friends, I am sure you will be — if you are not already — with us in developing many other initiatives that could be set up to improve the world. For this we count very much on you, on your particular sensitivity to these issues, a sensitivity that leaves us certain of your indispensable contribution.

And from this very moment I thank you from my heart for your friendship and for the commitment that you offer.

To the Youth

A united world: an ideal that becomes history

> Address to the fourth international festival (Genfest) of "Youth for a United World," Palaeur sports stadium, Rome, 31 March 1990.

The Movement "Youth for a United World" began officially five years ago with the 1985 Genfest.

Thanks to the Gen, totally committed young men and women who witness to the highest values and who are the main driving force behind this Movement, it has quickly spread around the planet. Today it includes youth of the greatest variety of races, of every nationality, who speak nearly sixty languages, who belong to the main Christian Churches or to one or another of the many world religions, or simply come from diverse cultural backgrounds.

The Movement's goal is at once ambitious and sublime. To some it may even appear to be a utopia, but it is not, because the overwhelming majority of its members rest upon a force that transcends it and enlightens it, that guides it and forever walks before it; the Movement rests upon God, who, it realizes, participates in the personal history of every man and woman and of all humanity.

The Movement is convinced that it is possible to make the world a better place. It believes that the world can one day become almost a single family, as if belonging to just one country, a world that lives in solidarity, even more, a united world. And it works toward this goal.

Its convictions and its action for this goal come in the first place from the evidence that today unity is a sign of the times, and from the awareness that it bears within itself (not for itself but for many), a gift that it has in common with the whole of the wider Focolare Movement and of which it is an expression. It is the gift, the charism of unity

And it finds its vision and its project confirmed by an analysis of the world at present.

Although aware of the tremendous and varied evils that even today afflict humanity, it is conscious that in the last decades the world is changing, and that our planet slowly but surely is turning towards a specific end: its unification.

Already in the Genfest of 1985 this phenomenon was examined and the signs were noticed: the outbreak of peace, as it was called then, in place of atomic war between the two superpowers, the formation of agencies that serve the interests of all the countries of the world, the coming together of States into single blocs, as with European unity (at that time only Western Europe was thought of), and in the field of religion openings unthinkable just a short time before, with dialogues among the Churches, with believers of other religions and with people of goodwill.

These were the observations that five years ago urged the young people of the Movement to do everything within their power to speed up the process.

And so we have seen them following the most varied "paths" to co-operate in constructing the unity of the world.

They have therefore, depending upon their capabilities and the requirements of their circumstances, mended torn relationships, put an end to divisions, plunged themselves into the most desperate rifts that pit one person against another, group against group; they have followed the way of unity among peoples, among races, between rich and poor, among the various ethnic groups, between generations....

And there has been a marvellous and rich flowering of actions, that are constant, daily, committed.

Aware, however, that all their work, however large, always produced but a drop in the sea of the world's needs, they entrusted themselves to the One who can do far more. And they decided before all else to walk along the Way par excellence. "I am the way" (Jn 14:6), Jesus said. They followed him, therefore, putting into practice his words.

And they were not disillusioned. In fact, they realized that while they were doing their small part, he, the Lord of history, intervened unquestionably by doing his part, a great one.

It is wonderful, and it makes the heart swell with joy to see how these past five years, since Genfest '85, have confirmed what you, Youth for a United World, proposed.

You are all familiar with the recent extraordinary events that cannot be attributed to human forces alone. You know of the changes, so widespread and radical, that have taken place in Eastern Europe which seem to have doubled the size of the European project, stretching it as far as the Ural Mountains. These changes are reflected now in other nations of the world, as in Central America and Asia. You know also the attempted changes in a large Asian country, unfortunately suppressed amidst bloodshed but no less significant for that, and a guarantee of hope for the future. You have also witnessed the collapse of racial barriers in Africa.

Yes, the world is changing, despite everything, despite everyone.

And behind all that happened — we must bear witness to it — is God. Referring to Eastern Europe, John Paul II said: "God won."[153]

And we agree with him.

God intervened, of course, through lesser figures whose names we all know from the headlines of the news.

Among these, in all this process that is shaking the world, there is another kind of figure that has not received due credit. It is not an individual but a category of persons: young people, yes, precisely, young people.

It is not true that today's youth have withdrawn into their own private world and, in general, have little interest in the large-scale problems of humankind.

There are many young people who, precisely because they are freer from conditioning and selfish interests, because of their need to believe in something authentic, because they long to renew the world, are sensitive to great ideals. And often among the young there is the most compelling and fascinating response to the thrusts of history.

Who do not have in their eyes and in their hearts the striking scene of Chinese youth in Tiananmen Square? With their extraordinary courage and faith in a better society, they strove to set in motion the great Beijing Spring. Who does not remember the unarmed young man who stopped a column of tanks, an image that stunned the world?

And who was not moved as they watched on television the great number of young people in the front line of demonstrations and political activities, who brought about the demolition of the Berlin Wall, or who gave life to the new springs of Prague, Budapest and Bucharest? And even before that, the Polish youth, crosses in hand, fingers raised in sign of victory, in Warsaw and Gdansk and in many other cities during the peaceful revolutions that have changed the face of Central and Eastern Europe? Or also the youth in the squares of Moscow, demanding the restoration of trampled human rights?

And we all recall clearly the fervour of the many youth involved in the non-violent people's revolts in Latin America: in Buenos Aires, São Paulo, Santiago, Montevideo and Asuncion, which led to the return of freedom after the oppression of military dictatorships.

Similarly we recall Korean youth who long for a single homeland, and those Palestinian and Lebanese youth who have acted non-violently. And there are many others. Forgive me if I do not mention everyone.

The huge number of young people participating last summer in the great pilgrimage to Santiago de Compostela, symbolic site of the spiritual unity of Europe, astounded public opinion. They were determined to promote a rediscovery of the Christian values that gave life to the civilization of the continent.

Young people are always in the front line of the great struggle to save nature despoiled by human activity, the necessary backdrop to a humanity at peace.

And young people have been and are in the front line when it comes to demanding peace.

And they are in the very front line when they make their time and energy available, completely freely, to give practical help to the peoples of the Third and Fourth Worlds. This, too, is another gigantic problem facing those who seek a united world.

Yes, young people today are active in every field.

Let us ask, then: among all of these what task do you, Youth for a United World, have? What is your specific contribution? What is your place?

Undoubtedly you, first of all, want to share your peers' hopes and struggles so that there may prevail the great values they champion, such as freedom, human rights, democracy, equality....

You have made the unequivocal decision to resolve problems in practical ways as you continue walking down the various paths to unity, supporting and setting up micro-projects, new initiatives that show those older than you what can be done on a larger scale, if the necessary tools, skills, experience, maturity are available.

But above all, you must offer the extraordinary, completely original contribution that is specifically yours because you are Youth for a United World.

You can give the most important element of all: you can give a "soul" to all who labour in this immense construction site which is our planet today.

You are aware of how requests for spiritual things, for spirituality, come from entire nations, especially those that have gone through the traumatic experience of atheistic materialism. Because of their great thirst for spirituality, whatever can be offered to them, even printed matter by the hundreds of thousands of copies, is sold out in a day. You have seen for yourselves, then, how the noblest aspirations of the human heart cannot be suffocated forever.

You have also observed that many people now looking towards the West can be harmed by another kind of materialism, no less dangerous.

This then is your task: to give what is most desired, satisfy the hunger for what is sacred and holy, for the spiritual element which every heart carries within it.

But how?

We know that God, the very height of the spiritual, is love.

Love, then, is the spiritual element most sought: the love that God, who made himself man, brought to earth.

Let us imagine passing before our eyes a few scenes symptomatic of today's world.

In Eastern Europe, in the nations that have recently seen changes, we observe people who are overjoyed by their newfound freedom. Beside them, however, others are frightened and disillusioned, depressed at the collapse of their ideals. We read on some faces threats of retaliation, revenge, even hatred.

Let us stop to think: what would Jesus say if he appeared among them? We can be certain: he would still speak today, as he did in his time, of love. He would say: "Love one another as I have loved you" (Jn 15:12). Only together, in harmony and in forgiveness, can a solid future be built.

Let us move on, as if watching a series of images fading in and out, to other locations, for example, to a country of Latin America. On one side we see skyscrapers, often modern cathedrals erected to the god of consumerism, and on the other we see shantytowns — the mocambos or favelas — with abject poverty, poverty both moral and physical, and diseases of every kind.

What would Jesus say about this scene of desolation? "I told you to love one another. You did not, and see now the consequences."

And if other pictures, as in a collage, were to flash before our eyes: cities known as the richest in the world, others with the most advanced technology, and panoramas of desert wastes with men, women and children dying of hunger. What would Jesus say if he appeared in the midst of it all? "Love one another."

Of if we were to see scenes of racial strife with massacres and violations of human rights... Or unending conflicts like those unfolding in the Middle East with houses collapsing, injuries, deaths and the endless, murderous rain of bombs or other deadly devices?... Let us ask ourselves once again: what would Jesus say in the face of such tragedy? "I said that you should love one another. Love one another as I have loved you."

Yes, this is what he would say looking upon these and the gravest situations in the world here and now.

But his words are not only words of regret for what has not been done. He truly repeats these words to us today. He has died but he is risen and — as he promised — he is with us every day, to the end of the world.

And what he said is of enormous importance. This sentence, "Love one another as I have loved you," is the master key to solve every problem; it is the fundamental answer to overcome every evil affecting humankind.

Youth for a United World can find no better way to fulfil their task of cooperating in giving a soul to the world than by bringing love back into it.

Certainly, it is not what it might seem at first glance; it is no easy task. It is exacting and challenging, but this love has the power to change the world.

Jesus called the commandment of love "mine" and "new." It is especially his since he filled it with unique and new content. "Love one another," he said, "as I have loved you." And he gave his life for us.

Therefore, our life is at stake with this love. It is a love ready to give its life, and that is what he asks us to do for our brothers and sisters.

Friendship or kindness towards others is not enough for Jesus, neither philanthropy nor solidarity alone. The kind of love that Jesus asks for is more than non-violence.

It is something active, dynamic. He asks that we no longer live for ourselves but for others. And this requires sacrifice, hard work. He asks everyone to change from spineless and egotistical individuals concerned only with their own interests, only with their own things, into small everyday heroes who, day after day, are at the service of their neighbours, ready to give even their lives for them.

Dearest young people, your vocation calls you to this if you do not want your ideals to vanish in utopian dreams.

You must love in this way, love one another in this way, first being witnesses to this love yourselves before you propose it to others.

Witnesses, models: may the world see how you love one another and repeat what was once said of the early Christians: "See how they love one another and are ready to give their lives for one another."[154]

Then a solid foundation will have been laid; the root of the tree we want to see blossom will have been planted.

This mutual love among you will, in fact, bring consequences that we could say have infinite value. Indeed, where there is love, there is God. As Jesus said: "Where two or three are gathered in my name [that is to say, in his love], I am there among them" (Mt 18:20).

You will have then Christ among you, Christ himself, the Almighty, and from him you can hope for all things.

He himself will work with you in your countries because he will, in a certain way, come again into the world wherever you meet, because you will make him present through your mutual love, through your unity.

And he will enlighten you about all that is to be done. He will guide you, he will sustain you, he will be your strength, your fervour, your joy.

Because of him, the world around you will be converted to living in harmony; every division will be healed. He said so: "May they all be one so that the world may believe" (see Jn 17:21).

The commitment you have made for yourselves is a magnificent one and no one but he can be your leader in the struggle.

Love, therefore, love among you and love sown in many corners of the earth among individuals, among groups, among nations; love sown by every means possible so that the invasion of love, of which we have spoken at times in the past, may become a reality and so that, also through your contribution, the civilization of love we all await may begin to take on solid form.

You have been called to this, and you will see great things.

Just think. If above all it is God who has won in the chapter of history we have just lived, what will it be like if to the direct action of God is added the action of young people, of many young people guided by Christ, present among them through love?

Go ahead then, without hesitation. Your youthfulness does not count the cost; it is generous. Make the most of it.

Go ahead, you Christians, you who believe in Christ.

Go ahead, you members of other religions, sustained by the very noble principles you hold.

Go ahead, you of other cultures who may not know God but feel in your hearts the need to spend all your energies for the ideal of a united world!

All of you, hand in hand, be certain of this: victory will be yours.[155]

To the children

> A previously unpublished address to the third Supercongress of "Youth for Unity," Rome, 26 May 2003.

Here you are in the city of Rome, full of sunshine, rich in history, centre of the Catholic Church, coming from ninety-two countries of the world, representing many cultures and many faiths: Jews, Muslims, Buddhists, Hindus, Sikhs, Zoroastrians, members of traditional African religions and Christians from fourteen different Churches.

Here you are in the shadow of the Coliseum, where so many Christians of the early centuries paid with martyrdom for their faith in Jesus.

Here you are to celebrate and to demonstrate in support of a truly huge ideal: peace.

Peace.

But does peace really matter here and now?

Certainly it does, and perhaps more than ever. And not only because of the dozens of wars raging here and there on our planet, but also because peace is now threatened in a different way, a more devious one.

You know it: although months have passed, for sure the deeply sad events of September 11th, when the Twin Towers were destroyed in New York, remain very much alive in your young hearts. And they are alive in a particular way just now, when new and similar threats of terrorism seem to be emerging. Well then, in the face of this situation and all the other forms of violence, the thinking of people who have been given responsibility and those who are enlightened is becoming more and more accepted. They think that all of this is the result not only of hatred between individuals and peoples, but it is also the effect of the dark force of Evil with a capital E, of the Shadows, as the Pope has said.

The situation, then, is serious. Because if things are like this, it is not enough to oppose such danger with human forces alone. It is necessary to commit the forces of Good with a capital G.

And you all know what this Good is. Before all else it is God and all that has its roots in him: the world of the spirit, of the great values, of true love, of prayer.

And here is the reason behind Assisi, last January 24th. On that occasion John Paul II invited representatives of the major religions of the world for a second time to the city of St. Francis to ask heaven for peace.

Today, however, true peace is so valuable that all of us, adults and youth, persons in office and ordinary citizens, have to commit ourselves to protecting it. And you young people too.

Naturally, in order to know what to do we need to understand thoroughly the deepest causes of the current tragic situation.

You too know how in the world justice does not reign, how there are rich countries and poor countries, starving people, while the plan of God for the human race is that we all should be brothers and sisters in one great family with one Father alone.

This imbalance is one of the factors, perhaps the most important, that generates resentment, hostility, revenge, terrorism.

And so how do we create greater equality, how do we bring about some kind of communion of goods?

It is obvious that goods do not move if hearts are not moved. We need, therefore, to spread love, that mutual love which generates a relationship of brothers and sisters among all. We need to invade the world with love! And we must start with ourselves.

And that means you, young people.

But someone here might ask me, "Is this love, this love for one another, compatible with the way of life handed down to us by our cultures?"

Yes, it is possible. Look in your Holy Books and you will find, nearly everywhere, the so-called Golden Rule. Christians recognize it in this form: "Do to others as you would have them do to you" (Lk 6:31). Jewish people say this: "What you hate, do not do to anyone" (Tb 4:15). Muslims say: "None of you truly believes until he loves for his brother what he loves for himself" (Hadith 13, Al-Bukhari). And Hindus say: "Do naught unto others which would cause you pain if done to you" (Mahabharata, 5:1517). All these sayings mean: respect and love your neighbour.

And if you, a Muslim young person, love; and if you, a Christian, love; and if you, a Hindu, love, you will certainly come to the point of loving one another. And so would it be for everyone. And here, now, we would find we have built one piece of universal brotherhood.

Then we need to love our other neighbours, and you in particular must love the young people you meet in your lives; since if like is attracted to like, young people will be better convinced and drawn to great ideals by other young people.

Love, therefore, is one of the great secrets of this moment.

Love with a special love. Not, of course, with that love reserved only for your own family or friends, but with love for everyone, likeable or not, poor or rich, young or old, from your county or from another, friends or enemies … towards everyone.

And be the first to love, taking the initiative, without waiting to be loved.

And love not just with words, but practically, with actions.

And love one another.

Dearest young people, if you do this, if we all do this, universal brotherhood will widen, solidarity will flourish, goods will be better distributed, and over the world will shine the rainbow of peace, a world which, in a few years, will be in your hands.

Epilogue

The vineyard of Jesus forsaken

"My vineyard, which is mine, is before me" (Sg 8:12, KJV).

We have always seen the Work of Mary as the vineyard of Jesus forsaken.

And now a thought returns to my mind.

After fifty-six years of the Movement's life, I can contemplate its leaves and branches spread across all the earth and its clusters bursting with juice that continue to nourish a *new people*.

And I remember the words I read with my first companions, perhaps as long ago as 1944, on the feast of Christ the King: "Ask of me, and I will make the nations your heritage, and the ends of the earth your possession" (Ps 2:8).

On that day, we asked for it with faith. The Movement has truly reached the very ends of the earth. And in this *new people* are *represented* the peoples of all the earth.

Their number is such that the wish of my bishop in 1956 … : "Would that there were a legion of Focolarini!" has now come true. He, who had hoped that standing by the Focolarini would help him to heaven, will be seeing this from above.

What, just now, would be my last wish? I wish that the Work of Mary, at the end of the ages, when it will be waiting, united, to appear before Jesus forsaken and risen, may be able to repeat to him, making its own words of the Belgian theologian Jacques Leclercq, words I always find moving: "On your day, my God, I shall come to you.… I shall come to you, my God … with my wildest dream: to bring you the world in my arms."[156]

"Father, may they all be one!"[157]

The secret

- *Is there a secret, a secret you would say is at the basis of all of this?*

Love.
It is everything!
God is love.
Love is everything![158]

Simply "Thank you"!

• *What do you imagine will happen when you come face-to-face with God?*

We have a song that puts something I wrote to music.

It goes like this: "When I will come to your door and you ask who I am, I will not say my name, I will say simply: "Thank you for everything and for always. That is my name."

This is how we see life.

We do not focus on either merits or sins.

We say simply, "Thank you." And I can say it with the Movement, which I have seen come to life.[159]

Bibliography

In Section One the abbreviations NCL and NCP refer to New City, London, and New City Press, New York respectively. Where editions are co-productions both abbreviations appear together. The dates refer to the latest edition.

In Sections Two and Three all works cited are published by Città Nuova, Rome, unless otherwise noted. Consistent with the style used by the Notes of this volume, the abbreviations CN, NU, UC stand for the journals "Città Nuova," "Nuova Umanità," "Unità e Carismi" respectively, and the abbreviation SS stands for *Scritti spirituali*. The publication dates for Chiara Lubich's original writings in Section Two and Igino Giordani's writings in Section Three show the date of first publication followed by the last publication, together with superscript numbers indicating the number of printings, current in 2006.

Section One
Chiara Lubich in English

Call to Love, A, NCP 1990 (contains *Our Yes to God, The Word of Life, The Eucharist*).
Challenges 99 x 4, NCL (in English, French, German and Dutch).
Charity, NCL 1980.
Christian Living Today: Meditations, NCP 1997.
Christmas Joy: Spiritual Insights, NCL and NCP 1998.
Cry, The, NCL and NCP 2001.
Diary 1964/5, NCP 1987.
Discovering the Present: Reflections from the Writings of Chiara Lubich (Audio CD), NCP 2006.
Eucharist, The, NCP 2005.
Heaven on Earth, NCP 2000.
Here and Now: Meditations on Living in the Present, NCL and NCP 2005.
Jesus: The Heart of His Message: Jesus Crucified and Forsaken, NCP 1997.
Jesus in Our Brother, NCL 1982.
Journey to Heaven, Spiritual Thoughts to Live, NCP 1997.

Living Presence, The, NCL 1997 (contains: *The Word of Life, The Eucharist, Where Two or Three*).
Love that Comes from God: Reflections on the Family, NCL and NCP 1995.
Manifesto, NCL 1981.
Man's Yes to God, NCL 1981.
May They All Be One, NCL and NCP 1981.
Mary, The Transparency of God, NCL and NCP 2003.
Meditations, NCL 2005.
New Way, A: The Spirituality of Unity, NCL and NCP 2006.
Only At Night We See the Stars: Finding Light in the Face of Darkness, NCL and NCP 2002.
Secret of Unity, The, NCL 1997.
Servants of All, NCL and NCP 1979.
When Our Love Is Charity, NCP 1991 (contains *When Our Love Is Charity, Jesus in Our Midst, When Did We See You, Lord?*).
Yes Yes No No, NCL 1981.

Section Two
Original Works by Chiara Lubich

1. Books

– **Meditations**

Meditazioni, Rome 1959, 2000[24].
Pensieri, Rome 1961, 1995[6].
Frammenti, Rome 1963, 1992[11].
Fermenti di unità, Rome 1963, 1978[4].
Saper perdere, Rome 1969, new ed. 1996[10].
Sì, sì. No, no, Rome 1973, 1981[3].
Disegni di luce. Meditazioni e immagini, Rome 1996.

– **Thematic presentations**

Tutti siano uno. Punti di spiritualità, Rome 1962, 1994[9].
La carità come ideale, Rome 1971, 1980[7].
Parola di vita, Rome 1975, 1993[7].
Dove due o tre, Rome 1976.
L'Eucaristia, Rome 1978, 1997[5].
Uomini al servizio di tutti, Rome 1978, 1978[2].
Gesù nel fratello, Rome 1979, 1995[5].
Il sì dell'uomo a Dio, Rome 1981, 1995[2].
L'unità e Gesù abbandonato, Rome 1984, 1998[9].
Una via nuova. La spiritualità dell'unità, 2002, 2003[2].

Maria trasparenza di Dio, Rome 2003, 2003³.
L'arte di amare, Rome 2005, 2005³.

– **Collections of spiritual writings**
SS/1. *L'attrattiva del tempo moderno*, Rome 1978, 1997⁴ (contains: *Meditazioni, Pensieri, Frammenti*).
SS/2. *L'essenziale di oggi*, Rome 1978, 1997² (contains: *Saper perdere, Sì, sì. No, no*).
SS/3. *Tutti uno*, Rome 1979, 1996⁴ (contains: *Tutti siano uno; La carità come ideale; Parola di vita; Dove due o tre*).
SS/4. *Dio è vicino*, Rome 1991, 1995⁴ (contains: *L'Eucaristia; Uomini al servizio di tutti; Gesù nel fratello; Il sì dell'uomo a Dio*).

– **Autobiographical writings**
Diario 1964/65, Rome 1967, new ed. 1985.
Incontri con l'Oriente, Intro and notes by E. M. Fondi, Rome 1986, 1987².
L'avventura dell'unità (intervista di Franca Zambonini), Paoline, Cinisello Balsamo 1991.
Il Grido, Rome 2000, 2003⁶.

– **Commentaries on scripture**
Essere la tua Parola/1, Rome 1980, 1980².
Essere la tua Parola/2, Rome 1982.
Costruire sulla roccia, Rome 1983, 1993⁴.
Parola che si fa vita. Commenti alla Scrittura, Rome 1989, 1990⁵.
Scrivere il Vangelo con la vita, Rome 1995².
L'amore vince, Rome 1998.

– **Collections of spiritual thoughts**
La vita un viaggio, Rome 1984.
In cammino col Risorto, Rome 1987, 1994⁴.
Cercando le cose di lassù, Rome 1992, 1992⁵.
Santi insieme, Rome 1994, 1995³.
Santità di popolo, Rome 2001.
Costruendo il "castello esteriore," Rome 2002.
In unità verso il Padre, Rome 2004.

– **To young people in the Focolare Movement**
Rivoluzione arcobaleno, Rome 1969.
Detti Gen, Rome 1969, 1999⁵.
Colloqui con i gen/1 – (1966-1969), Rome 1998.
Colloqui con i gen/2 – (1970-1974), Rome 1999.
Ai gen 3 – 1971-'75, Rome 1979, 1991³.
Ai gen 3 – 1975-'80, Rome 1994.

– **Various Anthologies**

E torna Natale ... , Rome 1987, 1991[8].
Una famiglia per rinnovare la società (coll. *Spazio Famiglia. Testi*), Rome 1993.
Cristo dispiegato nei secoli. Testi scelti e presentati da F. Ciardi, Rome 1994, 1994[2].
Perché mi hai abbandonato? - Il dolore nella spiritualità dell'unità, D. Fratta (ed.), Rome 1997, 1998[3].
Dove la vita si accende. Dialoghi sulla famiglia, Rome 1998, 1999[2].
La parabola del corpo, Rome 2000, 2000[3].
Ogni momento è un dono. Riflessioni sul vivere nel presente, Rome 2001.
L'economia di comunione. Storia e profezia, Rome 2001.

2. Selected articles

"Al consiglio d'Europa per il Premio europeo dei diritti dell'uomo," in NU, 20 (1999/5), 119, 529-31.

"Amare, dunque, amare, amare, amare," talk at the Giornata per la Vita (Day for Life) 1986, in *Firenze, Europa, cultura: Prima di tutto la Vita*, Movimento per la Vita, Florence 1986, 27-41.

"A tu per tu con Chiara – Risposte alle domande dei giovani," in *Speciale Genfest '95*, CN, 39 (1995), 11, 32-6.

"Come concorre il Movimento dei Focolari alla nuova evangelizzazione," in "Gen's," 22 (1992/1), 3-9.

"Conferimento della laurea honoris causa in teologia della vita consacrata," in NU, 27 (2005/1), 157, 5-16.

"Dimensione petrina e dimensione mariana," in *La Famiglia Cristiana nell' insegnamento di Giovanni Paolo II – Dieci anni di pontificato di Karol Woytila – Testimonianze*, Famiglia Cristiana, Milan 1988, 207-08.

"Discorso tenuto all'Università di Lublino," in NU, 18 (1996/3-4), 105-106, 313-26.

"Focolari tra le religioni - Un'esperienza di dialogo interreligioso in India," in "Il Regno," 46 (2001/10), 881, 303-05.

"Frutti ed effetti della vita del Vangelo nel Movimento dei Focolari," in UC, 1 (1991/2), 3-10.

"Gesù in mezzo a noi. Rendere visibile la presenza del Risorto nella Chiesa," in NU, 27 (2005/3-4), 159-160, 407-18.

"Giovani per il Duemila," in CN, 40 (1996), 10, 30-3.

"Igino Giordani, focolarino," in CN, 24 (1980), 9, 22-5.

"Igino Giordani: il confondatore," in NU, 17 (1995/1), 97, 5-10.

"Il Movimento dei Focolari e il Vangelo," in UC, 1 (1990/3), 3-8.

"Il Movimento dei Focolari e la Famiglia Francescana," in UC, 10 (2000/6), 10-17.

"Il Movimento dei Focolari nei suoi aspetti politico e sociale," in NU, 20 (1999/5), 119, 521-28.

"Il Movimento Parrocchiale: a servizio della parrocchia," in "Quaderni di Gen's/1," 16 (1986), 5-11 e in CN, 19 (1986), 9-10, 46-56.

"I media e il carisma dell'unità," in NU, 19 (1997/2), 110, 203-09.
"Incontro con amici musulmani – La preghiera, la meditazione e l'unione con Dio," in NU, 22 (2000/1), 127, 11-20.
"Incontro con la comunità ebraica in Argentina," in NU, 20 (1998/3-4), 117-118, 374-384. *I santi e l'unità*, in "Gen's," 15 (1985/4), 5-12.
"La Chiesa-comunione e la spiritualità dell'unità – Intervento al Congresso internazionale delle Religiose," in CN, 40 (1996), 9, 30-31.
"La comunione tra i Movimenti," in "Gen's", 29 (1999/6), 202-05.
"La donna artefice di pace e di unità, in Donna: genio e missione – Atti del Convegno sulla *Mulieris Dignitatem*," Vita e Pensiero, Milan 1990, 27-36.
"La famiglia. A colloquio con Chiara Lubich," in *Dieci sfide per i nostri giorni*, A. Campoleoni, L. Guglielmoni (eds.), Milan 2000, 19-32.
"La fraternità in politica: utopia o necessità?" in NU, 26 (2004/6), 156, 773-82.
"La fraternità politica nella storia e nel futuro dell'Europa," in NU, 24 (2002/4), 142, 407-16.
"La legge di Loppiano," in CN, 24 (1980), 14, 24-7.
"L'amore al prossimo," in NU 24 (2002/6), 144, 709-19.
"L'amore reciproco: nucleo fondamentale della spiritualità dell'unità," in "Gen's," 20 (1990/3-4), 77-83.
"L'annuncio di Dio Amore," in NU, 25 (2003/3-4), 147-8, 313-23.
"L'ansia del nostro tempo. Discorso al Katholikentag," in CN, 26 (1982), 18, 36-9.
"La radicale novità e la profonda libertà di Gesù nel rapporto con le donne," in "Quaderni dell'Osservatore Romano," 9 (1989), 125-29.
"La spiritualità per un vivere insieme. Intervento alla VII Assemblea della Conferenza Mondiale delle Religioni per la Pace," in NU, 22 (2000/2), 128, 147-56.
"L'avete fatto a me. Intervento al Congresso Internazionale Religiosi," in CN, 39 (1995), 10, 30-2.
"La vie spirituelle des laïcs. Témoignage," in *Éléments pour une Théologie du Laïcat*, Pontificio Consiglio dei Laici, Città del Vaticano, 1979, 79-80, 84-5, 90-4.
"Le parole che tu hai dato a me, io le ho date a loro", in UC, 9 (1999/3-4), 8-11.
"L'esperienza 'Economia di Comunione': Dalla spiritualità dell'unità una proposta di agire economico," in NU, 21 (1999/6), 126, 613-19.
"L' Europa unita per un mondo unito," in NU, 25 (2003/2), 146, 139-51.
"Lo Spirito Santo e i carismi," in NU, 6 (1984/2) 32, 3-6.
"Lo Spirito Santo e il Movimento dei Focolari - I," in "Gen's," 20 (1990/5), 161-8; "II: Effetti e doni," in "Gen's," 21 (1991/6), 184-91.
"Lo spirito di fratellanza nella politica come chiave dell'unità dell'Europa e del Mondo," in NU, 24 (2002/1), 139, 15-28.
"L'unione con Dio," in NU, 26 (2004/3-4), 153-54, 327-39.
"L'unità e Gesù crocifisso e abbandonato fondamento per una spiritualità di comunione," in NU, 25 (2003/1), 145, 21-36.

"Messaggio al 1° Incontro Internazionale degli Amici musulmani a Castel Gandolfo," in CN, 36 (1992), 13, 34.
"Messaggio per la Conferenza Mondiale delle Religioni per la Pace," NU, 7 (1985/1), 37, 3-5.
"Molte vie per un mondo unito," in CN, 19 (1985), 7, 31-8.
"Momento di Dio. Messaggio al Genfest '80," in CN, 24 (1980), 11, 26-9.
"Nella Moschea di Harlem," in NU, 19 (1997/6), 114, 703-11.
"Per una civiltà dell'amore, uomo e donna nella città," in "Il nuovo Aeropago," 18 (1999/1-2), 332-39.
"Per una civiltà dell'unità," in CN, 32 (1988), 12, 30-6.
"Possono le religioni essere partner sul cammino della pace?" in NU, 26 (2004/2), 152, 161-74.
"Realizzarsi nella gioia," in CN, 28 (1984), 9, 25-9.
"Segni di speranza per la Chiesa del futuro," in *Ein Koch-Buch: Anweisungen und Rezepte fur eine Kirche der Hoffnung; Festschrift zum 50. Geburstag des Bischofs Dr. Kurt Koch*, Kanisius Verlag, Freiburg Schweiz 2000, 95-106.
"Spiritualità e Movimenti," in *La voce dei Laici al Sinodo*, Pontificio Consiglio dei Laici, Città del Vaticano 1988, 171-7.
"Spiritualità dell'unità e vita trinitaria. Lezione per la laurea honoris causa in teologia," in NU, 26 (2004/1), 151, 11-20.
"Una spiritualità per la Chiesa - Intervento al Convegno Internazionale Movimento Parrocchiale," in CN, 40 (1996), 11, 30-2.
"Unione con Dio e con i fratelli nella spiritualità dell'unità," in NU, 24 (2002/5), 143, 553-64.
"Uomo del dialogo. La figura del presbitero oggi," in "Quaderni di Gen's/3," 17 (1987), 29-34.
"Verso l'unità delle nazioni e l'unità dei popoli," in NU, 20 (1998/1), 115, 57-65.
"Verso una nuova umanità," in CN, 26 (1982), 7, 23-9.
"Vita trinitaria," in NU, 24 (2002/2-3), 140-1, 135-7.

Section Three
Secondary Literature and Other Sources on the Spirituality of Unity in Various Languages

1. About Chiara Lubich and the spirituality of unity

Back, J.P., *Il contributo del Movimento dei Focolari alla koinonia ecumenica. Una spiritualità del nostro tempo al servizio dell'unità*, Rome 1988.

Cerini, M., *God Who Is Love*, New City Press, New York 1992.

Coda, P., *Viaggio in Asia. Con Chiara Lubich in Thailandia e Filippine*, Rome 1997.

____, *Nella moschea di Malcom X. Con Chiara Lubich negli Stati Uniti e in Messico*, Rome 1997.

____, *Le luci della menorah. Con Chiara Lubich in Argentina e Brasile*, Rome 1998.

Fondi, E. – Zanzucchi, M., *Un popolo nato dal Vangelo. Chiara Lubich e i Focolari*, Cinisello Balsamo 2003.

Gallagher, J., A *Woman's Work: The Story of the Focolare Movement and Its Founder*, New City Press, 1998.

Paolo VI al Movimento dei Focolari. Parole di saluto, esortazioni e insegnamenti rivolti dal S. Padre ai gruppi del Movimento dei Focolari partecipanti alle Udienze Generali 1965-1978, Rome 1978.

Pedrini, I., *Marilen. Semplicemente vivere*, Rome 2000.

Pelli, A., *L'abbandono di Gesù e il mistero del Dio Uno e Trino. Un'interpretazione teologica del nuovo orizzonte di comprensione aperto da Chiara Lubich*, Rome 1995.

Povilus, J.M., *"Gesù un mezzo" nel pensiero di Chiara Lubich. Genesi, contenuti ed attualità di un tema della sua spiritualità*, Città Nuova, Rome 1981 (con numerosi scritti inediti).

____, *United in His Name*, New City Press, New York 1992.

Pree, B., *Mitgliedschaft in kirchlichen Vereinigungen. Die Fokolar-Bewegung* (Linzer Kanonistische Beiträge 9), Linz 2000.

Robertson, E., *Chiara*, Christian Journals, Belfast 1978.

Salierno, L.M., *Maria negli scritti di Chiara Lubich*, Rome 1993.

Sgariglia, A. (ed.), *Contemplare Cristo con gli occhi di Maria*, Rome 2003.

Sorgi, T., *Un anima di fuoco. Profilo di Igino Giordani*, Rome 2003.

Tobler, S., *Jesu Gottverlassenheit als Heilsereignis in der Spiritualität Chiara Lubichs. Ein Beitrag zur Überwindung der Sprachnot in der Soteriologie*, Berlin/New York (Walter de Gruyter) 2003.

Vandeleene, M., *Io, il fratello, Dio nel pensiero di Chiara Lubich*, Rome 1999.

Various authors, *Esperienze,* Rome 1959.

____, *Il Movimento dei Focolari. L'unità è la nostra avventura*, Rome 1986.

Zamboni, D. (ed.), *Glimpses of Gospel Life: The "Little Flowers" of Chiara and the Focolare Movement*, New City, London, and New City Press, New York, 2004.

____, *Quando Dio interviene. Esperienze da tutto il mondo*, Rome 2004.

Zambonini, F. *Chiara Lubich: A Life for Unity*, New City, London, and New City Press, New York 1991.

Zanzucchi M., *Da Trento al mondo, dal mondo a Trento*, Rome 2001.

____, *Mille lune. In India con Chiara Lubich*, Rome 2001.

____, *I santuari sulle rocce. Con Chiara Lubich in Medio Oriente*, Rome 2000.

____, *Fontem un popolo nuovo*, Rome 2002.

____, *Il progetto di NetOne. Media e spiritualità dell'unità*, Rome 2004.

____, *Una visita a Loppiano*, Rome 2004.

2. Inspired by the spirituality of unity

Baggio, A.M. *Lavoro e dottrina sociale cristiana. Dalle origini al Novecento*, Rome 2005.

____, *Etica ed economia. Verso un paradigma di fraternità*, Rome 2005.

____, (ed.), *Meditazioni per la vita pubblica. Il carisma dell'unità e la politica*, Rome 2005.

Bruni, L., *Economia di comunione. Per una cultura economica a più dimensioni*, Rome 1999.

____, *L'economia la felicità e gli altri*, Rome 2004.

____, *The Economy of Communion: Toward a Multi-Dimensional Economic Culture*. New City Press, New York 2002.

Bruni, L., Moramarco, V. (eds.), *Verso un agire economico "a misura di persona." L'esperienza dell'Economia di Comunione*, Vita e Pensiero, Milan 2000.

Bruni, L., Crivelli, L. (eds.), *Per una economia di comunione. Un approccio multidisciplinare*, Rome 2004.

Cambón, E., *Trinità modello sociale*, Rome 1999.

Ciardi, F., *Koinonia. Spiritual and Theological Growth of the Religious Community*, New City Press, New York 2001.

____, *Fuoco è la Tua parola. Come vivere il Vangelo*, Rome 2003.

Coda, P., *Evento Pasquale. Trinità e Storia*, Rome 1984.

____, *Magnifica il Signore anima mia*, San Paolo, Cinisello Balsamo 2000.

____, *Il logos e il nulla. Trinità, religioni, mistica*, Rome 2004.

Coda, P., Tapken. A. (eds.), *La Trinità e il pensare. Figure, percorsi, prospettive*, Rome 1997.

Coda, P., Zák, L. (eds.), *Abitando la Trinità. Per un rinnovamento dell'ontologia*, Rome 1998.

Coda, P., Hennecke Ch. (eds.), *La fede. Evento e promessa*, Rome 2000.

Fondi E., *Le beatitudini*, Rome 1965.

Foresi P., *Teologia della socialità*, Rome 1963.

____, *Appunti di filosofia. Sulla conoscibilità di Dio*, Rome 1967.

____, *Parole di Vita*, Rome 1964, 1969[2].

____, *Conversazioni con i focolarini*, Rome 1967.

____, *Fede, speranza e carità nel Nuovo Testamento. Spunti di meditazione*, Rome 1968.

____, *Il testamento di Gesù*, Rome 1982.

____, *L'esistenza cristiana. Spunti di meditazione biblica*, Rome 1989.

____, *Conversazioni di filosofia*, Rome 2001.

____, *Note di filosofia*, Rome 2004.

Giordani, I., *La divina avventura*, Garzanti, Milan 1953; Città Nuova, Rome 1960, 1993[28].

____, *La carità. Principio sociale*, Figlie della Chiesa, Rome 1955.

____, *Le due città*, Rome 1961.

____, *Cristianizzare la politica*, Rome 1962.

____, *Laicato e sacerdozio*, Rome 1964.

____, *Maria modello perfetto. Via di vita interiore*, Rome 1967, 1989[6].

____, *La rivoluzione cristiana*, Rome 1969.

____, *Famiglia comunità d'amore*, Rome 1969.
____, *L'unico amore*, Rome 1974.
____, *Diario di fuoco*, Rome 1980, 19927.
____, *Diary of Fire*, New City, London 1981
____, *Memorie di un cristiano ingenuo*, Rome 1981, 19842.
____, *Il laico Chiesa. Pagine scelte*, T. Sorgi (ed.), Rome 1987, 1988[3].
Hegge, Ch., *Rezeption und Charisma. Der theologische und rechtliche Beitrag Kirchlicher Bewegungen zur Rezeption des Zeiten Vatikanischen Konzils*, Echtir Verlag, Würzburg 1999.
Hemmerle, K., *Vie per l'unità. Tracce di un cammino teologico e spirituale*, Rome 1985.
____, *Ausgewählte Schriften*, vols. 1-5, R. Feiter (ed.), Herder, Freiburg i. Br., 1995/96.
____, *Scelto per gli uomini. Profilo del sacerdote*, Rome 1995.
____, *Tesi di ontologia trinitaria. Per un rinnovamento del pensiero cristiano*, Rome 1996.
____, *Partire dall'unità. La Trinità come stile di vita e forma di pensiero*, Rome 1998.
Leahy, B., *The Marian Profile: In the Ecclesiology of Hans Urs von Balthasar*, New City Press, New York 2000.
Lubich, G., *Intervista al Movimento dei Focolari*, Rome 1975.
Marchetti, G., *Vangelo da vivere*, Rome 1973.
____, *Uniti nel suo nome*, Rome 1977.
____, *... Perché Dio è Amore*, Rome 1977.
Mitchell, D.W., *Spirituality and Emptiness: The Dynamics of Spiritual Life in Buddhism and Christianity*, Paulist Press, New York 1991.
Pochet, M., *Bel Amour. Esperienza interiore di un artista*, Rome 1978.
Pozzi, N., *Tra cielo e terra. La famiglia alla luce della spiritualità dell'unità*, Rome 1998, 1999[2].
Rossé, G., *Il Grido di Gesù in croce. Una panoramica esegetica e teologica*, Rome 1984; 1996[2].
____, *Ecclesiologia di Matteo. Interpretazione di Mt 18, 20*, Rome 1987.
____, *La spiritualità di comunione negli scritti giovannei*, Rome 1996.
Siniscalco, F., Zanzucchi, M., *Comunicazione e unità*, Rome 2003.
Sorgi, T., *Costruire il sociale. La persona e i suoi piccoli mondi*, Rome 1991, 1998[3].
____, *Giordani, segno di tempi nuovi*, Rome 1994.
Vandeleene, M. (ed.), *Egli è vivo! La presenza del Risorto nella comunità cristiana*, Rome 2006.
Various authors, *Dio e il suo avvento*, Rome 2003.
____, *Dio Amore nella tradizione cristiana e nella domanda dell'uomo contemporaneo*, Rome 1992.
____, *La Trinità. Vita di Dio. Progetto dell'uomo. Per una risposta alla sfida dell'oggi*, Rome 1989.

Yzaguirre, J. and C., *Thriving Marriages: An Inspirational and Practical Guide to Lasting Happiness*, New City Press, New York 2004.

Zanghí, G.M., *Dio che è amore. Trinità e vita in Cristo*, Rome 1991.

Zanzucchi, M. (ed.), *Tutta rivestita di Parola. Il mondo della comunicazione si specchia in Maria*, Rome 2004.

3. Articles about the spirituality of unity or inspired by it

Atti del convegno Social-One, in NU 27 (2005/6), 162.

Araujo, V., "Economia di Comunione e comportamenti sociali," in NU, 19 (1997/2), 110, 301-13.

____, "Il carisma dell'unità e la sociologia," in NU, 18 (1996/3-4), 105-6, 355-63.

____, "La cultura del dare," in NU, 21 (1999/5), 125, 489-510.

Atzori, M.C., "*Risurrezione di Roma*. Un approccio linguistico allo scritto di Chiara Lubich - I," in NU, 24 (2002/4), 142, 431-60.

____, "*Risurrezione di Roma*. La metafora del "Fuoco": alcuni spunti di analisi testuale - II," in NU, 24 (2002/5), 143, 591-612.

Back, J.P., "Un'esperienza ecumenica internazionale nell'ambito della Chiesa cattolica: Il Movimento dei Focolari" in *Orientamento Spirituale dell'Europa. Il Contributo del Cristianesimo Orientale ed Occidentale* (Atti del IV Simposio Intercristiano. Alessandropoli, 3 - 7 settembre 1995), Edizioni Kyomanos, Thessaloniki 1997, pp. 255-76.

____, "Mary in the Focolare Movement's Spirituality of Unity. Some emerging Ecumenical insights," in "New Humanity Review" 2004, n. 8, p. 15-32.

____, "Spunti per una riflessione su Gesù abbandonato in relazione alla riconciliazione fra i cristiani," in NU 23 (2001/1), 133, 31-49.

Baggio, A.M., "Le moment d'agir selon Chiara Lubich," in "Christus," 191, juillet 2001, 323-31.

____, *Trinità e politica. Riflessione su alcune categorie politiche alla luce della rivelazione trinitaria*, in NU, 19 (1997/6), 114, 727-97.

____, *Verità e politica*, in NU, 22 (2000/3-4), 129-130, 333-56.

Biela, A., "Una rivoluzione copernicana per le scienze sociali," in NU, 18 (1996/6), 108, 699-708.

Blaumeiser, H., "All'infinito verso la disunità: Considerazioni sull'inferno alla luce del pensiero di Chiara Lubich," in NU, 19 (1997/5), 113, 557-70.

____, "Un mediatore che è nulla," in *NU*, 20 (1998/3-4), 117-18, 385-407.

____, "Attraverso la trasparenza del nostro nulla: Riflessioni sulla mediazione ecclesiale alla luce di alcuni scritti di Chiara Lubich," in NU 20 (1998/6), 120, 667-87.

Cerini, M., "Alcuni aspetti mistici della spiritualità del Movimento dei Focolari o 'Opera di Maria,' " in *Mistica e misticismo oggi*, Rome 1979, 406-19.

____, "Aspetti della mariologia nella luce dell'insegnamento di Chiara Lubich," in NU, 21 (1999/1), 121, 19-28.

____, "La realtà di Maria in Chiara Lubich," in NU, 19 (1997/2), 110, 231-42.

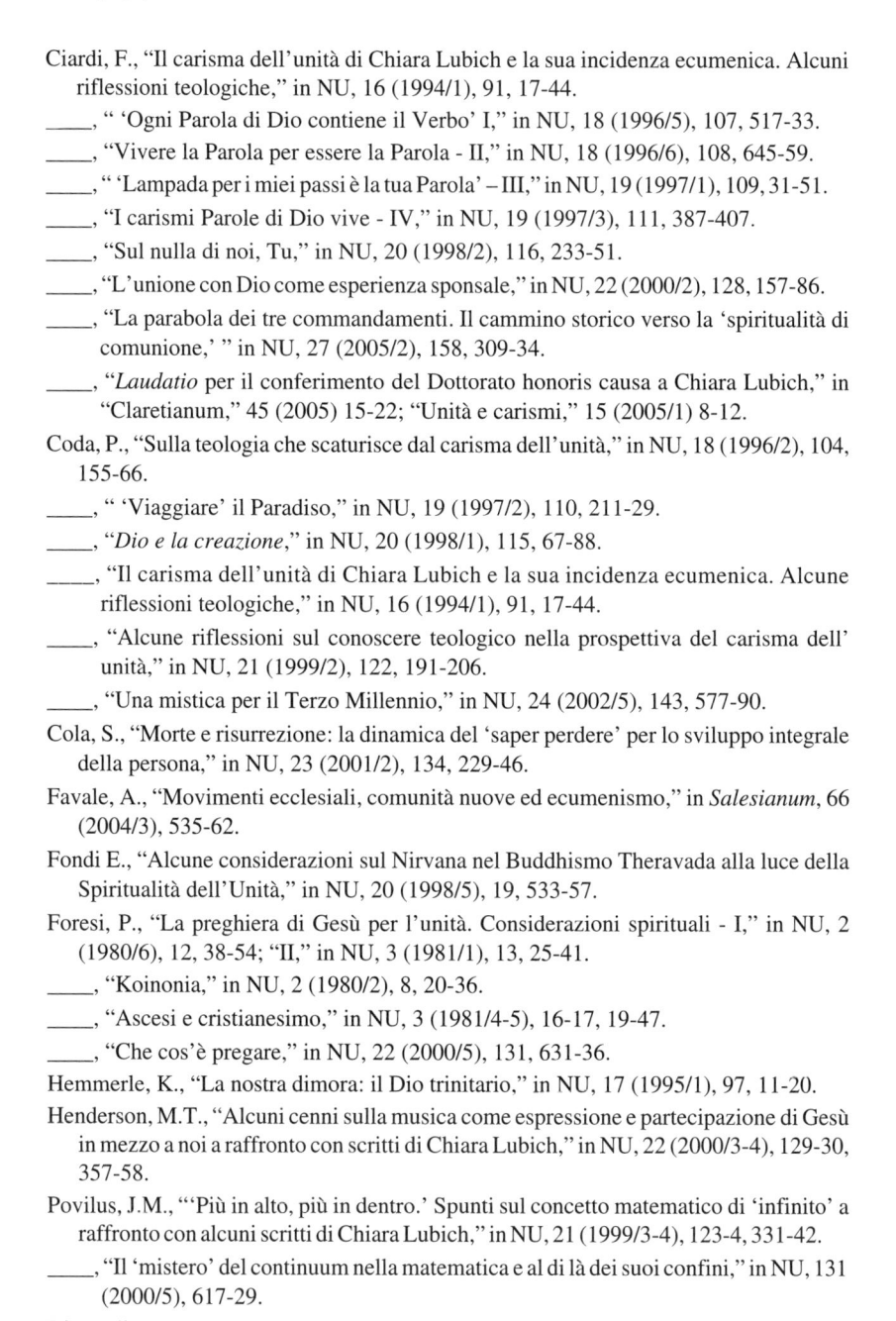

Ciardi, F., "Il carisma dell'unità di Chiara Lubich e la sua incidenza ecumenica. Alcuni riflessioni teologiche," in NU, 16 (1994/1), 91, 17-44.

____, " 'Ogni Parola di Dio contiene il Verbo' I," in NU, 18 (1996/5), 107, 517-33.

____, "Vivere la Parola per essere la Parola - II," in NU, 18 (1996/6), 108, 645-59.

____, " 'Lampada per i miei passi è la tua Parola' – III," in NU, 19 (1997/1), 109, 31-51.

____, "I carismi Parole di Dio vive - IV," in NU, 19 (1997/3), 111, 387-407.

____, "Sul nulla di noi, Tu," in NU, 20 (1998/2), 116, 233-51.

____, "L'unione con Dio come esperienza sponsale," in NU, 22 (2000/2), 128, 157-86.

____, "La parabola dei tre commandamenti. Il cammino storico verso la 'spiritualità di comunione,' " in NU, 27 (2005/2), 158, 309-34.

____, "*Laudatio* per il conferimento del Dottorato honoris causa a Chiara Lubich," in "Claretianum," 45 (2005) 15-22; "Unità e carismi," 15 (2005/1) 8-12.

Coda, P., "Sulla teologia che scaturisce dal carisma dell'unità," in NU, 18 (1996/2), 104, 155-66.

____, " 'Viaggiare' il Paradiso," in NU, 19 (1997/2), 110, 211-29.

____, "*Dio e la creazione*," in NU, 20 (1998/1), 115, 67-88.

____, "Il carisma dell'unità di Chiara Lubich e la sua incidenza ecumenica. Alcune riflessioni teologiche," in NU, 16 (1994/1), 91, 17-44.

____, "Alcune riflessioni sul conoscere teologico nella prospettiva del carisma dell' unità," in NU, 21 (1999/2), 122, 191-206.

____, "Una mistica per il Terzo Millennio," in NU, 24 (2002/5), 143, 577-90.

Cola, S., "Morte e risurrezione: la dinamica del 'saper perdere' per lo sviluppo integrale della persona," in NU, 23 (2001/2), 134, 229-46.

Favale, A., "Movimenti ecclesiali, comunità nuove ed ecumenismo," in *Salesianum*, 66 (2004/3), 535-62.

Fondi E., "Alcune considerazioni sul Nirvana nel Buddhismo Theravada alla luce della Spiritualità dell'Unità," in NU, 20 (1998/5), 19, 533-57.

Foresi, P., "La preghiera di Gesù per l'unità. Considerazioni spirituali - I," in NU, 2 (1980/6), 12, 38-54; "II," in NU, 3 (1981/1), 13, 25-41.

____, "Koinonia," in NU, 2 (1980/2), 8, 20-36.

____, "Ascesi e cristianesimo," in NU, 3 (1981/4-5), 16-17, 19-47.

____, "Che cos'è pregare," in NU, 22 (2000/5), 131, 631-36.

Hemmerle, K., "La nostra dimora: il Dio trinitario," in NU, 17 (1995/1), 97, 11-20.

Henderson, M.T., "Alcuni cenni sulla musica come espressione e partecipazione di Gesù in mezzo a noi a raffronto con scritti di Chiara Lubich," in NU, 22 (2000/3-4), 129-30, 357-58.

Povilus, J.M., "'Più in alto, più in dentro.' Spunti sul concetto matematico di 'infinito' a raffronto con alcuni scritti di Chiara Lubich," in NU, 21 (1999/3-4), 123-4, 331-42.

____, "Il 'mistero' del continuum nella matematica e al di là dei suoi confini," in NU, 131 (2000/5), 617-29.

Riccardi, A., "Presentazione editoriale: Jim Gallagher, *Chiara Lubich. Dialogo e profezia*, San Paolo, Cinisello Balsamo 1999," in NU, 22 (2000/1), 127, 120-6.

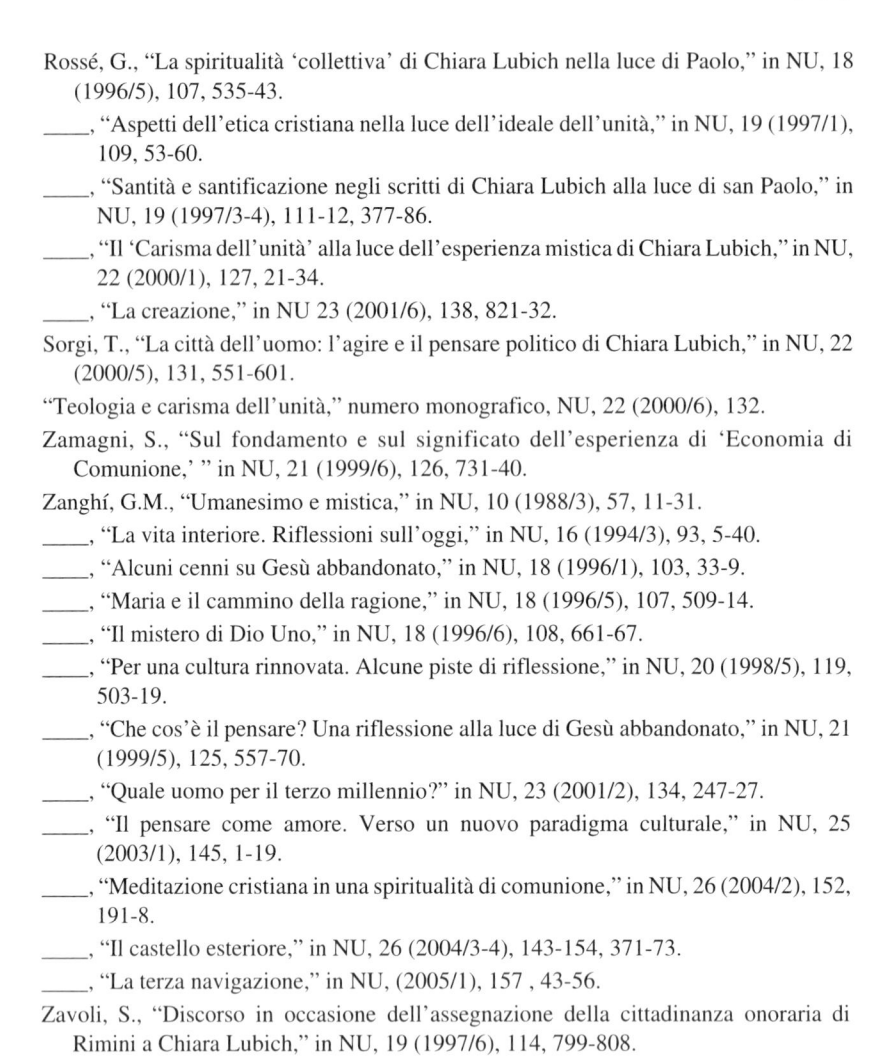

Rossé, G., "La spiritualità 'collettiva' di Chiara Lubich nella luce di Paolo," in NU, 18 (1996/5), 107, 535-43.

———, "Aspetti dell'etica cristiana nella luce dell'ideale dell'unità," in NU, 19 (1997/1), 109, 53-60.

———, "Santità e santificazione negli scritti di Chiara Lubich alla luce di san Paolo," in NU, 19 (1997/3-4), 111-12, 377-86.

———, "Il 'Carisma dell'unità' alla luce dell'esperienza mistica di Chiara Lubich," in NU, 22 (2000/1), 127, 21-34.

———, "La creazione," in NU 23 (2001/6), 138, 821-32.

Sorgi, T., "La città dell'uomo: l'agire e il pensare politico di Chiara Lubich," in NU, 22 (2000/5), 131, 551-601.

"Teologia e carisma dell'unità," numero monografico, NU, 22 (2000/6), 132.

Zamagni, S., "Sul fondamento e sul significato dell'esperienza di 'Economia di Comunione,' " in NU, 21 (1999/6), 126, 731-40.

Zanghí, G.M., "Umanesimo e mistica," in NU, 10 (1988/3), 57, 11-31.

———, "La vita interiore. Riflessioni sull'oggi," in NU, 16 (1994/3), 93, 5-40.

———, "Alcuni cenni su Gesù abbandonato," in NU, 18 (1996/1), 103, 33-9.

———, "Maria e il cammino della ragione," in NU, 18 (1996/5), 107, 509-14.

———, "Il mistero di Dio Uno," in NU, 18 (1996/6), 108, 661-67.

———, "Per una cultura rinnovata. Alcune piste di riflessione," in NU, 20 (1998/5), 119, 503-19.

———, "Che cos'è il pensare? Una riflessione alla luce di Gesù abbandonato," in NU, 21 (1999/5), 125, 557-70.

———, "Quale uomo per il terzo millennio?" in NU, 23 (2001/2), 134, 247-27.

———, "Il pensare come amore. Verso un nuovo paradigma culturale," in NU, 25 (2003/1), 145, 1-19.

———, "Meditazione cristiana in una spiritualità di comunione," in NU, 26 (2004/2), 152, 191-8.

———, "Il castello esteriore," in NU, 26 (2004/3-4), 143-154, 371-73.

———, "La terza navigazione," in NU, (2005/1), 157, 43-56.

Zavoli, S., "Discorso in occasione dell'assegnazione della cittadinanza onoraria di Rimini a Chiara Lubich," in NU, 19 (1997/6), 114, 799-808.

Significant Dates and Events

22 January 1920

> Chiara Lubich is born in Trent, Italy, and baptized "Silvia." Her mother is a practising Catholic; her father, a printer by trade, is a socialist. Her brother Gino will become an anti-Fascist resistance fighter, and later write for "L'Unità," the official newspaper of the Italian Communist Party.

1938

> Qualified as a primary school teacher, she begins her career at Castello and at Livio, small villages in the Val de Sole near Trent. Later, she will teach in Trent itself. She begins studies in philosophy at the University of Venice, but the Second World War will prevent her from completing them.

1939

> During a programme for young people of Catholic Action she visits the Marian shrine at Loreto, where she discovers her vocation. It would be the "focolare," a community of both virgins and married people who give their lives, even if in differing ways, completely to God.[1]

1943

> As a member of the Franciscan Third Order, attracted by the radical choice of God by Clare (in Italian, "Chiara") of Assisi, she takes the name "Chiara" as her own.

7 December 1943

> She gives herself to God with a perpetual vow of chastity. This date has come to be considered the birth of the Focolare Movement.

13 May 1944

> The aerial bombardment of Trent. Chiara Lubich's house is damaged and her family has to flee. She decides to remain in the city so as to

sustain the small group growing up around her. After a short time, they are offered an apartment in Piazza Cappucini, which, recalling her experience at Loreto, she calls the "little house of Nazareth." She and her first companions take up residence there, becoming in fact the first "focolare."[2]

1947

The Movement receives its first diocesan approval. Carlo de Ferrari, Archbishop of Trent, recognizes that "Here, there is the hand of God."

1948

The first men's focolare opens, in Trent.

In Rome, in the Italian Parliament building, she meets the Honourable Igino Giordani, a father of four, an elected representative, writer, journalist, and ecumenical pioneer. He later will become the first married focolarino. She sees him as a co-founder of the Movement because of his contribution to the spirituality of unity's incarnation in society and to its developments in the field of ecumenism.

1949-1959

Beginning in the summer of 1949, each year she and her first companions go to the mountains near Trent. More and more persons join them. They find themselves becoming the temporary presence of a new society based on the gospel: the *Mariapolis* (the city of Mary). In 1959, more than 10,000 people from 27 nations, and from as far away as Taiwan and Brazil, gather at Fiera di Primiero, near Trent.

1953

She founds the branch of the married focolarini, who are consecrated to God according to their state in life. Later, they become part of the women's and men's focolares. In time, they come to lead the *New Families* Movement.

1954

She founds the branch of the diocesan priests and of members of religious orders who take part in the Movement.

Pasquale Foresi, the first priest focolarino, is ordained by the Archbishop of Trent. Chiara Lubich also sees him as a co-founder because of his role in developing the Movement: for instance, in furthering theological studies, in drawing up the statutes, in setting up the first publishing house, and in establishing Loppiano, the first of the Movement's little towns.

1956

The mimeographed first edition of *Città Nuova* (New City), the Movement's magazine, is issued.

During the year when the Soviet Union invades Hungary, she promotes the *Volunteers of God*, lay men and women committed to bringing God, the source of freedom and unity, into every corner of society.

1959

The first collection of her spiritual writings, *Meditations*, is published, marking the start of the *Città Nuova* publishing house.

1960

As the result of a meeting in 1954 with refugees from what was then Czechoslovakia, she begins spreading the Focolare in the countries of Eastern Europe under communist rule.

1961

In Darmstadt, Germany, she meets some Lutheran pastors who wish to learn about her gospel-based spirituality: the start of the Movement's ecumenical activities.

1962

The Movement receives its first Papal approval. Pope John XXIII recognizes it with the name *The Work of Mary*.

1964

At Rocca di Papa, near Rome, Chiara Lubich inaugurates the first *Mariapolis Centre* for the formation of the Movement's members; at Incisa Valdarno, near Florence, she establishes Loppiano, the first of the Movement's little towns which give witness to the life of the gospel.

1966

In London, she is received by Dr. Michael Ramsey, Archbishop of Canterbury and Primate of the Anglican Communion. He encourages the spreading of the Focolare spirituality within the Church of England. Subsequently, she will meet his successors: Drs. Donald Coggan, Robert Runcie, George Carey, and Rowan Williams.

She establishes the *Gen*, the branch of the Movement for young adults.

In Fontem, Cameroon, she lays the cornerstone for a hospital dedicated to lowering the high rate of infant mortality among the Bangwa tribe. A little town is begun. It gives witness to the unity and the working together of the Focolare Movement and the Bangwa people. In 2000, she launches a widespread project to spread gospel-based values to neighbouring peoples as well.[3]

1967

In Istanbul, she meets with the Ecumenical Patriarch of the Orthodox Church, His All Holiness Athenagoras I. Between 1967 and 1972 she travels to Istanbul 8 times, and is received on 23 occasions by the Patriarch. Subsequently, she will meet with his successors, Dimitrios I and Bartholomew I.

She founds the *New Families* Movement.[4]

1968

She founds the *Gens*, a branch for seminarians.

1970

She founds a movement for children and younger teenagers — the *Gen 3,* the third generation of the Movement.

1971

At a historic meeting with Chiara, Pope Paul VI gives his blessing to the *Women Religious, Adherents to the Focolare Movement.*

1975

During the Holy Year, she presents to Pope Paul VI 20,000 young people from five continents, gathered for the *Genfest*, an international youth festival repeated every five years.[5]

1976

There begins a series of international meetings for *Bishops Friends of the Focolare Movement*, promoted by Klaus Hemmerle, Bishop of Aachen, Germany. These events allow the bishops to deepen the spirituality of unity and to have a lived experience of "effective and affective" collegiality. Chiara Lubich considers Bishop Hemmerle a co-founder of the Movement for his doctrinal contributions as well as for bringing to life the branch of the bishops, which has spiritual ties with the Movement. It will receive Papal approval in 1998.

1977

In London, before representatives of many faith traditions, she receives the Templeton Prize for Progress in Religion. Dialogue with world religions gets under way.

1981

In Tokyo, Rev. Nikkyo Niwano, founder of a lay Buddhist renewal movement, the Rissho Kosei-Kai, invites her to speak in its great temple before 10,000 people. A dialogue begins that continues to develop through efforts to provide humanitarian relief and to promote peace.

1982

At the request of Pope John Paul II, *Bishops Friends of the Focolare* from various Churches hold their first annual meeting.

1984

She founds the movement for younger children, the *Gen 4*.

Pope John Paul II visits the International Centre of the Movement in Rocca di Papa, near Rome.

1985

She is named consultant to the Pontifical Council for the Laity.

She participates in the extraordinary Synod held on the 20th anniversary of the Second Vatican Council. Subsequently, she will be invited to the 1987 Synod on the vocation and mission of the laity, as well as to the 1990 Synod for Europe.

1988

She receives the Augsburg Peace Prize, given by the city of Augsburg, Germany.

1990

The Pontifical Council for the Laity approves the updated *General Statutes of the Work of Mary,* also known as *The Focolare Movement.*

Working together with Bishop Klaus Hemmerle, she establishes at the Centre of the Movement the *Abba School*, to explore the doctrinal ramifications of the charism of unity.[6]

1991

In *Mariapolis Ginetta*, near São Paolo, Brazil, responding to the deep division between the rich and the poor, she establishes the *Economy of Communion*,[7] which soon spreads throughout the world.

1994

She is named one of the honorary presidents of the World Conference on Religion and Peace (WCRP).[8]

1996

In Naples, Italy, with a group of politicians, she forms the *Movement for Unity in Politics*. She proposes that they, although having differing political affiliations, base their lives and their political duties on fraternity.[9]

From the University of Lublin, Poland, she receives an honorary doctoral degree in Social Sciences for the innovative influence of the spirituality of unity. Subsequently, she will receive thirteen other honorary doctoral degrees: Theology (in the Philippines and in Taiwan, 1997; Slovakia, 2003),[10] Social Communications (Thailand, 1997),[11] Humane Letters (USA, 1997), Philosophy (Mexico, 1997),[12] a joint degree from all thirteen Academic Faculties (Argentina, 1998), Humanities and the Science of Religion (Brazil, 1998), Economics (Brazil, 1998; Italy 1999),[13] Psychology (Malta, 1999),[14] Education (USA, 2000),[15] Theology of Consecrated Life (Rome 2004).

In Paris, she receives the UNESCO Prize for Peace Education.[16]

1997

In Bangkok, Thailand, she meets with the Supreme Buddhist Patriarch of Thailand, His Holiness Somdet Phra Nyanasamvara, who encourages dialogue and cooperation between Buddhists and the Focolare Movement.

At Chiang Mai, Thailand, she presents her spiritual experience to a sizable number of monks, nuns, and lay Buddhists.

In Manila, she speaks of the Focolare Movement to the general assembly of the Philippine Bishops' Conference. Following this she will make presentations to the Bishops' Conferences of Taiwan, Switzerland, Argentina, Brazil, Croatia, Slovenia, Poland, India, the Czech Republic, Slovakia, Austria, India, and Ireland.

In New York, at the Glass Palace of the United Nations, she speaks on the unity of peoples to a symposium organized by the WCRP.

Invited by its founder, Imam W. D. Muhammad, she speaks before 3,000 African-American members of the American Muslim Society at the Malcolm X Mosque in Harlem, New York.

The first International Ecumenical Congress meets at Castel Gandolfo, Italy. Set up by the Focolare Movement, it gathers 1200 participants representing 70 Churches and 56 nations.

At Graz, Austria, she sets forth the spirituality of unity as "an ecumenical spirituality" at the opening of the Second European Ecumenical Assembly, sponsored by the Council of European Bishops' Conferences and by the Conference of European Churches, including the Orthodox, Anglican and Protestant Churches.[17] In 2002 she also presents this concept to the World Council of Churches in Geneva, Switzerland.

1998

At Castel Gandolfo, Italy, she addresses a conference on "Dialogue with People of Various Convictions." It attracts nearly 200 participants, many with no particular religious affiliation, who have been drawn for some time by the spirit of the Movement, particularly by the universal values it promotes. She proposes that they work together to bring about universal brotherhood.[18]

At Buenos Aires, Argentina, she meets with the Jewish community.

The President of Brazil confers on her the "Cruziero do Sul" (Southern Cross) for her efforts on behalf of the most disadvantaged and for promoting the Economy of Communion.

In Rome, at St. Peter's Square, before more than 350,000 participants, she is one of four founders who speak at the first international meeting of Ecclesial Movements and New Communities. Pope John Paul II entrusts to her the development of a path to communion among the Movements. Subsequently, among Churches at the local and national level, there will be large-scale meetings which by 2006 reached 282, involving more than 325 Movements and more than a half-million people.[19]

In Strasbourg, France, she receives the 1998 Human Rights Prize from the Council of Europe.

In Bern, Switzerland, she makes a presentation as part of the celebration of the 150th anniversary of the Swiss Constitution.

1999

In Strasbourg, France, she speaks to the Conference for the Fiftieth Anniversary of the Council of Europe. In her address, "*A Market-based Society, Democracy, and Solidarity,*" she presents the experience of the Economy of Communion as the basis of a new way of conducting business.

In Speyer, Germany, she brings a message of encouragement from Pope John Paul II to a meeting of the founders and leaders of 41 Ecclesial Movements and New Communities, organized by the Community of St. Egidio and the Renewal in the Holy Spirit.

In Augsburg, Germany, she joins in the ceremony of signing the historic Joint Declaration on the Doctrine of Justification, and meets with the highest authorities of the worldwide Lutheran Federation.

2000

She receives honorary citizenships from Rome and from Florence. In recent years, she had received seventeen such honours, including those from Palermo, Genoa, Turin, Milan, and Buenos Aires.

She receives the "Bundesverdienstkreuz" (Great Cross of Merit) from the Federal Republic of Germany.

In Rothenburg, Germany, she meets with representatives of fifty Evangelical Lutheran Movements.

In Washington, D.C., she speaks to a gathering of more than 5,000 people, including Christians and members of the American Muslim Society. A fraternal dialogue begins in many different cities across the United States, a development of particular significance considering the tensions in the United States following September 11, 2001.[20] There are forty mosques in open dialogue with the Movement.

In Rome, at the Italian parliament's Palazzo San Macuto, she presents to a large crowd of politicians the ideals of the *Movement for Unity in Politics*.[21] Following that event, she will meet with groups of representatives and mayors in Bratislava, Slovakia; Barcelona and Madrid, Spain; Dublin, Ireland; London, England; and Bern, Switzerland.

In Assisi, she advocates a journey towards communion among old and new charisms, beginning with the different branches of the Franciscan family. In Montserrat, Spain, she does the same with the Benedictine family.

2001

In Coimbatore, Tamil Nadu, India, she receives the Defender of Peace Prize from two Gandhian organizations, the Shanti Ashram and the Sarvodaya Movement. She also shares the story of her spiritual journey at the Somaya University, Mumbai. These events mark the beginning of deep dialogue with Hindus.

In Prague, the Czech Republic, she meets with President Vaclav Havel.

In Zurich, Switzerland, she speaks of the spirituality of unity at the Grossmünster, the ancient birthplace of the German-speaking Swiss Reformed Church. In 2002, she also speaks in Geneva at the Cathedral of St. Peter, birthplace of the Reformation as it developed under the influence of William Farel and John Calvin.

At Innsbruck, Austria, she participates at the Convention, "1000 Cities for Europe." It is also attended by the then-President of the European Commission, Romano Prodi, by the President of Austria, Thomas Klestil, and by more than 700 mayors and local administrators from 35 countries in both Eastern and Western Europe. She is invited to speak on fraternity as a political concept.[22]

2002

At the Day of Prayer for Peace in the World, held in Assisi, together with Andrea Riccardi, founder of the Community of St. Egidio, she speaks as a representative of the Roman Catholic Church. This event, arranged by Pope John Paul II, includes leaders of the twelve principal world religions.

In Castel Gandolfo, Italy, she supports the first symposium on interreligious dialogue among members of the Abba School and authoritative scholars and professors of Hinduism. There will follow another symposium with Hindus (2004) and symposiums with representatives of Buddhism (2004 and 2006), Judaism (2005), and Islam (2005).

2003

In Mumbai, she deepens the dialogue with Hinduism that began during her first visit to India in 2001. She speaks at the Somaya College, an Indian institute of higher learning dedicated principally to interreligious dialogue; at the Bharatiya Bidya Bhavan, a centre founded to rediscover the cultural roots of Hinduism; and with the Swadhyaya Family, a Movement of more than 8 million adherents spread throughout India.

Invited by Cardinal Dias, in Mumbai she also presents the spirituality of unity to priests, members of religious congregations, and lay movements. At the request of Archbishop Conceçao, she repeats the presentation in Delhi.

Responding to Pope John Paul II's request that the Focolare Movement take responsibility for promoting the year dedicated to the Rosary for the peace of the world, she promotes an International Marian Congress at Castel Gandolfo. Based on that event, 157 other Congresses, local as well as national, will follow on all five continents, at both local and national levels.

2004

The president of the Republic of Italy presents her with the insignia of a "Cavaliere di Gran Croce" (Knight of the Great Cross).

A daylong celebration, "Together for Europe," is held in Stuttgart, Germany, to mark the widening of the European Union to 25 nations. It emerged from the developing communion among more than 150 Movements and Communities from various Churches, including

Lutheran, Orthodox, Anglican, and Free Churches. Many political figures join the 9,000 participants, as well as another 100,000 who follow the event via live satellite transmission at 163 meetings taking place at the same time in other European cities.

2006

She is asked by the Pontifical Council for the Laity to speak on behalf of all the Ecclesial Movements and New Communities during their meeting with Pope Benedict XVI in St. Peter's Square on the vigil of Pentecost.

The Focolare Movement

Origin

Trent, 7 December 1943.

The spirituality of unity[1]

Gives life to the Movement as a whole. It is shared in various ways by those who belong to the Movement, those who participate in its activities, and those sympathetic to its goals. It is the soil from which its many activities and projects draw sustenance.

Purpose

To contribute to building universal brotherhood and to recompose the human family in unity as Jesus prayed: "May they all be one" (Jn 17:21). This comes about through five dialogues:

- within the Roman Catholic Church, or for other Christians within their own Churches
- with other Christian Churches and ecclesial communities
- with those who follow other religions
- with those who do not subscribe to any particular religious conviction
- in various areas of culture as a whole

Extent

- The Movement has spread to 182 nations, of which 89 have established centres in the following locations: Europe (29), Africa (25), South and North America (19), Asia (13), Australia and the Pacific Islands (3).
- It first spread beyond Italy into the rest of Europe in 1952, to the Americas in 1958, to Africa in 1963, to Asia in 1966, and to Australia in 1967.

Membership

- Within the various structures of the Movement: 140,300
- Those who do not feel called to be part of the various structures, but share closely in the Movement's life and work: 2,055,000

- approximately 47,000 from 350 Churches and ecclesial communities
- more than 30,000 from world religions, including Jews, Muslims, Buddhists, Hindus, and Sikhs
- approximately 10,000 of convictions with no specifically religious origin
- An unquantifiable number of several million people touched by the Movement's life and spirit.

Structure

The Movement is led by a president. Its Statute specifies that this position will always be held by a woman, assisted by a co-president and by a council formed by the men and women who oversee the general aspects of the Movement,[2] the various geographical areas, and its various branches.

Although the Movement remains a single entity, the variety of persons who make it up (celibate men and women, families, young people, priests, men and women religious from various congregations, and bishops) comprise eighteen distinct subgroups:

- Two principal sections, the men (focolarini) and women (focolarine), form the "backbone" of the Movement.
- Ten branches, which are identified in "Significant Dates and Events."[3]
- Six movements with widespread membership: *New Families, New Humanity, the Parish Movement, the Diocesan Movement, Youth for a United World,* and *Youth for Unity.*

The Movement is also divided geographically into "zones," currently 90.

Cultural and social developments

The *Abba School* began in 1990. It seeks to explore the doctrinal implications of the charism of unity. It includes Chiara Lubich and thirty or so scholars from various academic disciplines. Since 1998, an additional 350 university lecturers and other academics from various nations have been involved in its work.

The dialogue that the Focolare Movement has undertaken between the spirituality of unity and the culture as a whole has given rise to new developments in a variety of fields that touch on human knowledge and life, including:

- Economics: the "Economy of Communion," a project in business and economics, began in 1991. It has led to the creation of more than 750 businesses in the service and manufacturing sectors, spread across the globe, and has given rise to seven business parks located near the Focolare's

"little towns." It has also had an impact on economics as an academic discipline. It has been studied in more than 140 doctoral theses and at academic conferences sponsored by universities and by national and international professional groups.
- Politics: the "Movement for Unity in Politics" emerged in 1996. It assumes that politics itself can be understood through the concept of fraternity, that is, from the realization that every person is a member of the one human family. It has spread throughout various European nations, particularly in Italy; and in South America, especially in Brazil, Argentina, and Uruguay. It is made up of politically committed people from a wide range of backgrounds: ordinary citizens, government employees, elected officials at a variety of levels, party activists, or members of the diplomatic corps. They believe in universal human values such as ecological awareness, justice, freedom, and the sanctity of human life and place fraternity at the basis of the way they live and exercise their political responsibilities.

Publications

- The first publishing house, "Città Nuova" (New City), was founded in Italy. It brings out over 85 titles per year.
- In other countries, 25 publishing houses bring out more than 215 titles per year in 18 languages.
- Three publishing houses serve the English-speaking world: New City, London, for the United Kingdom, Ireland, the Commonwealth and European countries; New City Press, New York, for the United States of America and Canada; and New City, Manila, for the Philippines and other English-speaking readers in Asia.
- The magazine "New City," called "Living City" in the United States, is published in many countries of the English-speaking world. In all there are 36 editions of the magazine in 25 languages.
- "Nuova Umanità" (New Humanity), a cultural review in Italian but with international contributions, is issued six times a year.
- Based on "Gen's" and "Unità e Carismi" (Unity and Charisms) published by the Movement's centres for priests and members of religious congregations, in many parts of the world journals are issued in a variety of languages six times per year.
- There are magazines for young people: "Gen" for young adults, "Gen 3" for younger teenagers and older children, and "Gen 4" for younger children. These are published in several languages.
- "Economia di Communione: Una cultura nuova" (Economy of Communion: A New Culture) is issued four times per year.

- Two million copies of the "Word of Life," a monthly leaflet with exegesis and spiritual commentary on a passage from scripture to be applied in everyday life, are published in 96 languages and dialects. It is also broadcast each month via radio, television, and the internet.
- The official international website is www.focolare.org; there also are 24 other sites in different countries.

Programs of formation

- The 31 "little towns" of the Movement offer a living witness to the spirituality of unity. They are located in Austria, Belgium, the Czech Republic, France, Germany (2), Great Britain, Ireland, Italy, Holland, Poland, Portugal, Spain, Switzerland (2), the Philippines, Lebanon, Pakistan, Cameroon, the Ivory Coast, Kenya, Mexico, the United States, Argentina (2), Brazil (3), Venezuela, and Australia. Of these, twelve are at the beginning stages of development. The most developed, Loppiano, is located in Incisa Valdarno, near Florence, Italy. It has an international character, with 900 inhabitants who come from 70 nations.
- The 63 "Mariapolis Centres" in 46 different countries provide Focolare members with spiritual and social formation. The international headquarters for the Movement is located in Castel Gandolfo, near Rome, Italy.
- Yearly gatherings of the Focolare community, for people from all walks of life who wish to experience society transformed by the gospel, take place in approximately 70 countries. These last several days and are called "Mariapolis."
- A variety of countries host schools that offer specialized training in inculturation, ecumenism, interreligious dialogue and social issues.
- An institute of higher learning, "Sophia," promotes the culture of unity.
- The St. Clare Centre produces and distributes audiovisual materials designed to promote communication throughout the Movement worldwide.
- There are several centres for the development of the arts. The best known are the Ave Centre, and the performing arts groups Gen Verde and Gen Rosso.
- "Incontri Romani" (Roman Rendezvous) provides tour services for visitors to Rome.

Large-scale international meetings, held at Rome and transmitted throughout the world via satellite

- The "Genfest," a festival for young adults is held every five years. The sixth, in 2000, with 25,000 participants from across the globe, launched "Project Africa."
- The "Supercongress," a festival for younger teenagers, is also held every five years. The fourth, in 2002, drew 9,000 participants from 92 nations.
- The "Familyfest." In 2005, the third, it was held simultaneously in more than 120 cities spread throughout every part of the world.

Projects to promote international solidarity

- "Action for a United World," a non-governmental organization, formed in 1986 to promote international cooperation and development, is recognized by the Foreign Ministry of Italy. It is generally identified as "AMU," an acronym of its name in Italian ("Azione per un Mondo Unito").
- "New Humanity" is a non-governmental organization recognized by the United Nations Economic and Social Council (ECOSOC).
- More than 1,000 other social projects and activities operate in various parts of the world.
- "Adoption at a Distance" provides for the needs of more than 14,000 children and supports 96 projects in 45 nations.

Approval by the Roman Catholic and other Christian Churches

The Focolare Movement, known officially as "The Work of Mary," was first approved by the Roman Catholic Church in 1962. The revised general Statutes were approved by a decree of the Pontifical Council of the Laity on 29 June 1990, which recognizes the Movement as a "universal private association of the faithful of pontifical right."

In 1981 the Archbishop of Canterbury appointed a bishop as Ecclesiastical Guardian for Anglicans in the Focolare Movement. Other Churches have recognized the Movement in ways suitable to their own structures.

Notes

Where there is no reference to another English translation, all translations belong to the current volume. The abbreviations CN, NU, UC, stand for the journals "Città Nuova," "Nuova Umanità," "Unità e Carismi" respectively, and the abbreviation SS stands for *Scritti spirituali.*

Introduction

[1] Henri Bergson, *The Two Sources of Morality*, Notre Dame, Indiana 2002 (trans. Audra, Brereton and Carter), 32.
[2] *Dei Verbum,* 8.
[3] Chiara Lubich, *The Cry*, New York 2001, 60-61.
[4] See *Insegnamenti di Giovanni Paolo II,* V (1982) 3, Vatican City 1983, 1671-83.
[5] David Walsh, "The Turn toward Existence as Existence in the Turn" in Charles R. Embry & Barry Cooper, eds., *Philosophy, Literature and Politics: Essays Honoring Ellis Sandoz,* Columbia, Missouri 2005, 3-27.
[6] Footnote, 176.
[7] Ibid.
[8] *Letter to Diognetus,* quoted in J. Quasten, Patrology, vol. 1, Westminster, Maryland 1950, 250-51.
[9] Interview with Imam Warith Deen Mohammed, Castel Gandolfo, Italy, 12 June 1998 (http://www2.focolare.org/En/WDMohammad.html).
[10] See pages 209-14.
[11] Invitation to Chiara Lubich, 10 October 2002. (http://www2.wcc-coe.org/pressreleasesen.nsf/index/info-02-11.html).
[12] *Dottrina Spirituale,* Rome 2001, 27-28 (author's translation).
[13] Wallace Stevens, "Esthétique du mal," *The Collected Poems of Wallace Stevens*, London 1984, 320.

Part One: *Mysticism for the Third Millennium*

[1] *Insegnamenti di Giovanni Paolo II,* XVIII (1995) 2, Vatican City 1998, 744.
[2] Wilhelm Mühs, *Parole del cuore,* Milan 1996, 82.
[3] NU, 18 (1996/6) 108, 639-44.
[4] A new translation taken from *Unità e Gesù abbandonato,* Rome 1998. See also *Jesus: the Heart of his Message,* New City Press, New York 1985 and *The Secret of Unity,* London 1997 (two translations of the same original).
[5] *Unità e Gesù abbandonato,* Rome 1998, 26-32.
[6] *Unità e Gesù abbandonato,* Rome 1998, 50-69.
[7] CN, 39 (1995), 7, 33-37.
[8] *The Wisdom of the Desert,* ed. Thomas Merton, London 1961, 29.
[9] *The Imitation of Christ,* I, XX, 1-6.

[10] Jesus Castellano, O.C.D., Letter to Chiara Lubich about the collective spirituality (the spirituality of unity) in the Work of Mary, 21 June 1992.

[11] Karl Rahner, "The Spirituality of the Church of the Future," in *Theological Investigations: Concern for the Church, v. 20,* trans. Edward Quinn, New York 1981, 150-52.

[12] See Cardinal Montini, *Discorsi sulla Madonna e sui santi (1955-1962),* Milan 1965, 499-500.

[13] See also *If your eye is simple,* 80, and *Thoughts: The inner Master,* 146.

[14] Lorenzo Giustiniani, *Disciplina e perfezione della vita monastica,* Rome 1967, 4.

[15] *Insegnamenti di Giovanni Paolo II,* XVIII (1995) 1, Vatican City 1997, 382.

[16] NU, 18 (1996/2), 104, 133-35.

[17] Taken from Gérard Rossé, "Santità e santificazione negli scritti di Chiara Lubich," NU, 19 (1997/33-4), 111-12, 379-80 (revised).

[18] See Jn 15:3; Jn 14:21; Jn 15:5.

[19] See John Paul II, Letter to Chiara Lubich, 16 October 2002.

[20] Paul VI, "Discorso alla parrocchia di Santa Maria Consolatrice," Rome, 1 March 1964, in *Insegnamenti di Paolo VI* (1965/II), Vatican City, 1073.

[21] See *Lumen Gentium,* 65.

[22] *Mystici Corporis,* 27 June 1943, 110. See also, John XXIII: "Precisely on Golgotha our Redeemer … sealed, as a supreme covenant, that his Mother should be also the Mother of all the redeemed: 'Behold, your mother' " (General Audience, 9 September 1961, in *Osservatore Romano,* 10 September 1961).

[23] *Thérèse of Lisieux, Autobiography of a Saint,* trans. Ronald Knox, London 1957, 156.

[24] See John the Geometer, "Discourse on the Assumption," n. 66, in A. Wenger, *L'assomption di le T. S. Vierge dans la tradition byzantine du V° au X° siècle,* Paris 1955, 410-12.

[25] *Lumen Gentium,* 53.

[26] See Teresa of Avila, *The Interior Castle,* Seventh Mansion, IV, 12.

[27] *Leggenda di santa Chiara Vergine,* 46, in *Fonti francescane,* Padova 1980, 2432.

[28] NU, 25 (2000/3-5), 149, 519-30.

[29] *Gen's,* 30 (2000), 2, 42.

Part Two: *A New Look at Faith*

[1] See Marisa Cerini, *God Who Is Love: in the Experience and Thought of Chiara Lubich,* New York 1992.

[2] *Insegnamenti di Paolo VI* (1968/VI) Vatican City, 302.

[3] Ibid., 303.

[4] SS/2, 147-49.

[5] Ibid., 134-35.

[6] See also Jim Gallagher, *A Woman's Work,* New York 2003, 22-3.

[7] *Gen,* 27 (1993), 3, 2-3 (revised).

[8] SS/1, 64-65.

[9] Ibid., 54-55.

[10] SS/ 2, 126.

[11] SS/1, 223.

[12] Ibid., 224.

[13] SS/2, 49.
[14] SS/1, 137.
[15] Ibid., 130.
[16] Ibid., 221.
[17] From a talk on 16 August 1962 (revised).
[18] SS/1, 269.
[19] Ibid., 222.
[20] Ibid., 228.
[21] Ibid., 222.
[22] Ibid., 270.
[23] Ibid., 225.
[24] Detti Gen, Rome 1999, 36.
[25] See NU, 18 (1996/5), 107, 538-39.
[26] SS/1, 227.
[27] Thérèse of Lisieux, *Scritto autobiografico,* A, 37, in *Gli Scritti,* Rome 1970, 70.
[28] Giovanni XXIII, *Il giornale dell'anima,* Rome 1964, 117.
[29] Letter 359, *Le lettere di S. Caterina da Siena,* in *Opere,* Firenze 1940, 230.
[30] The Ascent of Mount Carmel, Book 1, XI, 3.
[31] *Spiritual Canticle,* XXXVIII, 3.
[32] *Treatise on the Love of God,* VIII, 7, trans. Henry Benedict Mackey, O.S.B., in "Library of St. Francis de Sales," vol. II, London and New York 1884.
[33] *Insegnamenti di Paolo VI* (1968/VI), Vatican City, 1154-55.
[34] See *Letter to Diognetus,* 6.
[35] SS/2, 141-45.
[36] SS/1, 100-02.
[37] SS/2, 194-95.
[38] CN, 22 (1978), 19, 40-1.
[39] SS/2, 200.
[40] Ibid., 26.
[41] SS/1, 63.
[42] Ibid., 137.
[43] Ibid., 129 (revised).
[44] Ibid., 265.
[45] Previously unpublished, ca. 1955.
[46] SS/1, 257 (revised).
[47] NU 19 (1997/2), 110, 227.
[48] SS/1, 37.
[49] See also *Charity*, London 1980 and *When Our Love Is Charity*, New York 1991 (two translations of the same original); *When Did We See You, Lord?* New York 1979 and *Jesus in Our Brother*, London 1982 (also two translations of the same original).
[50] SS/1, 74-5.
[51] SS/2, 180.
[52] SS/1, 92-3.
[53] Ibid., 164-65 (revised).
[54] See SS/1, 153.
[55] SS/1, 33.
[56] NU 18 (1996/5), 107, 515.
[57] SS/1, 48 (revised).
[58] Ibid., 110.

[59] *Insegnamenti di Paolo VI* (1970/VIII), Vatican City, 1311.
[60] SS/2, 127-28.
[61] SS/1, 274.
[62] Ibid., 51 (revised).
[63] Ibid., 66-7.
[64] SS/2, 184.
[65] SS/1, 276-77.
[66] Ibid., 130.
[67] Ibid., 229.
[68] Ibid., 133.
[69] *Detti Gen*, Rome 1995, 58.
[70] SS/1, 275.
[71] Ibid., 140.
[72] Ibid., 27.
[73] Ibid., 134.
[74] See also *The Secret of Unity*, London 1997; *Jesus: The Heart of His Message: Jesus Crucified and Forsaken*, New York 1997 (two translations of the same original) and *The Cry*, London and New York 2001.
[75] SS/1, 80-1.
[76] SS/2, 167.
[77] SS/1, 28-30.
[78] Ibid., 78-9.
[79] SS/2, 78.
[80] Ibid., 104
[81] SS/1, 43.
[82] A passage written in 1962. See *The Cry*, London and New York 2001, 83-4.
[83] SS/1, 41.
[84] Ibid., 169.
[85] 20 September 1949. See *The Cry*, London and New York 2001, 61-2.
[86] SS/1, 42.
[87] SS/4, 210.
[88] SS/1, 143.
[89] Ibid., 132.
[90] Ibid., 233.
[91] Ibid., 228.
[92] Ibid., 223.
[93] *Unità e Gesù abbandonato*, Rome 1998, 83.
[94] SS/1, 135.
[95] NU 19 (1997/5), 113, 570.
[96] SS/1, 44.
[97] See also above 16-19; and *Dove due o più*, Rome 1976, *Unità e Gesù abbandonato*, Rome 1998; J. M. Povilus, *"Gesù in Mezzo" nel pensiero di Chiara Lubich. Genesi, contenuti e attualità di una tema della sua spiritualità,* Rome 1981 (containing many previously unpublished texts) and *United in His Name*, New York 1992.
[98] SS/1, 251-52.
[99] Ibid., 49.
[100] SS/2, 53.
[101] SS/1, 103-5.

[102] Ibid., 108-9.
[103] Ibid., 251-52.
[104] Ibid., 90-1.
[105] Ibid., 70-1.
[106] Ibid., 116-19.
[107] *Unità e Gesù abbandonato*, Rome 1998, 33-4.
[108] SS/1, 136.
[109] Ibid., 273.
[110] Ibid., 276.
[111] Ibid., 136.
[112] 1950, previously unpublished.
[113] NU 21 (1999/5), 125, 500.
[114] NU 18 (1996/3-4), 105-6, 361.
[115] NU 19 (1997/6), 114, 121.
[116] See also *Uomini a servizio di tutti*, Rome 1976, *Servants of All*, New York 1978 and London 1979 (two translations of the same original); *Cristo dispiegato nei secoli*, Rome 1994, ed. Fabio Cardi.
[117] SS/1, 72-73.
[118] Ibid., 217-18.
[119] SS/2, 12-13.
[120] *Insegnamenti di Paolo VI* (1966/VI), Vatican City, 813-15.
[121] SS/2, 48.
[122] *La Rete* 1 (1957) 4, 8 (revised).
[123] SS/1, 61-62.
[124] Ibid., 76-7.
[125] SS/2, 205-6.
[126] See SS/1, 127.
[127] Ibid., 279.
[128] Ibid.
[129] Ibid., 280.
[130] Ibid., 53.
[131] *Insegnamenti di Paolo VI* (1967/V), Vatican City, 936.
[132] SS/2, 37.
[133] SS/2, 18-9.
[134] CN 22, 1978, 6, 41.
[135] CN 12, 1968, 18, 41.
[136] SS/1, 46.
[137] SS/2, 16.
[138] SS/1, 39-40.
[139] Ibid., 263.
[140] Ibid.
[141] Ibid., 143.
[142] NU 18 (1996/5), 107, 530.
[143] SS/1, 143.
[144] NU 20 (1998/6), 120, 679.
[145] NU 19 (1997/1), 109, 50.
[146] SS/1, 34.
[147] NU 19 (1997/1) 109, 51.

[148] From 1976, in an internal document of the Focolare Movement, *L'amore risana*, Rome 2000, 239-40.
[149] SS/2, 72-3.
[150] SS/1, 47.
[151] Ibid., 68-9.
[152] Ibid., 154-55.
[153] SS/1, 278.
[154] Ibid., 132.
[155] Ibid., 38.
[156] See L. M. Salierno, *Maria negli scritti di Chiara Lubich*, Rome 1993 (with a wide-ranging collection of Chiara Lubich's writings on Mary).
[157] SS/1, 114-15.
[158] SS/2, 164-65.
[159] CN 3 (1959), 13, 3 (revised).
[160] SS/1, 31-32 (as revised in 1978).
[161] Ibid., 171.
[162] Ibid., 242.
[163] SS/2, 39.
[164] *Diario 1964-1965*, Rome 1985, 46. See also *Diary 1964/65*, New York 1987, 39-40.
[165] SS/1, 58.
[166] NU 18 (1996/1), 103, 15-17.
[167] SS/1, 161-62.
[168] *Sequence* from the Mass of Pentecost.
[169] SS/2, 66.
[170] SS/1, 106-07 (revised).
[171] Ibid., 149.
[172] SS/2, 196.
[173] SS/1, 200.
[174] *Cercando le cose di lassù,* Rome 1992, 60.
[175] *Unità e Gesù abbandonato*, Rome 1998, 84-5.
[176] Diary entry 22 May 1972, cited in *Gen's* 29 (1999), 1, 7.
[177] SS/1, 254 (revised).
[178] Ibid., 250.
[179] *In cammino col Risorto*, Rome 1987, 138.
[180] NU 22 (2000/1), 127, 24.
[181] NU 19 (1997/1), 109, 56.
[182] SS/1, 250.
[183] See *La parabola del corpo*, Rome 2000.
[184] SS/2, 182-83.
[185] SS/1, 156-57.
[186] SS/1, 159-60.
[187] Ibid., 84-5.
[188] Ibid., 145-46.
[189] Ibid., 266-67.
[190] Ibid., 258-59.
[191] See *Perchè mi hai abbandonato? Il dolore nella spiritualità dell'unità,* ed. D. Fratta, Rome 1997.
[192] SS/1, 111-13.

[193] SS/2, 177.
[194] SS/1, 206-7.
[195] Ibid., 246-47.
[196] L. Boros, *Dio — uomo — mondo*, Brescia 1970, 83.
[197] *Della prima considerazione delle sacre sante istimate,* in *Fonti francescane*, Assisi 1977.
[198] SS/2, 216-20.
[199] Preface to the funeral Eucharist as used by various Churches.
[200] SS/2, 86.
[201] SS/1, 222.
[202] Ibid., 127.
[203] SS/2, 57-8.
[204] NU 19 (1997/5), 113, 562.

Part Three: *Reflections of Light upon the World*

[1] SS/1, 27.
[2] Ibid., 150-51.
[3] Ibid., 82-3.
[4] Ibid., 97-9.
[5] Written 29 October 1949, in NU 17 (1995/6), 102, 5-8.
[6] 2 December 1946.
[7] *Gen's* 28 (1998), 2, 35-42.
[8] See also *Una famiglia per rinnovare la società*, Rome 1993 and *Dove la vita si accende. Dialoghi sulla famiglia*, Rome 1998.
[9] SS/1, 254-55.
[10] See Synod of Bishops, *Messaggio alle famiglie cristiane nel mondo contemporaneo*, 13, Vatican City, 25 October 1980.
[11] CN 25 (1981), 19, 26-9.
[12] CN 37 (1993), 12, 30-1.
[13] See Igino Giordani, *Laicato e sacerdozio*, Rome 1964, 178.
[14] E. Mounier, *Le personnalisme,* in *Oeuvres,* Paris 1961, 455.
[15] See "Matrimonio e famiglia in un antropologia trinitaria" in NU 6 (1984/1), 31, 17.
[16] Letter to families, in *Insegnamenti di Giovanni Paolo II*, XVII (1994) 1, Vatican City 1996, 261.
[17] From a sermon in the military prison of Berlin, on the occasion of a wedding, 1943.
[18] See Tomaso Sorgi, *Costruire il sociale, la persona e i suoi piccolo mondi*, Rome 1991.
[19] See Various authors, *Familyfest, una proposta per il 2000*, Rome 1993, 11.
[20] Found in C. and L. Gentili, *Per stare bene in famiglia*, Rome 1998, 11.
[21] See G. Di Nicola and A. Danese, *Amici a vita*, Rome 1997, 39.
[22] *Chiesa locale e famiglia*, "Agenzia di informazione e documentazione di pastorale famigliare," 13 (1995), 49, 15.
[23] T. Bovet, *Situazione dei cristiani nel mondo*, Zurich 1944.
[24] *Chiesa locale e famiglia*, "Agenzia di informazione e documentazione di pastorale famigliare," 14 (1996), 52, 8.
[25] H. U. von Balthasar, *Solo l'amore è credibile*, Turin 1991, 143.
[26] I. Giordani, *Famiglia comunità d'amore*, Rome 1994, 15.

[27] I. Giordani, *Il laico chiesa*, Rome 1988, 107.
[28] NU 21 (1999/5), 125, 475-87.
[29] Teresa of Avila, *The Way of Perfection* (First Edition), IV, 1.
[30] See *Mulieris dignitatem*, 13.
[31] Ibid., 18.
[32] Ibid., 19.
[33] See Ibid., 4-5.
[34] Ibid., 4.
[35] Ibid., 5.
[36] *Redemptoris mater*, 45.
[37] Statement to the Cardinals and Prelates of the Roman Curia (22 December 1987), in *Insegnamenti di Giovanni Paolo II*, X (1987), 3, Vatican 1988, 1483.
[38] CN 39 (1995), 1, 27-31.
[39] See above 28-29.
[40] From *Per una filosofia che scaturisce dal Cristo,* NU 19 (1997/3-4), 111-12, 363-68.
[41] Speech given at the International Mariapolis Centre, Rocca di Papa, near Rome (19 August 1984) in *Insegnamenti di Giovanni Paolo II*, VII (1984) 2, Vatican City 1984, 222-26.
[42] See *Gaudium et Spes* 22, 24.
[43] "Mary's relationship with the Trinity," in *Insegnamenti di Giovanni Paolo II*, XIX (1996) 1, Vatican City 1998, 47.
[44] *Teologica*, Milan 1992, 22. See *Theo-Logic*, San Francisco 2000.
[45] See Saint Augustine, *Commentary on the Gospel of John*, Homily 21, 8-9.
[46] Thomas Aquinas, *De Veritate*, 29, 7-11.
[47] From *Discorso tenuto all'università di san Tomaso di Manila*, NU 19 (1997/1) 109, 22-29.
[48] See Jacques Maritain, *Existence and the Existent*, New York 1966, and E. Przywara, *Filosofia e teologia dell'Occidente*, Rome 1970.
[49] See *Being and Time*, Albany, Oxford 1962 and New York 1996. This reference cited from G. Reale, D. Antiseri, *Il pensiero occidentale dalle origini a oggi/3*, Brescia 1983, 449.
[50] From *Per una filosofia che scaturisce dal Cristo*, NU 19 (1997/3-4), 111-12, 368-75.
[51] CN 31 (1987) 9, 33-6.
[52] NU 23 (2001/5-6), 135-36, 341-52.
[53] CN 30 (1986), 11, 29-31.
[54] Abraham H. Maslow, *Motivation and Personality*, New York 1987, 271-72.
[55] NU 21 (1999/2), 122, 177-89.
[56] SS/1, 158.
[57] SS/1, 210-13.
[58] SS/1, 88-9.
[59] SS/1, 256.
[60] SS/1, 137.
[61] SS/1, 277.
[62] SS/1, 133.
[63] SS/1, 252.
[64] T. Sorgi, Letter to Chiara Lubich, 7 February 1962, unpublished document.

[65] NU 22 (2000/5), 131, 603-16.
[66] The Schuman declaration, 9 May 1950.
[67] *Osservatore Romano*, 2-3 April 1990, 6.
[68] NU 24 (2002/1) 139, 15-28.
[69] SS/1, 240.
[70] *Rerum Omnium*, 3.
[71] SS/2 155-60.
[72] SS/2, 210-11.
[73] NU 21 (1999/1), 121, 7-18.
[74] To the Polish Bishops during their *ad limina* visit (12 January 1993), in *Insegnamenti di Giovanni Paolo II*, XVI (1993).
[75] From texts on the Economy of Communion, see www.edc-online.org.
[76] *Laborem Exercens* 25-27.
[77] *Gaudium et Spes* 39.
[78] "Questo foglio," in *La Rete*, 1 (1957), 1
[79] From a message to a group of Polish bishops, 14 February 1998. *Insegnamenti di Giovanni Paolo II*, XXI (1998) 1, Vatican City 2000, 269-81.
[80] Message of the Holy Father for the XXXII World Communications Day, 14, 1998, 5.
[81] See NU 23 (2001/2), 133, 11-22.
[82] See above 294-95.
[83] See above 296.
[84] See NU 25 (2003/6), 150, 673-80.
[85] SS/1, 203-5.
[86] SS/1, 195-97.
[87] Ibid., 282.
[88] *Gravity and Grace*, Lincoln, 1952, 137.
[89] See above 304-05.
[90] See below 320ff.
[91] See *Fiume in Vaticano*, Alba 1998, 10.
[92] Paul VI, *Message to Artists* (8 December 1965), in *Insegnamenti di Paolo VI* (1965/III), Vatican City, 755.
[93] General Audience, 12 August 1998.
[94] *Gaudium et Spes*, 62.
[95] *I fondamenti spirituali della vita*, Turin 1950, 11.
[96] *To Artists* (20 May 1985), in *Insegnamenti di Giovanni Paolo II*, VIII (1985) 1, Vatican City 1985, 1567-68.
[97] Acceptance for the Nobel Prize in literature, 10 December 1957.
[98] See above 204.
[99] See above 175-76.
[100] *Paradiso*, canto XXXII, 85-6.
[101] *Rime*, 18.
[102] *Rime e Trionfi*, 366.
[103] *Rime sacre*, 218.
[104] NU 21 (1999/3-4), 123-24, 317-330.
[105] *The Idiot*, Part III, ch. 5.
[106] *Novo Millennio Ineunte*, 43
[107] Ibid., 45. Italics added by the author.
[108] Ibid., 42.

[109] Ibid.

[110] See *Lumen Gentium*.

[111] John Paul II, *Meeting with Ecclesial Movements and New Communities*, 30 May 1998.

[112] *Message of Pope John Paul II for The World Congress of Ecclesial Movements and New Communities*, 27 March 1998, 5.

[113] Rocco Buttiglioni, Italian minister for Europe Affairs.

[114] Adam Schultz, S.J., Chair of the Council of Polish Movements.

[115] Cardinal K. Lehmann, President of the German Episcopal Conference and Archbishop of Mainz.

[116] Prof. Tadeusz Mzowiecki, Former Prime Minister of Poland, the first after the fall of Communism.

[117] Zofia Dietl, Director of the Organizing Committee.

[118] President of the Pontifical Council for the Laity, the office of the Roman Catholic Church that oversees the new ecclesial Movements and the various lay associations.

[119] President of the Pontifical Council for Promoting Christian Unity.

[120] See the World Council of Churches, Faith and Order paper 153, *Confessing the one faith*, Genevre 1991.

[121] Pontifical Council for Promoting Christian Unity, *Directory for the Application of Principles and Norms on Ecumenism*, 92.

[122] John Paul II, *Ut Unum Sint*, 77.

[123] "L'avenir de l'ecuménisme" in *Proche Orient Chrétien*, 25 (1975), 1, 14-5.

[124] The Catholic-Orthodox Dialogue, "Il mistero della Chiesa e dell'Eucaristia alla luce del mistero della Santa Trinità," in *Enchiridion Oecumenicum*, vol. 1, 2190.

[125] See Consultation on "Christian Spirituality for Our Times," World Council of Church, Iasi, Romania, May 1994.

[126] R. Bertalot, "La riconciliazione nei dialoghi fra le Chiese," in *Studi Ecumenici*, 14 (1996), 3, 359.

[127] *Crossing the Threshold of Hope*, New York 1994, 167.

[128] Ibid.

[129] *Ad Gentes*, 11.

[130] *Nostra Aetate*, 2

[131] See above 121-22.

[132] Frank Whaling, *Christian Theology and World Religions: A Global Approach*, London 1986, 130.

[133] NU 19 (1997/5) 113, 543-56.

[134] See above 121-22.

[135] Pinchas Lapide, quoted by Hans Waldenfels, *Gesù crocifisso e le grandi religioni*, Naples 1987, 35.

[136] Ibid.

[137] Commission of the Holy See for Religious Relations with the Jews, *We Remember: A Reflection on the Shoah*, 16 March 1998.

[138] Abraham Heschel, *Man is not Alone*, New York 1951, 123.

[139] NU, 20 (1998/3-4), 117-18, 374-84.

[140] See in particular *The City of God*, but also the sermons in which St. Augustine speaks of the fall of Rome (nos. 81, 105, 296, 397).

[141] Wilhelm Mühs, *Parole del cuore*, Milan 1996, 82.

[142] Frank Whaling, *Christian Theology and World Religions: A Global Approach*, London 1986, 130.

[143] *Address of his Holiness Pope John Paul II to the Representatives of the World Religions*, Assisi (24 January 2002), in *Insegnamenti di Giovanni Paolo II,* XXV (2002) 1, Vatican City 2004, 104.
[144] *Address of John Paul II on the Occasion of the Meeting with the Exponents of Non-Christian Religions*, Madras, 5 February 1986, 4.
[145] Personal letter from Archbishop Michael Fitzgerald, 28 February 2003.
[146] In the years immediately following this talk other symposia were held. In 2004 at Castel Gandolfo, Rome, there was the first Buddhist-Christian symposium and in the year after that the Muslim-Christian and Jewish-Christian symposia took place. The second Buddhist-Christian symposium was at Osaka and Mount Hiei, Japan, in 2006.
[147] See above 339-41.
[148] See *Novo Millennio Ineunte*, 56.
[149] *Assisi: Giornata Mondiale di Preghiera per la Pace*, October 1986, in *Insegnamenti di Giovanni Paolo II,* IX (1986) 2, Vatican City 1986, 1252-53.
[150] NU 26 (2004/2) 152, 161-74.
[151] CN 36 (1992) 13, 34.
[152] CN, 35, 1991, 15-16, 34.
[153] "Thanksgiving to Our Lady of Jasna Gora for the Gift of Many Historical Changes," *Osservatore Romano,* 22 February 1990.
[154] Tertullian, *Apologetics*, 39, 7.
[155] CN 34 (1990), 7, 34-9.
[156] Quoted in Wilhelm Mühs, *Dio nostro Padre. 365 pensieri sulla paternità di Dio*, Rome 1998, 64.
[157] *Il grido*, Rome 2000, 129-30.
[158] Interview with F. Morandi, *I carismi*, SAT 2000, 1997.
[159] Interview P. Damosso, "TV7," 15 April 2001.

Significant Dates

[1] See pages 49-52.
[2] Ibid.
[3] See pages 245-47.
[4] See pages 180-94.
[5] See pages 360-66.
[6] See page 204.
[7] See pages 274-78.
[8] See pages 344-47.
[9] See pages 236-47.
[10] See pages 204-9.
[11] See pages 290-303.
[12] See pages 209-14.
[13] See pages 274-78.
[14] See pages 225-29.
[15] See pages 219-24.
[16] See pages 12-15.
[17] See pages 325-33.
[18] See pages 354-59.
[19] See pages 320-25.
[20] See pages 344-48.

[21] See pages 236-43.
[22] See pages 247-64.

The Focolare Movement

[1] See "A New Way of Christian Living," pages 12-15.
[2] See pages 177-78.
[3] See pages 383-93.

Index

(prepared by Kathleen Strattan)

abandonment:
- Christ as abandoned, 55, 190–191, 253, 329
- fears of, 55

Abba School, 204, 210, 243, 311, 315
abortion, 189
Absolute Being, 210
addiction, 190, 192
Adenauer, Konrad, 238, 251
adolescents, 224–225
    See also children; youth
adoption:
- Christians as adopted, 69
- the Persons of the Trinity and, 141

Africa, 337
African-American Muslims, 345
agape, 204, 339
Algeria, 266
the All-Beautiful, 141–142, 316–317
- *See also under* Mary: beauty of

American Muslim Society, 341
Americas
- *See also* North America; South America spread of Focolare Movement in, 9

Anglicans and Anglican Church, 8–9, 260, 330
the Annunciation, 44
Anselm of Canterbury, 208
apostles, 32, 59–60, 138, 148, 323
- See also *individual names*
- Mary and, 46, 148
- successors of, 148

Aquinas, St. Thomas.
    See Thomas Aquinas, St.
Archbishop of Canterbury.
    See individual names
Arsenius, Abba, 27
art:
- artistic vocation, 317–319
- charism of unity and, 304–319
- collective spirituality and, 11
- *Letter to Artists,* 307

art of loving, 14, 77
ascent, ways of, 36–37
asceticism of love, 57
Asia, 9, 311, 332, 337, 361–362
    See also *specific locations*
Assisi, 342, 367
- *See also* Francis of Assisi, St.
atheism, 179, 206, 305, 363
Athenagoras I, Patriarch of Constantinople, 9
attire. *See* dress
Augustine of Hippo, St., 28, 58, 207–208, 337
Australia, 311
Austria, 247, 325–333
authenticity, 252, 283
- *See also* truth
- human demand for, 162, 193
awards:
Author of the Year Prize, 27
- Prize for Peace Education, 12
- Turrita d'Argento Award, 3

Baden-Powell, 188

413

balance, 125
Bangkok, Thailand, 290
Bangwa Tribe, 245–246, 344
baptism, 9, 44, 271, 326, 331
Baptists and Baptist Church, 9
Barber, Benjamin R., 264–268
Bartholomew I, Patriarch of Constantinople, 9
Bea, Cardinal, 8, 328
the beatitudes, 107, 125–126, 218
beauty, 157–158, 232, 304–319
 – See also art; specific topics, e.g., family; Mary
 – and being loved, 55
 – of creation, 213
 – of the faith, 172
 – God as, 307
 – of the gospel, 202, 274
 – living a beautiful life, 73, 76–77, 100
 – of a mother's love, 124
 – in our eyes vs. in God's eyes, 157–158
 – physical, human, 80, 107, 122
 – seeing, 157–158
 – suffering and, 152
 – of this world, 57, 64
 – true, 318
 – truth and, 152, 313
 – various beauties, 158
being and non-being, 127, 205, 211–213, 315
Benedictines, 323
Benedict of Nursia, St., 249–250
Berlin Wall, 362
Bernard of Clairveaux, 208
biogenetic experiments, 189
birth of Jesus, 44–45
bishop friends of Focolare, 32, 308
bishops, 112, 144, 198, 320, 322
 – European Union, conference of, 324
 – and Focolare Movement, 351, 369
 – Polish Bishops' Conference, 324
 – Synod of Bishops, Rome, 198

Blaue Reiter, der (the Blue Rider), 313
Blessed Virgin Mary.
  See Mary, Blessed Virgin
Boccaccio, 316–317
Body of Christ, Mystical.
  See Mystical Body of Christ
Bologna, discourse at, 3–11
Bonaventure, St., 208
Bonhoeffer, Dietrich, 187
boredom, 66, 69, 80, 98, 145, 151–152, 170
Brazil, 232, 274–275, 278
Bride of Christ, 112–119
Bridget of Sweden, St., 250
brotherhood, universal, 235–236
 – See also fraternity
Brussels, 252–253
Buber, Martin, 336
Buddhists and Buddhism, 9, 332–333, 340–341, 344–346, 350, 353, 366
Buenos Aires, Argentina, 333, 346, 362

camel: "It is easier for a camel to go through the eye of a needle….", 126–127
Cameroon, 245–247, 344
Campidoglio, 237
Cana, wedding feast of, 50, 302
Canterbury, Archbishop of.
  See individual names
Canticle of Canticles (Song of Songs), 24
Carey, Dr. George, Archbishop of Canterbury, 9
Carmelites, 113
Caruso, Igor, 226
Castel Gandolfo, Italy, 236, 278, 286, 290, 298, 307–308, 317, 348, 354, 358
 – Marian Congress, 38
Castellano, Father Jesus, 28
St. Catherine Centre, 240–241, 243
Catherine of Siena, St., 67, 197, 250, 270
Catherine of the Blood of Christ, St., 114

Index 415

Catholic Action, 323
Catholic Charismatic Conference, Fiuggi, Italy, 320–325
Catholic Church, 83, 170, 260, 270, 366
– *See also* Church; Mystical Body of Christ
– Chiara Lubich and, 201
– dialogue within, 320–325
– and Focolare Movement, 3, 26, 320–323, 350 (*see also* Work of Mary)
– in politics, 235
Catholic Movements, 321–322
– *See also* ecclesial Movements
Catholic University of America, 219
celibacy. *See* virginity
Centesimus Annus, 277
Central America, 311, 361–362, 364
Chamber of Deputies, Italy, 236, 238
charismatic Movements, 252, 320–325
charism of Focolare, 26, 31–32, 38, 177, 202, 298, 322, 338, 348, 350, 360
charisms, 32, 44–46, 50, 112, 198–200, 320, 323–324
– *See also* unity, charism of
charity:
– and being made "beneficiaries," 274
– inappropriate, burdensome to recipient, 84
– *See also* love
chastity, 216
– *See also* virginity
– of God, maintaining, 81
– Joseph and, 182
– quality of, 216
children, 366–368
– *See also* family; youth; *specific topics*, e.g., education
– discipline of, 216–217
– of God, 86
– Jesus as teacher, 215–219
– "my little children," 59–60
– need for love, 224–225

– procreation of, 187
– "the little way," 113
China, 362
Christ. *See* Jesus Christ
Christian community, 229
– and communion, 229
– the first, 288
Christianity
– See also *specific topics*, e.g., spiritualities
– central point of, 358
– the Christian adventure, 104
– cross of the Christian, 78
– Providence and, 273
"Christianize," the term, 283
Christians and Christian life, 12–15
– *See also* under *specific topics*, e.g., love
– "actualized," 270
– baptism and, 271
– "developing," 271
– dialogues with other, 325–333
– early, 27, 247
– perfect, 56
– "real Christians," 270
– responsibility of, 172–173
– underdeveloped, 269–273, 270
Church
– *See also* Catholic Church; Mystical Body of Christ; *specific topics*
– authorities, and Focolare Movement, 7
– beauty of, 114, 130
– Bride of Christ, 112–119
– as communion, 110–119, 288
– description of, 129
– and the Eucharist, 129
– living in, 203
– Mary and, 43
– as Mother, 111
– as offering help, 14
– "outpouring" of Holy Spirit on, 321

- passion for, 112–113
- social doctrine of, 277
- through the centuries, 114

Cicero, 187
Città Nuova, 291
the city, 262
city of God: secret that builds, 104–105
Clare of Assisi, St., 44, 47, 197, 291
cloister, 102–103
clothing. *See* dress
Coggan, Dr. Donald, Archbishop of Canterbury, 9
cohabitation before marriage, 189
collective prayer, 31
collective sanctity, 117
collective spirituality, 3, 11, 28, 30, 33, 314
- *See also* spirituality of communion/ unity

Comenius, 220
commandments, 218
- *See also* Golden Rule
- of Jesus, 6, 19, 27–28, 55, 81, 141, 199, 202
- of Old Testament, 205

common good, 240, 247, 262–263, 276, 283, 291, 342
communication
- *See also* media
- guiding principles of (Focolare Movement), 295–297
- Mary and, 298
- root of, 294–295
- worldwide, 293

communion, 210–211, 226, 228
- *See also* unity; *specific topics,* e.g., politics
- the Christian community and, 229
- the Church and, 199, 203
- the Church as, 110–119
- the family and, 183–185, 188, 193, 224

- with God, 180
- love and, 100–101, 177
- in marriage, 186, 193
- need for, 199
- refusal to enter into, 228
- spirituality of, 27–35, 177, 331–332

Communion, Economy of.
   See Economy of Communion
communion of goods, 368
Communion of Saints, 99
Communists and Communism, 237, 351
communitarian dimension of Focolare Movement, 3–4, 13, 27, 203
communities, ecclesial Movements and.
   See ecclesial Movements
community, Christian.
   See Christian community
companionship, human thirst for, 152–153
companions of Chiara Lubich, 17, 20n, 318, 369
competition: media and, 293
conjugal communion, 186, 193
consecration, 72
- of Chiara Lubich, 20
- consecrated virgins, 144
- Focolare Movement and, 49, 244
- of Mary, 42
- the Spouse of God, 119

contemplation, 113
Council of Europe, 242
Councils of the Church, 203
- *See also* Vatican Council, the Second

courage, 64, 122, 160–161, 170, 175, 209, 218, 252, 325
- peace and, 14

creation, 212
- beauty of, 213

the *Creed,* 55
the cross, 14, 22, 57–58, 86, 89–91
- *See also* Jesus forsaken

Index 417

- suffering of the Christian, 78
- love for, 202
- taking up one's own, 241

Crossing the Threshold of Hope (John Paul II), 328–329

crucifixion of Jesus.
    See cross; Jesus forsaken
culture of giving, 184, 247, 267, 275, 277–282, 285
culture of love, 280
Cyril, 250
Czechoslovakia, 220n

Dante, 316
dark night of the senses, 46
Day of Interdependence, 264–265
Day of Peace, 195
death and dying, 58, 63, 65, 67, 75, 78, 81, 103, 108, 154, 157–165, 315
- *See also* Jesus forsaken
- as approach to heaven, 158–159, 162–163
- as beginning of Life, 161
- as day of our birth into heaven, 163
- the Eucharist and, 213–214
- of Jesus, 60, 89, 136, 161, 165, 190–191, 329, 336
- Jesus and, 173
- living death, 94
- living in the present at time of, 351
- love as passing from death to life, 83
- of loved ones, 75, 152, 158–159, 164
- and a mother's love, 136
- in order to multiply, 8, 26, 134, 157–158
- the prospect of, 171–172
- sadness about, 163, 170
- saints and, 86, 115
- sanctity and, 88
- to self, 36, 175, 340, 347
- a silence, 175
- the soul and, 153
- thinking of, 158–159

- those who build unity and, 147
Declaration of Human Rights, 189
Declaration of Interdependence, 264
De Ferrari, Archbishop Carlo (Bishop of Trent), 17n
De Gasperi, Alcide, 238, 250
Demetrios I, Patriarch of Constantinople, 9
the Desolate (Mary desolate), 35, 42, 46, 139, 299–302
Dewey, John, 223
dialogue, interreligious, 15, 200, 204, 252–253, 259–265, 267, 320–359
- within the Catholic Church, 320–325
- with Eastern religious traditions, 260
- Focolare Movement's experience with, 344–347
- Golden Rule and, 253
- Holy Spirit and, 355
- Jewish-Christian, 333–336
- love and, 355
- with Muslims, 348–354
- with other Christians, 325–333
- with people of convictions not based in religion, 354–357
- with the world religions, 337–344

Dialogues (Plato), 308–309
diplomacy, divine, 233–234
discipleship, 32
discipline, of children, 216–217
"divine adventure," 67, 69, 165
divorce, 189
doctors of the Church, 270
Dolomite Mountains, Italy, 231, 244
Dominicans (order of), 113, 203
Dostoyevsky, 318
dress, 30, 84, 157, 310

East, religious traditions of, 206
Easter mystery, 173
Eastern Europe, 361–362, 364
Eastern Orthodox, 9
ecclesial Movements, 252–253, 260, 282, 320–325

- characteristics of, 283
economy:
- charism of unity and, 269–289
- collective spirituality and, 11
- divine, 22–23
- economics in Western world, 259
- healthy, 357
- single, in family, 183
- work, detachment from, 287
Economy of Communion, 10, 184, 243, 267–269, 274–289
- aims of, 276, 279–280
- beauty of, 283
- characteristics of, 276–277
- fundamental concepts of, 278–285
- Providence and, 277
- work done by, 286–289
economy of the cross, 85
ecstasies, 272
Ecumenical Councils, 203
ecumenism, 41, 233n, 325–333, 326, 329–330
education, 11, 298, 359
- of children, 83, 183
- definition of, 219
- and Economy of Communion, 285
- Jesus as teacher, 215–219
- moral, 221
- need for, 285
- in society, 184
- unity and, 215–229
- "Woman educator for peace," 195–200
ego, 226, 368
- collective egos, 231
egoism, 356
Egypt, flight to, 45
Elizabeth, 44
encyclicals, 269
enemies, 7, 122, 220, 227, 235, 248, 252, 368
engaged couples, 225

England, 232, 257, 337, 344
England, Church of.
  See Anglicans and Anglican Church
envy, 80, 170
Ephrem the Syrian, St., 41n
equality: "liberty, equality, fraternity," 244, 249, 258
ethical relativism, 293
Eucharist, 19, 43, 49, 81, 271, 330
- Church and, 129
- daily nourishment with, 203
- death and, 213–214
- importance of, 199, 203, 205, 213–214
- institution of, 19
- Jesus in, 129–134, 208
- Mary in, 140
- purpose and task of, 129
Europe, 249, 251, 253, 256, 311, 325, 337, 361–364
- See also *specific locations*
- Council of Europe, 242
- new ecclesial Movements in, 252
- Second European Ecumenical Assembly, 325–333
- of the spirit, 261
- through the centuries, 256–257
- Together for Europe, 324
- unity, European, 249–251, 257, 260
- vocation of, 257
European Coal and Steel Community (ECSC), 250–251
European Union, 238, 250
  bishops' conference of, 188
euthanasia, 189
evangelical spirit of Focolare Movement, 3
existential unity, 221

faith, 13, 71
- love and, 263
- politics and, 263
family, 179–194, 246, 284
- beauty of, 181, 185–186, 191, 193

Index 419

- current situation of, 188–190
- and Ideal of Focolare Movement, 48
- International Year of the Family, 188
- as living cell, 179
- love and, 180–182
- New Families Movement, 180–185, 215–219
- original beauty of, reacquiring, 191–194
- as our future, 185–194
- parenthood, 187
- as protector of life, 187
- and society, 183–185, 187–188
- spirit of, 48
- Trinitarian roots of, 186
- unity of human, 262
- universal, 232, 236, 243, 248, 251, 262, 264–266, 268, 271, 279, 360, 367

Familyfest '93, 292
Father, God as, 13–14
fatherhood, 13–14
- *See also* family; parenthood
- a father's love, 99
- words of fathers, 98–99

Fathers of the Church, 40, 203, 208, 330–331
Fatima, Portugal, 232
fear, 319
Fiera di Primero (Dolomite Mountains, Italy), 231, 244
fire, 173–174
- becoming bearers of, 102
- being on fire, 56
- "between two fires," 48–50
- of communion, 291
- of Jesus, 103–105
- of love, 59, 96, 111, 185

Fiuggi, Italy, 320–325
Fiume, Salvatore, 312
flight to Egypt, 45

Florence, Italy, 224, 308n, 354
Focolare Movement, 3–11
- *See also under* gospel: living; spirituality of unity; *specific topics*
- as about unity, 3
- accusations against, 351
- approval by Church authorities, 7
- beauty and, 309–317
- birth of, 3–11, 16–17, 20, 49–52, 202, 261, 266–267, 369
- and Church, teachings of, 203
- co-founder, Igino Giordani as, 236–237
- communitarian dimension of, 3–4, 13, 27, 203
- effects of, 10–11
- evangelical spirit of, 3
- Holy Spirit and, 5, 17, 26, 28, 43, 265
- Ideal of, 48
  and interreligious dialogue, 344–347
- life of, 51
- main ideas of, 202–203
- Mary in, 38–47, 49–52
- and media, 290–291
- motto of, 357
- religions involved in (many), 3
- "sign" of, 267
- spread of, 9, 265, 292, 338
- three stages of, 311–212
- vocation of, 16, 267, 357
- as "Work of Mary," 26 (*see also* Work of Mary)

"Focolarine," 17n
Fon Defang of Fontem, 245–246
Fontem, Cameroon, 245–247
Fontem, Dr. Lucas Njifua, 246
forgiveness, 101, 170
- *See also* reconciliation
- love and, 85

"fourth way," 49
France, 250, 252

Franciscans, 16, 17n, 113, 252, 311, 323
Francis de Sales, St., 67, 270
Francis of Assisi, St., 44, 114, 118, 160, 163, 203, 207, 210, 311n
fraternal love, 6, 78–79, 81, 90, 102, 125, 252, 328
– *See also* love
fraternity, 341
– *See also* fraternal love, above; Movement for Unity in Politics
– author of, 253
– fraternal communion, 100
– fraternal unity, 31
– interdependence based on, 264–268
– Jesus as our brother, 59–61
– as needing continual renewal, 31
– and peace, 343
– political prospects for, 254–257
– primary source of, 252
– universal brotherhood, 235–236
freedom:
  "liberty, equality, fraternity," 244, 249, 258
  marriage and, 189
French Revolution, 244, 249, 258
Friedrich, Johannes (Evangelical Lutheran bishop), 323
friendship, 51, 152–153, 183, 187, 217, 225, 227, 248, 365
– desire for, 153

Gandhi, Mahatma, 248
"generating" through mutual love, 40
Geneva, 323–324
Genfest, Gen Movement, 292, 360–361
– *See also* youth; Youth for a United World
Germany, 8, 250, 252, 260, 323–324
Giordani, Igino, 194, 225, 236–237, 263, 283, 317
Giustiani, St. Lawrence, 30
giving, culture of. *See* culture of giving
globalization, 253, 259, 293, 297, 337

God
– *See also* Trinity; will of God; specific topics, e.g., love
– beauty of, 34, 57–58, 90
– belief in, 13
– confidence in, 70–71
– as everything, 154
– as Father, 13–14
– Focolare Movement and (awareness of God), 13
– "giving God," 146
– as Ideal, 4, 13
– listening to (communing with), 63–65
– as love, 55–65, 84, 204, 220, 266–267
– loving the One who is Love, 58–59, 62–63, 146
– as omnipotent, 60–61
– outside of self, 33, 49–51
– people of, 230
– power of, 60–61
– within self (in us), 5, 33–34, 49–51, 57–58
– trust in, 70–71
– unity as Father, 13, 18
– as what matters, 154–155
– will of, 5–6, 18
God-Love, 4, 56
Golden Rule, 121–123, 248, 267, 331–333, 339, 349, 354, 368
– and dialogue, interreligious, 253, 346
– mutual love and, 346–347
good: doing good, 86
Good Friday, 92
goodwill, 86
gospel, 7, 170
– *See also under* Focolare Movement: birth of
– answers in, 5–8
– beauty of, 202, 274
– the Church and, 113

- as credible, 6
- Focolare Movement and, 13, 38, 202
- giving witness to, 274
- "gospel illiterates," 127
- as including everyone, 122
- laity and, 283
- living, 7–9, 37–38, 40, 84, 120, 274, 280–285, 295, 345
- most profound law of, 299, 301–302
- nature of, 7
- put into action, 351 (*see also under* Focolare Movement: birth of)
- radicalism of, 252, 269, 283
- and spirituality of unity, 3
- truth of, 6

government
- *See also* nations; politics
- more wisdom in, 235

grace, 319
gratitude, 22, 41, 132–133, 370
Graz, Austria, 325–333
Greece, 256
growth: improving always, 75–76

happiness. *See* joy
Harlem, New York, 10, 345
hatred, 170
heaven, 99
- beauty of, 157–158
- death as approach to, 158–159, 162–163
- death as day of birth into heaven, 163
- on earth, 133–134
- life as rehearsal for, 164–165

Heidegger, 213
hell, 165
Hemmerle, Klaus, Bishop of Aachen, 186, 204
hermits, 27
Heschel, Abraham, 336
Hindus and Hinduism, 332, 340, 344, 346, 350, 366, 368

history, 114, 231, 247, 268
- See also *specific topics*
- Europe through the centuries, 256–257

holiness, 29, 50, 73, 115, 203, 270–273, 287–288, 316, 324
Holy Family, 49, 182
Holy Father. *See* Pope; *individual Popes*
Holy Land, 286
Holy Spirit, 143–149, 207–208
- *See also under* Focolare Movement: Holy Spirit and; Trinity; *specific topics,* e.g., laity
- and ecclesial Movements, 252–253
- and gospel of love, 130
- love and, 341
- and Mary, 38, 40, 143–144, 147
- "outpouring" on Church, 321
- and sanctity, 144
- and unity, 12, 28

Holy Trinity. *See* Trinity, Holy
Horace, 189
House of Nazareth, 49–52, 286
human beings
- See also *specific topics*
- companionship, human thirst for, 152–153
- created as gifts for each other, 88
- human way of seeing things, 89
- need for love, 224–225
- as only given one life, 116

human rights, 10, 336, 338, 362–364
- Declaration of Human Rights, 189

humility, 18, 146
the "hundredfold," 7, 109, 277, 284, 287
Hungary, 242

Ibn Arabi, 349
Ideal:
- God as, 4, 13
- the term, 7n

Ignatius of Loyola, St., 207–208
imagination, 315–316
The Imitation of Christ, 27

immigrants, 256
improving always, 75–76
inculturation, 340, 347
individualism
- *See also* self
- individualistic culture, 188
- refusal to enter into communion, 228
individual spiritualities, 27–30
injustice, 189, 191, 282, 300
Innsbruck, Austria, 247
intelligence, 116
interdependence, 262
- Day of Interdependence, 264–268
- Declaration of Interdependence, 264
- fraternity and, 268
"interest groups," 228–229
"interior castle," 31–32
international solidarity, 200, 343
International Year of the Family, 188
interreligious dialogue.
  See dialogue, interreligious
"inundations," 243
Islam. *See* Muslims
Italy, 170, 232, 237, 239, 252, 254, 261, 311
- See also *specific cities and locations,* e.g., Rome; Trent

Japan, 333, 344–345
jealousy, 170
Jean-Baptiste de La Salle University, 201
Jerusalem, 45, 206, 217, 302, 321
Jesuits, 115
Jesus Christ
- *See also* cross; God; prayer for unity Trinity; *specific topics,* e.g., Eucharist
- beauty of, 90, 93–94
- birth of, 44–45
- characteristics of, 60
- in each person, 19
- as everything, 34
- as God and Man together, 358–359
- imitation of, 218, 253

- to "live Christ," 19
- Mary, relationship with, 138–139
- as our brother, 59–61
- public life of, 46
- Risen (*See* Risen Jesus)
- as teacher, 215–219
- in the Temple, 45
- unity, and presence of, 102
- as Word of God, 113
Jesus forsaken, 16, 19–26, 31, 34–35, 88–97, 190–191, 206, 211–212
- disunity experienced by, 241–242
- as key to unity, 31
- as the secret, 221–222
Jesus Forsaken-and-Risen, 253
Jesus in the midst, 30–31, 49, 51, 103, 129, 147, 202, 214, 222–223, 285, 288, 315, 318, 325, 330, 335
- and unity, 102
Jesus suffering, 8, 20–25
Jewish-Christian dialogues, 333–336
Jewish people, 216, 252, 258, 331–336, 340, 344, 346, 366, 368
Joan of Arc, St., 197
John Chrysostom, St., 243, 298
John of the Cross, St., 67
John Paul II, Pope, 32, 333, 338, 343, 347, 367
- on art and human genius, 313
- on Church divisions, 327
- and communion, spirituality of, 29n
- on dialogue, 343
- on discipleship, 32
- on Eastern Europe, 362
- and Economy of Communion, 277
- on the family, 186
- and Focolare Movement, 38
- on global interdependence, 266
- on the laity, 282
- *Letter to Artists,* 307
- on love, 204
- and Mary, year dedicated to, 38

- on Mary, 207
- on the media, 293
- on the millennium, 320
- and mysteries of light, 38
- and "spirituality of communion," 29n, 253
- at UN anniversary, 11
- on unity, 251
- unity, as personification of, 12
- on unity and plurality, 329

John the evangelist, 42, 125, 163, 299, 327, 348
John XXIII, Pope, 67, 272
Joseph (husband of Mary, foster father of Jesus), 182, 286, 302, 353
joy, 66–68
- acquiring through suffering, 89, 200
- of others, sharing, 233
- perfect, 68
- rejoicing with others, 48
- sharing, 233
- source of, 171

jubilee year, 297
judging others, 170
Jung, Carl, 228
justice, 23, 70, 116, 183–184, 244, 288, 336, 338, 343, 345, 357, 367
- for women, 196

Kasper, Cardinal, 325
King, Martin Luther, 263
koinonia. *See* communion
Kolbe, St. Maximilian, 227

laity, 8, 51–52, 112, 117, 198, 282–284
- Holy Spirit and, 146, 282

Lambeth Palace, 9
La Salle University, 201
Latin America, 311, 361–362, 362, 364
Lebanon, 323, 362
Leclerq, Jacques, 369
Letter to Artists (John Paul II), 307
life, 150–156

- call to, 78
- death as beginning of, 161
- humans as only given one, 116
- as important passage, 164–165
- lives (of many people) that are not lived, 88–89
- living life, 150–156
- living only for love, 82
- love as passing from death to life, 83
- as rehearsal, 164–165
- the secret for a great life, 68
- as trial, 79
- a true, full life, 145

Life, Word of. *See* Word of Life
light, 34, 210
- love as, 84

light, mysteries of, 38
liturgical prayer, 31
liturgy, 130
living water, "torrents of," 243
"living within," 63, 174
London, 257, 337
loneliness, 55, 71, 81–82, 95, 158
Loppiano, Italy, 9, 308, 345, 354
Loreto, Italy, 49, 286
losing and knowing how to lose, 34, 299, 301–302, 315–316
Lourdes, France, 232
love
- *See also* charity; fraternal love; mutual love
- alive, 146
- art of loving, 14, 77
- asceticism of, 57
- "being love," 87
- being loved, 55
- belief in God's love, 13
- as blind, 144
- Christian, 235, 237
- the Church and, 114
- communication of, need for, 146
- communion generated by, 100–101

- the cross and, 91
- culture of, 280
- and dialogue, 355
- disinterested, 356
- distillation of, 148
- and doing good, 86
- doing things "for love" vs. "being love," 84
- as enlarging our hearts, 81
- evangelical, 280
- faith and, 263
- and the family, 180–182
- a father's love, 99
- "foolishness" of, 96–97
- and forgiveness, 85
- fraternal, 78–79, 81, 90, 102, 125, 328
- friendship, 319
- giving, 281
- for God, 145
- God as, 55–65, 84, 144, 204, 220, 266–267
- and goodwill, 86
- gospel-based, 339–340
- and holiness, 273
- Holy Spirit and, 341
- human, seasons of, 187
- human need for, 224–225
- as Jesus loves, 81–82
- the kind Jesus asks for, 365–366, 368
- as law of everything, 88
- laws of, 186
- as light, 84
- living only for love, 82
- as to love and be loved, 80
- loving Jesus in one's neighbour, 82
- loving relationships, description of, 226
- loving the One who is Love, 58–59, 62–63
- many kinds of, 56–57
- a mother's love, 124
- in motion, 146

- need to love, 281
- for neighbour, 79–81, 202
- nothing as small if done out of, 86–87
- nothingness of (*see* nothingness)
- as not love, 144–145
- as organized, 109
- as passing from death to life, 83
- politics and, 263
- politics as love of all loves, 254
- reciprocal (*see* mutual love)
- "ripeness" in, 270–271
- as the secret, 369
- seven main expressions of, 177
- the soul and, 82, 124–125
- and suffering, 14, 85
- supernatural, 124
- true, 356
- and truth, 86, 101
- vs. burdensome charity, 84
- as watchful, 125
- as what matters, 83–84
- without speaking, 353–354

Lubich, Chiara
- See also *specific topics*
- companions of (*see* companions of Chiara Lubich)
- consecration of, 20

Lutherans and Lutheran Church, 8–9, 260, 323

Madonna of Czestochowa, 232
Madonna of Michelangelo, 304–305, 310
Madrid, 259, 261
Magisterium of the Church, 203, 207
the Magnificat, 40, 44, 137, 269, 300
Malta, 225
man. *See* human beings
Manila, Philippines, 201
Margaret Mary Alacoque of the Sacred Heart, St., 114
Marian Congress, Castel Gandolfo, 38
Marian profile of the Church, 324
Marian year, 303

Index 425

marriage, 254, 352–353
- *See also* family
- bond of, 189
- communion in, 186, 193
- freedom and, 189
- living together before, 189
- and procreation, 187
- stable, 189

martyrdom, 59, 172–173, 367

Mary, Blessed Virgin, 15, 135–142, 154, 206–207
- and the apostles, 46, 148
- beauty of, 40–43, 47, 94, 135, 137–142, 182, 304–305, 316–317
- as bond of unity among nations, 231–233
- Cana, wedding feast of, 50, 302
- and the Church, 43, 51–52, 112, 207
- and communication, 298
- Desolate, 35, 42, 46, 139, 299–302
- events in life of, 44–47
- as "explanation" of God, 136–137
- in Focolare Movement, 38–47, 49–52
- Holy Spirit and, 38, 40, 143–144, 147–148
- imitating, 203
- Jesus, relationship with, 138–139
- as knowing how to lose, 299–301
- "little Marys," becoming, 49
- as Mother, 139–140
- *Theotokos*, 41, 200, 330
- and the Trinity, 40, 207
- and unity, 244
- as virgin, 119, 138
- Way of Mary *(Via Mariae)*, 44–47
- and the Word of God, 40–41
- year dedicated to, 38

Mary, Work of. *See* Work of Mary

Mary Magdalene, 60, 85, 119

materialism, 78, 322, 332, 336, 363

matrimony. *See* marriage

"May they all be one."
  See prayer for unity

media, 189, 259, 269, 290–303, 337
- *See also* communication
- and charism of unity, 290–297

meditation, 63–64, 123, 286

Meditations, 291

meekness, 115

mercy, 85
- God's, 217
- truth and, 101
- works of mercy, 79

Methodius, 250

Mexico City, 201

Milan, Italy, 27

miracles, 272

missionaries, 113, 172, 235

mistrust, 170

modern times, 169–178

monasticism, 27n, 249–250

Monnet, Jean, 251

Montini, Cardinal Ludivico, 29

moral education, 221

Mother, Church as, 111

motherhood
- *See also* family; Mary, Blessed Virgin; parenthood
- a mother's love, 124
- qualities of, 296
- spiritual maternity, 353
- task of mothers, 15

Mounier, Emmanuel, 185

Mouvement de la Jeuness Orthodoxe, 323

Movement for Life, 224

Movement for Unity in Politics, 230, 236–247, 254–256, 261–264, 268, 285
- *See also* fraternity
- beginning of, 254
- as political expression of the Focolare, 261

Movements, ecclesial.
  See ecclesial Movements

Mulieris Dignitatem, 195, 197, 200
Munich, 323
Muslims and Islam, 252–253, 266, 331–333, 340–341, 344–346, 348–354, 368
– African-American, 345
mutual love, 14, 202, 328
– and building unity, 18, 330
– and the Golden Rule, 346–347
– love as to love and be loved, 80
mysteries of light, 38
Mystical Body of Christ
– *See also* Church; *specific topics,* e.g., spiritualities
– building up, 102
– era of, 230
– illuminating, 99
– Jesus as head of, 34–35
– Mary and, 51–52, 112, 207
– *Mystici Corporis,* 17
mystical experiences, 62
Mystici Corporis, 17
mystics, 29, 46–47, 329
mythology, 212, 271

Nairobi, Kenya, 348
Naples, Italy, 257
narcissism, 226
nations, 3–4, 17, 200, 243, 260, 262, 264, 343, 369
– *See also* politics; *specific locations*
– divisions between, 241
– Economy of Communion, 276
– and globalization, 253
– interdependence among, 265
– international organizations, 262
– love among, 366
– Mary as bond of unity among, 230–233, 244
– media and, 337
– and politics, 255–257, 259 (*see also* Movement for Unity in Politics)
– and spirituality, 363
– spread of Focolare Movement, 265, 292, 338
– United Nations, 260–261
nature, laws of, 186
Nazareth, House of, 49–52, 286
neighbour
– *See also specific topics,* e.g., forgiveness
– attitude toward, previous, 27
– God in, 18–19
– having one idea of, 19
– love for, 202
– loving as self, 79–81
– loving Jesus in, 82
– making self one with, 233
– who "neighbour" is, 5, 19
Net*One,* 298
New Families Movement, 180–185, 215–219
New Humanity Movement, 242
"new people," 275, 279, 282, 285, 369
New Testament, 328
– *See also* gospel; *specific topics*
New York. *See specific topics and locations,* e.g., Harlem; September 11
Nicene-Constantinopolitan creed, 325
night of the senses, 46
Niwano, Rev. Nikkyo, 344
North America
– *See also* United States
– spread of Focolare Movement in, 9
Nostra Aetate, 333
nothingness, 17, 21–22, 74, 115, 191, 302, 340, 346–347
– God as everything, 154–155
– and Jesus forsaken, 211
– and making yourself one with others, 346–347
– self-emptying, 228
Nova Millennio Inuente, 253, 320–321

obedience, 16, 72, 138, 182, 216
old self/new self, 31, 296, 350

Old Testament, 282, 333–334
orders, 11, 114–115
– See also *specific Orders*
original sin, 74, 123
Orthodox Churches, 9, 42, 230, 260

pain. *See* suffering
Palace of Westminster, 257
Palestine, 266, 362
paradise. *See* heaven
Paradiso (Dante), 316
parenthood, 187
– *See also* family; fatherhood; marriage; motherhood
Paris, 324
patience, 123
Paul, St., the apostle, 8, 18, 30n–31, 41, 206, 213, 293–294, 332, 337, 340, 353
– on death, 158
– "new people," 275
– "old self," 31, 296, 350
– on sanctification, 71
– Word of Life, 30n
Paul VI, Pope, 68
– on the *Creed*, 55
– "generating" through mutual love, 40
– on love, 83
– on "passion for the Church," 112
– on the true life of Christians, 68
– and unity, 12, 198
– on the word of God, 120
peace, 341, 367
– being a peacemaker, 170
– courage and, 14
– Day of Peace, 195
– fraternity and, 343
– human longing for, 171
– the Lord as, 232
– need for, 262
– peace-building, 343
– and suffering, 14
– and unity, 12

– World Day of Peace, 266
Penance, sacrament of, 271
penances, 27, 29
Pentecost, 148
Pentecost 1998, 252, 321
people of God, 230
perfection, 270
– perfect Christians, 56
– and unity, 109
perfect joy, 68
Peter, St., 46, 50, 78, 288
Petrarch, 317
philosophy, 20n, 135, 201–204, 242, 278, 298, 304–305, 313–314, 318
– charism of unity and, 209–214
Piacenza, Italy, 274
Pius XI, Pope, 270
Pius XII, Pope, 17, 42, 230–231
Plato, 308–309
politics
– *See also* fraternity; Movement for Unity in Politics
– based on communion, 257–264
– charism of unity and, 230–268
– faith and, 263
– of Jesus, 243
– love and, 263
– as love of all loves, 254
– vocation, political, 254
Pontifical Council for the Laity, 322
the poor and poverty, 3, 5–6, 10, 15–16, 20, 44, 61, 85–86, 106, 114, 126–127 171, 189, 206, 368
– 1 Corinthians 13:3, 121
– and heaven, 126
– helping, 275, 282, 357
– poor countries, 189, 259, 262, 274, 342, 367
– the poor in spirit, 113, 173, 347
– relief to, 357
Popes, 115
– See also *individual Popes*

Populorum progressio, 269
Portugal, 232
Poupard, Cardinal, 307
poverty. *See* poor, the
Prague, Czech Republic, 262
prayer, 352
 – collective, 31
 – communing with God, 63–65
 – liturgical, 31
 – and vocation, 319
prayer for unity ("May they all be one") 6, 16–19, 26, 202, 205, 279, 344
 – significance of, 248–249
priesthood, 19, 72, 111–112, 119
 – institution of, 19
 – our "royal priesthood," 158
Prize for Peace Education, 12
procreation, 187
Prodi, Romano, 324
prodigal son, 217
proselytism, 341, 347, 356
Protestants, 351
Providence, 68, 76, 152, 162, 197, 202, 241, 277, 281, 287, 298
 – Christianity and, 273
 – detachment and, 287
 – and Economy of Communion, 277
Przywara, 212
Pseudo-Dionysius the Aeropagite, 36
psychology:
 – psychological illnesses, 227–228
 – unity and, 225–229
purgatory, 31, 116

Qur'an, 351–353

radicalism. *See under* gospel: radicalism of
Rahner, Karl, 29
Ramsey, Dr. Michael, Archbishop of Canterbury, 9
reciprocal love. *See* mutual love
recollection, 76
reconciliation, 130, 327
 – *See also* dialogue, interreligious; forgiveness
re-evangelization, 127–128
relativism, ethical, 293
religion
 – *See also* dialogue, interreligious; ecumenism; *specific religions and topics*
 – embracing parallel values, 12
 – religions involved in Focolare Movement, 3
resignation, Christian, 69
resolutions, making, 146
"respectful proclamation," 340–341, 347
Riccardi, Andrea, 323
the rich, 86, 126–127, 171, 200, 216, 269, 282
 – rich countries, 259, 262, 342, 367
Risen Jesus, 214, 325
Rissho-Kosei-kai, 341, 344–345
Rita of Cascia, St., 197
Roman Empire, 247
Rome, Italy, 7–8, 102, 180, 183, 188, 237n, 264, 292, 321, 323–324, 360, 366
 – "Resurrection of," 173–176, 316
Rose of Lima, St., 197
Rumi, the poet, 348
Runcie, Dr. Robert, Archbishop of Canterbury, 9
Rylko, Monsignor Stanislaw, 325

Sacred Heart Catholic University (Piacenza, Italy), 274
Saints, Communion of, 99
saints and sainthood, 27, 41, 44, 72–74, 86, 88, 90–92, 104, 114–118, 154
 – See also *individual names*
 – becoming a saint, 72
 – becoming saints as Church, 117–118
 – calling to be saints, 56
 – cross, saints as understanding, 90
 – description of saints, 74
 – future, currently being shaped, 146

Index

- lives of, 21, 115–116
- "real Christians," 270
- and reliving Christ in themselves, 92
- and suffering, 92

sanctity, 23, 29, 31, 49, 51, 71–73, 88, 224
- collective, 117–118, 224
- Holy Spirit and, 144

Santiago de Compostela, 362
Sâo Paulo, Brazil, 278, 362
Schuman, Robert, 238, 250–251
science: and theology, 209
Scouts (World Scout Movement), 188
scripture, 199, 280, 328, 331, 348–350
- See also *specific topics*

seasons of love, 187
Second European Ecumenical Assembly (Graz, Austria), 325–333
Second Vatican Council. See Vatican Council, the Second

secret:
- Jesus forsaken as, 221–222
- love as, 369
- for a great life, 68
- that builds the city of God, 104–105

secularism, 322, 332, 336
self, 225–229
- genuine consciousness of, 211
- God in us, 33–34, 49–51, 57–58
- making yourself one with others, 233, 346–347
- old self/new self, 31, 296, 350
- safeguarding, 228

self-affirmation, 227
self-emptying, 228
self-fulfilment, 226
selfishness, 80
September 11, 248, 259, 264–267, 342, 367
sexuality, 188, 224
- individualistic culture and, 188
- sexual anarchy, 189

the Shoah, 335–336
Simeon, 45
sin:
- and Jesus forsaken, 206
- original (*see* original sin)

social revolution, 188
society: the family and, 183–185, 187–188
solidarity, 274, 354
- See also Economy of Communion

solitude, 29
Soloviev, Vladimir, 313
Song of Songs, 24
sorrow
- See also suffering
- of Mary (*see under* Mary, Blessed Virgin: Desolate)
- sharing, 233

the soul, 33–34, 80, 88–89
- being possessive of one's own soul, 80
- the cross and, 91
- God and, 124–125, 153
- love and, 124–125
- presence of Jesus in, 120
- as seeking love, 82
- two souls meeting, 109

South Africa, 266
South America, 311, 361–362, 364
"spiritual director," 50
spiritualities, Christian, 27, 29
- See also spirituality of communion, below
- collective, 30, 33
- historic development of, 27n
- individual, 27–30

spirituality of communion/unity 3, 12, 16, 27–28, 34, 36, 40, 47, 50n, 228–229
- characteristic elements of, 33–34
- communitarian dimension of, 27

main ideas of, 202–203
Spouse of Christ, 321
- See also Bride of Christ

St. Catherine Centre, 240–241, 243
St. Egidio, 321, 323
St. Peter's Square, Rome, 321
Stein, Edith, 250
stigmata, 118
Strasbourg, 261
Stuttgart, Germany, 324
suffering, 8, 14, 85, 351–352
 – *See also* cross; Desolate (Mary desolate); Jesus forsaken
 – and beauty, 152
 – joy and, 89, 200
 – love and, 14, 85
 – Muslims and, 351
 – of others, sharing, 14, 233
 – with others, 48
 – prayer and, 352
 – as precious, 351
 – reverence for, 92
 – saints and, 92
 – and truth, 152
 – welcoming suffering, 104–105
 – what to do when it comes, 352
 – will of God during, 352
superficiality, 84
supernatural love, 124
Switzerland, 185, 344
Synod of Bishops, Rome, 198

Talmud, 335
Tasso, 317
teenagers. *See* young people
Templeton Prize for Progress in Religion, 344
temptations, 78
Teresa, Mother, 227
Teresa of Avila, St., 31, 49, 51, 72, 160, 196, 270
terrorism, 259, 264, 337, 341–342, 342, 367
Tertullian, 247, 292
Testament of Jesus, 16, 18, 24, 38, 199, 224, 238, 266, 328, 336, 344

Thailand, 290, 333, 345, 353
thanksgiving. *See* gratitude
theology, 28, 176n, 201–214, 242, 295, 314, 331
 – charism of unity and, 204–209
 – and science, 209
Theotokos, 41, 200, 330
Thérèse of Lisieux, St, 67, 113–114
Third World, 269–273
Thomas Aquinas, St., 203, 208, 270, 282
Together for Europe, 324
Tokyo, Japan, 344–345
tolerance, 355
Torah, 335
"torrents of living water," 243
"transforming union," 47
Trent (northern Italy), 238, 261, 267, 334
 – *See also under* Focolare Movement: birth of
 – Day of Peace, 195
Trinity, Holy, 129, 174–175, 182, 186, 203–207, 223–224, 298, 330, 358
 – and God in us, 33–35
 – love and, 212
 – love as essence of, 204
 – Mary and, 40, 207
 – and unity, 109
trust:
 – in God, 70–71
 – mistrust, 170
truth, 120–121
 – *See also* authenticity
 – and beauty, 152, 313
 – of gospel, 6
 – Jesus as, 201
 – love and, 86, 101
 – and mercy, 101
 – personified, 127
 – suffering and, 152
Turrita d'Argento Award, 3
Twin Towers. *See* September 11

Index 431

UELCI (Union of Italian Catholic Publishers and Booksellers), 27
underdeveloped Christians, 269–273, 270
UNESCO, 12–15, 242, 324
– address to, 12
unhappiness, 171
United Nations, 260–261
United States, 248
– See also *specific topics*
– spread of Focolare Movement in North America, 9
United World Fund, 247, 251
unity
– See also Jesus in the midst
– building, mutual love and, 18
– complete, 101–102
– as divine word, 98
– *existential unity,* 221
– Focolare Movement as about, 3
– Holy Spirit and, 12
– instruments of, 252–253
– and Jesus forsaken, 25–26, 31
– Jesus' prayer for (*see* prayer for unity)
– living unity, 109
– Mary and, 244
– "may they all be one" (*see* prayer for unity)
– and peace, 12
– and perfection, 109
– signs of world's longing for, 259–260
– spirituality of, 3
the Trinity and, 109
– way of, 36–37
unity, charism of:
– and the arts, 304–319
– culture of, 242
– and economy, 269–289
– and education, 219–224
– effect on individuals, 44
– and the media, 290–297
– and philosophy, 209–214

– and politics, 230–268
– and psychology, 225–229
– and theology, 204–209
University of Malta, 225
University of Santo Tomas, 201

vanity, 84, 165
Vatican Council, the Second, 199, 205, 282–283, 316–317, 321, 333
– See also *specific topics*
– on art, 312–313
– and Church as communion, 288
– and Mary, 148
– and unity, 12, 29, 130
Via Mariae (Way of Mary), 44–47
violence
– See also terrorism
– evangelical, 115
– in history, 231
virginity, 118–119, 119, 138, 144, 352–353
– beauty of, 118
– consecrated virgins, 144
– Mary as virgin, 119
– virgins, foolish and wise, 119
Virgin Mary, Blessed.
See Mary, Blessed Virgin
visions, 272
vocation, 79
– artistic, 317–319
– of Europe, 257
– of Focolare Movement, 16, 267, 357
– political, true and proper, 254
– prayer and, 319
Volunteers of God, 242
Von Balthasar, Fr. Hans-Urs, 191, 207

Warsaw, Poland, 242, 362
watching, being watchful, 125
water: "torrents of living water," 243
Way of Mary *(Via Mariae),* 44–47
wealth, 151
– See also poverty

- distribution of, disparity in, 189, 200
- producing for benefit of those in need, 275
- the rich, 126–127

Weil, Simone, 308
Western Europe, 361
Western world, 188–189, 217
- economics in, 259

Westminster, Palace of (London), 257
Westminster Central Hall (London), 337
Wetter, Cardinal Friedrich, 323
Willebrands, Cardinal, 326
will of God, 68–76, 202
- and birth of Focolare Movement, 6
- as coinciding with love, 226
- discerning, 6
- and our resolutions, 146
- in times of suffering, 352

Wojtyla, Cardinal Karol of Cracow. *See* John Paul II, Pope

women:
- justice for, 196
- talents and gifts of, 195–200

Word of God, 34, 120–128
- Jesus as, 113
- Mary and, 40–41

Word of Life, 30, 291, 295

work
- *See also* economy; vocation
- detachment from, 287

Work of Mary, 26, 43, 47, 139, 147, 177–178, 207, 357
works of mercy, 79
world, 212
- See also under *specific topics,* e.g., unity
- beauty of, 57, 64
- as increasingly interdependent, 262

World Conference for Religion and Peace, 12
World Council of Churches, 12, 324, 326
World Day of Peace, 266
"world people," 356
World Scout Movement, 188
World War II, 17n, 49, 237, 266, 334

Year of the Family, 188
youth, young people, 8, 11, 162, 242, 245, 251, 290, 292n, 360–368
- *See also* children

Youth for a United World, 360–361, 363, 365
Youth for Unity, 366–368
Zamboni, Doriana, 20n